The What, Where, When, How & Why
Of Gardening In Colorado

Colorado

GARDENER'S
GUIDE

JOHN L. CRETTI

**COOL
SPRINGS
PRESS**

Nashville, Tennessee

A Division of Thomas Nelson, Inc.
www.ThomasNelson.com

Cretti, John L.
    Colorado Gardener's Guide: the what, where, when, how & why of gardening in Colorado / John L. Cretti

    p.   cm.
    Includes bibliographical references (p.   ) and index.
    ISBN 1-888608-48-X
    1. Landscape plants -- Colorado 2. Landscape gardening -- Colorado
    3. Gardening -- Colorado I. Title
635.9--dc20
Cre

Published by Cool Springs Press, a Division of Thomas Nelson, Inc., P.O. Box 141000, Nashville, Tennessee 37214.

First printing 1998
Printed in the United States of America
10 9 8 7 6 5 4

Horticultural Nomenclature Editor: Robert F. Polomski,
    Extension Consumer Horticulturist, Clemson University

On the cover (clockwise from top left): Red Hybrid Tea Rose, Lilac, Aspen, Rocky Mountain Columbine

Map (found on last page of color insert) provided by Agricultural Research Service, USDA

Visit the Thomas Nelson website at: www.ThomasNelson.com

DEDICATION

*T*O MY LOVING WIFE JERI, for her gardening spirit and patience, and to my wonderful children, Jason, Justin, Jinny, and Jonathan, for their patience and understanding as I worked overtime on this project.

To my mother, Angelina L. Cretti, who gave me the opportunity to garden and experiment in the "ranch" garden as a child, and who taught me the value of hard work. To my aunts and uncles for their love and support, and for buying me my first seeds, bulbs, and butterfly bush. To the loving memory of my grandmother, "Nonnita," for passing on her love of making things grow. To the memory of my best friend, "Bronson," for his unconditional love, inspiration, and companionship.

PREFACE

*G*ARDENING IS AN INEXACT SCIENCE, AND SUCCESSFUL GARDENERS ARE MADE, NOT BORN. I firmly believe that the best way to develop the truly valuable gardening skills is to practice the old 4-H Club motto: "Learn by Doing!"

Some Coloradoans tell me, "I don't know *anything* about gardening," and they let it go at that! They have been so intimidated by the great number of gardening books with enticing colorful pictures and mostly scientific and arcane information that they throw up their hands in defeat. Others are unable to resist the urge to get outdoors, work the earth, and plant a garden. That's how my interest in gardening began.

I began my avocation in gardening and entomology as a child growing up on a small ranch in Colorado—but who knew at that time that I would eventually pursue a career in horticulture?

My grandmother, whom I called "Nonnita," was instrumental in nurturing my love of gardening. Every day she tended to her garden nestled below the "hogbacks," a range of mountains to the north of Silt Mesa in beautiful western Colorado. Hers was a community garden, shared with deer, rabbits, chipmunks, squirrels, and birds. Even some of the chickens would find their way up the hill to scratch for seeds; they would eat some of the insect pests as they browsed through the plants. All in all, it was a piece of earth that produced a dandy crop of vegetables for canning. A small fruit orchard stills holds a special place in my heart. Despite the threat of springtime frosts when the apricots and Italian plums were in bloom, these fruit trees usually produced a generous crop for drying and canning. Nonnita's rock-faced root cellar was chock-full of homegrown goodies. We didn't have all the modern-day conveniences back then. We had no electricity and there was no indoor plumbing. Refrigeration was provided by an icebox, later to be replaced by a propane-powered refrigerator. So all those canned vegetables and fruits were a necessity—and they sure were good!

An old-fashioned lilac with a sweet fragrance bloomed at the back door; there were fresh green pastures, blossoming fruit trees, and busy honeybees. All these, and much more, inspired me to

Preface

become a Rocky Mountain horticulturist. There is no substitute for
spending time in your garden, using all your senses to learn about
what is going on in nature. You'll have to learn some gardening
basics first, but the more you garden, the more you will know what
works and what doesn't.

Use the recommendations in the *Colorado Gardener's Guide* as a
starting point, experiment, and try to learn as much as you can
about your particular area. After all, gardening is "down-to-earth,"
not all scientific. I don't think that we'll ever know all there is to
know about gardening. I'm just content knowing there's a tiny
miracle in a seed or a bulb. I believe in an old saying: "The Kiss of
the Sun for Pardon, the Song of the Birds for Mirth; One Is Nearer
God's Heart in a Garden Than Anywhere Else on Earth."

Above all, have fun, and you may find that you begin, like me,
to *think like a plant*.

John L. Cretti
Colorado's Doctor Green Thumb

ACKNOWLEDGMENTS

*O*VER THE YEARS OF GARDENING AND GARDEN
COMMUNICATIONS, I have been fortunate to have the
support and encouragement of many special people. Like a seed,
this *Colorado Gardener's Guide* could not have germinated and grown
without them. Thanks to Roger Waynick and Hank McBride of Cool
Springs Press for their intuition that a book like this—a first of
its kind for Colorado—would be a resource for beginning and
seasoned gardeners, alike. I'd like to gratefully acknowledge Jan
Keeling for her superb job of reviewing the manuscript and offering
helpful suggestions. Thanks to Bob Polomski, horticulturist at
Clemson University, for serving as horticultural editor and sharing
his knowledge and experience.

I am grateful to the many Colorado gardeners who generously
shared their knowledge during the preparation of this book.
Special thanks to Dave and Steve Woodman for reviewing the
chapters on trees and shrubs, Eleanor Welshon for her insight
on growing perennials, and Jo Kendzerski for sharing her secrets
on growing roses.

Thanks to all of you who read my newspaper columns, attend
garden programs, and listen to Colorado's Green Thumb Garden
Talk radio show. You have posed many interesting and important
questions about gardening in Colorado and the Rocky Mountain
region.

CONTENTS

INTRODUCTION

Colorado Gardening

$\mathscr{G}$ARDENING IN COLORADO IS AN ADVENTURE. Some may tell you that gardening in our state is a difficult challenge, but this Colorado native does not agree. Take our unique challenges and turn them into opportunities. Discover the lay of the land and the diversity of our native plants; take advantage of the natural and human-created microclimates around your home; and begin a journey to successful gardening in Colorado.

DESIGNING YOUR LANDSCAPE

When it comes to the different aspects of gardening, few are as intimidating as garden design. I suppose part of the problem is our belief that landscape design is a practice best left to trained garden experts who have artistic skills. But we all design things every day, from arranging furniture in our homes and setting the table to placing books on the bookshelf and hanging pictures on the wall.

There's nothing really mysterious about the process of designing a functional landscape. In the gardens we've developed over the years, we've marked the outline of a proposed flower bed with a garden hose, grouped shrubs together, and chosen sites for shade trees. These practices are all part of landscape design. Like an artist, you control what goes on the landscape canvas, choosing a variety of adaptable plants for the palette, creating a garden of distinction and diversity that reflects your gardening style and personality. Remember that as beginning gardeners we may already be nervous about all the stuff we don't know; don't confuse this "beginner's nervousness" with an inability to design.

Start small and grow with confidence. Attempting too much too soon can quickly lead to frustration. Don't feel as if you have to tackle everything at once. Let your landscape evolve along with your knowledge, skills, and interests. You will find that landscaping in phases is a lot easier on your bank account, too.

COLORADO SOILS

Get a group of gardeners together and the conversation will inevitably turn to the topic of "dirt." To be technically correct, we should call it *soil*.

Introduction

The physical properties of Colorado soils are varied. A description of a soil type will generally include the percentage of organic matter, the kind and percentage of soil particles (sand, silt, clay), information on mineral content, soil consistency (the amount of resistance to cultivating), and soil structure (the kind and amount of soil particle aggregates). Most soils in our state are alkaline with a pH of 7.2 to 8.3.

Colorado soils can pose problems for some plants. Most landscape plants from other parts of the country do best in organically rich soils. Except for the soil in many mountain communities, the organic content of Colorado soil is generally low, ranging from 0.8 to 1.4 percent. Native soils have sufficient potassium for normal plant growth, and micronutrients such as iron, manganese, copper, and zinc should be sufficient, but the high pH or alkalinity of our soil makes these nutrients unavailable to the plants. The yellowing of foliage in some plants is often caused by an iron deficiency, a condition known as *iron chlorosis*; it usually occurs because our high-calcium (calcareous) soils hold the iron in a form unavailable to the plant. Adding iron such as ferrous sulfate to the soil is, at best, a temporary solution, as the soil will soon make this source unavailable, too. An alternative solution? Try to select plants that are tolerant of Colorado's alkaline soils.

Most soil-improvement advice is geared toward traditional plant types and comes from sources unfamiliar with our state. These sources usually advocate the addition of lime, gypsum, vitamins, and liquid soil conditioners to the soil. This advice should be disregarded; these additives are not in themselves the answer to our soil problems. (Remember this adage: "If it sounds too good to be true, it usually is.")

But without some soil modification, Colorado soils cannot sustain many of the traditional plants that are introduced from other parts of the United States. Since little can be done to modify our dry air and wind, the secret to successful gardening in Colorado is in the soil. In most situations, the best soils for growing plants have a good balance of minerals, air, and moisture. Whether your soil is too

Introduction

sandy, rocky, or high in clay, the solution is essentially the same: add a high-quality organic amendment.

Never forget that soil modification can pose problems in Colorado soils. Our semi-arid, highly alkaline soils can accumulate natural soluble salts if too much organic matter is added. When these salts stay in the amended soil layer around the root zone, plant roots can be injured. It is important to loosen the soil as thoroughly and as deeply as possible; this will make it more porous so that the salts will be leached away with watering.

Plants will have trouble making their roots explore compacted clay soil, and roots cannot obtain enough moisture in fast-draining sand or crushed granite. Gardeners often compound the problem by overwatering, which displaces oxygen in the soil and waterlogs the plant. It is a strange paradox that in our semi-arid climate, trees and shrubs are doomed by too much water as often as they are doomed by drought.

WATERING

Water has become an increasingly precious resource throughout Colorado, so we encourage a water-thrifty landscape that is in harmony with your surroundings. But you don't have to deprive yourself of a carpet of lawn for you, your children, and your pets to play and relax on, and you don't have to deny yourself the pleasure of growing a favorite flowering shrub or flower garden. There are many creative ways to design your home landscape so that it includes native plants as well as adaptable plants from regions of the world that have climates similar to our own.

It seems simple enough to water outdoor plants, but most gardeners either overwater or underwater. Watering properly depends upon the type of soil you inherit or create. Sandy soils drain so well that water for such soils must be applied more frequently but in lower quantities. Clay soils hold water longer; they should be watered less often, or plants can become subject to waterlogging. As you "learn by doing," get a feel for your soil; your observations will be the best judge in determining when and how much to water.

Introduction

MULCHING

If you take a walk through the forest, you will notice that the soil beneath our native vegetation is covered with aspen leaves, pine and spruce needles, and other woodland debris. Take a lesson from nature and imitate forest conditions in your landscape by using organic mulches.

Mulch acts like a blanket. It keeps moisture in the soil, prevents roots from becoming too hot or too cold, and reduces weed growth; the plants will respond with healthier growth. As organic mulches break down, they enrich the soil with humus and provide valuable nutrients. The ideal mulch will permit water and air to penetrate the underlying soil. One of my favorites is pine needles—I call it *Rocky Mountain mulch*. Even though evergreen needles are acidic, there's no need to worry about their making the soil "too acid." Most Colorado soils are alkaline and resistant to quick transformation. Shredded leaves, dried grass clippings, pole peelings, wood chips, straw, and shredded wood are some other mulch materials.

Soil is alive and it needs oxygen. Don't cover the soil around plants with black plastic. Use a top-quality fabric weed barrier. Cover the fabric with mulch to prevent rapid degradation from sunlight.

PESTS AND DISEASES

The same conditions which allow our gardens to thrive also make an ideal environment for insects and diseases. Luckily, the abundance of sunshine, low humidity, and dry winters in Colorado save us from much grief over plant diseases. As we often say on our radio shows: "A healthy plant is the best defense against pests." Plants that grow vigorously can quickly overcome insect damage, and plants that are not stressed by environmental conditions can resist most diseases. A stressed plant, on the other hand, is more susceptible to insect and disease attack.

Many of the plants chosen for this book have strong resistance to insects and diseases. If you follow my suggestions about proper placement and care of the plants, you should rarely have to use pesticides. Remember, successful gardens are by nature "user-friendly" when it comes to the gardener, wildlife, pets, and the environment.

BOTANICAL NAMES

You may wonder why it is necessary to become familiar with the scientific names of plants. The answer is simple: We want you to make sure the lilac you select for your landscape is the same sweet-smelling lilac you admired in your parent's, grandparent's, or neighbor's garden. There's no doubt that a botanical name can be hard to pronounce, but unlike a common name, which can be applied to several very different plants, a scientific designation is specific and unique.

Throughout this book you will find both scientific and common names. A plant's scientific name consists of the genus (the first word) and an epithet. For example, all lilacs belong to the genus *Syringa*. The epithet (in our example, *vulgaris*) identifies a specific kind of lilac. *Syringa vulgaris* is the common lilac.

A third word or phrase in the name may refer to a special variety of the plant, termed a cultivar. This name is important because it designates a superior selection known for more vigor, bigger blooms, better foliage, or some other noteworthy characteristic. A cultivar name is set off with single quotation marks, as in the name *Syringa vulgaris* 'Charles Joly', a double-flowered lilac that has magenta blooms. Armed with a knowledge of both scientific and common names, you will be able to acquire the best plants for your Colorado garden.

PLANT HARDINESS AND LIGHT REQUIREMENTS

The United States Department of Agriculture (USDA) Plant Hardiness Zone map (found on the last page of the color insert) was created with weather data that was used to divide our country into minimum-temperature zones. For each plant we have listed the zones in which it can survive winter conditions. This means that if a plant is listed as hardy to Zone 5, but you live in Zone 4 (where colder winter temperatures can occur), that particular plant may not survive a severe winter in your area without additional protection.

Introduction

The USDA Plant Hardiness Zone map in this book reflects a new view of changing climatic conditions. Zones designated as "A" are 5 degrees cooler than those designated "B." These additional designations show differences in local climate and microclimates of specific areas. A and B plant hardiness is not specified in the text of this guide, however, because current, reliable USDA information on the hardiness of all the plants listed is not yet available. Ongoing research is leading to the development of new data, including extremes of cold and heat in which landscape plants will thrive. The zone ratings given in this book can serve as a guideline for selecting plants suited to your geographic region's climatic conditions.

Keep in mind, however, that conditions other than zone hardiness can determine whether a plant will thrive in your landscape in the winter. The lay of the land, wind, sunlight intensity, rainfall, exposure, humidity, soil, pH, drainage, and microclimates can all affect plant hardiness. Valleys or low areas can frequently be expected to have late-spring frosts. City dwellers will generally find their average temperatures are warmer than those in surrounding rural areas. The plants recommended in this book are good performers in many parts of Colorado, but do remember there is a wide range of weather conditions across our state. With a little ingenuity, you might be able to create a spot in your landscape that replicates conditions suited for certain plants that are native to other areas. Plants don't know geography; they only know if they are happy in the site you've chosen.

Take the time to analyze a planting site, the amount of sun it gets, and its soil, wind exposure, and soil drainage. Try to match the plant to the site; this will give the plant the best chance of staying healthy and vigorous, which is the best way for it to resist pests and diseases.

Introduction

We have also provided symbols for the amount of sunlight suitable for each plant's growing requirements. The following symbols indicate full sun, partial shade, and shade.

Full Sun   Partial   Shade
            Shade

CONCLUSION

This book was written both as a guide for the beginning Colorado gardener and as a refresher for the seasoned gardener. Gardening in Colorado presents tremendous opportunities. Even though we must cope with drying winds, unpredictable storms and frosts, long dry spells, and a growing population of browsing deer, Colorado gardeners are a resourceful lot. With a little ingenuity, you will discover that our climate allows us to grow many traditional plants as well as an exciting range of native plants.

Good Gardening!

CHAPTER ONE

Annuals

*I*F YOU'RE LOOKING FOR A RIOT OF COLOR that appears in a short amount of time, then annuals are your answer. Not only do they bloom abundantly and profusely, they do it quickly and with little effort on your part.

Early in my gardening career, I grew annuals by the bucketload. Who could resist the double petunias and crackerjack marigolds that sold for $1.29 for a baker's dozen at the local greenhouse and florist? Nowadays, you're not likely to find such great prices, but annuals are still popular among Colorado gardeners.

There are many ways you can use annuals in your landscape. They are good fillers for barren spots, and they can be planted in a mixed border, used in mass plantings, or used to add a touch of summer color in front of the mailbox. They make a fine addition to the perennial border. There are many annuals that make wonderful cut flowers, so if you have the room, plant an annual cutflower garden. Annuals make ideal container plants that can be set on the deck or patio, in windowboxes, or in a sunroom for the winter months.

An annual is a plant that completes its entire life cycle in one season: it starts from seed, grows, flowers, reproduces seeds, and dies when the appearance of frost ends its growth period. Some annuals, such as marigolds, morning glories, and zinnias, will reward you if they are grown in suitable sites and soils. At season's end, they may self-sow seeds that will winter over in the ground and sprout in the spring, starting the cycle over again.

Most seed companies classify annuals based on the temperature needed for germination, healthy growth, and bloom. They divide annuals into three categories: hardy, half-hardy, and tender. The hardy annuals are those plants that can withstand a reasonable degree of frost. Though they die back in the fall, their seeds survive outside and germinate in the spring. In fact, the alternate freezing and thawing of late winter will not harm them and is often necessary for germination. Sweet pea, calendula, and cleome are among the hardy annuals. Half-hardy annuals are generally damaged, stunted, or killed by continued exposure to frost, but they will stand up to an occasional light frost and cooler temperatures. A few half-hardy annuals are snapdragon, petunia, and marigold. Tender annuals, such as impatiens, coleus, and cosmos, are those that are immediately killed by frost. They need warm soils for germination and to achieve vigorous growth.

Annuals will start to bloom soon after they are planted, bringing excitement and color to the garden in a relatively short time. They generally grow in the top six inches or so of soil. They are less demanding of elaborate soil preparation than are the perennial plants in your landscape.

Planting and Caring for Annuals

If you purchase annuals as "bedding plants" instead of growing your own, look for healthy plants with dark-green leaves that are neither too spindly nor too compact. It is preferable to choose plants that are not in bloom. Annuals will have less transplant shock and come into bloom faster in your garden if they are not in bloom when planted. If you can't plant them right away, keep them in a lightly shaded spot and water as needed to keep them from wilting. Carefully lift or punch the plants from their individual cell-packs or containers, keeping the rootball together to prevent damage. If the roots have grown extremely compacted, loosen them gently before planting or score the rootball with a pocketknife. This will allow the roots to spread out readily once they make contact with the soil. Dig the planting hole slightly larger than the root system, set the plant at the same level it was growing in the container, and gently firm the soil around the roots. Water-in thoroughly after planting. Until the plants are well established, water thoroughly whenever the top two inches of the soil begins to dry out. An application of a high-phosphorous fertilizer (5-10-5) will get the transplants off to a good start.

Cleome

Cleome hassleriana

Height: 4 to 5 ft. **Flowers:** Pink, lavender, purple, rose, white **Bloom Period:** Midsummer to frost **Zones:** 4, 5, 6	**Light Requirement:**

*I*f you desire an airy, colorful tall annual, you will appreciate the colorful, floriferous cleome. Cleome, or spider plant, gets its name from its spider-like flowers with their long, waving stamens. As the flowers mature, attractive seedpods appear. Cleome is wonderful for informal, sunny gardens. It can be used behind other plants in a flower border or planted in a bed all its own. Whether you plant it from seed or from transplants, cleome will grow rather quickly to 4 ft. or more, and it spreads about 2 ft. wide. Its globe-shaped flowers appear in midsummer and are quite interesting with their curving stamens. Because it self-seeds so prolifically, cleome may not be for the gardener who detests pulling out volunteer plants.

WHEN TO PLANT

Cleome can be sown directly outdoors in late spring as the soil warms. You can start seeds indoors 4 weeks before the last killing frost and harden young transplants before setting them into the garden. Young transplants may be available at garden retailers.

WHERE TO PLANT

Locate cleome in a sunny, well-drained soil. This annual will produce more blooms when it has more sun, but it will tolerate light shade. Since it grows so tall, keep it in the background. It works well behind a border of perennials or shorter-growing annuals.

HOW TO PLANT

Space plants or thin seedlings 18 to 24 in. apart. When sowing seeds outdoors, plant them at the depth recommended on the seed packet. Transplants should be set at the same level they were growing in their original containers. Gently firm the soil around the roots and water-in well. After planting, apply an all-purpose 5-10-5 granular fertilizer, lightly scratching it into the soil.

Care and Maintenance

Cleome is an easy-to-grow annual that thrives in hot weather. It is tolerant of dry soils, but it should be watered during hot, dry spells to ensure vigor and blooms. If you plant cleome in poor soil, apply an all-purpose fertilizer such as 5-10-5 or 10-10-10 a couple of times during the summer. You can deadhead spent flowers to encourage additional blooms and to reduce self-seeding. Mature flowers will develop interesting seedpods later in the season.

Additional Information

Cleome can grow quite tall and require staking in wind-prone areas. This annual is usually free of serious pests or diseases. Use cleome as an annual screen or grow it against a wood fence or retaining wall.

Additional Species, Cultivars, or Varieties

Cleomes in the 'Queen' series (4 ft.) are available in shades of pink, rose, purple, lilac, and white.

Cosmos

Cosmos bipinnatus

Height: 12 in. to 4 ft. **Flowers:** Pink, white, rose, lavender **Bloom Period:** Midsummer to frost **Zones:** 3, 4, 5, 6	**Light Requirement:**

The tall, wispy stems and daisy-like flowers of cosmos are favorites in an old-fashioned garden. Cosmos is one of the easy-to-grow annuals that can be grown from seed sown directly in the garden in late spring. It is dependable and will grow quickly to several feet tall. Its blooms consist of flower petals which are actually separate ray flowers with notched edges that look as if they were trimmed with pinking shears. The bright-yellow centers of the blooms are really disk flowers. Cosmos make excellent cut flowers and are good in floral arrangements. They are reliable and will bloom from July to frost. Children can have success growing these annuals. The plants are grown easily from seed and can quickly stretch taller than the young gardeners who plant them. Cosmos will almost thrive on neglect and poor soils, requiring very little in the way of care. Give them an occasional drink of water during hot spells. They are native from Mexico to Brazil and perform best in warm weather.

WHEN TO PLANT

Sow cosmos seeds directly in the garden in spring as soon as the soil is workable. Transplants can be set out after the last spring frost, and they will establish themselves quickly as the soil warms.

WHERE TO PLANT

Cosmos prefer a location in full sun and well-drained, average-to-poor soils. Soils that are too rich make for lush leafy growth and sparse flowers. Use these plants as background for other annuals and for perennials, where their graceful stems will wave in the breeze. Grow cosmos in cutting gardens or in mass plantings all by itself. The fern-like foliage, branching form, and height create an old-fashioned, romantic effect. Cosmos are great annuals for those hot, sunny spots that might stress more heat-sensitive plants.

How to Plant

Space cosmos plants 10 to 15 in. apart. They will grow and branch out freely, so allow plenty of room. Young transplants should be pinched back to encourage bushier growth and branching. Set transplants at the same level they were growing in their original containers. Gently firm the soil around the roots and water-in well.

Care and Maintenance

Cosmos are generally not bothered by insects or disease. Good air circulation is essential to reduce problems with powdery mildew in late summer. Avoid wetting the foliage in the evening. Too much fertilizer produces rank foliage and sparse flowering, so don't use plant food with these annuals. During dry periods, water as needed. Cosmos can tolerate dry conditions. Deadhead spent flowers to keep the flowerbed tidy and to encourage more blooms. This will also reduce self-seeding.

Additional Information

This annual will self-sow readily, but the flower colors may not be exactly the same as those of the parent plants. You may want to yank out volunteer seedlings and plant new ones each year, or experiment and enjoy the show.

Additional Species, Cultivars, or Varieties

'Picotee' (30 in.) is one of our favorites, with its icy-white blossoms that are boldly bordered, splashed, or stippled with crimson. If you want something different, try 'Seashells' (3 ft.), which has petals that curve inward like fluted sea shells around a button-like center. Plants in the 'Sonata' series produce 3-in. flowers on relatively small plants (24 in.); they are well suited for smaller gardens. *Cosmos sulphureus* 'Ladybird Mixed' (10 in.) is a collection of scarlet red, tangerine, and yellow with semi-double flowers. 'Sunny Orange Red' (12 in.) produces bold semi-double blossoms in hot-orange to red.

Dusty Miller

Senecio cineraria

Height: 6 to 15 in.
Flowers: Grown for its silvery
gray foliage
Zones: 3, 4, 5, 6

Light Requirement:

*T*he word senecio comes from the Latin for "old man," a name given in recognition of the thick mat of white whiskers that covers this plant's leaves. If the colors in your garden are overwhelmingly bright, plant dusty miller among the bright ones. The silvery gray foliage will cool the bold reds, oranges, and yellows of many annuals and perennials. Dusty miller is wonderful for edging flower beds and borders and for creating patterns. It can be grown successfully in full sun or part shade. Plants can be kept compact and within bounds with periodic pinching or pruning throughout the summer. For a cooling effect, combine dusty miller with pink geraniums in a border planting or a half whiskey barrel. The foliage is nice in floral arrangements. This easy-to-grow annual is tolerant of heat and cool conditions, and will often overwinter if the weather is mild.

WHEN TO PLANT

Plant dusty miller transplants in late spring. You can purchase transplants from most garden retailers.

WHERE TO PLANT

Dusty miller will grow well in full sun, and it will tolerate filtered sun. Our soil is a sandy loam, and plants thrive here. Whether your soil is sandy or clay, dusty miller does best in well-drained soils. Heavy, compacted clay soil or extremely sandy soil should be amended with compost before planting. Dusty miller's foliage, which is silvery white to gray, is effective as a foil for other bedding plants. It is excellent for edging, for formal bedding, and to create patterns.

HOW TO PLANT

Compacted soils should be improved with organic matter such as compost before you plant. Incorporate 2 to 3 in. of compost into the soil to a depth of 6 in. or more. Once the soil has been worked, remove transplants from their containers and set them at the same level they were growing at the nursery. Gently firm the soil around the roots and water-in well. If you desire, apply an all-purpose 5-10-5 or 10-10-10 fertilizer around the plants and lightly rake it in. Mulch with a few inches of shredded cedar or aspen mulch.

CARE AND MAINTENANCE

Dusty miller is virtually insect- and disease-free. To encourage bushier growth, pinch back flowers as soon as they appear. If the plant starts to grow leggy, prune back once or twice during the summer for a neat and attractive appearance. Our plants continue to maintain their handsome foliage into late autumn, even after a frost.

ADDITIONAL INFORMATION

Dusty miller will often survive a mild winter. Though the top of the plant may die back, the crown will survive and sprout new growth the following spring. If live buds are present, cut the dead foliage within 2 in. of ground level in spring and wait for regrowth. This half-hardy annual is invaluable for adding contrast to the garden palette.

ADDITIONAL SPECIES, CULTIVARS, OR VARIETIES

There are several varieties of dusty miller available. Some, like 'Silver Dust' (8 in.), have deeply cut leaves. 'Silver Dust' is covered with dense, woolly white hairs. *Senecio cineraria* 'Cirrhus' has spoon-shaped leaves that are woolly and silvery white. It can grow to 15 in. tall. 'Silver Queen' is a French strain (8 in.) with delicate lacy leaves in silver-white. It is excellent for windowboxes, container gardening, and borders.

Flowering Cabbage

Brassica oleracea

Height: 10 to 18 in. depending on variety
Flowers: Grown for its colorful leaves in
   white, cream, purple, maroon
Bloom Period: Late summer through fall
Zones: 3, 4, 5, 6

Light Requirement:

*I*f you live in the high country, flowering cabbage or kale is an annual that is well worth growing. It thrives in cool weather, putting on a dramatic display. In the High Plains or at lower elevations, this plant begins to show its true colors in late summer through autumn. The waxy green heads are pink, red, white, cream, or maroon in the centers. Flowering cabbage will retain its crispy foliage well into the fall, despite cool weather and brushes with frost. It should be used in mass plantings to make a bold display. Plant single colors of your choice to outline beds of other cool-tolerant plants such as pansies, calendulas, and dianthus.

WHEN TO PLANT

The best time to acquire transplants of flowering cabbage or kale is early spring. Some garden retailers may stock them in summer and early fall.

WHERE TO PLANT

Flowering cabbage and kale are good plants to use near an entry or any place you want attractive color. Plant in flower beds near the driveway or curb. They are especially effective when planted as a single color in groups of 6 or more. To achieve the best foliage color, plant in full sun and well-drained soils. In many Colorado resort mountain communities, you will often see flowering kale planted in large containers for immediate eye appeal. Do not plant in compacted clay soil without first improving it with organic matter.

HOW TO PLANT

Flowering cabbage and kale perform best in well-drained compost-enriched soil. Loosen the soil to a depth of 6 in. or more and work 2 to 3 in. of compost uniformly into the soil. Rake the planting area level and dig planting holes wide enough to accommodate the root system. Position the transplants at the same level they were growing in their containers. Gently firm the soil around the roots and water thoroughly. Scatter an all-purpose fertilizer like 5-10-5 or 10-10-10 throughout the planted bed and lightly rake the fertilizer into the soil. Then apply a 2-in. layer of organic mulch over the entire annual bed. If planting in containers, use a high-quality compost-based potting soil.

CARE AND MAINTENANCE

Flowering cabbage and kale are easy to grow and generally require little attention. Provide ample water during the heat of summer and throughout the growth cycle. Avoid overwatering, as water-logging will kill the plants. Using mulches will maintain moisture and keep the soil cool. You may have to remove an occasional unsightly or old leaf throughout the growing season. Unlike edible cabbage, ornamental cabbage is usually not bothered by cabbage loopers or aphids. This is a great asset for an annual. If caterpillars should become a problem, engage in bacteria warfare by using *Bacillus thuriengensis* (called *Bt*). Read and follow label directions.

ADDITIONAL INFORMATION

In many parts of Colorado, flowering kale and cabbage may provide color in the landscape into early winter, depending upon weather conditions. It is often listed as "edible" and some people use it as a garnish. I find the leaves a bit too bitter.

ADDITIONAL SPECIES, CULTIVARS, OR VARIETIES

You will find various forms of flowering cabbage and kale at garden retailers. They are commonly sold as white, pink, or mixed colors. Some have lobed leaves, while others are deeply cut or fringed. You can order seeds from mail-order sources as well. Try 'Nagoya' hybrid mix and 'Tokyo' hybrid mix.

Geranium

Pelargonium × *hortorum*

Height: 12 to 24 in.
Flowers: Pink, red, magenta, white,
    salmon, bicolors
Bloom Period: Early summer to frost
Zones: 3, 4, 5, 6

Light Requirement:

Geraniums continue to be among the most popular annuals for containers and borders. Every year without fail, we strive to overwinter pots and pots of summer's geraniums in the sunniest window of our basement. The bright globes of clustered flowers are a welcome sight in the midst of winter. From the time the plants are set outdoors in late spring, geraniums put on a show of continuous color until a hard frost. By summer's end, the plants may have become woody; they will benefit from a good pruning if you plan to bring them indoors. This makes for a tidy plant and the development of fresh, new foliage. To keep the plants blooming vigorously, it helps to deadhead the spent flowers regularly. There is a wide variety of colors and leaf forms available, both locally and from mail-order sources. Geraniums with darker markings around the leaves are called zonal geraniums. Seed-grown geraniums with single flowers have gained popularity in mass plantings.

WHEN TO PLANT

Geraniums are planted in late spring. They are readily available at local garden retailers as transplants of blooming size.

WHERE TO PLANT

Plant in a sunny place that has well-drained soil. Geraniums can be effectively used in containers, in flower beds, as accent plants, and in windowboxes.

HOW TO PLANT

Before planting geraniums, enrich the soil with compost to retain moisture and improve drainage. Loosen the soil in a prepared bed to a depth of 6 in. or more. Scatter an all-purpose 5-10-5 or 10-10-10 fertilizer over the bed and lightly rake it in. Dig the planting hole wide enough to accommodate the root system and position the plants at the same depth they were growing in their containers. Gently firm the soil around the roots and water-in well. Space plants 12 to 15 in. apart. To conserve moisture and reduce weed growth, apply a mulch of shredded cedar or aspen around the plants.

CARE AND MAINTENANCE

Geraniums will thrive in Colorado's bright sunshine and cool evenings. Provide them with water throughout the growing season and apply a general flower fertilizer every 3 weeks according to the manufacturer's recommendations. Avoid watering in late evening as the flower clusters tend to stay wet and become more susceptible to fungus problems. Remove faded flowers to encourage more blooms. Under these proper growing conditions, geraniums are usually trouble-free and will bloom until a hard frost visits the garden.

ADDITIONAL INFORMATION

Geraniums are frequently attacked by a notorious pest known as tobacco/geranium budworm. The tiny caterpillars tunnel into the developing buds and reduce flowering. If this should be a problem, you may have to treat the geranium plants early in the season with a systemic insecticide. Read and follow label directions.

ADDITIONAL SPECIES, CULTIVARS, OR VARIETIES

There are so many geraniums to pick from—let your individual taste determine the colors you like best. For a bold display, plant groups of the same color. Scented geraniums are prized for their fragrant foliage. Peppermint, lemon, rose, nutmeg, and apple are a few tempting possibilities to try in your garden. Plant them near the patio or deck where you can brush up against them to release their charming fragrance. *Pelargonium × domesticum*, Martha Washington geranium, is a gorgeous plant with large individual blossoms between 2 and 3 in. wide. It requires cooler temperatures and partial shade to bloom dependably. The ivy geranium, *Pelargonium peltatum*, is excellent for hanging baskets underneath the patio or covered deck. Trailing stems spill over the containers with brilliant-colored blooms.

Impatiens

Impatiens wallerana

Height: 6 to 18 in.
Flowers: Red, pink, scarlet, orange, striped white, white, bicolors
Bloom Period: Summer to frost
Zones: 3, 4, 5, 6

Light Requirement:

*S*o you have a shady garden and you say you can't grow flowers. Have you tried impatiens? These brightly colored annuals will dress up a shady spot, making an especially big splash around the base of a large shade tree. Use impatiens in containers or windowboxes and watch the bright blossoms spill over the sides. The older varieties are well adapted to shade, while some of the newer varieties will tolerate some sun. Single plants can grow into a flower-covered mound up to 18 in. tall and equally as wide. Impatiens will bloom all summer until touched by frost. Look for double impatiens which have flowers that resemble fluffy miniature roses. Experiment with various color combinations from hot pink or orange to the softer lavender or pink blooms. In late summer and early fall, collect the seedpods and watch them disperse their seeds. Place one in a child's palm and the youngster will be fascinated with the way the light-green seedpod splits open and launches tiny seeds.

WHEN TO PLANT

Set transplants outdoors after the danger of frost has passed in your area, usually late May to mid-June. Impatiens are tender annuals that grow best after the soil has had a chance to warm. Plants set out in cool soil will sulk.

WHERE TO PLANT

Impatiens are ideal as mass plantings in the shade of trees and shrubs. Plant them in containers on the shaded patio or deck. These annuals make excellent companions for other shade plants such as ferns, hostas, pulmonaria, and lungwort. They will flower more profusely where they receive at least some morning sun; the newer varieties can tolerate even more sunlight. Soil should be rich in humus and well-drained. In heavy clay or sandy soils, add compost before planting for the best results.

How to Plant

Impatiens can be spaced from 10 to 12 in. apart. Position transplants at the same level they were growing in their containers. Gently firm the soil around the roots and water-in well. After planting, fertilize with an all-purpose 5-10-5 or 10-10-10 plant food. Do not use a high-nitrogen food, as this will result in more foliage and scarce flowers.

Care and Maintenance

Impatiens in shade should be watered sparingly to avoid waterlogging the soil. If they are growing in more sun, they will require more attention to watering. Mulch after transplanting to conserve and maintain moisture in the soil. Fertilize with an all-purpose plant food, the same kind used at planting time, every 3 to 4 weeks if desired. Impatiens can be plagued by slugs. If you begin to see leaf damage, take appropriate control measures.

Additional Information

Plant impatiens in shady spots to brighten the landscape. Use the paler colored impatiens in shade, brighter colors where there is more sun. If you desire, impatiens can be overwintered indoors. Rather than taking in the whole plant, take cuttings in August, root them in perlite or sand, and after they have rooted, transplant them into potting soil. They will flower indoors if placed in a cool spot that has bright light.

Additional Species, Cultivars, or Varieties

There are many cultivars to choose from. 'Blue Pearl' is a delightful pastel blue-lilac shade with flowers borne on compact plants (8 to 10 in.). 'Super Elfins' are available in 11 colors and are earlier to bloom than many others. 'New Guinea' impatiens have variegated leaves and larger blooms, and tolerate more heat. They are spectacular in hanging containers, but they will need daily watering during hot, dry periods. *Impatiens oncidioides* bears 2-in. golden blossoms perched above deep-green foliage. The garden balsam, *Impatiens balsamina*, is an old-fashioned garden favorite with double flowers in yellow, pink, or salmon. Its common name, touch-me-not, comes from the way its ripe seedpods erupt when pressure is applied.

Love-in-a-Mist

Nigella damascena

Height: 12 to 18 in.
Flowers: Blue, rose, white
Bloom Period: Early summer to frost
Zones: 3, 4, 5, 6

Light Requirement:

ove-in-a-mist, or fennel flower, is an old-fashioned favorite. Its romantic name comes from the pastel-colored blossoms that hover above soft, green, fern-like foliage. The most beautiful forms of this annual are those that have clear sky-blue or delphinium-blue blossoms, an uncommon color for flowers. It is best used as a filler in perennial beds, cottage gardens, and herb gardens, and in the cutflower garden, where it is grown for its dainty flowers and distinctive seedpods. The horned seedpods give this plant another common name, devil-in-a-bush. These inflated seedpods are actually quite attractive with their maroon stripes and can be used, both fresh and dried, in floral arrangements and in herbal wreaths. Each seedpod contains many black seeds that can be shared with friends or allowed to self-sow. The seeds are aromatic and are used by cooks and physicians in Asian countries. The leaves and seeds are used in India to prevent moths from chewing clothing.

WHEN TO PLANT

As soon as the soil can be worked in spring, love-in-a-mist is easy to grow from seeds sown in the garden. The seeds will germinate in about 2 weeks.

WHERE TO PLANT

Plant in average garden soil with good drainage in full sun to part shade. Use in the perennial garden to fill in open spots, or let *Nigella* self-sow in the vegetable and herb garden for special accents.

HOW TO PLANT

Nigella has a taproot and resents being transplanted. Sowing seed directly in the garden will give the best results. Love-in-a-mist will tolerate cooler temperatures and can be sown as soon as the soil is workable in spring. Thin the seedlings to 6 to 8 in. apart. If you are transparenting from cell-packs, be careful not to disturb the roots. Set at the same level they were growing in their cells.

CARE AND MAINTENANCE

When planted early, love-in-a-mist will provide the greatest show before the hot temperatures of summer. The plants reach maturity in about 6 weeks; then blooming will slow down. Successive sowings made from spring through early summer can prolong the blooming period. When planted in average garden soil, extra fertilizer will not be needed. This annual will thrive on the normal watering provided neighboring plants. It is truly an easy-grower.

ADDITIONAL INFORMATION

Ripening seedpods inflate like balloons crowned with jester's caps, except they don't have bells. Pick the pods just as the maroon color has begun to develop. If you wait too long, the pods will not be as striking. Love-in-a-mist may find a good home in an unusual place such as a rose garden where the delicate plants and flowers will accent the roses and will not significantly compete for water or nutrients.

ADDITIONAL SPECIES, CULTIVARS, OR VARIETIES

Some cultivars worth seeking out are 'Miss Jekyll' with bright blue, semi-double flowers; 'Miss Jekyll Alba', a pure white; and 'Persian Jewels', which has pink, white, and lavender-blue double flowers. The single color selections, which are best for planned color combinations, may have to be ordered from seed catalogs. 'Oxford Blue' (to 30 in.) is a tall, double-flowered form that can add a unique deep-blue color and delicate grace to a perennial garden. 'Mulberry Rose' (15 in.) is a beautiful single pink. *Nigella hispanica* (16 in.) has black centers and scarlet stamens.

Marigold

Tagetes spp.

Height: 6 to 36 in.	**Light Requirement:**
Flowers: Yellow, lemon, orange, mahogany, creamy white	
Bloom Period: Early summer to frost	
Zones: 3, 4, 5, 6	

*M*arigolds appeal to both beginning and experienced gardeners who like a riot of color in orange, yellow, and mahogany. Even red-and-yellow-striped cultivars are available. The rounded full flowers resemble small carnations or chrysanthemums. Marigolds are the sunshine of the annual flower bed, and they end the season with a burst of vigor. Plants grow from just a few inches tall to 3 ft. The French marigold, *Tagetes patula*, ranges in height from 6 to 14 in. and has fern-like foliage. Flowers may be single, double, or crested. Colors are solid or bicolored with orange, gold, yellow, or mahogany-red combinations. African marigolds, *Tagetes erecta*, grow as tall as 3 ft. and are best planted in masses. 'Crackerjack mixed' produces bold flowers of orange, gold, and lemon. 'Galore' hybrids (16 to 18 in.) are self cleaning, which means spent flowers disappear under new blooms. 'Discovery' hybrids are the compact African (10 in.). Plants can be grown easily from seed started indoors in spring or sown directly outside in mid- to late May. Children enjoy starting marigold seeds, as they sprout reliably.

WHEN TO PLANT

Seeds of marigolds can be started indoors 4 to 6 weeks before the last frost date. Direct-sow outdoors in mid- to late May. Transplants are readily available from local garden retailers.

WHERE TO PLANT

Marigolds prefer full sun, but they will tolerate some light shade. Well-drained soils of average to poor fertility suit this annual just fine. The tamed growth habit of these plants makes them excellent for edging or massing in open flower beds. Some of the smaller varieties are superb for containers.

How to Plant

Space marigolds 6 to 15 in. apart, depending on the type. Position transplants slightly deeper than they were growing in their containers. In heavy clay or sandy soils, add some compost to the soil before planting. This improves drainage and aids in moisture retention. After planting, apply an all-purpose 5-10-5 fertilizer. Seeds sown directly in the garden will germinate in 7 to 10 days, depending upon soil temperature.

Care and Maintenance

Marigolds prefer warm weather. Wait until the soil begins to warm up if you are going to direct-seed outdoors. If the soil is too rich, or if you use high-nitrogen fertilizers, marigolds generally grow lush foliage but few flowers. Keep plants watered as the soil dries out. Try not to get water on the flowers; this will shorten their life. Deadhead or remove faded flowers often to prevent seed development and to keep the plants tidy.

Additional Information

Many gardeners interplant their vegetable garden with marigolds in the belief that these annuals repel pests. The pungent, distinctive aroma of the old-fashioned species seems to be the most effective. Marigolds are long-lived cut flowers, so enjoy them freely.

Additional Species, Cultivars, or Varieties

Look at any seed catalog and you will be mesmerized by the many interesting marigold cultivars. The single French marigolds are becoming popular again, with some heirloom selections available. 'Tiger Eyes' is one of our favorites; it has a scarlet "skirt" and a prominent chrysanthemum-flowered crest. The African marigolds have quilled or rolled petals, which are actually ray flowers. Among them are the popular 'Inca' (14 to 16 in.) and 'Discovery' (10 to 12 in.) hybrids. *Tagetes tenuifolia*, the signet marigolds (6 to 10 in.), bear single flowers on handsome ferny foliage and are particularly useful as edging in a border.

Morning Glory

Ipomoea purpurea

Height: 8 to 10 ft., depending upon variety **Flowers:** Blue, white, purple, pink, red **Bloom Period:** Summer to frost **Zones:** 4, 5, 6	**Light Requirement:**

*M*orning glories are favorite annual flowering vines that Colorado gardeners have grown for generations. The vigorous, quick climbers twine around upright supports such as chain-link fences, trellises, pergolas, and branches of dead trees to provide a temporary summer screen. The handsome heart-shaped leaves provide a contrast to the large, showy trumpet-like flowers that grow up to 5 in. across. Morning glories will bloom prolifically in bright, sunny spots. Each flower lasts for a day, but a new flower appears every day. These are among the few plants that bloom in mid- to late summer when other plants are winding down. If you want to get the plants to grow and bloom earlier, try starting seeds indoors 4 weeks before they can be safely be sown outdoors in the garden.

When to Plant

Sow morning glories in the spring after the danger of frost is past and the soil is warm. Seeds can be started indoors a month before the last frost date in your area.

Where to Plant

Morning glories prosper in sunny locations and well-drained soils. To bloom profusely, they need a minimum of 6 hours of sun daily. Avoid heavily shaded areas or poorly drained soils. These annual vines are useful for summertime flowering screens. Plant them around gazebos, trellises, chain-link fences, posts, and other garden structures.

How to Plant

Seeds planted directly outdoors will germinate in 10 to 20 days. One way to hasten germination is to nick the pointed ends of the seeds with a file, pocketknife, or grinder. You can also soak the seeds in warm water for 24 hours before planting. These procedures will speed up and increase the percentage of seed germination. If you live in an area that has heavy clay soil, amend the soil with compost before planting. This will improve drainage and help to retain moisture. Add 2 to 3 in. of compost to the planting area and incorporate it to a depth of 6 inches or more. Morning glories can be successfully grown in a large pot in which you have erected an upright structure or trellis. Fill the container with a compost-based potting soil and make sure there is proper drainage at the bottom or sides of the container.

CARE AND MAINTENANCE

Morning glories are not bothered by many insect pests or diseases. Regular watering is necessary to prevent stress and severe wilting, which can delay flowering. No pruning is needed, but you can train the vines to grow in specific directions. They don't require lots of fertilizer. Use an all-purpose 5-10-5 or 10-10-10 fertilizer in spring to get them started. Those growing in pots can be fertilized every 3 to 4 weeks.

ADDITIONAL INFORMATION

Morning glories don't get the respect they deserve. They are hard-working annual vines that provide a quick and colorful accent or screen. They often self-sow, and volunteers return in subsequent years.

ADDITIONAL SPECIES, CULTIVARS, OR VARIETIES

There are many cultivars of morning glories, including some double-flowering types. A few favorites are 'Heavenly Blue' with true-blue trumpets (3 to 5 in. across); 'Sapphire Cross' and 'Flying Saucers', both blue-and-white-striped hybrids; 'Cardinal', which bears red flowers; white 'Pearly Gates'; and 'Minibar Rose', a unique plant that has rosy-red blooms edged in white. 'Scarlet O'Hara' is an All-America winner with large, rich-crimson flowers. *Ipomoea* × *multifida* is the best climber. It has delicate, deeply fringed foliage and glowing scarlet 2-in. tubular blooms. Plant it to attract hummingbirds.

Moss Rose

Portulaca grandiflora

Height: 4 to 6 in.	**Light Requirement:**
Flowers: Red, pink, white, orange, yellow	
Bloom Period: Early summer to frost	
Zones: 3, 4, 5, 6	

oss rose is an annual that is able to survive and bloom in the most inhospitable places. Neither dry, parched, poor soils or the heat of the sun will slow the vigorous growth of this attractive annual groundcover. Its bright glowing flowers with satiny petals in red, yellow, scarlet, magenta, orange, and white bloom in profusion on succulent reddish stems. The creeping stems hug the ground, making this an excellent groundcover when grouped in front of a perennial bed or along a sidewalk or driveway. When other plants are wilting in the summer's heat, portulaca grows on, creeping and spreading to cover a spot where nothing else dares to grow. Flowers range in size from 1 to 2 in. and are available in singles or doubles. Moss rose is noted for its ability to self-sow and return the following season. Second-year flowers may not be quite as vigorous or colorful as the originals. If you don't like the look, pull out these volunteers and replant with new plants.

WHEN TO PLANT

Young transplants can be purchased and set out in the garden after danger of frost has passed and the soil has warmed. Seeds can be started indoors 6 weeks before the last frost date in your area.

WHERE TO PLANT

In order to thrive and bloom profusely, moss rose requires full sun. It will tolerate poor soil, but the site should be well-drained; avoid areas that remain wet. Plant it in problem spots where you want a flowering groundcover. Use it in front of perennial borders, between paving stones or surrounding bricks, and for edging pathways and driveways.

HOW TO PLANT

Plant young plants 6 to 8 in. apart. If you start seeds indoors, mix the fine seed with sand for easier sowing and do not cover, as portulaca needs light for germination. After setting outdoors, apply an all-purpose 5-10-5 or 10-10-10 fertilizer. This is the one and only time you will have to fertilize; these plants don't require supplemental food. Water the soil as it becomes dry.

CARE AND MAINTENANCE

Moss rose is quick to establish, sprawling and trailing its way along the ground. It blooms profusely with a minimum of care. Portulaca can withstand drought conditions, but it should be watered regularly to maintain vigorous growth. Avoid fertilizing with any high-nitrogen fertilizer, or flowering will diminish. Since it has no serious pest or disease problems, this annual is an excellent choice for beginners and for the lazy gardener.

ADDITIONAL INFORMATION

Its fleshy leaves help this plant adapt to dry, exposed locations. It is a good plant for rock gardens or for containers in hot spots. Moss rose is a good companion for dusty miller, providing a nice contrast to the fuzzy foliage. Other good buddies for moss rose are petunias.

ADDITIONAL SPECIES, CULTIVARS, OR VARIETIES

Seed catalogs list several cultivars of moss rose. Some, such as 'Kariba' mixed, have extra-large double flowers. 'Sundial' hybrid mix produces double flowers in colors of cream, fuchsia, pink, orange, scarlet, yellow, and white. A Park Seed® introduction, 'Afternoon Delight' has flowers that stay open all day, even during the hottest days.

Pansy

Viola × wittrockiana

Height: 6 to 10 in.
Flowers: Blue, violet, purple, white,
   splotched, orange, mahogany,
   multicolored
Bloom Period: Spring and fall
Zones: 3, 4, 5, 6

Light Requirement:

---

*P*ansies are old-fashioned flowers that perform with gusto in spring and fall. They make wonderful filler plants to disguise the old or ripening foliage of perennials. Plant them to cover an area that was recently planted with daffodils and tulips. There have been numerous improvements in pansies over the years. They come in a multitude of colors—blue, purple, violet, rose, gold, yellow, orange, lavender, white, bicolored—and many types have markings that create a cheerful tiny face. Although they grow like perennials, pansies are best treated as annuals since they begin to lose their vitality by the second year. Fall-planted pansies will continue to flower through November and even poke their faces out of melting snow in winter. If mulched over the winter, they will revive and begin to bloom at the first hint of spring.

WHEN TO PLANT

Set out transplants 2 to 3 weeks before the last frost. Plants are readily available in September for flowers in autumn and the following spring. Apply a mulch of evergreen boughs over fall-planted pansies after the ground freezes.

WHERE TO PLANT

Pansies will thrive in sun to light shade. Exposure to afternoon sun will make them dry out faster. Plant in well-drained soils that have been amended with compost. Avoid heavy clay soils that stay wet all winter. Use pansies in flower beds, plant them in masses, or grow them in containers. In autumn, plant them over newly planted bulb beds. They will bloom into early winter and return in spring with colorful flowers skirting the bases of daffodils, tulips, and other bulbs.

How to Plant

Set transplants 6 to 8 in. apart. Try them in a checkerboard pattern for a dramatic effect. Position the plants at the same level they were growing in their containers. Gently firm the soil around the rootball and water-in well. Apply an all-purpose 5-10-5 fertilizer throughout the prepared bed and lightly rake it in. Mulch with shredded cedar or pole peelings to conserve moisture and keep the soil cool.

Care and Maintenance

Pinching off spent flowers will encourage more blooms and keep the flower bed tidy. Pansies do best in cool weather and are well suited to high-altitude gardens. Partial shade in summer will help prolong bloom; mulch to keep the soil cool. Provide water on a regular basis; these plants resent dry, hot periods. We have cut our pansies after the big flush of bloom, and this stimulates the plants to regrow and repeat-bloom in fall.

Additional Information

Pansies with cheerful faces are favorites of children; encourage kids to plant a 12-pack. Slugs can become a problem—they cherish the tender leaves. You can surround the plants with wood ashes to repel these pests.

Additional Species, Cultivars, or Varieties

There are a wide variety of pansies available. 'Joker' has petals of light violet, white, and dark purple fading into a yellow throat. 'Antique Shades' is gorgeous with silky flowers (up to 3 in. across) in tones that range from apricot to rose. 'Crystal Bowl', 'Universal', and 'Maxim' are very cold tolerant. One of my personal favorites is *Viola tricolor* Johnny-jump-up (10 to 12 in.), which is always a welcome sight in the garden. Its tricolored flowers are purple, yellow, and white, and about 3/4 in. long. There are various cultivars of *V. tricolor* available—'Bowles Black' has blooms of near black and a tiny yellow eye in the center.

Petunia

Petunia × hybrida

Height: 4 to 18 in. **Flowers:** White, pink, purple, red, lavender, light blue, rose, bicolors **Bloom Period:** Early summer to frost **Zones:** 3, 4, 5, 6	**Light Requirement:**

etunias are among the most common bedding plants sold by garden retailers in the spring. Their wide range of colors and long season of bloom make them a dependable annual for Colorado gardens. Even if they are shredded or beaten down by a summer hailstorm, these resilient plants grow back to continue flowering until a hard frost. They are remarkable in the high country, as they thrive in cool conditions and display bright colors at higher elevations. Petunias also take the heat in stride. There are many new introductions which offer advantages over the older petunias. 'Purple Wave', an All-America winner, was the first groundcover petunia, producing a dense carpet of burgundy-purple blooms on compact plants (4 in.). One plant will spread 3 ft. or more in a flower bed or hanging basket. Petunias come in all kinds of colors and flowers may be veined or striped, ruffled, single, or double. The name petunia comes from the Brazilian name for tobacco, a close relative. With their velvety texture, funnel-shaped flowers, and distinctive fragrance, petunias work well in annual flower beds as well as in hanging baskets and containers.

WHEN TO PLANT

Purchase transplants to plant in spring. Petunias are more tolerant of cold weather than many annuals, so they can be planted outdoors a few weeks before the last frost date. Plants grown in greenhouses can be "hardened-off" before setting out in the garden. Hardening-off is a process of growing the plants outdoors in filtered sun during the day, and bringing them indoors at night. Follow this schedule for 7 to 10 days to allow the plants to become accustomed to outdoor conditions. If there is no danger of frost at night, leave the plants outdoors. Those that have been hardened-off will adjust to being outside more easily.

WHERE TO PLANT

Petunias prefer sunny locations that have at least 6 hours of daily sun. Partial shade is acceptable, but flowering may be sparse. Plant them in humus-enriched, well-drained soil. Heavy clay and sandy soil should be amended with compost before planting.

HOW TO PLANT

Space petunia plants 6 to 12 inches apart, depending on the cultivar. After planting, apply an all-purpose 5-10-5 or 10-10-10 fertilizer. Set the plants at the same depth they were growing in their containers. Gently firm the soil around the roots and water-in well. Pinch off the flowers to promote a bushier plant.

CARE AND MAINTENANCE

Petunias are easy-to-grow annuals that thrive in the heat of summer. Keep the soil watered regularly during hot, dry spells. Avoid watering late in the evening, as plants that stay wet overnight can be more susceptible to diseases. Fertilize about once a month to keep the foliage vigorous and flowers developing. Remove faded blooms to encourage new growth and more flowers. This can be accomplished by pinching off spent flowers, making sure you remove the seedpods. Petunias that become tall and scraggly can be sheared in early July to rejuvenate the plants and promote another flush of bloom. Cut such plants back by half, and then fertilize.

ADDITIONAL INFORMATION

Petunias are well suited to sunny garden beds. They are good companions for sweet alyssum and plants with silver foliage such as artemisia, dusty miller, and lamb's ears. Petunias can be bothered by the tobacco/geranium budworm. This pest will tunnel through the flower beds and reduce flowering; use an appropriate systemic control to keep it at bay.

ADDITIONAL SPECIES, CULTIVARS, OR VARIETIES

There are so many petunia cultivars, it would take another chapter to do them all justice. Choose colors and growth habits that fit your garden.

Pot Marigold

Calendula officinalis

Height: 12 to 24 in. **Flowers:** Orange, yellow, cream **Bloom Period:** Early summer to frost **Zones:** 3, 4, 5, 6	**Light Requirement:**

*T*he pot marigold or calendula is an easy-to-grow annual that was grown in every medieval garden; it was thought to possess wondrous medical virtues. Seeds of this annual can be sown in early spring, even as the snow melts, and they will easily germinate and grow. In 6 weeks, calendula will be putting on a display of silky-petaled flowers, blooming from late spring to late fall. It thrives with cool nights and is outstanding for high-altitude gardens. In the heat of summer, calendula may take a rest from blooming because it lacks heat resistance. If you plant it in light afternoon shade, you can prolong its summer bloom period. Its flowers have been long used for culinary, cosmetic, and medicinal purposes. Today's flower types include single and semi-double to fully double; some varieties have a contrasting maroon center. The flower petals possess a silky sheen and are soft to the touch. Plant calendula in annual beds, containers, cottage gardens, and herb gardens. Sow a row in the vegetable garden if you have space to grow extra flowers for cutting. They are excellent cut flowers, lasting up to 2 weeks in a vase. The brightly colored flowers blend easily with other hot colors, and we like to combine them with purple and blue flowers. For a wonderful blue-and-orange combination, sow seeds of blue larkspur at the same time you sow pot marigold seeds.

WHEN TO PLANT

Seed can be sown directly into the garden in early spring. This annual is tolerant of cooler temperatures and can be sown a few weeks before the frost-free date.

WHERE TO PLANT

Calendula will thrive in full sun, but it will tolerate a bit of shade, particularly during the heat of summer. Sow seeds in moderately moist and well-drained soil. Heavy clay and sandy soils should be improved with some compost before planting. Use calendula in an annual flower bed, cutting garden, herb garden, and containers. It is very effective when planted in masses. Some good companions are love-in-a-mist, orange nasturtiums, borage, and 'Dark Opal' basil.

How to Plant

Sow seeds directly outdoors as soon as the ground can be worked; they will germinate in 10 to 14 days. Plants should be thinned 6 to 10 inches apart, depending on the variety. Keep the flower bed moistened daily to ensure good germination. Once the plants have been thinned, apply a light mulch of compost around them to conserve moisture and keep the soil cool.

Care and Maintenance

Calendula will begin to languish in the heat of summer, but don't fret. Trim the plants back by half to stimulate new growth, and they will repeat-bloom when cool weather returns in late summer and fall. Deadhead or remove spent flowers to stimulate the plants to produce more blooms. Keep the plants watered regularly during the hot, dry summer weather. Pot marigold prefers the cooler temperatures of spring and fall and will flower profusely until a hard frost.

Additional Information

Calendula is quite cold tolerant and will continue to bloom into late autumn when other flowers are waning. It will self-sow generously and produce an abundance of volunteers. You should thin plants to encourage vigorous growth and better flowering.

Additional Species, Cultivars, or Varieties

There are some compact-growing calendulas (12 in.) that work well in borders. Two of these are 'Fiesta Gitana' and 'Double Lemon Coronet'. The 'Pacific' series grows taller (24 to 30 in.) and makes wonderful cut flowers. 'Touch of Red' (14 to 16 in.) is outstanding with its silky flower petals that are edged in dark red, giving it an antique look.

Snapdragon

Antirrhinum majus

Height: 6 to 36 in. **Flowers:** White, orange, pink, red, yellow, purple, bicolors **Bloom Period:** Early summer to frost **Zones:** 3, 4, 5, 6	**Light Requirement:**

olorful snapdragons are perfect plants for children who want to learn about plants and flowers. Snaps are lots of fun as children play with the blossoms, pushing the "dragon jaws" open and then allowing the jaws to snap shut. These old-fashioned favorites are easy to grow, either from seed or from young transplants. The spikes loaded with flowers in a variety of colors are useful as edging and bedding. They are also excellent cut flowers and should be planted in the cutting garden. Position taller varieties toward the middle to back of a border and the smaller snapdragons at the front of beds. The dwarf and intermediate types do not require staking. Snapdragons range in height from under 12 in. to several feet tall. Some cultivars, such as the 'Butterfly' series, produce double flowers. Some of the dwarf kinds, such as 'Floral Carpet' and 'Tahiti', are excellent for containers as they grow into a mass of bright colors.

WHEN TO PLANT

Sow seeds in mid- to late spring. You can purchase and plant transplants in the spring. Snapdragons can tolerate cooler conditions, so they can be planted a few weeks before the last frost date.

WHERE TO PLANT

Plant snapdragons in full sun and well-drained soil. The soil should be enriched with compost for moisture retention and to improve drainage conditions. Loosen the soil to a depth of 6 in. or more. Avoid planting in heavy clay. Snapdragons are especially suited to old-fashioned gardens; use them for background in perennial beds and in cutting gardens.

HOW TO PLANT

Space plants 8 to 10 in. apart depending on the plant's ultimate size. Transplants should rest at the same depth they were growing in their containers. After setting out transplants, fertilize with a 5-10-5 all-purpose flower food. If you sow seeds outdoors, make a shallow trench in the prepared soil and lightly cover ($1/4$ in.) with fine compost or peat moss. Water lightly and keep the seedbed moist so the seeds will germinate quickly. Snapdragons can be pinched back to make them grow bushier.

Care and Maintenance

Once the plants are established, snapdragons will produce bright, long-lasting blooms with little effort on your part. Fertilize the plants with a balanced plant food such as 5-10-5 or 10-10-10 early in the season, but don't fertilize again until after the first flush of bloom; then cut back the spent flower spikes and fertilize. Snapdragons dislike conditions that are too wet or too dry; with trial and error you can find the right balance. To conserve water, apply mulch around the plants when they are young. Taller types may need to be staked in windy areas. Deadhead regularly to keep them tidy and to redirect energy to new plant growth.

Additional Information

Snapdragons are dependable plants that will bloom well into autumn if deadheaded regularly. They will self-seed if the flowers are left to mature. A disease called rust can infect the older types of snapdragons; it appears as tiny, brownish, powder-filled dots on the undersides of the leaves. Try to select varieties that are resistant to rust. Improve air circulation around the plants by adequate spacing and pinching, and this will help to reduce a severe disease problem.

Additional Species, Cultivars, or Varieties

There are many varieties of snapdragons to choose from. The dwarf plants (12 in.) in 'Double Sweetheart Mix' look like tiny azalea flowers, and they are rust resistant. The vigorous-flowering 'Royal Carpet Mix' (8 to 12 in.) is also rust resistant. The 'Liberty' series produces sturdy, extra-long spikes (18 to 24 in.), making them superb cut flowers.

Zinnia

Zinnia elegans

Height: 6 to 40 in. **Flowers:** White, yellow, red, orange, pink, lavender, striped **Bloom Period:** Summer to frost **Zones:** 3, 4, 5, 6	**Light Requirement:**

*O*ld-fashioned zinnias are among the most popular annual bedding plants. They make wonderful cut flowers, and butterflies and hummingbirds love them. The brightly colored flowers come in various shapes and colors. The dahlia-flowered types have wide petals that form a rounded flower head up to 6 in. across. Giant tetraploid varieties such as 'State Fair' have huge blooms and good disease resistance. Cactus-flowered types, with blooms up to 6 in., have quilled, ruffled petals. Dwarfs like 'Thumbelina' grow no more than 8 in. and will bloom when only a few inches tall. Burpee® Seeds offers a 'Cut and Come Again' series that produces double flowers (2½ in. across) on long stems; the more flowers you pick, the more flowers are produced. *Zinnia angustifolia*, or classic zinnia, is different from traditional zinnia. Its narrow, dark-green foliage supports a multitude of small daisies (about 2 in. across) that have orange centers. They are heat and drought tolerant, and flower profusely until frost. Both classic and common zinnias are dependable when grown from seeds sown directly in the garden, or when grown from transplants.

When to Plant

Zinnias are not frost tolerant and their seed won't germinate in cold soils. Plant seed in mid- to late spring after danger of frost has passed. Transplants are available from garden retailers in the spring.

Where to Plant

Zinnias do best in full sun and well-drained soils. Work compost into the soil before planting. The classic zinnia is more tolerant of poor, dry soils than is the common zinnia. Plant zinnias in annual flower beds, borders, and cutting gardens. Avoid shady areas and locations where air movement is restricted.

How to Plant

Seeds can be sown directly outdoors after the soil has warmed; they will germinate in 7 to 10 days. Thin common zinnia 10 to 15 in. apart and classic zinnia 6 to 10 in. apart, depending on the mature height and the effect you desire. Good air circulation is essential for reducing powdery mildew disease on the foliage. Transplants from the garden store are easy to transplant. Set them at the same level they were growing in their containers. Gently firm the soil around the roots and water-in well. Keep transplants well watered to lessen transplant shock.

Care and Maintenance

Zinnias will produce more flowers if you regularly remove their spent blossoms. The common zinnia should be pinched to promote bushy, well-branched plants. Some of the taller types may require staking in wind-prone areas. Zinnias are susceptible to foliar diseases, including powdery mildew. Water at ground level to avoid wetting the leaves. These plants will thrive in hot, dry summers, but regular watering is necessary for good flowering during dry spells. Classic zinnia is more drought tolerant than common zinnia, and it does not require deadheading or support.

Additional Information

The classic zinnia is virtually pest- and disease-free. Common zinnia does best with regular deadheading and may need support. Powdery mildew can become a serious problem; increase air circulation and take appropriate control measures.

Additional Species, Cultivars, or Varieties

There are many zinnias to choose from, including the 'Peter Pan' series, 'Peppermint Stick' mixed, 'Envy Double', 'Scabious Flowered', 'Giant Cactus', and 'Parasol' hybrids, to name just a few. Look for mildew-resistant zinnias. Several selections of classic zinnia are available; 'Crystal White' bears large white flowers, and the 'Star' series comes in gold, orange, and starbright mix. *Zinnia angustifolia*, narrowleaf zinnia (12 to 18 in.), is a water-thrifty plant with trailing stems. It works well in beds and borders, and as an annual groundcover. 'Golden Orange' and 'Tropic Snow' are two favorite cultivars. A related species is *Sanvitalia procumbens*, creeping zinnia (4 to 6 in.); it is great for groundcover, edging, rock gardens, and container gardens. 'Mandarin Orange', 'Golden Carpet', 'Yellow Carpet', and 'Flore Pleno' (double form) are a few suggested cultivars.

CHAPTER TWO

Deciduous Trees

*W*HEN PLANTED IN THE PROPER LOCATION, a tree will live for generations, silently cleaning the air while providing shade, beauty, and shelter for wildlife. A tree can be a living link between the past and the future. To plant a sapling maple in spring and watch it grow in twenty years or more into a stately tree is a most satisfying investment in our children's future. Though this may be unrealistic for most of us in our society of frequent movers, a tree will still last long as a living memory.

SELECTING A TREE

The most important part of growing trees successfully in Colorado and the Rockies is to choose the right type of tree for your site and needs. What is it that you are looking for? An evergreen for year-round greenery? Maybe a tree that has an ever-changing seasonal display? A tree just for shade? Or do you want a tree that will grow fast for both privacy and shade? After a long chilly winter, who does not look forward to the beauty of a flowering redbud or crab apple?

Trees are functional all year long. They sharpen our awareness of the changing seasons, from the first green buds in spring through their cool, lush summer foliage. The brilliant autumn yellow and gold of Colorado's native aspen trees stirs visitors and residents alike to take trips to the mountains. As winter arrives, deciduous trees can bring dramatic sculptural interest to an otherwise stark landscape.

Deciduous trees give us shade in the summer, cooling our living environment by blocking out the hot sun. Bare of their leaves in winter, the same trees allow sunlight and warmth to reach us when we need it most. They remove carbon dioxide and pollutants from the air and return oxygen to the air we breathe.

PLANTING

Trees are available with their rootballs wrapped in burlap (called "balled and burlapped"). The root system is usually held together with a wire basket. It is important to remove the top third to half of the wire basket after the tree is situated in the planting hole. Don't forget to cut away the nylon twine entirely, as this material will not decompose and can girdle roots and the trunk of the tree years later.

Bare-root trees are grown in a nursery field, harvested when dormant (early spring or late fall), and then made available to gardeners. Once dug, these trees should be planted as soon as possible so the roots don't dry out, preferably before the leaves emerge.

Container-grown trees are also available at local garden retailers and nurseries. Look for signs of healthy new growth when selecting these trees. When planting a containerized tree, first check the root system. If the roots have grown into a mass encircling the rootball, they should be teased or even cut at planting to encourage lateral growth. The nice thing about container-grown trees is that they can be planted almost any time of the year—but the ideal time is spring, as soon as the ground can be worked. Remember that so-called "plantable" containers are really *not* plantable; take the tree out of its container before planting.

As is true for all types of plants, the secret to growing trees successfully is to start with good soil. Few trees will thrive in clay, heavy, compacted, or poorly drained soils; the lack of oxygen to the roots will result in stunted growth or eventual death. Nor will trees survive drought if they are planted in sandy or rocky soils that have no ability to retain moisture. Trees produce vigorous, healthy growth if they are planted in soil that is well drained, loosened as deeply as possible, and amended with organic matter. There is one caveat: don't overamend the soil with too much "stuff"! If too many amendments (or too much of any one amendment) are added to the planting hole, the tree's roots may decide to remain within the hole and never explore the surrounding soil. Remember, roots will grow and move into soil that contains more oxygen, so the best recommendation is to dig the planting hole *much wider* than deep; and be sure to thoroughly loosen the soil around the planting hole as well.

So how much organic matter should be added to Colorado soils? A *Green Thumb rule of thumb* is to use up to four cubic yards of organic matter for every thousand square feet of area to be planted.

If you are moving to a new homesite that is not yet landscaped, the ideal way to prepare the soil is to incorporate organic amendments into the soil as deeply as possible and adjust the planting height. A tractor with a plow or disk attachments works best for large areas; a heavy-duty rototiller is good for smaller areas. When planting trees in existing landscaping or when replacing trees, amend the soil taken from the planting holes. Mix one-quarter to one-third compost or sphagnum peat moss by volume to the native soil.

TREE PLANTING MYTHS

You don't have to cut the branches back by one-third to balance the top of a tree with its roots. The branch tips on a small tree produce plant hormones that direct the growth of the roots. If you prune too much, the tree's energy will go into replacing the lost foliage, and root growth will temporarily stop. This is exactly the opposite of what the new tree should do. Except to remove broken, damaged branches, or to correct shape, don't prune a new tree for a year after planting.

You don't have to feed the tree with vitamins and hormones at the time of planting. Vitamins and hormones will impede root growth by increasing the soluble salt levels in the planting hole. A tree manufactures its own vitamins and hormones, so why waste your money?

After planting, spread a two- to three-inch layer of mulch around the planting hole. Mulching helps reduce weed growth, keeps the soil cooler, and maintains and conserves moisture. Water deeply and thoroughly to moisten the rootball and the surrounding soil. This will encourage new roots to move out into the native soil. Don't fertilize trees for the first year after transplanting; the soil will provide enough nutrients for the first growing season.

FERTILIZING TREES

A soil test can help determine when it is necessary to apply fertilizer to trees. You can also look for symptoms of nutrient deficiency, including small leaves, light-green or yellow leaf color, stunted or short shoot growth, dead twigs at the end of branches, and a general lack of vigor. If these symptoms are present and are not a result of other variables such as drought stress, root injuries, herbicide damage, or diseases, then tree fertilization may be necessary.

Tree fertilizer should be applied when environmental conditions are most favorable for root growth. In Colorado, this is best done in late spring or early summer when the soil is moist and temperatures are between 68 and 84 degrees Fahrenheit.

Fertilizer applications are most effective and best utilized by the tree when they are applied to the soil surface over the root system (the tree's dripline and several feet beyond this area). Research has shown that surface placement of a complete fertilizer (N-P-K such as 14-5-5 or 10-5-5) is as good as, or better than, subsurface applications to shade trees growing outside of lawn areas. Trees growing within lawn areas will benefit from the applications of lawn fertilizer (do not use weed-and-feed formulations), and they generally do not need additional tree fertilizer applications. Trees can absorb nutrients applied to the soil surface because the nutrients move downward with the water that percolates through the soil; tree roots near the soil surface can absorb the migrating nutrients. A rate of one to two pounds of actual nitrogen per 1,000 square feet per growing season will supply the nutrient needs of most trees. Just remember, fertilizer applications are not to be used as a rescue effort for stressed, injured, or declining trees.

Since the root zone of most trees lies just below the soil surface (6 to 12 in.), applying fertilizer to the surface of the soil is the easiest and most effective method of getting nitrogen to the root zone. Scatter the fertilizer at the dripline of the tree and several feet beyond this area, using the required amount to cover the desired square feet. Water-in thoroughly after application to allow the nutrients to reach the root system. **Caution:** Do not use too much fertilizer. If you apply more than the manufacturer's recommendations, tree roots can be burned or killed and this will stress the tree.

PRUNING TREES

You would be surprised to know how much outdated information on the pruning of trees can still be found in gardening books. Two common outdated pruning procedures are: "Prune flush with the trunk" and "Paint the cut to prevent the wood from rotting." Research has shown that both of these old recommendations will cause more harm than good to the tree.

The larger cut which results from pruning flush with the trunk will take longer to heal or close over. A large cut also eliminates the growing zone, called the branch collar. When pruning, try to cut the branch so as to maintain the branch collar. Make pruning wounds as small as possible so the tree can close the wounds more quickly. The longer a wound remains open, the greater the chance there is for development of decay.

Trees do not heal wounds the way people do. Trees grow callus tissue in response to pruning. This tissue grows over the wound or injured area, but the damaged tissues are not repaired. Trees chemically wall off the wounded tissue, a process called compartmentalization. Wound dressings or paints will inhibit a tree from healing itself. If a tree is pruned at the proper time and pruned correctly, the plant will heal itself quickly. Do not leave stubs sticking out from the trunk. They will die back into the trunk and cause the heart wood to decay.

When to Prune

Trees can be pruned any time of year, but pruning at different seasons will cause different plant responses. Late winter to early spring after a general warming trend is a good time to prune, because callus tissue will form rapidly at this time. This is the period of fastest readjustment to pruned limbs.

"Bleeding" (dripping sap) is generally not harmful to a tree, but you may wish to avoid the bleeding by trimming trees such as maples, birches, and walnuts in late summer or early fall. Removing large quantities of foliage after (not during) a flush of growth, such as late spring or early summer, will tend to dwarf a tree. Sometimes this dwarfing is desired. If more rapid development is wanted, pruning prior to leaf emergence in spring is better.

Pruning in late summer or early fall can cause vigorous regrowth, which in some species will not allow the tree time to harden off by winter. Pruning in late fall or early winter subjects the tree to a greater incidence of dieback around the cut, and the wound will close more slowly.

WHAT TO PRUNE

Prune to remove dead, diseased, or damaged wood, to eliminate rubbing, interfering, or poorly placed branches, and to shape the tree. Dead wood should be cut back to but not into live wood. You may prune out diseased wood to stop the spread of a disease. When pruning diseased wood, make a thinning cut into the healthy wood well below the infected site. Disinfect your pruning equipment between each cut with seventy percent alcohol or rubbing alcohol. Do not use chlorine bleach because it will rust tools. Cut damaged branches back to another branch (the damage may be previous poor pruning cuts or stubs). Select the main scaffold branches as early as possible. Cut off branches that will eventually rub or grow in the wrong direction.

Narrow "V" crotches (bark inclusions) occur when a layer of bark gets squeezed between two branches growing very close together. Bark inclusions may cause one of the limbs to split under strong winds or under a heavy snow or ice load. Cut off one of the trunks or branches. Prune the tree to the shape desired, trying to accentuate the tree's normal shape.

Water sprouts or suckers sometimes emerge when a tree has been severely pruned, and they almost always grow from a stub cut. Some species are notorious for producing many vigorous shoots. These shoots are generally poorly placed and interfere with growth. Prune them off when young or physically rub them off when they are small.

PROTECTING TREES IN LATE FALL AND WINTER

You can protect young trees from sunscald injury and wildlife damage by wrapping $1\frac{1}{2}$-inch-diameter white plastic swimming pool hose around the trunk. Cut the hose to a length equal to the distance between the ground and the first branch. Make a vertical cut the length of the hose, pry it open, and snap the hose around the trunk. A *Green Thumb rule of thumb*: Apply reflective tree wraps around Thanksgiving and remove the wrapping around Easter.

Amur Maple

Acer ginnala

Height: 18 to 25 ft. with a spread comparable to the height (a wider spread is typical on multistemmed specimen trees)	**Light Requirement:**
Type: Small deciduous shade tree	
Zones: 3, 4, 5, 6	

One of the outstanding characteristics of amur maple is its brilliant red foliage in autumn. If you lack red colors in the fall, this tree is a must for the Colorado homescape. The winged samara seeds are quite attractive in the summer and will persist through the winter, though they often become a nuisance. They may drop into the flower bed and into cracks of the sidewalk, where they will germinate the following spring. The foliage is a handsome, dark, glossy green. The amur maple's smaller size is desirable for a tree that will occupy a patio setting; it may be used for screening, grouping, accenting a blank wall of the house or garden shed, or gracing the entryway.

WHEN TO PLANT

The best time to plant amur maple is in spring once the ground has thawed. It can be planted in the early fall while the soil remains warm and will encourage strong root growth before winter. Container-grown nursery stock and balled-and-burlapped specimens can be found at many local nurseries and garden centers.

WHERE TO PLANT

The amur maple is not a large maple tree, so it can be utilized in small landscapes quite well. It is adaptable to most Colorado soils but grows best in moist, well-drained areas. It can be planted near entryways. This tree responds quite well to heavy pruning; prune yearly in late spring to keep it within bounds.

HOW TO PLANT

The roots of amur maple tend to grow shallow, and they quickly explore surrounding soil. It is important to dig the planting hole 3 times wider than the rootball. In fact, if you have the energy, dig the hole 4 to 5 times wider and it will pay off with a more vigorous and healthy specimen tree. If you plant in the summer months, be sure to provide ample moisture to prevent scorched leaves. If you locate this tree in wind-prone areas, mist the foliage periodically morning and evening; this practice will help the tree become more strongly established in its early years.

CARE AND MAINTENANCE

Amur maple will grow gracefully without much pruning. Minor pruning can be done in late spring or early summer to remove branches that are crisscrossing and to allow for good air circulation. Fertilize in spring after leaf emergence, and use a chelated iron source if yellowing of the leaves caused by iron chlorosis becomes a problem. Regular watering in the summer is a must. You can add a mulch of pine needles or wood chips to help conserve moisture and to keep the root system cool.

ADDITIONAL INFORMATION

A common problem in midsummer is the appearance of yellow leaves as the tips of the leaves become scorched. Yellowing may be an indication that the tree is suffering from iron chlorosis. Though there is iron in Colorado soils, the high pH makes it unavailable. This problem can be remedied by applying a chelated iron source. Overwatering or underwatering can also contribute to yellowing foliage. Scorched leaves usually indicate that not enough water is getting to the leaves. Determine whether the problem is lack of available water in the soil or that the soil is too compacted, and correct the condition.

ADDITIONAL SPECIES, CULTIVARS, OR VARIETIES

There are some fine selections of amur maple for the home landscape. Check with your local supplier for *Acer ginnala* 'Compactum', which grows vigorously and has larger leaves that are dark green. Its autumn color is brilliant red-purple. 'Flame' is very hardy in our region and has excellent red fall foliage. It is not very tolerant of high-alkaline soils, so amend the soil with sphagnum peat or compost at time of planting.

Eastern Redbud

Cercis canadensis

Height: 20 to 30 ft. (spread 25 to 30 ft.)
Type: Small deciduous tree
Zones: 4, 5, 6

Light Requirement:

*A*mong the most striking sights of early spring are the redbuds clothed in a profusion of magenta-pink flowers. These smaller, somewhat spreading trees flower before their leaves appear—a redbud has the ability to produce flower buds on older wood, a feature known as "cauliflory." It is not uncommon to see a mature tree with older, gnarled branches covered with small reddish-purple buds each spring. The foliage is delicate and emerges with reddish tones, gradually becoming green. Redbud makes an attractive specimen, especially when placed against a background of darker-green evergreens. It is considered a small tree and can be used quite effectively in limited spaces. Seedling trees grow rapidly and transplant well. In autumn, papery 2- to 3-in. brown pea-like pods appear. These can be a nuisance to clean up on a patio or deck, and the seeds will germinate in flower beds the following spring. Redbud will not tolerate poorly drained sites or heavy clay soils. Find the proper location, and this tree will make a beautiful addition to your landscape.

WHEN TO PLANT

Plant redbud trees in early spring as soon as the soil can be worked. Container-grown trees can be planted any time they are available, but avoid the heat of summer unless you can provide proper moisture and care.

WHERE TO PLANT

Full sun encourages the best shape and the most prolific flowering, but redbud will grow quite well in partial shade. This tree does not like heavy soils or poorly drained sites. Avoid planting near streets, sidewalks, or driveways that may be salted in winter; redbud is sensitive to salt accumulations in the soil.

How to Plant

Amend the soil to improve drainage and porosity before planting. Add a high-quality compost or compost/sphagnum peat mixture, up to 30 percent of the volume of the existing soil. Redbud is highly sensitive to soluble salts, so avoid using manure or cheap soil amendments. Dig the planting hole at least 2 to 3 times wider than the rootball. It is important to get the tree established early in its life so it will adapt and survive. If your soil is a heavy clay, dig the planting hole 2 in. shallower than the depth of the soilball. In sandy soils, the hole should be no deeper than the rootball. In heavy or poorly drained soils, set the rootball 2 in. above the surrounding grade. This will allow for some sinking or settling of the rootball, but will ensure good root growth in the top $1/3$ of the planting hole and surrounding area. Mulch the soil around the planting area with a few inches of compost or shredded cedar mulch.

Care and Maintenance

Redbud is a vigorous grower once it gets started, but it slows down with age. Keep the soil uniformly moist by deep-watering on a regular basis, but avoid waterlogging the soil. A light fertilizer application of 14-5-5 can be made in late May or early June by broadcasting around the dripline of the tree. Water-in thoroughly. During the first 3 to 5 years of establishment, protect from sunscald injury in the winter by shading the trunk or applying a light-colored tree wrap. Remove the wrapping in the spring. A *Green Thumb rule of thumb*: Apply tree wrap around Thanksgiving and remove the wrap around Easter.

Additional Information

The redbud is an excellent tree for limited space and will thrive in a somewhat protected location. Its early blanket of rosy-pink blooms in early spring is beyond compare. The flowers of redbud are edible and can be used as a garnish in salads and desserts.

Additional Species, Cultivars, or Varieties

You may run across several cultivated varieties, but not all are adapted to Colorado's climate. When selecting a tree at a nursery or garden store, inquire about the seed source or region where the tree originated; trees from the South will usually suffer in our climate. The cultivars 'Alba' and 'Royal White' have white blossoms.

Flowering Crab Apple

Malus spp.

Height: 15 to 25 ft. (spread 10 to 25 ft.)
Flowers: White, pink, rose-red
Bloom Period: Spring
Zones: 4, 5, 6 (3 if planted in
    protected location)

Light Requirement:

Flowering crab apples are among the most popular ornamental landscape trees in Colorado and the Rockies. Their primary growth habit is that of a deciduous tree, but over the past 12 years of evaluating crab apple varieties for disease resistance, we have found some forms to be more shrub-like and very attractive in the landscape. Fireblight, a bacterial disease, is a common problem and is particularly destructive to this tree's ornamental value. Some of the new selections have shown good resistance to fireblight.

WHEN TO PLANT

Crab apples are available as bare-root nursery stock in early spring. You can find them container-grown in pots from spring through fall, and larger specimens can be purchased with the roots balled and burlapped. Planting in the spring is preferred, but containerized trees and balled-and-burlapped stock can be planted from spring through fall. If you plant in the fall, be sure to supply adequate moisture to the root zone throughout the autumn and winter during extended dry spells.

WHERE TO PLANT

To achieve the best growth, prolific flowering, and bright fruit, crab apples should be planted in full sun. Examine the planting site for trees that may eventually grow and shade the crab apple over a period of years. It is best to locate the tree far enough away from other trees so that shade and root competition will not become a perennial problem. Crab apples are adaptable to a wide range of soil conditions, but they do best in soils that are well drained.

HOW TO PLANT

The planting hole should be at least 2 to 3 times wider than the rootball or spread of the roots. You can amend the soil with 1/4 to 1/3 compost, but avoid adding too much organic soil amendment since this will make the soil too rich and will impede good root development. If you plant a balled-and-burlapped tree, set the tree in the planting hole first, orient the tree in the desired position, and then remove any nylon twine or rope and at least the top half of the wire basket around the rootball. The top of the rootball or container root system should be planted level with the surrounding soil grade. In Colorado clay soils, plant the top of the rootball 2 in. above the surrounding grade. Mulch around the root zone with shredded bark or cedar shavings to a depth of 2 inches. Water the soil thoroughly and check every few days. Water the soil when it begins to dry out 6 to 8 in. deep. Avoid overwatering, as crab apples do not appreciate wet feet.

CARE AND MAINTENANCE

Once a crab apple tree is established, it will thrive with little care. If planted in a lawn, it will not require additional fertilizer since it will utilize nutrients from lawn fertilization. It is important to avoid the use of "weed and feed" fertilizer combinations to avoid potential herbicide contamination to the tree. To maintain tree health, proper air circulation, and beauty, prune every few years in late winter or early spring. Avoid pruning heavily after mid-June or you'll find you have removed many of the following year's flower buds.

ADDITIONAL INFORMATION

Most crab apple cultivars are grafted to a more vigorous rootstock that will often sprout growth off the base of the trunk. These sprouts or suckers can be removed as soon as they appear. Because fireblight disease can be transmitted by pruning tools, it's a good idea to have a bottle of denatured alcohol available when pruning trees. You can easily clean pruners and saw blades with the alcohol after each pruning cut.

ADDITIONAL SPECIES, CULTIVARS, OR VARIETIES

Some of our favorite varieties have shown superior resistance to fireblight disease. *Centurion* has red buds that open to rose flowers, red fruit, and reddish-purple foliage that ages to green. *David* has pink buds that open to pure white. *Indian Summer* has large rose-red flowers and large 5/8-in. fruit; its bronzy foliage changes to green. *Profusion* starts with deep-red buds that open to a deeper pink. Its fruit is maroon; its new foliage is purplish and fades to bronze with age. *Molten Lava* has a weeping form and abundant red-orange fruit. Avoid the following because of disease susceptibility: 'Hopa', 'Bechtel', 'Royalty', 'Brandywine', 'Eleyi', 'Dolgo', 'Kelsey', 'Radiant', 'Snowcloud', 'Beverly', and 'Vanguard'.

Goldenrain Tree

Koelreuteria paniculata

Height: 25 to 40 ft. (spread 20 to 30 ft.)
Type: Deciduous tree
Zones: 4 , 5, 6

Light Requirement:

The goldenrain tree is one of the few trees that flower in midsummer. It has panicles of fragrant yellow flowers followed by clusters of papery, lantern-like seedpods. It is the perfect size for a smaller landscape, though it grows relatively fast, but it does not grow so large as to overpower a house or a small landscape. The compound leaves are purplish red as they emerge and later mature to green, changing to orange-yellow in fall. This is an attractive ornamental tree, so place it where it can be enjoyed from a window, or near the flow of pedestrian or automobile traffic. It will grow best at elevations below 5,000 ft., including the High Plains and western Colorado. It is not uncommon for a young tree to experience winter die-back for a few years until the root system becomes firmly established.

When to Plant

The best time to plant is in early spring to allow for good root development, or in early autumn while the soil is still warm. Avoid planting in midsummer, as the heat will stress the tree. The foliage requires more moisture than the roots can possibly supply in the heat of summer.

Where to Plant

Plant the goldenrain tree in full sun for the best flower development, in a semi-protected spot away from prevailing winds and temperature fluctuations. It is adaptable to our alkaline soils and will tolerate air pollution.

How to Plant

Dig the planting hole 3 times as wide as the rootball, though it need not be any deeper than the depth of the rootball. Once the rootball is placed in the hole, cut away nylon twine and as much of the wire basket that holds the rootball as you can. Add half of the backfill soil and water thoroughly to eliminate air pockets; once this has soaked in, add the remaining soil and water again. Construct a dike or water basin just beyond the edge of the planting hole. Check soil moisture weekly by digging down 4 to 6 in. near the edge of the dike. If the soil is drying out, fill the water basin and soak the soil. Mulch with 2 to 3 in. of compost or other suitable organic material to maintain and conserve moisture. Misting the foliage in the morning and evening will help to reduce heat stress and leaf scorch during the establishment of this tree.

CARE AND MAINTENANCE

Once the tree has become established in the landscape, it is beneficial to apply an all-purpose fertilizer such as 14-5-5 in late spring or early summer. A 1-pound coffee can holds about 2 lb. of granular fertilizer. Broadcast the fertilizer around the dripline of the tree (and beyond) and water-in thoroughly. If you prefer, you can scatter the fertilizer granules in 8- to 12-in. holes placed around the dripline. Trees located in lawn areas generally do not require supplemental fertilizer, as they receive some nutrients from applications of lawn food. Avoid the high-nitrogen fertilizers that may induce soft growth that is more susceptible to breakage. Young trees can suffer from sunscald injury—splitting or cracking of the bark. You can protect young trees by wrapping $1^1/2$-in.-diameter white plastic swimming pool hose around the trunk. Cut the hose to a length equal to the distance between the ground and the first branch. Make a vertical cut the length of the hose, pry it open, and snap the hose around the trunk.

ADDITIONAL INFORMATION

Its growth rate and habit can make this tree weak-wooded, so be on the watch for weak branch attachment and prune accordingly. Early snowstorms may result in some storm damage. Brownish-black seedpods will drop in the fall and seedlings will sprout the following spring. These can be dug and shared with friends.

ADDITIONAL SPECIES, CULTIVARS, OR VARIETIES

'Fastigiata' is a goldenrain tree with a columnar growth habit, but it reportedly seldom flowers. 'September' grows with a broad-rounded crown and produces flowers later in summer. It requires protection from extreme exposures of winter sun and wind.

Green Ash

Fraxinus pennsylvanica

Height: 50 to 60 ft. (spread 25 to 30 ft.)
Type: Deciduous shade tree
Zones: 3, 4, 5, 6

Light Requirement:

The green ash has become one of the most dominant trees in Colorado landscapes because of its adaptability and drought tolerance. In some cases, green ash has become overplanted, and the trees can be compromised should a disease outbreak occur. Green ash is adaptable to alkaline soils and is relatively fast growing. It grows into a pyramidal tree when young and becomes broadly oval as it matures. The dark-green compound foliage turns a radiant yellow in autumn. The maturing gray-brown bark is rather attractive with its furrows that resemble diamond shapes separated by narrow ridges. Green ash is very heat and cold tolerant, making it an ideal landscape tree for Colorado.

WHEN TO PLANT

Container-grown trees can be planted from spring through early fall. If planting during the heat of summer, be sure to provide adequate moisture for good establishment.

WHERE TO PLANT

Locate the tree where it will receive full sun for the best growth and development. Green ash is very adaptable to Colorado's varied soil conditions and it will survive up to 8500-ft. elevation. Some outstanding selections are available for street plantings or specimen shade trees in the landscape.

HOW TO PLANT

The planting hole should be dug 3 times as wide as the rootball. If your soil is a heavy clay, dig the planting hole 2 in. shallower than the rootball. In sandy soils, the hole should be no deeper than the rootball. Trees have a hard time establishing in clay, compacted, or poorly drained soils. Amend the soil by adding 25 to 30 percent compost or well-rotted manure by volume to the planting area.

Work the organic matter deeply into the soil by hand spading or rototilling. Larger trees that are balled and burlapped should be placed in the planting hole; then remove any twine and roping that is wrapped around the rootball. The wire basket should be cut away; you need not remove the entire basket, but cut away at least the upper half to ensure good root development. In heavy or poorly drained soils, set the top of the root system 2 in. above the surrounding grade. Mulch with compost or pole peelings after planting.

CARE AND MAINTENANCE

While the green ash is a popular shade tree, it has often been overplanted in commercial plantings. Maintaining tree vigor and health is important. Avoid overwatering the soil, which can waterlog the soil and displace oxygen, causing a rapid decline of the tree. It is best to water deeply with a soaker hose or "frog-eye" sprinkler on a regular basis throughout the growing season. You can protect young trees by wrapping $1^1/2$ in.-diameter white plastic swimming pool hose around the trunk. Cut the hose to a length equal to the distance between the ground and the first branch. Make a vertical cut the length of the hose, pry it open, and snap the hose around the trunk. During extended dry periods in late fall and winter, water the tree every 5 to 6 weeks when temperatures are above freezing.

ADDITIONAL INFORMATION

Vigorous trees that are properly maintained will generally resist insect problems. It is common, however, for green ash to be attacked by the ash-lilac borer, particularly if the tree is drought-stressed. Pheromone traps are available to attract and capture the adult clearwinged moth borer. Monitoring insect pests will help alert you when it's time to take appropriate control measures.

ADDITIONAL SPECIES, CULTIVARS, OR VARIETIES

There are a number of promising selections, including 'Cardan', which was developed by the USDA for farmstead and windbreak planting and is reported to have better resistance to ash borer. 'Patmore' has an oval growth habit and is hardier than 'Marshall Seedless'. 'Cimmaron' has an upright oval form with dramatic reddish fall foliage; it is tolerant of alkaline soils. 'Newport' is noted for its straight trunk and strong branching.

Hawthorn

Crataegus spp.

Height: 15 to 25 ft. (equal spread)
Type: Small deciduous tree
Zones: 3, 4, 5, 6

Light Requirement:

The hawthorns are a group of small trees that have a wide range of adaptability to Colorado soils. They are tough, hardy, and easy to grow, and they grow where few other trees will survive, making them of great value in difficult sites. But don't overlook their ornamental qualities in the landscape, as they can also make nice specimen trees. Hawthorns are good choices for areas with limited space. Their clusters of showy white flowers are followed by apple-like fruit in late summer that persist through fall. The fruit is favored by many wild birds. Fall foliage color ranges from bronze to red-orange. *Crataegus laevigata* 'Crimson Cloud' is a delightful low-branching tree with an upright growth habit. This is one cultivar that can survive in compacted soils with poor aeration. Blossoms of crimson-red flowers with white star-shaped centers appear in late spring. There are many desirable varieties that grow well throughout our area.

WHEN TO PLANT

Plant in spring through fall. Container-grown nursery stock can be planted any time they are available, but it is best to avoid late-fall planting.

WHERE TO PLANT

Plant in a full-sun location to promote vigorous growth and prolific flowering. Performance is best in moist, well-drained soils, but trees will adapt to dry conditions once established. Most hawthorns are pH adaptable, but an occasional selection may develop chlorosis.

HOW TO PLANT

Dig the planting hole 2 to 3 times wider than the rootball. Larger balled-and-burlapped specimens should have twine, rope, and as much of the wire basket removed as possible after being placed in the planting hole. This will allow the upper portion of the root system to become established. Be sure the top of the rootball or container root system is planted level with the surrounding grade. In heavy clay soils, the planting hole can be dug 2 in. shallower than the rootball. Mulch after planting with 2 to 3 in. of compost or other suitable organic mulch.

CARE AND MAINTENANCE

Hawthorns are among our favorite trees for landscaping, and they offer a wide range of possibilities. Once established, they require little maintenance, needing only periodic pruning in late winter or early spring. Water deeply and infrequently. In soils with a high pH, hawthorns can develop a problem with iron chlorosis (even though iron is in our Colorado soils, it is unavailable to trees). You can apply a chelated iron source by punching holes 8 to 10 in. deep around the dripline, spacing the holes 12 in. apart. Broadcast the fertilizer over the area and water-in well.

ADDITIONAL INFORMATION

Trees that become stressed may become susceptible to fireblight, rusts, leaf spots, cedar hawthorn rust, aphids, and mites. Some suckering around the base of the tree may occur occasionally, but these suckers can be pruned away as they grow.

ADDITIONAL SPECIES, CULTIVARS, OR VARIETIES

Cockspur hawthorn, *Crataegus crus-galli*, has glossy bluish green leaves that turn to purplish red in fall. This is a small spreading tree with sharp red thorns that can be grown single- or multi-stemmed. It is a good wildlife habitat tree and good for traffic control; the variety *inermis* is a thornless type. *Crataegus laevigata*, English hawthorn, has an upright growth habit that matures to a rounded crown with dense branching. 'Crimson Cloud' has unique crimson-red flowers with white star-shaped centers. It has good resistance to leaf blight. *Crataegus mollis*, Downy hawthorn, has serrated leaves. *Crataegus rivularis*, river hawthorn, is a small tree with a dense, upright oval growth habit; it is adapted to alkaline soils. Do not plant it near junipers that are susceptible to juniper-hawthorn rust. *Crataegus × mordenensis* 'Toba' is a hybrid with a handsome upright-rounded form and double white flowers that fade to showy pale pink. *Crataegus ambigua*, Russian hawthorn, is an attractive broad-crowned tree with a moderate growth rate. It is very hardy to Zone 3 and its gnarled growth habit makes an interesting silhouette in the landscape.

Hedge Maple

Acer campestre

Height: 15 to 25 ft. (spread equal to height)
Type: Deciduous shade tree
Zones: 4, 5, 6

Light Requirement:

*M*any gardeners are not familiar with the hedge maple, but this is a good tree to plant in the Colorado landscape. Even though it is a slow-growing tree, its unique foliage and lightly ridged bark makes it a great choice for a smaller landscape. The attractive dark-green leaves change to a yellow-green or yellow in the autumn. One of its merits is its ability to adapt to our alkaline soil conditions; it does not exhibit iron chlorosis as other maples often do. It makes a great choice for a water-wise landscape, for it is tolerant of dry soils and soil compaction.

WHEN TO PLANT

Plant your new hedge maple in early spring through fall. Container-grown trees can be planted as soon as they become available in spring, but be sure to provide extra care during the heat of summer, supplying ample moisture for proper establishment.

WHERE TO PLANT

The hedge maple is not a large tree, so it can be planted near sidewalks, driveways, and entrances where it can be appreciated by visitors. It is quite adaptable to a wide range of soils, but prefers a rich, well-drained location. Soils that are typically alkaline do not seem to bother this fine tree, and it will soon become tolerant of dry soil conditions after a few years of establishment. It does best if planted in full sun or light shade.

HOW TO PLANT

The planting hole should be at least 3 times as large as the rootball, though it need not be deeper than the depth of the rootball. Roots are shallow, allowing for healthy root development. Use a good soil conditioner such as compost or sphagnum peat moss, incorporating into the soil a volume of it equal to 25 to 30 percent of the native soil. You need not bring in topsoil, for it can be variable and often contains high-soluble salts which can stunt or damage roots. If you plant a larger specimen, place the tree in the planting hole and then cut away nylon twine or rope and as much of the wire basket as possible. Fill the hole halfway with soil and water thoroughly. Once the water has soaked in, add the remaining soil and water again. Spread a 2-in. layer of shredded cedar mulch or pine needles over the planting area.

CARE AND MAINTENANCE

Once your hedge maple becomes established in a few years, you will find it is a low-maintenance tree. It is relatively disease- and pest-free. Fertilizer can be applied in late spring or early summer. When applying tree fertilizer, it is important to distribute it to as much of the root zone as possible. Broadcasting is the simplest method of fertilizer application, or you can punch holes at the dripline with a crowbar and scatter the fertilizer in this area. Water-in thoroughly. Light pruning, if needed, can be done during the summer months; avoid pruning in late fall and winter.

ADDITIONAL INFORMATION

The hedge maple attracts no serious pests and is relatively disease-free. Occasionally, a few caterpillars may chew on the foliage, but they are easy to control with biological or insecticidal soap sprays.

ADDITIONAL SPECIES, CULTIVARS, OR VARIETIES

You will have to take time to look for this tree, as it is not available in every retail nursery—but it is worth the effort needed to find it. There are at least 4 varieties that are recognized in the trade: *A. austriacum, A. hebecarpum, A. leiocarpum,* and *A. tauricum.* One of our favorites in our landscape is the cultivar 'Queen Elizabeth', noted for its strong branch development and darker-green leaves. 'Fastigiatum' is upright-growing with corky branches and 5-lobed leaves.

Kentucky Coffee Tree

Gymnocladus dioica

Height: 50 to 60 ft. (spread 40 to 50 ft.) **Type:** Deciduous shade tree **Zones:** 4, 5, 6	**Light Requirement:**

One of the most stately trees in the winter landscape, the Kentucky coffee tree is a strong tree that is very hardy in our region. Its distinctive rough bark is deeply furrowed. As the bark matures, it develops scaly, recurving ridges that provide seasonal interest. Female trees will bear greenish white panicles of flowers followed by long, bean-like pods that persist through the winter. Male flowers are smaller and less fragrant. It is one of the latest trees to leaf out in the spring and generally avoids late spring frosts. Its foliage has a purplish tinge when emerging, and gradually changes to dark bluish green in summer. Kentucky coffee tree has a narrow growth habit when young but will mature to an open, broad, spreading crown. It makes an excellent shade tree with superior drought endurance.

WHEN TO PLANT

Container-grown Kentucky coffee trees can be planted in early spring or early fall.

WHERE TO PLANT

Even though the Kentucky coffee tree may grow slowly, it will eventually reach a larger size that requires plenty of room to develop. Locate it in full sun. It is adaptable to a wide range of soil types and is tolerant of drought conditions. The fruits on the female trees and the large leaf stalks that support the many leaflets will drop in masses and require periodic cleanup throughout the year.

HOW TO PLANT

The planting hole should be 2 to 3 times as wide as the rootball. If your soil is a heavy or compacted clay, dig the planting hole 2 in. shallower than the rootball. In sandy soils, the hole should be no deeper than the rootball. To prevent settling, place the rootball on undisturbed soil. Once a balled-and-burlapped tree is situated in the hole, remove any twine, rope, or metal wire that is wrapped around the rootball, especially around the top $1/3$ of the rootball where the feeder roots will develop. Be sure the top of the rootball (or container root system) is planted level with the surrounding grade. Place backfill soil into the planting hole and water slowly to eliminate any air pockets. With extra backfill soil, make a temporary dike or water basin just beyond the rim of the hole. Check the soil moisture weekly by digging down 4 to 6 in. near the edge of the dike. If the soil is becoming dry, water thoroughly. Mulch after planting with a few inches of a good organic mulch.

CARE AND MAINTENANCE
The Kentucky coffee tree is a very hardy, disease-free tree with few insect pest problems. Once this tree becomes established in your landscape, it requires a minimum of care. Soak the root zone deeply but infrequently. Use a twin-eye or "frog-eye" sprinkler to soak the soil. Set the sprinkler at the dripline and water each area for 15 to 20 minutes. Move around the tree until the watering is completed. Prune only to remove dead and broken branches. You may have to remove basal suckers that emerge around the bottom of the trunk. Trees that are planted in lawn areas rarely need additional fertilizer, since they will receive some nutrients from applications of lawn food.

ADDITIONAL INFORMATION
Kentucky coffee tree makes a good permanent shade tree and should be planted more often. It has a majestic presence in the winter landscape. Its superior tolerance of drought makes it a great water-thrifty tree, too!

ADDITIONAL SPECIES, CULTIVARS, OR VARIETIES
There are a few fruitless male trees such as 'Stately Manor' and 'Espresso'. You will have to check with local nurseries for their availability. As work continues on propagation via root cuttings and micropropagation techniques, new cultivars may soon be on the market.

Linden

Tilia spp.

Height: 50 to 60 ft. (spread 30 to 45 ft.)
Type: Deciduous shade tree
Zones: 3, 4, 5, 6

Light Requirement:

inden trees are remarkably attractive; heart-shaped leaves grace these uniformly pyramidal trees. The fragrant flowers that droop from the branches appear in midsummer, acting as a magnet for honeybees. In fall, clusters of tiny pea-sized fruits hang delicately from papery bracts. The littleleaf linden, *Tilia cordata*, is an excellent street, lawn, or specimen tree with a dense pyramidal form. The American linden, *Tilia americana* , will generally grow larger, but it has the same pyramidal growth habit of littleleaf linden. These trees are very tolerant of our alkaline soil conditions and their foliage has a handsome golden color in autumn.

WHEN TO PLANT
Plant in the spring through early fall. If planting in midsummer, be sure to provide ample moisture to prevent stress and subsequent leaf scorch.

WHERE TO PLANT
Locate linden in full sun for best growth and development. Lindens are adaptable to a wide range of soils, including alkaline conditions. They will, however, grow more vigorously in moist, well-drained soil, and will not tolerate excessively wet locations.

HOW TO PLANT
Prepare the planting site by digging the hole 2 to 3 times wider than the tree's rootball. After placing a balled-and-burlapped specimen tree in the planting hole, remove all nylon twine and as much of the wire basket as possible with a bolt cutter. This is critical so that the upper portion of the rootball will achieve good root development. If your soil is a heavy compacted clay, dig the planting hole 2 in. shallower than the rootball. In sandy soils, dig the hole no deeper than the rootball. To prevent settling, set the container-grown or balled-

and-burlapped tree in the hole on undisturbed soil. Add backfill soil to the hole, and water slowly to eliminate any air pockets. Use some of the extra soil to make a dike or water basin for future watering. When the soil begins to dry out in the 4- to 6-in. layer, fill the water basin to thoroughly soak the soil. Mulch after planting with 2 to 3 in. of compost or other suitable organic material.

CARE AND MAINTENANCE

Lindens are generally pest- and trouble-free. They are not very tolerant of extreme drought conditions. It is important to water during dry periods because stressed trees are more susceptible to spider mites and leaf scorch. A newly transplanted tree can suffer from sunscald in the late winter and can be protected by wrapping the trunk in late November. You can protect a young tree by wrapping $1^1/_2$-in. diameter white plastic swimming pool hose around the trunk. Cut the hose to a length equal to the distance between the ground and the first branch. Make a vertical cut the length of the hose, pry it open, and snap the hose around the trunk. Sucker growth at the base of the tree can be a nuisance with some cultivars; this can be easily remedied by pruning the suckers off on a periodic basis.

ADDITIONAL INFORMATION

When linden trees are in full blossom, they will attract bees. You may want to take this into consideration when selecting the site for planting.

ADDITIONAL SPECIES, CULTIVARS, OR VARIETIES

There are several cultivars of American and littleleaf lindens that grow well in our area. Among the most popular littleleaf lindens are *Tilia cordata* 'Greenspire', which has a dense, formal shape and spicy, fragrant flowers in June to July; 'Chancellor', which has a more upright, narrow pyramidal form and is fairly resistant to drought and storm damage; and 'Glenleven' *Tilia* × *flavescens*, a fast-growing selection with an open habit, reaching a height of 40 ft. and a spread of 30 ft. American lindens to look for include *Tilia americana* 'Bailyard', 'Boulevard', 'Legend', and 'Redmond'. *Tilia tomentosa*, the silver linden, is a great species with its large, heart-shaped leaves that are two-toned, dark green on top and silvery white on the bottom; its foliage is resistant to aphids.

Norway Maple

Acer platanoides

Height: 30 to 50 ft. (usually rounded except as noted for certain varieties) **Type:** Deciduous shade tree **Zones:** 3, 4, 5, 6	**Light Requirement:**

*N*orway maples mark the beginning of spring with their greenish yellow flowers that emerge in April before the leaves appear. They signify the end of the growing season with colorful yellow and reddish foliage. Norway maple is a good choice for dense shade. An attractive rounded outline is common in both young and older trees. It will adapt to clay or sandy soils and will withstand hot, dry conditions better than sugar maple. The winged seeds are fun to watch as they "helicopter" down from the branches in the fall.

WHEN TO PLANT

Plant in spring through early fall. Fall planting should be done as early as possible to allow for strong root growth before winter. Container-grown and balled-and-burlapped trees are available at many retail nurseries.

WHERE TO PLANT

Norway maple does best with lots of space, so plan accordingly. It has a shallow root system, which may limit its use in lawn areas as the tree matures. It prefers a well-drained, moderately moist and fertile soil. The rounded, symmetrical crown will provide dense shade.

HOW TO PLANT

Dig the planting hole 2 to 3 times wider than the rootball. If your soil is a heavy clay, the planting hole can be dug 2 in. shallower than the depth of the soilball. In sandy soils, the hole should be no deeper than the rootball. Incorporate into the soil a quantity of a high-quality soil conditioner such as compost and sphagnum peat moss that is equal in volume to 25 to 30 percent of the existing soil. Position the tree in the planting hole on undisturbed soil. If the rootball is being held by a wire basket, cut away the upper half of the basket, using a bolt cutter to cut through the stiff wire, and remove nylon twine. Put backfill soil into the hole and water slowly to eliminate air pockets. Use extra soil to form a water basin or dike just beyond the edge of the planting hole. Water when the soil begins to dry at 4 to 6 in. deep. Add a few inches of mulch on the surface of the root zone to maintain and conserve moisture.

CARE AND MAINTENANCE

To keep the tree healthy and growing, water it on a regular basis during the summer with a twin-eye or "frog-eye" sprinkler placed at the dripline. Let the water run for 25 to 30 minutes, then move to another area for good overlap. During dry, windy conditions in late fall and winter, be sure to water when temperatures are above freezing and the soil is unfrozen. Water early in the day to allow the water to soak in before nightfall. Trees growing in lawns usually do not need additional fertilizer.

ADDITIONAL INFORMATION

The Norway maple has shown good tolerance to the varied range of soils in Colorado and is recommended over the soft or silver maple selections.

ADDITIONAL CULTIVARS AND SPECIES

One of the Norway maples that are most common in Colorado landscapes is 'Schwedleri', with its reddish-purple foliage in spring that transforms to dark green in summer. Another notable variety is 'Deborah', which has a straight leader and reddish-purple spring leaf color that eventually turns dark green. This rounded-crown tree is a favorite choice for shade. 'Crimson King' is one of the oldest cultivars and has maroon leaves all season. Its flowers are maroon-yellow in early spring. 'Superform' is a rapidly growing tree with a straight trunk and a more upright growth habit. 'Cleveland', 'Emerald Queen', and 'Summershade' are other cultivars that are desirable for the home landscape.

Oak

Quercus spp.

Height: 15 to 60 ft. (comparable spread)	**Light Requirement:**
Type: Deciduous shade tree	
Zones: 3, 4, 5, 6	

Throughout history, oaks have been recognized as symbols of strength and durability. If it were not for their slow growth rate, they would have more prominence in our landscapes. Most oak trees are not tolerant of highly alkaline soils and will become chlorotic in soils that have poor drainage. We have found it important to add a good source of organic amendment to help neutralize a high pH and create a more favorable growing environment. Compost, sphagnum peat, or a combination of the two can be added to the growing area prior to planting. Our native Rocky Mountain oak, *Quercus gambelli*, is noted for its durability and adaptability to dry conditions and alkaline soils. It can be grown as a small tree or large shrub and is hardy to an elevation of 8,000 ft. In autumn, its red-orange, reddish-purple to maroon foliage is a nice accent to the golden aspen. Bur oak, *Quercus macrocarpa*, is one of the best suited for Colorado soils and drier conditions. Swamp white oak, *Quercus bicolor*, adapts well to heavy clay soils, but it can become chlorotic if drainage is a problem. Applications of granular or powdered chelated iron (Sequestrene 330 WP) can help reduce severe iron chlorosis in oaks that are prone to this problem. A smaller landscape may not accommodate the large size of an oak very well, but if you have space and plan accordingly, try using this majestic tree in your Colorado landscape; it will leave a living legacy for future generations.

WHEN TO PLANT

The best time to plant oaks is early spring. They are somewhat temperamental when transplanted in late summer or fall, but with care this can be done. It is best to select smaller trees to minimize transplant shock and to help ensure successful establishment.

WHERE TO PLANT

Locate in full sun and allow plenty of room for these trees to develop. Place them away from buildings that would eventually become engulfed by trees that are planted close by. Trees are best placed in open areas so they can grow into larger specimen trees.

How to Plant

The planting hole should be at least 2 to 3 times as wide as the rootball or container. After placing a larger balled-and-burlapped trees in the planting hole, remove any twine or metal wire that is wrapped around the roots. This is especially important for the upper portion of the rootball so there will be good root establishment. The top of the rootball should be set level with the surrounding grade. Mulch after planting with a few inches of pine needles or other organic mulch.

Care and Maintenance

The oaks recommended for our area are quite adaptable to varied soil conditions and can be found in sandy soils to more compacted clay soils. Depending on the cultivar selected, oaks will readily establish if watered on a regular basis. To avoid an accumulation of soluble salts in the root zone, it is best to thoroughly water trees and avoid shallow watering. Use a soaker hose or "frog-eye" sprinkler to apply enough water, and allow it to soak down deeply. Oaks that begin to develop iron chlorosis (or severe yellowing of the foliage) can be treated with chelated iron in the spring. This will help to maintain healthy green leaves.

Additional Information

Some oak species are susceptible to oak gall and aphids, though these problems generally do not cause considerable damage nor do they affect tree health.

Additional Species, Cultivars, or Varieties

Some of the more adapted oaks for Colorado are *Quercus gambelii*, Gambel oak, our native which can be grown as a small tree or large shrub; *Quercus macrocarpa*, bur oak, which tolerates urban conditions and varied soil types; *Quercus robur*, English oak, which does best in soils that have a pH less than 8; 'Fastigiata', with its columnar growth habit (15 to 20 ft. width) that makes it well suited for smaller spaces; *Quercus coccinea*, scarlet oak, with its deeply lobed leaves that turn purple in autumn; and *Quercus rubra*, red oak, which is easily transplanted in Colorado soils.

Ohio Buckeye

Aesculus glabra

Height: 20 to 35 ft.	**Light Requirement:**
Type: Deciduous tree	
Zones: 3, 4, 5, 6	

*O*ne of the showiest trees in the spring landscape is the Ohio buckeye. It has a rounded growth habit and strong ascending branches that form a dense crown. Its greenish-yellow spring flowers are borne on 4- to 6-in.-long and 2- to 3-in.-wide terminal panicles. These blooms look like yellow trumpets against the dark-green foliage. Ohio buckeye is one of the first trees to leaf out in spring and also one of the first to drop its leaves in fall. Its autumn color is a bright yellow to orange-red. What makes the tree unique are its compound leaves that consist of 5 large leaflets (3 to 6 in. long) that have finely toothed edges. Some outstanding specimens can be seen in Denver's city parks, where they thrive with plenty of room to spread. Buckeye produces fruit in the form of prickly, reddish-tan capsules; when the capsules crack open, they reveal seeds that resemble a "buck's eye." As a child, I gathered pocketfuls of these shiny seeds in the park. The only problem is that these fruit are poisonous, though the squirrels don't seem to mind as they hoard the seeds and hide them in the grass.

When to Plant

The best time to plant Ohio buckeye is in the spring as soon as the soil can be worked. Avoid planting in the heat of summer, as this tree is vulnerable to leaf scorch.

Where to Plant

Locate the tree where it has adequate space to develop and spread (15 to 25 ft.). It prefers full sun and will tolerate slightly alkaline soils that are well-drained. It makes an excellent shade tree and can be used for screening and in a windbreak.

How to Plant

The Ohio buckeye is a bit temperamental about heavy clay or alkaline soils, and prefers a richer, loamy soil. Take care to find the right location, and amend the soil if necessary. Amending the soil with sphagnum peat moss (adding a volume equal to 30 to 40 percent of the volume of existing soil) will help buffer the alkalinity, creating a more favorable growing environment. The planting hole should be dug 2 to 3 times wider than the rootball. If your soil is a heavy or compacted clay, dig the planting hole 2 in. shallower than the rootball. In sandy soils, the hole should be no deeper than the rootball. Place the rootball on undisturbed soil, which will prevent it from sinking too deep. If you plant a balled-and-burlapped tree, remove twine, rope, and the wire that holds the rootball. This is especially critical around the top half of the rootball where the feeder roots will develop. Shovel backfill soil into the planting hole, and water slowly to eliminate any air pockets. Use the extra backfill soil to make a temporary dike or water basin at the edge of the planting hole. Check the soil moisture weekly by digging down 4 to 6 in. near the edge of the dike. If the soil is becoming dry, fill the water basin to soak the soil thoroughly. Mulch after planting with shredded wood chips, pine needles, or cedar shavings.

CARE AND MAINTENANCE

The buckeye grows naturally in moist locations, but once established, it will do well almost anywhere as long as it receives occasional deep waterings. Leaf scorch will occur if the tree is subjected to continuous drought-stress, and it can drop its leaves prematurely. The Ohio buckeye fruit can become a nuisance, especially if you hate the constant cleanup required. Fertilizer may be applied in late spring or early summer. Broadcaast the fertilizer at the dripline and beyond, and water-in.

ADDITIONAL INFORMATION

Its dense shade and relatively small stature make Ohio buckeye a good choice for smaller yards. Remember that the seeds are poisonous even though they are a source of food for squirrels.

ADDITIONAL SPECIES, CULTIVARS, OR VARIETIES

The yellow buckeye, *Aesculus flava*, has leaves that are dark green above and yellow-green beneath. It grows quite large (50 to 60 ft.) and is suited for larger areas. The common horsechestnut, *Aesculus hippocastanum*, also grows larger (50 to 70 ft.) and has white flowers.

Poplar

Populus spp.

Other Name: Cottonwood
Height: 30 to 70 ft. (spreads vary
   from 20 to 50 ft.)
Type: Deciduous shade tree
Zones: 3, 4, 5, 6

Light Requirement:

---

*N*ewcomers to Colorado are always asking for trees that will grow fast and provide "instant" shade. Many are awed by the fall gold seen in the high country and they want aspen, *Populus tremuloides*, somewhere in their landscapes. But these desires can eventually lead to having problem trees that are weak-wooded, subject to storm damage, and susceptible to insects and diseases. It is important to learn about the various members of the *Populus* group and make appropriate choices for your landscape. One of our pioneer native species, *Populus deltoides* spp. *monilifera*, grows along streams and rivers, surviving quite well. In the home landscape, cottonwoods can be a hazard because of their weak, brittle branches, and female trees will produce inordinate amounts of cottony seeds. Poplars are especially useful for planting in wet sites, but their fast growth rate and rapidly expanding crowns and vigorous greedy roots make them poor candidates for placing near buildings, septic systems, sewers, underground drainage pipes, or wherever water is not freely available. The trees do best in moist, deep, loamy soils.

WHEN TO PLANT

Plant from spring through fall. Bare-root trees are available from some local nurseries or mail-order sources, and they should be planted as soon as the soil can be worked in the spring.

WHERE TO PLANT

Locate in an open area away from buildings and sewer systems. Some species such as *Populus alba* 'Pyramidalis' (with its spread of 15 to 20 ft.) have a narrow growth habit and can be utilized for screening. This is a good replacement for the short-lived Lombardy poplar.

How to Plant

Prepare the planting hole 3 times wider than the spread of roots or the rootball. In most soil conditions it is helpful to add a soil amendment such as well-aged manure or compost, at a volume equal to 1/3 of the volume of the existing soil. Mix uniformly with the existing soil to allow for vigorous root development. After being placed in the hole, a balled-and-burlapped tree should have nylon twine, rope, and wire basket removed. Otherwise, trunk and roots may eventually become girdled. Spread a 2- to 3-in. layer of shredded wood chips or other mulch around the planting area to maintain and conserve moisture during establishment of the trees.

Care and Maintenance

Prune to maintain tree health and safety on an annual basis and following storm damage. These trees need regular watering to maintain vigor and health and to reduce leaf scorch during drought periods. They will grow fast and vigorously with proper watering. Water deeply and as infrequently as possible to discourage shallow rooting.

Additional Information

The poplar family is notorious for producing sucker growth in lawns, gardens, and flower beds. The tree must be carefully sited to prevent such problems. Female trees produce catkins, followed by cottony seeds which becomes a nuisance and may require frequent cleanup. Diseases and insect pests are common. At lower elevations, quaking aspen is highly susceptible to poplar twiggall fly; there are no effective control measures.

Additional Species, Cultivars, or Varieties

Populus deltoides × nigra 'Robusta' is a hybrid cottonless selection that is adapted to alkaline soils. It grows into a large tree with a broad oval growth habit (50 ft. with a 40-ft. spread) and is good for windbreak, shelterbelt, and shade. *Populus alba*, or silver poplar, has chalky-white bark with leaves that are dark green on top and silvery white on the bottom. *Populus × acuminata*, or lanceleaf cottonwood, is a native tree with an upright rounded crown. It will grow up to a 7500-ft. elevation, as will the narrowleaf cottonwood, *Populus angustifolia*, which has narrow, willow-like leaves that turn a golden yellow in autumn. *Populus tremula* 'Erecta' or upright European aspen has a narrow columnar growth habit and is less susceptible to diseases, winter dieback, or chlorosis. *Populus tremuloides*, our native quaking aspen, grows beautifully at elevations above 7,000 ft.

Quaking Aspen

Populus tremuloides

Height: 20 to 30 ft. **Type:** Deciduous tree **Zones:** 2, 3, 4, 5, 6	**Light Requirement:**

*W*hat would Colorado be without aspen? It appears that every home owner wants to plant an aspen or a grove of aspens to create that "mountain woodland" effect. The characteristic smooth white bark, leaves that quake in the breeze, and golden-yellow fall foliage make aspens a Colorado favorite. They are indeed native to our region, but there are limitations for their use. Aspen trees do best at elevations of 7,000 ft. and above. When planted at lower elevations, aspen trees are vulnerable to a wide range of problems including insect pests, spider mites, and diseases—the most frequently asked question on our Green Thumb radio programs is what to do about aspen disease! Because they grow relatively fast and have a small ornamental scale, aspens are good for use in foundation plantings to soften the front of buildings and entryways. As these trees grow, however, a multitude of roots expands into the surrounding area and "suckers" appear everywhere. Just try to pull out those stray sprouts that poke through the lawn and flower beds! Aspen trees bear either male or female flowers. The male tree forms fuzzy catkins while the female forms cottony tassels with seeds. Take this into account when choosing the proper location. Viewing or growing aspen trees in the mountains is the most reliable way to enjoy this Colorado native.

WHEN TO PLANT

The best time to plant aspen trees is in the spring, which will allow for good root establishment. The second-best time is in the fall after the trees have become dormant. Fall planting requires careful monitoring of moisture during dry spells through fall and winter.

WHERE TO PLANT

Aspen trees do best in full sun and well-drained soils. To reduce the incidence of leaf diseases, choose a location that has good air circulation. The smaller scale of these trees makes them useful for foundation planting or as a temporary screen in the landscape.

How to Plant

In their native habitat, aspen trees grow in soils that have been naturally enriched with lots of humusy leaf mold. When planting in your landscape, amend the soil with a moisture-retentive compost to simulate mountainous conditions. These trees need ample moisture to thrive and stay healthy. Container-grown trees and balled-and-burlapped specimens are both readily available. Dig the planting hole 2 to 3 times wider than the rootball. Position the tree in the hole at the same level it was growing in its container. For a balled-and-burlapped tree, make sure the rootball is sitting on solid soil and planted about 1 in. higher than soil grade. Remove the top half of the wire basket and cut away nylon twine. Add backfill soil about halfway around the roots and water-in, making sure there are no pockets of air underneath the root system. After the water has soaked in, add the remaining soil to complete the planting, and water again. Apply a mulch of shredded bark or cedar to maintain and conserve moisture.

Care and Maintenance

To keep aspen trees healthy and growing vigorously, don't let them become stressed. Provide ample watering throughout the growing season, particularly during long, hot dry spells. These are shallow-rooted trees that can be easily watered with a twin-eye or "frog-eye" sprinkler placed at the dripline. Run the sprinkler for 15 to 20 minutes, then move it to another location until you have soaked the entire root zone. An application of 14-5-5 fertilizer with chelated iron can be applied in spring during leaf expansion.

Additional Information

Aspen trees are beautiful in the high country of Colorado at elevations of 7,000 ft. or more. At lower elevations, these trees are susceptible to canker diseases, poplar twig-gall, leaf spot diseases, and scale insects. Maintaining tree vigor and health can help reduce serious problems.

Additional Species, Cultivars, or Varieties

If you've tried growing aspen trees but they have been short-lived, you might want to try *Populus tremula* 'Erecta'. It is an upright European aspen with a narrower growth habit, and it does not have a tendency to sucker. It is also less susceptible to cultural problems.

River Birch

Betula nigra

Height: 25 to 35 ft. (spread 20 to 30 ft.) **Type:** Deciduous tree **Zones:** 4, 5, 6	**Light Requirement:**

One of the most interesting and eye-catching characteristics of the river birch is its bark. The young tree has a reddish-brown bark; as the tree matures, it begins to peel and expose an inner bark in colors of buckskin to cinnamon-brown. It is very showy during the fall and winter. At maturity the tree can reach 30 to 35 feet in height and has a rounded crown. The fall color is a rich yellow. While many trees need adequate space to grow without competition, the river birch can be used to create a dramatic effect in group plantings or as a multi-stemmed specimen. This tree prefers moist areas; it can be effectively planted in lower, wet areas of the landscape and will adapt to most Colorado soil conditions except those that are highly alkaline with a pH over 8. An attractive combination is river birch planted with *Cornus stolonifera* (redosier dogwood), which also prefers moist soil conditions. The reddish stems and flaking bark of the birch make a nice contrast to the redosier. During the winter, the river birch makes a handsome statement if located near the evergreen foliage of the Colorado blue spruce, *Picea pungens f. glauca.*

WHEN TO PLANT

Plant in early spring through early summer. Be sure to provide ample water during the heat of summer for good root establishment.

WHERE TO PLANT

Locate in full sun or partial shade. River birch is most effective when grown as multistemmed specimens. Single-stem trees can be used for smaller landscapes and can be spaced 15 ft. apart so that the canopies intertwine. Lower branches can be removed to permit foot traffic if needed.

HOW TO PLANT

Prepare the planting hole 2 to 3 times wider than the rootball. If you purchase balled-and-burlapped trees, remove any nylon twine and the upper portion of the wire basket after the tree is situated in the hole. This is critical for the proper establishment of the top third of the rootball where the feeder roots will develop. In heavy or poorly drained soils, plant the top of the rootball a few inches above the surrounding grade. Some settling of the rootball will generally occur in these situations. Once the tree is planted, apply a 2- to 3-in. layer of pine needles or other organic mulch.

CARE AND MAINTENANCE

The river birch does best in moist soils; it will survive in drier conditions, although growth will be slower. Late fall and winter watering are a must to ensure tree survival, especially when there is a lack of natural precipitation or when snowcover is lacking. Use a "frog-eye" or twin-eye sprinkler to soak the root zone every 5 to 6 weeks. Water when temperatures are above freezing and the soil is unfrozen. The trees can develop iron chlorosis in highly alkaline soils (pH of 7.8 or higher). This can be remedied by applying chelated iron periodically. Avoid pruning in early spring, or "bleeding" of sap will occur. The best time to prune is during the summer. In our dry climate, it is helpful to mist the foliage on a regular basis in early morning and evening; this will reduce the severity of heat stress and leaf scorch.

ADDITIONAL INFORMATION

The male river birch produces slender, dark-brown catkins, adding to its ornamental value. Trees will vary in amount of exfoliating bark, so it is wise to purchase trees that have started to exhibit showy bark. The river birch is not bothered by bronze birch borers as is the European white birch.

ADDITIONAL SPECIES, CULTIVARS, OR VARIETIES

The patented selection *Heritage* has good resistance to bronze birch borer and appears to be more tolerant of clay soils than paper birch. The bark starts to exfoliate on smaller trunks and reveals a salmon-white bark which eventually darkens to buckskin as the tree ages.

Serviceberry

Amelanchier alnifolia

Height: 18 to 20 ft. (spread 10 to 15 ft.) **Type:** Small deciduous tree **Zones:** 3, 4, 5, 6	**Light Requirement:**

While many other native plants grow taller in moist, semi-shaded locations, serviceberry is one of our natives often seen grown as small, multistemmed shrubs in dry conditions. This is an attractive plant, with fragrant white flowers and serrated foliage. The blooms appear before full leaf emergence, and this adds to its landscape interest. It is known to produce many sucker shoots, but it can be trained into a multitrunk tree. The sweet blue fruit is treasured by birds and humans alike. In autumn, leaves range from yellow to orange-red. The small size of *Amelanchier* makes it perfect for smaller landscapes and for use in patio plantings and as a foundation plant. It is a good choice for naturalized plantings when grouped in a mass where the clumping or suckering habits of the tree and bountiful fruit attract wildlife to the landscape.

WHEN TO PLANT

Plant serviceberry in spring or early fall. With proper moisture and misting of the foliage, serviceberry can be planted during the summer months.

WHERE TO PLANT

Locate in full sun to partial shade. Trees planted in full sun will have more blossoms and more intense fall colors. Soils need to be well drained and will benefit from the addition of some organic matter.

HOW TO PLANT

Dig the planting hole 2 to 3 times as wide as the rootball. If your soil is a heavy clay, the hole should be made 2 in. shallower than the soilball. In sandy soils, the hole should be no deeper than the rootball. Remove the plastic or fiber pot. After placing a larger balled-and-burlapped specimen tree in its planting hole, remove twine and as much of the wire basket as possible; use a bolt cutter to cut through the stiff wire and carefully pull it away. This will allow the upper portion of the rootball to develop healthy roots. The top of the rootball or container root system should be planted level with the surrounding grade. Place backfill soil into the planting hole and add water slowly to eliminate air pockets. Use some of the extra soil to form a dike or water basin beyond the edge of the planting hole before watering the newly planted tree. Water again when the soil begins to dry at 4 to 6 in. deep. Avoid frequent, light waterings. Mulch after planting with a few inches of shredded cedar shavings or pine needles.

CARE AND MAINTENANCE
The serviceberry needs regular watering during long, hot, dry periods. Soak the soil thoroughly with a twin-eye or "frog-eye" sprinkler placed at the dripline, and water each zone for 15 to 20 minutes. Move the sprinkler as needed until you have watered the entire root zone. This small ornamental tree is relatively low maintenance, but it will require periodic pruning of suckers at the base if you intend to keep it as a single or multistemmed specimen. Avoid fertilizing with a high-nitrogen fertilizer, since this can produce soft growth which is susceptible to fireblight disease.

ADDITIONAL INFORMATION
One of the desirable features of serviceberry is the reddish-purple fall color that appears every year. It can be grown in limited space, or as a large, multiple-trunked shrub. Birds just love the ripening fruit, and this is an exceptional landscape plant for developing a wildlife habitat.

ADDITIONAL SPECIES, CULTIVARS, OR VARIETIES
The Shadblow serviceberry (*Amelanchier canadensis*) has a desirable upright growth habit well suited for limited spaces. Showy white flowers in spring are followed by red fruit that is quickly eaten by birds. *Amelanchier* × *grandiflora* 'Robin Hill' has an upright oval form with clusters of pink buds that open to white flowers followed by reddish-purple fruit. It is well adapted to our soil conditions. *Amelanchier laevis* 'Cumulus' has an orange-scarlet fall color and flowers that are larger than those of other cultivars.

Thornless Honeylocust

Gleditsia triacanthos var. *inermis*

Height: 30 to 50 ft. (comparable spread)	**Light Requirement:**
Type: Deciduous shade tree	
Zones: 3, 4, 5, 6	

The thornless honeylocust is one of the most adaptable trees for Colorado landscapes, though it is often overplanted. Noted for its wide-spreading habit and filtered shade, honeylocust can be grown successfully in our various soils. It is tolerant of alkaline soil conditions and has proven to be tolerant of salt as it grows along streets and highways. The foliage has a feathery appearance; the leaves are pinnately compound, bright green in spring and summer, and yellow in early fall. Honeylocust has fine-textured foliage which casts light shade, allowing some turfgrasses to grow beneath the tree. When the leaves drop in the fall, they are small enough to be mowed and mulched and don't generally require raking.

WHEN TO PLANT

Plant in spring through early fall. Small bare-root nursery stock will be available locally or through mail-order sources and will transplant easily. Container-grown and balled-and-burlapped trees are widely available and can be planted any time during the growing season.

WHERE TO PLANT

Locate the tree in full sun. Honeylocust is a good lawn tree, or it can be used as a street tree.

HOW TO PLANT

Dig the planting hole 2 to 3 times wider than the spread of the roots or rootball. For container-grown trees, be sure to remove the container after placing the tree in the hole. Balled-and-burlapped trees, after being situated in the hole, should have any twine, rope, or metal wires that are wrapped around the rootball removed. This will permit stronger root growth and reduces the chances of root girdling.

Care and Maintenance

Since honeylocust has been overplanted in some areas of the state, it is important to keep trees healthy to avoid problems with disease and insect outbreaks. Stressed trees are susceptible to canker disease and will often succumb. Young trees can suffer from "southwest disease" (cracking of the bark on the south and west sides of the trunk) in winter. You can protect young trees by wrapping $1^1/_2$-in.-diameter white plastic swimming pool hose around the trunk. Cut the hose to a length equal to the distance between the ground and the first branch. Make a vertical cut the length of the hose, pry it open, and snap the hose around the trunk. Trees should be watered deeply and infrequently to maintain vigor and to prevent shallow root development. If the tree is planted in a lawn, it is not necessary to provide supplemental fertilizer.

Additional Information

Honeylocust is an attractive landscape tree, but it can be plagued with problems if it becomes stressed from drought, hail, or bark injuries. Keep grass from growing around the base of the trunk where a condition known as "lawn moweritis" can occur. Nicking the bark with a lawn mower or weed trimmer will make the tree susceptible to diseases and insect attack. Honeylocust can be attacked by leafhoppers that cause distortion to the leaf tips. A systemic insecticide can help prevent severe hopper damage.

Additional Species, Cultivars, or Varieties

There are many honeylocust selections, with different color variations and growth habits. Some nice varieties for our region are 'Moraine', a fruitless and thornless tree with dark-green foliage that changes to golden yellow in fall; 'Halka', with a widely oval form and strong horizontal branches capable of bearing snow loads; 'Skyline', with a stately upright pyramidal form, uniform branching, and dark-green foliage; and 'Imperial', a more compact grower that has a symmetrical growth habit and bright-green leaves that turn golden in autumn. 'Suncole' is a good choice for smaller landscapes. 'Sunburst' is noted for its bright golden leaves in early spring that fade to lime green as the foliage matures; it grows irregularly rounded and is both seedless and thornless.

Western Catalpa

Catalpa speciosa

Other Name: Northern Catalpa **Height:** 40 to 60 ft. (spread 25 to 30 ft.) **Type:** Deciduous shade tree **Zones:** 4, 5, 6	**Light Requirement:**

One of the most dramatic large shade trees for the home landscape is the western catalpa. It grows tall and has huge, light-green, heart-shaped leaves. Its clusters of bell-shaped flowers fill the air with a sweet scent in early summer. During the winter, the tree's rugged silhouette reveals short, wide-angled branches that will carry snow loads quite comfortably. Bean-like seedpods are generally persistent on the tree throughout the winter. This is a tree that should be used more frequently for a water-wise landscape. It withstands hot, dry conditions and will survive with deep, infrequent waterings once it becomes established.

WHEN TO PLANT

Plant container-grown catalpa trees in spring, summer, or early fall. Provide ample water during the heat of summer for good root establishment.

WHERE TO PLANT

To enjoy this tree's unique shape and size, allow plenty of space when finding a spot for it in your landscape. Avoid planting near sidewalks and driveways; the seedpods can accumulate, and if crushed, they will stain concrete surfaces. Western catalpa is very tolerant of both wet and dry alkaline soil conditions.

HOW TO PLANT

Dig the planting hole wide enough to encourage good root growth during the tree's early development. If your soil is a heavy clay, dig the planting hole 2 in. shallower than the soilball. In sandy soils, the hole need not be dug any deeper than the root system. You can add a high-quality soil amendment such as compost or sphagnum peat moss in a volume equal to 25 to 30 percent of the volume of the native soil. Once a larger balled-and-burlapped specimen tree is positioned in the planting hole, cut away nylon twine and as much of the wire basket as possible; use a bolt cutter to cut through the stiff wire and carefully pull it away from the root mass. Fill the hole halfway with backfill soil, and water thoroughly to eliminate any air pockets. After this water has soaked in, add the remaining backfill soil and water again. Apply a mulch of coarse compost or shredded wood shavings to maintain and conserve water during establishment.

CARE AND MAINTENANCE

Western catalpa is well adapted throughout the state and is tolerant of varied soil conditions. Water deeply and infrequently to maintain tree health and vigor. It does not seem to be bothered by insect pests or diseases. Small branches are quite brittle and are easily broken off in ice and snow storms or during high winds. If a heavy, wet snow is threatening, take caution to go outdoors and carefully knock the snow off the drooping branches. Do not push downward, as this will cause more breakage. Instead, gently push upward to remove the accumulation of snow.

ADDITIONAL INFORMATION

The western catalpa is a wonderful tree if you have the space to plant it. It is so adaptable, and its huge leaves are a bright lime-green in early spring. It can produce lots of bean-like fruit, which has given this tree the common name "Indian Bean" tree. Children love to play with the fruit, though it can be messy on concrete if crushed by car tires.

ADDITIONAL SPECIES, CULTIVARS, OR VARIETIES

The availability of western catalpa may be somewhat limited, so check with your local garden retailer early in the season. They may be able to order it for you. Another species, *Catalpa bignonioides*, southern catalpa (30 to 40 ft.), is hardy to Zone 5 and flowers later than western catalpa. The cultivar 'Aurea' has rich yellow color and holds its foliage longer. 'Nana' is a compact form that has been grafted on a standard to create a globe shape.

Western Hackberry

Celtis occidentalis

Height: 50 to 60 ft. (equal spread)	Light Requirement:
Type: Deciduous shade tree	
Zones: 2, 3, 4, 5, 6	

The western hackberry is well adapted to Colorado's climate extremes and varied soil conditions. This Colorado native can be found growing throughout our region in clay, sandy, and rocky soils. Under more favorable growing conditions, hackberry can grow quite large with a large, straight trunk. In less favorable sites, the tree tends to be more open, developing an irregular growth habit and widely spreading branches. Its bark is light gray and is noted for its corky knobbed texture. Drying winds don't seem to faze this tough survivor. It is a great tree selection for the lower elevations of the High Plains and can be grown successfully in the higher elevations of mountain communities. Its foliage is light green. Hackberry produces small, dark reddish-purple berries in late summer that will persist for several weeks; these berries are a favorite food source for wild birds.

WHEN TO PLANT

Plant in early spring through early fall. Small bare-root nursery stock can be easily transplanted in the spring. Container-grown and balled-and-burlapped trees can be planted throughout the growing season.

WHERE TO PLANT

Plant in full sun for best growth and development. This tree is very adaptable to Colorado's alkaline soil conditions; it will tolerate wind and drought conditions and withstand city pollution.

HOW TO PLANT

Prepare the planting hole 2 to 3 times wider than the rootball. Though this tree is tolerant of a wide range of soils, heavy clay or extremely sandy soils will benefit from a soil amendment. Add a high-quality compost or well-aged manure at a volume equal to 25 to 30 percent of the volume of the native soil. Dig the planting hole

2 in. shallower if your soil is heavy clay; in a sandy soil, the hole should be no deeper than the rootball. After placing a balled-and-burlapped tree in its hole, remove the nylon twine and metal wires that are wrapped around the rootball. You can use a bolt cutter and carefully tug the wire basket away in sections. This will allow for better root development and reduce the chances of root girdling in the future. Add backfill soil into the hole and water slowly to eliminate air pockets. Use some of the extra soil to make a dike or water basin at the edge of the planting hole for watering later on. Reapply water when the soil begins to dry at 4 to 6 in. deep. Mulch with wood chips or pine needles.

CARE AND MAINTENANCE

Once it becomes established after a few years, western hackberry is a low-maintenance tree. Small amounts of fertilizer can be applied in late spring or early summer if the tree is not planted in a lawn area. Scatter a 14-5-5 fertilizer around the tree's dripline and beyond and water the area thoroughly to move the nutrients to the root zone. Trees situated in lawns generally do not need additional fertilizer since they can make use of lawn fertilizer. Water deeply every 2 to 3 weeks during the growing season and periodically during a dry fall and winter.

ADDITIONAL INFORMATION

The light-green compound leaves are susceptible to hackberry nipple-gall, which is primarily a cosmetic concern. This nuisance pest lives in symbiosis with the tree and causes no harmful damage; therefore, controls are not necessary.

ADDITIONAL SPECIES, CULTIVARS, OR VARIETIES

The common species of western hackberry is probably the best and most adapted choice for Colorado landscapes. A cultivar called 'Prairie Pride' has nice glossy foliage and is said to be less susceptible to gall problems. The sugar hackberry, *Celtis laevigata* (Zone 5), has a more desirable upright growing habit much like American elm. The bark on this tree is smooth, not ridged and corky like the western hackberry's bark. It is tolerant of wet or dry soils.

White Ash

Fraxinus americana

Height: 50 to 60 ft. (spread 40 to 50 ft.) **Type:** Deciduous shade tree **Zones:** 3, 4, 5, 6	**Light Requirement:**

*T*he white ash adds superior ornamental value to the landscape with its glossy green leaves that turn reddish-purple in autumn. This tree's fall coloration highlights the landscape. Though it is not as adaptable to heavy soils as green ash is, it can be grown on soils that are improved with a good soil conditioner. Its growth habit is pyramidal when young, but as the tree matures, it develops a well-rounded crown. The white ash is unique in its maintenance of a straight trunk with even distribution of branches. The handsome gray-brown bark has characteristic diamond-shaped furrows and forked ridges. It is well suited for use in open lawn areas or landscapes that have space to accommodate its height and its open, spreading branches. It is important to provide good growing conditions for this tree to keep it healthy and make it more resistant to insect invasions. It grows best in full sun and soils that are neither too wet nor too dry.

WHEN TO PLANT

Plant container-grown nursery trees from early spring through early fall. If planting in the heat of summer, take care to provide adequate moisture and mulch to conserve water.

WHERE TO PLANT

Allow plenty of space for this tree, keeping it far enough away from any building that may interfere with its large spread. Before planting, make sure the soil is well drained.

HOW TO PLANT

The planting hole should be at least 2 to 3 times as wide as the rootball. After a larger balled-and-burlapped tree is placed in the planting hole, remove any twine and a good portion of the wire basket. This is especially important for the upper portion of the rootball. Be sure that the top of the rootball or container root system is planted level with the surrounding grade. If your soil is heavy clay, elevate the rootball so that its top is 2 to 3 in. above the surrounding grade. Apply a 2-in. layer of organic mulch or compost around the root zone after planting.

CARE AND MAINTENANCE

While the white ash is favored for its burgundy to purple fall color and lustrous green foliage, it is susceptible to various problems in Colorado's fluctuating climatic conditions. The ash-lilac borer can be a serious pest of drought-stressed trees or those planted in poor soil conditions. Frost cracks are also common on white ash, but these are generally not fatal if tree vigor and health are maintained. You can protect young trees by wrapping $1^1/_2$-in.-diameter white plastic swimming pool hose around the trunk. Cut the hose to a length equal to the distance between the ground and the first branch. Make a vertical cut the length of the hose, pry it open, and snap the hose around the trunk. It is also important to water in late fall and winter when there is little or no snowcover. Ash borers can be monitored by hanging pheromone traps that will attract and capture the adult clear-winged moths. Monitoring insect population levels will alert you when it is time to take appropriate control measures.

ADDITIONAL INFORMATION

After reading about its potential problems, one may wonder if white ash has any place in the landscape—but this tree *is* a good choice for Colorado landscapes. It is truly a handsome tree in autumn and can be grown successfully with a smidgen of care and attention.

ADDITIONAL SPECIES, CULTIVARS, OR VARIETIES

'Autumn Purple' is one of the most readily available cultivars in our area. It has superior, long-lasting reddish-purple to maroon fall color. Its summer foliage is glossy green on top and paler beneath. 'Elk Grove' is an introduction that has an upright growth habit and leaves that turn purple in fall. Its bark is more resistant to frost cracking than that of other cultivars.

Willow

Salix spp.

Height: 35 to 40 ft. (comparable spread)
Type: Deciduous trees and shrubs
Zones: 3, 4, 5, 6

Light Requirement:

*W*illows are a diverse group of deciduous trees and shrubs in the Rocky Mountain region. They are extremely vigorous and grow rapidly under moist conditions. This fast-growing trait makes their wood brittle, so care must be taken when locating a planting site in the landscape. Globe willow, *Salix matsudana* 'Umbraculifera', is common on the western slope of Colorado, and has bright green leaves and a globe crown. On the eastern slope, this same willow will suffer from freeze injury and temperature fluctuations. Willows can be quite effective in moist sites, but allow plenty of room for growth. They are usually messy trees as they age since they drop twigs onto the lawn when the wind blows.

WHEN TO PLANT
Container-grown willows can be planted from spring through fall. Bare-root nursery stock should be planted in spring as soon as the soil can be worked. Willows are quick to establish if moisture is readily available to the immediate root zone.

WHERE TO PLANT
Plant in full sun to partial shade. Willows are best adapted to moist sites and loamy soils. Trees will require additional moisture during extended dry periods, including late fall and winter when there is little or no natural precipitation.

HOW TO PLANT
The planting hole should be 2 to 3 times as wide as the rootball (or spread of the roots in bare-root nursery stock). If your soil is a heavy, compacted clay, the planting hole should be dug 2 in. shallower than the soilball. In sandy soils, dig the hole no deeper than the rootball. In heavy clay or sandy soils, add a generous supply of compost (25 to 30 percent by volume) to the native soil to improve

drainage and moisture retention. This will help in vigorous establishment of the root system. Place backfill soil into the planting hole and water slowly to eliminate any air pockets. Use some extra soil to construct a dike or water basin for future watering at the edge of the planting hole. Water the newly transplanted trees when the soil begins to dry out 4 to 6 in. deep. Fill the water basin to thoroughly soak the soil. Apply a 2- to 3-in. layer of organic mulch in the planting area to maintain and conserve moisture.

CARE AND MAINTENANCE

Willows love moisture and have extensive root systems. They must be watered on a regular basis to maintain health and vigor. As they mature, trees will commonly shed small branches and twigs onto the ground. This can become a nuisance and will mean more raking of the lawn.

ADDITIONAL INFORMATION

Willows are afflicted with a variety of insect pests and diseases. Trees that become stressed are susceptible to canker diseases and may be short-lived. Aphids can become a problem in late summer when their natural predators are not around. Hose them off with a strong stream of water, or use a homemade soap spray to control the "beasties."

ADDITIONAL SPECIES, CULTIVARS, OR VARIETIES

Globe willow—*Salix matsudana* 'Navajo' or 'Umbraculifera'—is praised for its round-topped crown and brilliant green foliage that turns golden in fall. It is a hardy tree that adapts well to western slope soil types. Golden weeping willow, *Salix alba* 'Tristis', is easily transplanted and has an attractive upright growth habit and drooping branches. Its distinctive golden bark makes it a handsome tree, though it is a favorite food source for aphids. *Salix pentandra*, laurel leaf willow, has an upright growth habit that forms a dense oval crown. It is a good choice for screening. Like most willows, it prefers moist locations.

CHAPTER THREE

Evergreens

*F*ROM THE HIGH PEAKS OF THE ROCKY MOUNTAINS at treeline (that ragged line where trees stop and tundra begins) where the twisted bristlecone pines reside . . . to the subalpine forest in the White River National Forest where spires of firs rise to the sky . . . to the montane forests with ponderosa pines growing on south-facing slopes and Douglas firs residing on wetter, north-facing exposures . . . to the juniper-pinyon woodland in western Colorado where pinyon and juniper grow in harmony . . . you can see the wonderful diversity of evergreens that endure both cold and drought. Some of the wind-sculptured bristlecone pines on Mount Evans have survived two thousand years or more.

Home owners may choose a variety of evergreen trees for the home landscape for privacy screening, wind abatement, and for year-round accent. Evergreens make highly effective windbreaks that buffer the force of the wind, absorbing it rather than redirecting it up over a fence or wall. To stop the force of the westerly winds in our High Plains windbreak, we planted many Austrian pines, whose branches grow all the way to the ground. When combined with deciduous trees and shrubs, evergreens provide ornamental interest and wildlife habitat through all the seasons.

SELECTING EVERGREENS

When you plan to plant evergreens in your landscape, keep their native habitat in mind. A pinyon pine planted in the middle of the lawn will soon develop weak branches, fall under borer attack, and be on its way to plant heaven. Similarly, our Colorado blue spruce will become stunted and struggle to survive if planted in a corner of the yard where snow seldom remains and water never appears. Finding an evergreen that looks good will be a disappointing memory if the tree does not survive. One important consideration is the tree's winter hardiness. The United States Department of

Chapter Three

Agriculture (USDA) has divided a map of the country into layers called hardiness zones based on their average minimum winter temperatures. These hardiness zone numbers are not always an exact guide, however. Even within a particular zone, there can be significant variations in soil, rainfall, exposure, and humidity that affect a plant's ability to acclimate to a certain locale. That's one of the reasons gardening can be an adventure in Colorado. If you can simulate the growing conditions of native evergreens in your landscape, you will enjoy experimenting with growing the various species.

You should be aware that some trees are more long-lived than others, and some trees are more susceptible to diseases and insect pests. The faster a tree grows, the shorter its life span in Colorado's fluctuating weather conditions. For example, poplars and willows have brittle branches and are subject to storm damage when a late-spring snow arrives, or when we get a late-summer or early-fall storm. These "limb breakers" are all too common along the Front Range of Colorado.

It is important to know the ultimate height and spread of an evergreen *before* you plant it. If you value a mountain view, don't plant a spruce in front of the living room window—it will eventually block the view. Look upward, as well, as evergreens can grow to block walkways, driveways, entranceways, utility areas, or overhead power lines. The spread of an evergreen is often referred to as its "skirt," and it can have negative consequences in your landscape without proper planning. The skirt of our Colorado spruce can grow to twenty-five feet or more. What a shame it is to prune a beautiful spruce by removing the lower branches to open up a view or driveway; raising a spruce's skirt is tree butchery, and can endanger the tree. Cutting away a large portion of the lower branches will also destroy the fulcrum of balance of the spruce, and it will be more likely to blow over when high winds hit your neighborhood.

PLANTING EVERGREENS
Evergreens are best planted in the spring, though fall planting can be successful if you can get it done by mid-October. Root growth

Chapter Three

slows down as soil temperatures approach forty-five degrees Fahrenheit. Trees planted in the fall will need to be mulched more heavily (four to six inches) in an effort to delay the freezing of the soil and allow more time for root development. Autumn and winter watering is absolutely essential before the freezing of the soil, and you should continue to monitor moisture in the soil, watering monthly when there is no snowcover during the winter.

Planting evergreens is relatively simple: dig a wide, shallow hole, add the backfill soil, water slowly to eliminate air pockets under the roots, cover the soil with an organic mulch, and water as needed after planting. Nothing else is really necessary. The old practices of digging a deep hole, adding lots of organic matter or fertilizer to the soil, and pruning back the top growth by one-third to compensate for root pruning are the result of myths. Research is now showing that a tree will acclimate to its new environment if planted in concert with native soil conditions.

Very few plants thrive in "contractor dirt," compacted clay, or poorly drained soils; these soils are deficient in the oxygen that is needed for root growth. Adding some organic matter is helpful for improving drainage and aeration, but don't add large amounts of organic matter into the backfill soil. If the soil is made too rich, the tree's roots may decide to remain within the planting hole and never attempt to explore the surrounding native soil. Roots will grow into soil that has a balance of oxygen and water, so the best recommendation is to dig the hole much wider than deep, and loosen the soil thoroughly.

So how much organic matter is good thing? For Colorado soils, mix in a volume of high-quality organic matter that is equal to one-fourth to one-third of the volume of soil removed from the planting hole. In our clay, alkaline soils, organic matter will provide the roots with better aeration. In sandy and rocky soils, organic matter will provide water-holding capacity to prevent drought stress to the root system.

Dig the planting hole two inches shallower than the height of the tree's rootball if you are planting in heavy clay soil. Planting shallow in clay soils prevents the tree from sinking in too deep. If your soil is sandy, the hole should be no deeper than the rootball. The idea behind this planting practice is to place the rootball on a solid foundation so the roots can grow in the top fifteen to eighteen inches of soil.

Now you're finally ready to plant. Remove the tree from its container and place it in the hole. If the roots have become potbound and compacted, growing in circles, tease out the roots by hand or score (nick) the sides of the rootball with a sharp knife. This will stop the roots from growing in a spiral pattern and encourage them to spread out into the soil.

A larger balled-and-burlapped evergreen tree should have the top half of its wire basket removed *after* the tree is situated in the planting hole. Cut off remaining nylon twine and rope as well. The burlap wrap around the top of the ball can be cut off, or tucked back into the soil, cutting several slits through it to permit the roots to venture into new soil. Shovel backfill soil into the hole about half full, and gently firm to keep the tree from tipping over. Then water slowly and allow the soil settle in, eliminating air pockets. Once the water has soaked in, add more backfill soil to complete the planting. Water again. Use the extra soil to construct a dike at the edge of the planting hole. In about four or five days, fill this reservoir with water. It is important not to overwater; more evergreens die from overwatering than underwatering. Give the soil a good soaking when it begins to dry out at four to six inches deep. Mulch the planting area (four to six inches deep) with old pine needles or shredded wood chips. In later years, an appropriate groundcover can be planted as a living mulch.

You don't have to add fertilizer during the planting operation or afterwards. Research has shown that no fertilizer is needed for the first growing season. After the second or third year, you can apply a 10-10-10 fertilizer in spring, around the dripline. Apply one cup of fertilizer per inch of trunk thickness; measure the thickness of the trunk four feet from the ground. Use a crowbar or an old ski pole to punch holes eight to ten inches deep at twelve-inch intervals, and scatter the fertilizer granules where the holes were punched. Water until the fertilizer granules are dissolved or washed into the holes.

American Arborvitae

Thuja occidentalis

Other Name: Eastern Arborvitae **Height:** 15 to 20 ft. (spread to 12 ft.) **Type:** Evergreen tree or large shrub **Zones:** 2, 3, 4, 5, 6	**Light Requirement:**

*A*borvitae tend to be small to medium evergreen trees or shrubs with soft and flattened branches. Some arborvitae are not preferred because they discolor and dehydrate in the winter from exposure to sun and wind. They are, however, adaptable to our alkaline soils and poor growing conditions. It is important to select the right one for your landscape needs, and it may be necessary to provide additional winter protection to keep them looking good. For limited space, consider some of the dwarf selections such as 'Globosa', which grows in a compact, rounded form and maintains this round shape with minimal pruning. Arborvitae are well suited as accent plants, informal hedges, screening, or group plantings.

WHEN TO PLANT

Plant in spring through fall. When planting in fall, be sure to water regularly when rain- and snowfall is scarce or lacking.

WHERE TO PLANT

Keep the plants away from roof lines, where sliding snow may result in branch damage. Locate in a semi-protected location in part sun or shade.

HOW TO PLANT

Container-grown plants are easy to transplant. After removing the plant from the container, carefully pull apart the compacted or circling roots that have built up in the container. Make sure the soil is thoroughly broken up; add additional compost in sandy soils to help retain moisture. If your soil is a heavy clay, dig the planting hole 2 in. shallower than the rootball. In sandy soils, the hole should be no deeper than the root system; it is more important to dig the hole much wider to encourage strong root development. When the rootball is set on undisturbed soil, there is less chance of the rootball settling too deep. After positioning the tree in the hole, add backfill soil and water slowly to eliminate air pockets. Take some of the extra soil and make a dike or water basin at the edge of the planting hole to use for future watering. When the soil begins to dry out 4 to 6 in. deep, fill the reservoir with water to soak the soil. It is best to avoid frequent light waterings. Mulch with shredded cedar or other suitable organic material.

CARE AND MAINTENANCE

Once established, arborvitae will withstand Colorado heat and tolerate drought conditions. They adapt well in deep, well-drained soils and benefit from deep watering periodically during prolonged periods of drought. If pruning is needed, it is best done in spring just as new growth begins. In mid- to late spring, you can apply a fertilizer around the dripline of the tree or shrub. Use a crowbar or metal rod to make a series of holes 8 to 10 in. deep and 12 in. apart, around the dripline and beyond. Broadcast the fertilizer over the area where the holes have been punched. Apply a fertilizer such as 14-5-5 at the rate of 1 to 2 lb. per 1,000 sq. ft., and water-in thoroughly.

ADDITIONAL INFORMATION

To provide protection from heavy snow loads, it is helpful to support the branchlets with twine or heavy plastic-coated wire wrapped in a spiral fashion around the plant to hold the foliage and stems together. The dense foliage of this evergreen will eventually hide the supports. If the foliage becomes chlorotic or pale yellow, apply chelated iron in spring and this will restore the green color for that growing season.

ADDITIONAL SPECIES, CULTIVARS, OR VARIETIES

There are several cultivars available in the nursery trade. Look for 'Emerald Green' with its narrow growth habit and bright, lustrous emerald-green foliage. It has good heat and cold tolerance. 'Techny' holds its evergreen color throughout the seasons. 'Smaragd' is emerald green and grows into a neat pyramid; it holds its color through the winter. 'Brandon' has handsome dark-green foliage with a bluish cast.

Bristlecone Pine

Pinus aristata

Height: 10 to 30 ft. **Type:** Alpine conifer **Zones:** 2, 3, 4, 5, 6	**Light Requirement:**

*T*he bristlecone pine is a beloved native that grows in the sub-alpine forests and at treeline, growing slowly in cold temperatures. Its dark-brown cones have small prickles on their scales, giving this pine its common name. Winds shape the bristlecone pines into twisted shapes and contorted forms. These uniquely shaped trees are called *krummholz*, from the German word for "crooked wood." Bristlecone pines in Colorado can be 2,000 years old, or older. They are among the oldest trees in the world. Their dark-green needles occur in fascicles of five and are densely clustered along the stems and branches, giving rise to another common name: foxtail pine. The needles are covered with tiny pitch nodules which are often mistaken for insect pests. Bristlecone pines will hold their needles for 10 to 15 years before a normal needle drop occurs. This pine is truly a tough species that endures in alkaline, rocky, poor, or well-drained soils, as well as windy conditions. Its irregular shrubby, spreading branches make this pine an ideal accent conifer, and it retains its growth habit with age. Plant *Juniperus horizontalis* at its feet for an extra-special effect.

WHEN TO PLANT

The preferred time to plant bristlecone pine is spring; this will give the pine a longer season to establish roots before winter. Fall planting can be successful if certain guidelines are followed (refer to the beginning of this chapter).

WHERE TO PLANT

Bristlecone pine does best in full sun in well-drained soils, and it will tolerate windy sites. Avoid areas that don't drain water; this will mean certain death for this native pine. Plant it as a specimen conifer, as a backdrop for a perennial garden, or in a rock garden setting. We have used it in foundation plantings because it grows slowly and has a picturesque growth habit.

How to Plant

Dig the planting hole at least 2 to 3 times as wide as the rootball or container. If your soil is heavy clay or poorly drained, plant the top of the root system 2 in. above the surrounding grade. When planting in sandy soils, the planting hole should be no deeper than the rootball. After positioning a balled-and-burlapped tree in its hole on undisturbed soil, remove any twine or rope and the wire basket around the top half of the rootball. This is important for the proper establishment of unimpeded feeder roots within the planting hole. Add backfill soil around the roots and water slowly to eliminate any air pockets underneath the root system; check later to see if additional soil is needed. Water again when the soil begins to dry out 4 to 6 in. deep around the edge of the planting hole. Mulch with pine needles or shredded bark to maintain soil moisture during establishment.

Care and Maintenance

Bristlecone pine can be a long-lived evergreen if it is not overwatered or overfertilized. Provide water during long, dry spells to maintain tree vigor; water deeply, but infrequently. You can apply 1 cup of a 10-10-10 fertilizer for each inch of trunk thickness in early spring after the first growing season. This will help to make it grow a bit faster. Be sure to water the fertilizer into the soil thoroughly after application. Bristlecone pines have unique growing characteristics and should not be pruned; allow them to grow and develop naturally.

Additional Information

The bristlecone pine is one of the slowest-growing pines you can plant in your landscape. You can expect to pay a premium for a larger specimen tree.

Additional Species, Cultivars, or Varieties

There is only one bristlecone pine. God had a plan in mind when this enduring conifer was created.

Colorado Blue Spruce

Picea pungens

Height: 60 to 100 ft. (spread 20 to 30 ft.) **Type:** Large evergreen **Zones:** 2, 3, 4, 5, 6	**Light Requirement:**

*T*he Colorado blue spruce is our state tree and a favorite for landscape use. This stately pyramid-shaped evergreen has blue glaucous color and stiff horizontal branches that sweep the ground. Seedling trees vary from bright-green to gray-green to silver-blue. Blue spruce is best planted as a specimen tree where it can grow to its full form. When selecting a spruce for your landscape, look for some of the grafted cultivars that have outstanding color and characteristics. Some of our favorites are 'Hoopsii', 'Fat Albert', 'Iseli Fastigiate', 'Montgomery', and 'Thompsonii'. Since it is native to rivers and streams throughout the Rocky Mountain region, spruce must be planted where it will receive adequate moisture. Give the blue spruce plenty of room to grow so you won't have to prune it later and destroy its natural growth habit.

WHEN TO PLANT

Plant in early spring through early fall. Container-grown and balled-and-burlapped nursery stock is readily available and easily transplanted. Seedling trees are available through mail-order nurseries, but be aware that not all will have "blue genes"!

WHERE TO PLANT

Allow plenty of space when picking a location for your blue spruce. Some cultivars grow more slowly and some have a columnar habit; these can be used for special situations. Spruce does best in full sun and prefers moist soils.

HOW TO PLANT

Prepare a planting hole equal in depth to the rootball and 3 to 4 times as wide. It is best to loosen the soil well beyond the rootball to provide more room in which new roots can grow. When planting container-grown trees, it is helpful to mix some compost or sphagnum peat moss with the backfill soil to reduce soil compaction and create a more favorable growing environment. If your soil is a heavy clay, dig the planting hole 2 in. shallower than the rootball. In sandy soils, the hole should be no deeper than the root system; it is more important to dig the hole much wider to encourage strong root development. When the rootball is set on undisturbed soil, there is less chance that it will settle too deep. After positioning the tree in the hole, add backfill soil and water slowly to eliminate air pockets. Take some of the extra soil and make a dike or water basin at the edge of the planting hole to use for future watering. When the soil begins to dry out 4 to 6 in. deep, fill the reservoir with water to soak the soil. It is best to avoid frequent light waterings. Mulch with a few inches of pine needles, compost, or other suitable organic matter.

Care and Maintenance

The first few growing seasons are important for establishing your blue spruce. Be sure to provide adequate moisture to keep the roots thriving and prevent heat stress. Spider mites can become a problem in the heat of summer; they can be controlled by syringing the tree with water or an appropriate miticide. The spruce adelgid is a pest that causes new growth to develop purple galls that turn brown by August. Avoid the application of "weed and feed" fertilizers near spruce trees; these herbicides can accumulate and result in distorted growth and possible dieback.

Additional Information

Be very cautious when using dormant sprays on spruce—oil sprays will remove the blue coloration. The spruce adelgid that causes gall formation can be controlled in early spring as the new growth begins to expand; use an appropriate insecticide and follow label directions.

Additional Species, Cultivars, or Varieties

The traditional spruce can grow to 100 ft. and have a spread of 30 ft. There are some cultivars such as 'Iseli Fastigiate' that have an upright, columnar growth and a narrow width of 6 ft. This selection is a good alternative to the overplanted upright junipers. 'Hoopsii' has an informal growth habit with a width of 15 to 20 ft. and bright-blue needles that make it a striking specimen evergreen. 'Fat Albert' has a broad pyramidal form with silver-blue needles. *Picea glauca* 'Conica', the dwarf Alberta spruce, is often planted near entries, but it does best with protection from intense sunlight and prevailing winds.

Creeping Juniper

Juniperus horizontalis

Height: 6 to 18 in. **Type:** Small evergreen shrub or groundcover **Zones:** 3, 4, 5, 6	**Light Requirement:**

The creeping juniper family is one of our favorites for Colorado landscapes because it so widely adaptable and will withstand the hottest, driest sandy soils imaginable. Overwatering is the biggest killer of this rugged tree. These incredible evergreens have adapted well by minimizing water loss—they have small, needle-like scales that are packed densely along the stems and a growth habit that shades the soil over the root system. After becoming established, they spread to form an impenetrable weed barrier. You will find cultivars with dark-green, steel blue, or bluish gray foliage; some produce attractive blue berries, and some will develop a striking plum-purple hue over the winter. Creeping juniper's toughness allows it to be put to work as a groundcover shrub in the water-thrifty landscape. Use creeping juniper to cover a steep slope, to fill in the "hellstrip" (that area between the sidewalk and the street), or anywhere you want winter interest. Its low horizontal growth habit is ideal for creative foundation plantings, and its salt tolerance makes it adapt well along sidewalks and driveways where de-icing salts are often used.

WHEN TO PLANT

Creeping junipers can be planted from spring through early fall. They are available at most garden retailers in early spring.

WHERE TO PLANT

This juniper performs best in full sun but will tolerate some light shade. Don't plant it in deep shade. Creeping junipers can be used in many difficult landscape situations from sandy, dry soils to heavy clay; just be sure the soil is well drained. Plant a grouping to cover a slope, fill in a rough spot, or cascade over a rock wall or in planters.

HOW TO PLANT

When using juniper as a groundcover, space the plants 2¹/₂ to 3 ft. apart; they will spread over time. Dig the planting holes as deep as the rootball or container and 3 times as wide. Remove the shrub from the container and, if possible, carefully loosen the crowded roots with your hands. If you have extremely rootbound plants that have built up a large mass of roots which encircle the rootball, score or nick the roots with a sharp pocketknife. Four or 5 cuts spaced evenly around the rootball will break the roots free and encourage their vigorous development into the soil. Position the plant so it is growing at the same depth it was in the container. Replace the back-fill soil around the roots, water slowly to eliminate any air pockets, and check again to see if additional soil is needed. Using extra back-fill soil, make a dike at the edge of the planting hole to form a water basin which will hold water when you need to water again. As the soil dries out 4 to 6 in. deep, fill the basin with water to slowly per-colate and moisten the soil. Apply a 2- to 3-in. layer of mulch (like shredded bark) around the plant to conserve moisture.

CARE AND MAINTENANCE

Once established, creeping junipers are long-lived. They should be watered deeply, but not frequently. As new growth begins in the spring, you can apply a high-quality, long-lasting slow-release fertilizer such as 14-5-5 with chelated iron. Water thoroughly after applying any fertilizer to avoid foliage burn. Spider mites may visit junipers during hot, dry periods. Hose them off with water regu-larly to prevent a severe problem, or use an appropriate control for mites.

ADDITIONAL INFORMATION

Creeping junipers will awaken with color in spring if you underplant spring-flowering bulbs through their low horizontal branches—try bulbs like crocus, botanical tulips, narcissus, and *Iris reticulata*.

ADDITIONAL SPECIES, CULTIVARS, OR VARIETIES

There are many cultivars of groundcover-type junipers for Colorado landscapes. 'Blue Chip' (8 to 10 in.) has attractive blue foliage, pur-plish winter color, and a low spreading habit. 'Wiltonii' or 'Blue Rug' grows very prostrate (4 to 6 in.), has a width of 6 to 8 ft., and has silvery blue foliage that turns plum in the winter months. 'Bar Harbor', 'Hughes', and many other cultivars are available with dif-fering heights, foliage color, textures, and winter coloration.

Douglas Fir

Pseudotsuga menziesii

Height: 30 to 60 ft. (spread 15 to 20 ft.)	**Light Requirement:**
Type: Evergreen tree	
Zones: 3, 4, 5, 6	

*T*he Douglas fir is a forest native that is harvested primarily for lumber. I recall childhood days of taking a winter trip to the mountains to cut a "Doug fir" for the family Christmas tree. This evergreen can be found growing in dense forests and benefits from thinning. It is often seen as an ornamental conifer in the landscape. It is effective when planted in groupings for a windbreak, as a garden backdrop, or as a single specimen tree in a large lawn area. The short, thin needles are a shiny green above with a whitish band beneath. One of the features of this evergreen is its downward-hanging cones with decorative 3-pronged bracts. It does best in moist, well-drained soils and is not tolerant of dry sites.

WHEN TO PLANT

Plant in early spring. Trees are available as balled-and-burlapped or container-grown nursery stock.

WHERE TO PLANT

Locate in full sun or partial shade. With a new planting, it is advisable to construct a burlap screen on the windward side of the tree to reduce the incidence of sunburn. (This will be needed only for the first few years as the tree is becoming established.) The Douglas fir can be planted as a specimen tree or planted as a backdrop or a screen.

HOW TO PLANT

Prepare the planting hole 2 to 3 times wider than the rootball. Loosen the soil well beyond the planting hole and add compost to the area. If your soil is a heavy clay, dig the planting hole 2 in. shallower than the rootball. In sandy soils, the hole should be no deeper than the root system; it is more important to dig the hole much wider to encourage strong root development. When the rootball is set on undisturbed soil, there is less chance that it will settle too deep. After placing a balled-and-burlapped tree in its hole, remove any nylon twine or rope and the uppermost part of the wire basket. This will permit strong root development within the planting site and reduce the chances of root girdling. After positioning the tree in the hole, add backfill soil and water slowly to eliminate air pockets. Take some of the extra soil and make a dike or water basin at the edge of the planting hole to use for future watering. When the soil begins to dry out 4 to 6 in. deep, fill the reservoir with water to soak the soil. It is best to avoid frequent light waterings. Mulch with shredded wood chips, pole peelings, or pine needles after planting.

CARE AND MAINTENANCE

Douglas fir can be a long-lived tree provided it receives adequate moisture. Soak the soil deeply on a regular basis with a soaker hose or twin-eye sprinkler placed at the dripline and beyond. Move the sprinkler every 15 to 20 minutes until you have watered the entire root area. If soils become compacted, aerate once or twice a year with a crowbar, metal rod, or old ski pole. Punch holes 10 to 12 in. deep all around the dripline to allow oxygen, water, and nutrients to be more available in the root zone. Trees growing in lawn areas will receive some nutrients from applications of lawn fertilizers. Do not apply "weed and feed"-type products near evergreens; herbicide contamination in the root zone can result in dieback.

ADDITIONAL INFORMATION

This tree serves as the winter host of the spruce gall adelgid, a pest that causes purplish-brown galls on blue spruce.

ADDITIONAL SPECIES, CULTIVARS, OR VARIETIES

The blue-needled form *P. menziesii* spp. *glauca* is a slow-growing type that is somewhat pyramidal. 'Pendula', the weeping Douglas fir, is a good choice for rock gardens, as is the dwarf cultivar 'Densa'.

European Larch

Larix decidua

Height: 70 to 80 ft. (spread of 25 to 30 ft.) **Type:** Deciduous conifer **Zones:** 2, 3, 4, 5, 6	**Light Requirement:**

*T*he larch belongs to a class of conifers which shed their leaves in autumn and remain barren throughout the winter. It is a native of northern and central Europe, but is extremely well adapted to Colorado climate and soils. It is unique and eye-catching in the fall with its golden-yellow color. In the spring, the branches are re-clothed in bright-green foliage. If you live in a passive solar house, larch is a good substitute for large spruces or pines. The broad pyramidal growth habit is typical when the tree is young and will become irregular with age. Larch is very cold hardy and tolerant of alkaline soils. If you have space in your landscape, plant this impressive deciduous conifer and enjoy its spectacular form. Its needles turn yellow to a rich golden-yellow in autumn, adding seasonal interest to the landscape.

WHEN TO PLANT
Container-grown larch specimens should be planted in early spring.

WHERE TO PLANT
Plant in an open area with full sun. Allow plenty of space, for larch will have a considerable spread. This tree prefers well-drained soils, so it is beneficial to amend the planting area with compost or other suitable organic matter.

HOW TO PLANT
Prepare the planting hole 2 to 3 times wider than the rootball. If your soil is a heavy clay, dig the planting hole 2 in. shallower than the rootball. In sandy soils, the hole should be no deeper than the root system; it is more important to dig the hole much wider to encourage strong root development. When the rootball is set on undisturbed soil, there is less chance of its settling too deep. After positioning the tree in the hole, add backfill soil and water slowly to eliminate air pockets. Take some of the extra soil and make a dike or

water basin at the edge of the planting hole to use for future watering. When the soil begins to dry out 4 to 6 in. deep, fill the reservoir with water to soak the soil. It is best to avoid frequent light waterings. After situating a larger balled-and-burlapped specimen tree in its hole, remove any nylon twine or rope and the upper part of the wire basket. This will ensure good root development in the root zone. Mulch with a few inches of compost or shredded wood chips after planting.

CARE AND MAINTENANCE

Larch is easy to establish provided you supply consistent moisture during the growing season. It is not tolerant of extreme drought conditions, so water to soak the soil deeply. Use a "frog-eye" sprinkler that is set at the dripline. Allow the water to soak in for 25- to 30-minute periods, and move the sprinkler to provide good overlap. If the tree is planted in a lawn area, it will receive some nutrients from applications of lawn fertilizers. Be sure to avoid applications of "weed and feed" products which will result in an accumulation of herbicides that can be absorbed by the tree roots.

ADDITIONAL INFORMATION

Larch is generally pest- and disease-free, but it is intolerant of extremely dry conditions. Water periodically throughout the winter, particularly when there is little or no snowcover. Apply water when temperatures are above freezing and the soil is unfrozen. Winter watering may be necessary every 5 to 6 weeks during extended dry spells in late fall and winter.

ADDITIONAL SPECIES, CULTIVARS, OR VARIETIES

If you have limited space but still want to grow this unusual deciduous evergreen, search out 'Fastigiata'. This cultivar has a narrow, columnar growth habit and short ascending branches.

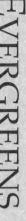

Japanese Yew

Taxus cuspidata

Height: 15 to 20 ft. (spread to 6 ft.) **Type:** Small evergreen tree or shrub **Zones:** 4, 5, 6	**Light Requirement:**

*Y*ews are among the most attractive evergreens for Colorado landscapes. They are best grown on an east or north exposure with protection from winter sun and wind. Some fine specimens can be seen in Fort Collins, Colorado, where their handsome dark-green needles create a nice contrast to the harsh university building walls. In the proper location, yews can be used in mass plantings, in shrub borders, or as foundation plantings. They need well-drained soils and prefer moist conditions, so shady locations are best. If desired, yews can be pruned into a more formal hedge, but the natural growth form is quite attractive. Planted in combination with other deciduous trees and shrubs, yews offer striking contrast in color and texture.

WHEN TO PLANT
Plant in spring through early fall. Container-grown plants transplant easily.

WHERE TO PLANT
Colorado has intense sunlight; choose an area that is part shade to shade. While perfectly hardy in our state, yews should be planted out of extremely exposed windy locations or winter sun, or the needles will surely brown. Avoid low areas where water accumulates and may cause root rot. The soil must be well drained.

HOW TO PLANT
Dig the planting hole 2 to 3 times wider than the rootball. Heavily compacted soils will need to be prepared by adding to the native soil a generous supply of compost, up to 40 percent by volume of the soil from the hole. Loosen the soil to break it up and improve soil porosity. If your soil is a heavy clay, dig the planting hole 2 in. shallower than the rootball. In sandy soils, the hole should be no deeper than the root system. It is more important to dig the hole

much wider to encourage strong root development. When the root-ball is set on undisturbed soil, there is less chance of its settling too deep. After positioning the tree in the hole, add backfill soil and water slowly to eliminate air pockets. Take some of the extra soil and make a dike or water basin at the edge of the planting hole to use for future watering. When the soil begins to dry out 4 to 6 in. deep, fill the reservoir with water to soak the soil. It is best to avoid frequent light waterings. Container-grown plants that have become rootbound in the pot should have the roots gently pulled apart to encourage vigorous, healthy root development.

CARE AND MAINTENANCE

This evergreen will not tolerate prolonged periods of drought, so be sure to water regularly during dry periods throughout the growing season, especially in late fall and winter if weather conditions are dry. Water when air temperatures are above freezing and when the soil is not frozen. In late spring or early spring, fertilize sparingly with a 14-5-5 with chelated iron or similar analysis according to label directions. A crowbar or metal rod should be used to make a series of holes around the dripline and beyond; make the holes 8 to 10 in. deep and 12 in. apart. Broadcast the fertilizer in this area and water-in thoroughly. Prune the longest growth in spring to maintain a natural look.

ADDITIONAL INFORMATION

Extreme exposure to winter sun and wind will cause the needles to turn yellow or brown, so consider location carefully. The needles are poisonous if eaten, as are the inner hard seeds of the red fruits.

ADDITIONAL SPECIES, CULTIVARS, OR VARIETIES

There are several varieties available; read the labels carefully to determine if the plant will be hardy in your landscape and eleva-tion. 'Capitata' is a pyramidal form that is well adapted for hedging, specimen planting, or planting as an accent. *Taxus* × *media* 'Hicksii' has a narrow, upright growth habit and soft green needles, and grows to 10 ft. in height and 6 ft. in spread.

Pine

Pinus spp.

Height: 15 to 80 ft. (spread 15 to 35 ft.) **Type:** Evergreen trees and shrubs **Zones:** 2, 3, 4, 5, 6	**Light Requirement:**

*P*ines can be found in all parts of Colorado. The gnarled bristle-cone pines on Mount Evans are a testimonial to their durability and strength. One of my favorites is the pinyon pine, *Pinus edulis,* a native that grows throughout western Colorado. Its pungent evergreen aroma brings back childhood memories—it was decorated for Christmas and lasted for weeks indoors. When cutting wood for the stoves, it was great fun to collect pine cones for a bountiful harvest of pinyon nuts. Pinyon is drought tolerant and can grow into picturesque forms with twisted trunk and limbs. Under cultivation in the home landscape, it will succumb to overwatering and often falls victim to pitch mass borers. Proper placement in the landscape is key to this pine's survival. Pines provide year-round color in the landscape, and the foliage makes a nice backdrop for many deciduous trees and shrubs. Combine with our native sumac, *Rhus trilobata,* for a spectacular autumn display. Pines can be grown as specimen trees or planted at the perimeter of a larger landscape for screening or windbreak.

WHEN TO PLANT
Container-grown specimen pines can be planted from early spring to early fall.

WHERE TO PLANT
Locate in full sun for the best growth and most uniform development. Well-drained soils are preferred, but pines adapt to clay soils that are made to drain with good soil preparation and modifications. Planting pines on raised berms in heavy soil sites will help ensure their survival and prevent overwatering.

HOW TO PLANT
The planting hole should be at least 2 to 3 times as wide as the root-ball or the container-grown root system. If your soil is a heavy clay,

dig the planting hole 2 in. shallower than the rootball. In sandy soils, the hole should be no deeper than the root system. It is more important to dig the hole much wider to encourage strong root development. When the rootball is set on undisturbed soil, there is less chance of the rootball settling too deep. After positioning the tree in the hole, add backfill soil and water slowly to eliminate air pockets. Take some of the extra soil and make a dike or water basin at the edge of the planting hole to use for future watering. When the soil begins to dry out 4 to 6 in. deep, fill the reservoir with water to soak the soil. It is best to avoid frequent light waterings. Mulch after planting with pine needles, shredded wood chips, or other organic material.

CARE AND MAINTENANCE

Pines are more tolerant of poor soil conditions than are spruces and firs. They are often treated with too much love and care; they will soon become stressed from overwatering, overfertilizing, and improper pruning. Pines can be pruned to maintain height and spread in mid- to late spring. Remove half of the new candle growth to keep it in bounds.

ADDITIONAL INFORMATION

Identifying pines in your landscape can be a fun family activity. Notice that the needles grow on the branch tips in bundles of 2, 3, or 5 individual needles. Pinyon pine has two needles per bundle, bristlecone pine has five needles per bundle, and Ponderosa pine has three.

ADDITIONAL SPECIES, CULTIVARS, OR VARIETIES

There are many pines well suited to landscape use. Allow plenty of room for the larger species; cultivars of dwarf pines are available for small spaces or rock gardens. Some of our favorites for Colorado landscapes are *Pinus cembroides* var. *edulis*, pinyon pine (18 to 25 ft. with a 12- to 15-ft. spread); *Pinus nigra*, Austrian pine (30 to 50 ft. in height with a 20- to 30-ft. spread); *Pinus ponderosa*, Ponderosa pine (40 to 60 ft. with a 20- to 35-ft. spread); *Pinus sylvestris*, Scotch pine (30 to 50 ft. with a 30- to 40-ft. spread); *Pinus flexilis*, limber pine (30 to 40 ft. and width of 25 to 30 ft.); *Pinus contorta* spp. *latifolia*, lodgepole pine (30- to 50-ft. height with a 15- to 25-ft. spread); *Pinus mugo*, Mugo pine (15- to 25-ft. height and 20-ft. spread); and *Pinus × reflexa*, southwestern white pine (40 to 60 ft. with a width of 30 to 40 ft).

Rocky Mountain Juniper

Juniperus scopulorum

Height: 15 to 35 ft.
Type: Evergreen tree or shrub
Zones: 3, 4, 5, 6

Light Requirement:

---

*O*ur native Rocky Mountain juniper is a strong survivor of Colorado's drought and alkaline soils. It has a natural pyramidal growth habit and characteristic grayish shaggy bark. It can withstand the cold of the high country and the extreme hot, dry, windy conditions of the canyons, deserts, and plains. It can be found throughout the state; many new cultivars have been selected for the landscape. Unless stressed from overwatering or bark injuries, it remains relatively untouched by insect pests. During the spring frenzy, many home owners take pruners in hand and shear their junipers, but this ritual can actually shorten the tree's life and turn the inside of this evergreen brown. Junipers are drought-enduring shrubs or trees, an integral part of the water-thrifty landscape. They provide cover for wildlife and their bluish-to-green berries are both attractive and a food source for birds. Junipers can be used as windbreaks, hedges, group plantings, foundation plants, and specimens. They are a diverse group that is easy to grow in a wide range of soils from sandy soils to clay with high pH; they will tolerate dry conditions once they become established.

WHEN TO PLANT
Container-grown plants can be planted from spring through early fall.

WHERE TO PLANT
Plant in full sun to avoid leggy, weak growth that often occurs in too much shade. Junipers are adapted to filtered light. Use as specimen plants, screening, or informal hedges. Junipers can be overused in the landscape, so try to strike a balance in making your landscape design.

HOW TO PLANT
Junipers are commonly available as container-grown plants and larger balled-and-burlapped specimens. The planting hole should be prepared 2 to 3 times wider than the containerized root system or rootball. Set the plant slightly higher than ground level in heavy

clay soils to allow for settling after watering. Once in the hole, remove nylon twine and as much of the wire basket as possible from around the rootball. This is important and will help in the growth and development of a strong root system within the planting hole; it will also ensure better drought tolerance in future years. In heavily compacted soils, it is beneficial to work compost into the surrounding soil so that root growth will be unimpeded. Form a raised dike of soil around the outer edge of the rootball. This will serve as a water reservoir for the root zone during plant establishment. Spread a few inches of wood chip mulch or pine needles over the planting site to keep the soil from baking and cracking and to conserve moisture.

CARE AND MAINTENANCE

Once established, Rocky Mountain juniper is a true survivor that can withstand dry conditions. Water periodically throughout the growing season, but water deeply and infrequently. Though junipers can be pruned or sheared for a more formal hedge effect, this will ultimately shorten their life span and results in the inner foliage turning brown. It is best to remove long branches or those growing out-of-bounds by pruning individual branches back to the main framework of the shrub; this will maintain a more natural look.

ADDITIONAL INFORMATION

Poor drainage, oxygen starvation to the roots, and bark injuries are the most common causes of decline in juniper plantings. Stressed trees are often attacked by spider mites in the heat of summer, but the pests can be controlled by spraying the foliage with water or an appropriate miticide.

ADDITIONAL SPECIES, CULTIVARS, OR VARIETIES

There are many selections of upright, conical junipers for landscape use. Some of the most readily available are 'Gray Gleam', with gray-green foliage, a height of 12 to 15 ft., and a 6- to 8-ft. spread; 'Blue Haven', with handsome blue foliage, a height of 15 to 20 ft., and a 10- to 12-ft. spread; 'Cologreen', with a rich green color, a height of 15 to 20 ft., and a 6- to 8-ft. spread; 'Moonglow', with a broader pyramidal form, compact silvery-blue foliage, a height to 20 ft., and a spread to 15 ft.; 'Wichita Blue', noted for its feathery blue foliage and wider pyramidal growth habit, reaching 15 to 20 ft. with a 6- to 8-ft. spread; and 'Skyrocket', which has blue-green foliage and a narrow width of 2 to 3 ft. *Juniperus virginiana*, or Eastern red cedar, grows larger in height, up to 35 ft., and is well adapted to Colorado landscapes. It tolerates a wide range of soil types and grows with a spreading habit yet withstands heavy, wet snows. Cultivars such as 'Canaertii', 'Hillspire', 'Idyllwild', and 'Manhattan Blue' are available.

White Fir

Abies concolor

Height: 30 to 60 ft. **Type:** Evergreen tree **Zones:** 3, 4, 5, 6	**Light Requirement:**

*A*re you looking for a great evergreen? The white fir with its beautiful tiered branches makes a bold statement in the Colorado landscape. Its soft, short, flattened needles make this native a favorite evergreen. This majestic tree can reach 60 ft. or more in height, and has a conical growth habit sporting bluish-green needles. It is notable among firs for its outstanding tolerance of hot, dry conditions. If you want a dwarf evergreen fir for the rock garden, be sure to check out *Abies concolor* 'Compacta' (3 ft.) with its beautiful silvery blue needles.

WHEN TO PLANT
Container-grown specimen trees can be planted from spring through early fall. If planting in the heat of summer, be sure to provide ample water and attention to avoid stress and severe transplant shock.

WHERE TO PLANT
Locate in a spot that receives full sun or afternoon shade, and allow enough room for this large evergreen to grow. White fir prefers moist, well-drained soils, but it will endure drought conditions if watered properly. Protection from prevailing winds and winter sun is helpful during the first 2 to 3 years of establishment.

HOW TO PLANT
Prepare the planting hole 3 to 4 times wider than the rootball. White fir does best in deep, rich, moist, well-drained soils, and it dislikes heavy clay. Clay soils will benefit from soil amendments like compost or sphagnum peat. If your soil is a heavy clay, dig the planting hole 2 in. shallower than the rootball. In sandy soils, the hole should be no deeper than the root system; it is more important to dig the hole much wider to encourage strong root development. When the rootball is set on undisturbed soil, there will be less chance of the

rootball settling too deep. Once a balled-and-burlapped tree is situated in its hole, remove nylon twine and the upper portion of the wire basket that is used to support the rootball—use a bolt cutter to cut through the wire and carefully tug away the wire basket. This will allow for the best root growth in the top third of the planting hole. After positioning the tree in the hole, add backfill soil and water slowly to eliminate air pockets. Take some of the extra soil and make a dike or water basin at the edge of the planting hole to use for future watering. When the soil begins to dry out 4 to 6 in. deep, fill the reservoir with water to soak the soil. It is best to avoid frequent light waterings. Mulch after planting with 2 to 3 in. of pine needles or other organic matter.

CARE AND MAINTENANCE

Water on a regular basis to help new trees become well established, especially before the ground freezes. The tree should be properly watered in the late fall and during long dry spells in winter; then it will have adequate moisture for retaining its needles throughout the winter when winds can have a freeze-drying effect on exposed evergreen plantings. Water regularly during the summer months, and aerate the soil if it becomes compacted. Trees growing in lawn areas will receive some nutrients from lawn fertilization and generally do not need supplemental fertilizer.

ADDITIONAL INFORMATION

The white fir is prized for its softer evergreen effect in the landscape and, as the tree matures, for its production of interesting purplish-brown cones. It is not bothered by diseases or insects. In windy and exposed sites, it is a good idea to construct a burlap screen on the windward side of the tree to reduce windburn.

ADDITIONAL SPECIES, CULTIVARS, OR VARIETIES

There are several cultivars available in the nursery trade. 'Candicans' is a good choice for a more narrow upright habit; it has bright silver-blue needles. 'Compacta' is a dwarf form with bright silvery blue needles. *Abies lasiocarpa*, Alpine fir, is a native of the high country, and it does best with some protection to the south and west exposures.

C H A P T E R   F O U R

Groundcovers

*T*HE DECORATIVE QUALITIES OF GROUNDCOVERS provide pleasing contrasts in color and texture. Groundcovers may be vines, shrubs, herbaceous perennials, roses, or even annuals that reseed themselves. These plants accomplish their groundcovering feats by means of specialized growth structures such as underground stolons or rhizomes which explore the soil and send up new shoots, or aboveground runners that do the same thing. Some spread by means of stems that creep along the ground and root, while others ramble along the ground with long stems.

Like lawn grasses, groundcovers are grown primarily for their usefulness in holding the soil, but they are also grown for their appealing foliage and if a groundcover covers itself in a carpet of blue flowers (as does Turkish veronica), who can possibly object?

Observe groundcovers that are used in your area, in both private and public gardens. Take note of the groundcover's height, color, texture, and overall ornamental value. Most of the herbaceous types are easy to propagate by dividing in the spring. Choose the appropriate groundcover for your exposure and growing conditions. Plants selected specifically for a site will have the best chance of survival, growing healthy and vigorous and creating a dense, weed-free groundcover.

The plants selected for this chapter are easy to grow, and once established should require little care. Groundcovers will reduce lawn maintenance on steep slopes, where mowing is an arduous chore. But don't think groundcovers are completely maintenance-free! They need some attention and an occasional grooming to keep them looking good. The groundcover-type junipers, *Juniperus horizontalis* and *J. procumbens*, are quite pleasing when planted on a slope or in the area between the street and sidewalk (that hard-to-landscape place we call the "hellstrip"). They will adapt well and thrive without a lot of watering in Colorado's humus-deprived soils.

Chapter Four

Groundcovers perform other functions, too. Their foliage can disguise the ripening foliage of spring-flowering bulbs. Once established, they grow so densely that they are eventually weed-free, which is good news for the lazy gardener. Evergreen groundcovers provide year-round greenery even in the dreariest months of winter.

With a few exceptions, the procedures for planting groundcovers are essentially the same as those for installing a lawn. Groundcovers are meant to be permanent plantings that will last for many years. Making sure you consider soil drainage, exposure, irrigation, and soil preparation is the secret to growing them successfully. Once a groundcover is established it becomes more difficult, and often costly, to alter its situation.

SOIL PREPARATION

If you have the opportunity, prepare the soil in the entire planting area before planting a groundcover. Thoroughly loosen the ground, remove rubble and trash, and work a high-quality organic conditioner deeply into the planting site. As monumental as this task may sound, it needn't be—in our Green Thumb landscape, we improved the soil in steps, doing a section of the property at a time. This ground preparation ensures healthy and long-lived plants. If you are unable to prepare the planting site in this manner, then digging planting holes and amending their backfill soil will do nicely. There is one lesson we want to share with you from the school of hard Colorado soils and bent spading forks: Don't skimp on soil preparation as you begin the planting process or you will be haunted by sick plants.

CONTROL THE INVASION OF THE WEEDS

No matter what kind of groundcover you plant, it will encounter some competition from weeds—especially from those perennial pests. Mulching with shredded bark, pole peelings, and other materials will help control most weeds, but hand-to-hand combat may be needed to remove some of the more persistent. We know it isn't the easy way—but it's the cowboy way! You can also apply selective pre-emergent herbicides that prevent the weeds from growing. This must be timed appropriately for the best results. Read and follow label directions carefully.

Bigroot Geranium

Geranium macrorrhizum

Height: 12 to 15 in.
Flowers: Magenta-pink, pink, white
Bloom Period: Summer
Zones: 3, 4, 5, 6

Light Requirement:

---

*T*he bigroot geranium's thick, fleshy roots enable it to withstand all kinds of adversity. Classified as a hardy geranium, it can form a dense groundcover that has the ability to adapt to dry shade, to overcome root competition, and even to endure drought. Its lobed leaves with scalloped edges are softly hairy and create a handsome texture over the surface of the soil. Rosy- to light-pink blooms rise above the foliage. The protruding floral parts create a delicate, wispy appearance. Add attractive foliage in the fall and you've got a perennial groundcover that should often have a place in Colorado landscapes. The leaves turn scarlet and bronze in autumn. Younger leaves remain semi-evergreen, adding winter interest. Bigroot geranium is ideal for planting with daffodils and other bulbs—its leaves expand to mask the bulbs' dying foliage.

WHEN TO PLANT

Plant container-grown bigroot geranium in spring through fall. Provide proper moisture and you can plant it in summer.

WHERE TO PLANT

Geranium macrorrhizum does best in partial shade and well-drained soil. It will grow in full sun if provided adequate moisture and if the soil has been prepared with moisture-retentive compost. Mulch to maintain and conserve moisture and to keep the soil cool. Avoid hot, dry locations or heat traps. Use this groundcover under shrubs or trees, in shade gardens, as an overplanting for bulbs, or in the perennial border.

HOW TO PLANT

Plant bigroot geranium 12 to 15 in. apart. Dig the planting holes wide enough to accommodate the roots without crowding. Position the plants so that the soil level is the same as it was in the container.

Gently firm the soil around the roots and water-in well. If the geranium is planted in sun, mulch to conserve moisture.

CARE AND MAINTENANCE

Bigroot geranium is tolerant of drought, but for best growth it should be watered during hot, dry spells. Plants in full sun require regular watering. Soils that have been improved with compost or other moisture-retentive organic matter will allow this groundcover to fill in more quickly. Fertilize in spring with an all-purpose 5-10-5 or 10-10-10 plant food. If plants become overcrowded, they can be divided in spring. Lift the clumps and break them apart. Separate the pieces, making sure each has a portion of thick stem and root. Rosettes of foliage on rhizome-like stems produce roots, so you can plant a section with few or no roots and still have growing success. These plants are very hardy. Firm the soil around new divisions and water as needed. A layer of mulch will help conserve moisture.

ADDITIONAL INFORMATION

The leaves of *Geranium macrorrhizum* have another unique feature. They are fragrant: their crushed leaves emit a fresh pine scent.

ADDITIONAL SPECIES, CULTIVARS, OR VARIETIES

There are several good cultivars of bigroot geranium. 'Bevan's Variety' has deep-magenta flowers with red sepals. 'Album' is white-flowered and has pinkish red sepals. 'Ingwersen's Variety' has pale-pink flowers over light-green foliage. Other hardy geraniums are useful as groundcovers. Dalmatian cranesbill, *Geranium dalmaticum* (4 to 6 in.), is a low carpeting plant with small light-pink flowers and good fall color. Another species to try is *Geranium* × *cantabrigiense* (8 to 9 in.), a naturally occurring hybrid of bigroot geranium and Dalmatian cranesbill. Its ground-hugging habit and multitude of pink flowers makes it desirable under trees and shrubs.

Carpet Bugleweed

Ajuga reptans

Height: 4 to 8 in.	**Light Requirement:**
Flowers: Blue-purple, pink, white	
Bloom Period: Mid-April to June	
Zones: 4, 5, 6	

*B*ugleweed is a great groundcover with glossy, deeply veined leaves that spread quickly over the soil's surface to form a rippled carpet of green, purple, bronze, or variegated foliage. It can be grown in sun or shade and adapts well to poor soils. From mid-April to June, spikes of blue-purple flowers appear above the low-growing leaves. It is the leaves, however, that make this a desirable ground-cover year-round. Use bugleweed in shady areas along sidewalks and driveways, or beneath shrubs, vines, or hedges. Bugleweed can be planted in a shady perennial garden, but it can be somewhat aggressive, and you may have to thin it out periodically. Carpet bugleweed spreads rapidly by means of runners which root in moist soil; it is appropriate for areas where a vigorous, weed-free groundcover is desired.

When to Plant

Plant from spring to early fall. Container-grown plants are readily available. Bare-root plants should be planted in early spring as soon as the soil can be worked; this will allow for good root establishment before the heat of summer.

Where to Plant

Ajuga prefers shade or part shade, but it will grow in full sun. It can suffer from leaf scorch in hot locations or from damage from winter wind. The soil should be moderately rich in organic matter and hold moisture. Heavy clay soils and extremely sandy, infertile soils should be amended with compost before planting the area. Bugleweed's foliage and low growth habit make it useful as a contrast to other landscape plants including shrubs, evergreens, hostas, and daylilies. Use it to border a pathway or the edges of a patio, sidewalk, or driveway where it will be contained by a hard surface.

How to Plant

Few groundcovers will grow vigorously in pure sand, and most are difficult to establish in heavy clay soils that have poor drainage. Add a high-quality soil amendment such as compost or sphagnum peat moss to retain moisture in sandy soils, and to improve drainage and porosity in clay soils. Prepare the soil with moisture-retentive compost (30 to 40 percent of native soil by volume) and mix uniformly with the soil. Dig the planting hole twice as wide as the rootball and set at the same level the plant was growing in the pot. Space plants 10 to 12 inches apart. Water after planting and during hot, dry periods until the plants are well established. Mulch around young transplants to conserve moisture.

Care and Maintenance

Bugleweed is generally a low-maintenance groundcover and requires only occasional watering during dry weather. If planted in full sun, it will need additional water to avoid severe wilt and scorch. Once established, *Ajuga* will tolerate dry shade if the soil has been properly prepared. An all-purpose 5-10-5 fertilizer can be applied in spring, and the plants can be cleaned up by a light shearing after flowering. This will encourage fresh, new foliage and improve the plant's appearance.

Additional Information

Bugleweed can be propagated by taking divisions; lift clumps and split them apart. The leafy rosettes (called "stolons") that form along the creeping stems can also be separated and planted for new plants.

Additional Species, Cultivars, or Varieties

There are several cultivars of bugleweed. 'Alba' has dark-green foliage and white flowers. 'Bronze Beauty' has glossy bronzy-purple leaves and purplish flowers. 'Rosea' is attractive with its green foliage and spikes of pink flowers on 8-in. stems.

Creeping Phlox

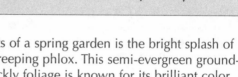

Phlox subulata

> **Height:** 4 to 6 in.
> **Flowers:** Pink, blue, white, magenta
> **Bloom Period:** April to June
> **Zones:** 3, 4, 5, 6
>
> **Light Requirement:**
>

*O*ne of the highlights of a spring garden is the bright splash of color provided by creeping phlox. This semi-evergreen groundcover with its mats of prickly foliage is known for its brilliant color as it tumbles over rock walls or boulders, or creeps along borders. It makes an excellent accent plant in the rock garden and mingles naturally with other perennial flowers. The foliage hugs the ground and provides a dark-green groundcover all year long. Once the plants become established, creeping phlox can withstand shaded dry areas. It is particularly effective planted around rocks or growing over rock walls.

WHEN TO PLANT

Plant container-grown phlox plants in spring or early fall. If you purchase bare-root plants from a mail-order nursery, plant these in the spring as soon as the soil can be worked.

WHERE TO PLANT

Choose a location that receives full sun. Creeping phlox will grow in part shade, but the flowers may not be as abundant. Plant it in rock walls, on terraces, on slopes, and as edging. It makes a good companion for *Aurinia saxatile*, basket of gold, and other spring-flowering bulbs.

HOW TO PLANT

Dig holes twice as wide as the rootballs and position the plants so that the soil is the same level it was in the containers. Few groundcovers will grow vigorously in pure sand, and most are difficult to establish in heavy clay soils that have poor drainage. Add a high-quality soil amendment such as compost or sphagnum peat moss to retain moisture in sandy soils, and to improve the drainage and porosity of clay soils. Prepare the soil with a volume of moisture-retentive compost equal to 30 to 40 percent of the volume of native soil and mix uniformly with the soil. Space the plants 12 to 15 inches apart. Water-in well and apply a mulch of compost, shredded cedar, or other organic material to help the plants stay moist during establishment.

CARE AND MAINTENANCE

Once creeping phlox is established, it will generally withstand drought and heat. To maintain the vigor of the plant, be sure to water deeply once a week during the summer. If you plant it in a humus-enriched soil, additional fertilizer is usually not necessary. Prune or shear back plants after blooming to encourage fresh new growth. As the plants get older, they will start to die out in the center. This is a good indication that it is time to lift and divide the plants. Do this in early spring or early autumn. Discard the center portion and keep new divisions from the outside of the clump. Replant in soil that has been amended with compost and water-in well. Newly set divisions will begin to grow quickly.

ADDITIONAL INFORMATION

Creeping phlox can be propagated by division. Lift the older plants and gently pull them apart into sections, leaving a good portion of roots on each division. Set these new transplants into the soil, firm the soil around them, then water and mulch.

ADDITIONAL SPECIES, CULTIVARS, OR VARIETIES

There are many varieties of creeping phlox available in various colors. A newer variety with beautiful two-tone flowers is 'Candy Stripes'. Eye-catching pink-and-white flowers blanket mounds of bright-green foliage in early spring. 'Emerald Cushion' has blue flowers; 'White Delight' produces pure-white blooms; and 'Atropurpurea' has reddish-purple blossoms.

False Rockcress

Aubrieta deltoidea

Height: 4 to 6 in.
Flowers: Rose, purple, bluish purple, white
Bloom Period: Spring
Zones: 2, 3, 4, 5, 6

Light Requirement:

One of our favorite groundcovers in our Green Thumb garden is false rockcress. As the weather warms up in spring, this plant amazes me each year with its loads of bright blooms. The hairy, grayish-silver evergreen foliage of *Aubrieta* is attractive in a front border or a rock garden, or as an underplanting for spring-flowering bulbs. In spring, small pink to purple blooms cover the plant. False rockcress has a spreading, mat-forming habit and makes a nice compact cover. 'Purple Gem' is a common variety found in Colorado gardens; it has small purple flowers held above a dense mat of grayish-green leaves.

WHEN TO PLANT

Plant container-grown plants from spring through early fall. If you purchase bare-root perennials from a mail-order catalog, plant them in spring as soon as the soil can be worked. This will allow for good root growth before the onset of summer heat.

WHERE TO PLANT

Choose a sunny spot with soil that is well drained. Loosen soil in the area that is to be planted. False rockcress can be planted in rock walls for a nice effect. Use in front of perennial borders and in combination with spring-flowering bulbs.

HOW TO PLANT

Dig the planting hole twice as wide as the container. Few groundcovers will grow vigorously in pure sand, and most are difficult to establish in heavy clay soils with poor drainage. Add a high-quality soil amendment such as compost or sphagnum peat moss to retain moisture in sandy soils, and to improve drainage and porosity in clay soils. Prepare the soil with moisture-retentive compost (30 to 40 percent by volume) and mix uniformly with the native soil. Set the plant at the same level it was growing in the container. Firm the soil around the roots and water-in well. Mulch with compost or shredded cedar. Space the plants 12 to 15 in. apart.

CARE AND MAINTENANCE

False rockcress is a widely adaptable plant that requires a minimum of care. Remember that it does best in well-drained sites. Be careful about watering, as this plant can succumb to crown rot; water sparingly as the soil begins to dry out. If you desire, apply a low-nitrogen organic fertilizer such as 5-10-5 in early spring. Scatter the fertilizer around the plants and carefully scratch it into the soil. Water-in well. After flowering is complete, deadhead the plants to keep them tidy and to encourage compact growth.

ADDITIONAL INFORMATION

This groundcover has performed admirably in our landscape over the years; it offers low evergreen mats of hairy green foliage and bright purple flowers in spring.

ADDITIONAL SPECIES, CULTIVARS, OR VARIETIES

There are several selections of *Aubrieta*. Look for 'Borsch's White', which produces white flowers. 'Variegata' has blue flowers contrasted with foliage that is margined in silvery-white. 'Gloriosa' has large, soft rose-like blossoms.

Heart-Leafed Bergenia

Bergenia cordifolia

Height: 12 to 15 in. **Flowers:** Reddish-pink **Bloom Period:** Spring **Zones:** 3, 4, 5, 6	**Light Requirement:**

*H*eart-leafed bergenia has handsome foliage and flowers. The plants grow with thick, creeping rhizomes that spread to produce nice solid clumps, but they are not invasive. Use them under shrubs or trees, or along pathways or in mass plantings. The paddle-shaped leaves are a bold, glossy dark-green. Strong stems bear clusters of waxy flowers in early spring. This groundcover prefers Colorado soils that have been loosened deeply. The cabbage-like leaves of bergenia combine well with the feathery-textured foliage of daylilies, Siberian irises, and ornamental grasses.

WHEN TO PLANT

Plant container-grown plants from spring through fall. If you purchase plants through mail-order catalogs, plant them in the spring as soon as the soil can be worked. This will allow them plenty of time to become established before the heat of summer.

WHERE TO PLANT

Bergenia prefer partial shade, but they can grow in sun if the soil is deeply prepared and well drained. The foliage will turn burgundy in autumn if the plants are grown in a sunny exposure. Use as border plants near shrubs and hedges and in other part-shade situations. Some good companion plants for bergenia are daylilies, Jacob's ladder, and Siberian irises.

HOW TO PLANT

Few groundcovers will grow vigorously in pure sand, and most are difficult to establish in heavy clay soils that have poor drainage. Add a high-quality soil amendment such as compost or sphagnum peat moss to retain moisture in sandy soils, and to improve drainage and porosity in clay soils. Prepare the soil with moisture-retentive compost (30 to 40 percent by volume) and mix uniformly with native soil. Dig the planting hole twice as wide as the container. Space plants 18 to 24 inches apart. Position in the hole at the same depth the plant was growing in its pot. Water-in well and mulch with compost or other suitable organic material. The first growing season is the most critical time for getting a groundcover established; keep the weeds out by hand-pulling or light cultivation. Mulches will help considerably in keeping weeds to a minimum.

CARE AND MAINTENANCE

Bergenia are not invasive and will thrive with a minimum of care. Provide water as needed during dry periods. Keep a layer of organic mulch around new plants to maintain and conserve moisture. Avoid overfertilizing, as this will result in soft, weak growth and fewer flowers. If plants become overcrowded, lift clumps and divide.

ADDITIONAL INFORMATION

Bergenia is a groundcover that will tolerate dry shade where tree or shrub roots grow near the surface. Use this groundcover beneath maturing deciduous elm and maple trees.

ADDITIONAL SPECIES, CULTIVARS, OR VARIETIES

Bergenia cordifolia purpurea has large, reddish cabbage-like leaves that become purple in winter. Reddish flower stalks support purple-red blossoms. 'Perfecta' grows taller than the species and has purplish foliage with rosy-red flowers.

Kinnikinick

Arctostaphylos uva-ursi

Height: 6 to 12 in.
Flowers: White, pink
Bloom Period: April to May
Zones: 2, 3, 4, 5, 6

Light Requirement:

innikinick is one of our favorite low-growing native evergreen groundcovers with handsome glossy, bright-green foliage. It is an excellent choice for planting beneath pines and spruce, as its broadleaf evergreen leaves contrast nicely with the evergreen needles above. Light-pink flowers appear in spring, followed by small red berries in fall. Kinnikinick makes an nice accent plant in the rock garden. It is a great choice for planting in a larger area and is drought tolerant once the plants become established. The glossy green foliage will turn bronze to reddish in fall and winter. Indians used this plant for medicine, tea, and tobacco, and for curing skin problems. Early settlers used the berries for cider and jelly. Though this plant may require some extra soil preparation, it is well worth the effort required to grow this native in your landscape.

WHEN TO PLANT

Plant kinnikinick in spring as soon as the soil can be worked. Select healthy container-grown plants from a reputable nursery or mail-order supply source.

WHERE TO PLANT

Kinnikinick is adaptable to sun or shade. An acidic soil is preferred, but plants are tolerant of most Colorado soils as long as they undergo some extra preparation. Amend the soil with compost or sphagnum peat moss to buffer alkaline conditions and improve drainage. Plant this groundcover in naturescapes or rocky slopes, or use it for naturalizing beneath trees and shrubs.

HOW TO PLANT

Good drainage is a must for kinnikinick, so it is important to loosen compacted soils and incorporate an acidic, moisture-retentive organic amendment such as compost or sphagnum peat moss. Prepare the soil with moisture-retentive compost (30 to 40 percent by volume) and mix uniformly with the native soil. This will help ensure good establishment. Space the plants from 1 to 2 ft. apart, depending on how quickly you want a full groundcover effect. I prefer to set transplants 12 to 15 in. apart. Water-in thoroughly and mulch new transplants with pine needles or compost. Water weekly the first season for good establishment. After the first season, plants will require a thorough watering only every 10 to 14 days.

CARE AND MAINTENANCE

Once established, kinnikinick is a durable, long-lasting groundcover. It requires little or no fertilizer, and pruning is generally not needed. It keeps its tidy appearance year after year. Kinnikinick can endure drought periods if you provide a good watering every 2 weeks or so. If fertilizer is needed, apply a light sprinkling of an all-purpose 5-10-5 or 10-10-10 fertilizer around the plants and water-in thoroughly. Young plants may need some protection from winter sun and drying winds until they are established.

ADDITIONAL INFORMATION

The year-round glossy evergreen foliage of Kinnikinick is one of its best features in our Colorado landscape. Let it naturalize in rock gardens, on slopes, or beneath pine trees.

ADDITIONAL SPECIES, CULTIVARS, OR VARIETIES

There are a few selections that may be available from local nurseries. Look for 'Point Reyes' with its more rounded leaves and pink flowers. You may also find 'Alaska' and 'Massachusetts' in the nursery trade.

Lily-of-the-Valley

Convallaria majalis

Height: 6 to 12 in.
Flowers: Pure-white
Bloom Period: Late spring
Zones: 3, 4, 5, 6

Light Requirement:

The sweet fragrance emitted from the nodding, bell-shaped flowers of lily-of-the-valley is unforgettable. As spring bulbs are blooming, the sturdy green shoots of lily-of-the-valley push their way up through the soil. By mid-May, dainty stalks bearing racemes of white buds will arch over the foliage. As the buds open, lily-of-the-valley releases a delicious fragrance that some gardeners claim to be the essence of spring. In well-drained soil and partial shade, this plant grows into an excellent easy-to-grow groundcover. It spreads quickly by underground stems or rhizomes. At times lily-of-the-valley grows so vigorously that it is considered invasive. Put it to work beneath shrubs to create a living mulch, or keep it in bounds with metal edging. Each plant has two pointed leaves up to 8 in. long and 3 in. wide; they give a stiff, somewhat coarse effect. In late summer, the foliage begins to look ratty, especially if the plants are grown in sun. Mature or ripened foliage can be pulled out to keep the area tidy.

WHEN TO PLANT

Divisions of lily-of-the-valley rhizomes should be planted in early spring. Underground stems with 2 to 3 pips (the "eyes" or shoots) should be planted in early spring as well. Container-grown plants can be planted from spring through fall.

WHERE TO PLANT

Lily-of-the-valley prefers humus-rich soils and moist conditions in full to partial shade. The soil should be prepared with a moisture-retentive compost, but it must be well drained. We have grown plants near the edge of the house where they receive full sun for a good portion of the day, but the leaves of these plants tend to turn yellow and brown as summer approaches. This groundcover does best in shaded areas that receive no foot traffic. Plant lily-of-the-valley on the north side of the house, in woodland settings, or shade gardens, and use it for covering north- or northeast-facing slopes to prevent erosion. We like to combine it with hostas, ferns, and astilbes.

How to Plant

Lily-of-the-valley plants that have been container-grown should be spaced 8 to 12 in. apart. Set the plants at the same level they were growing in their original containers. Gently firm the soil around the roots and water-in well. Divisions can be set 6 in. apart about 1 to $1^1/2$ in. deep. If the soil is heavy clay or sandy, amend with compost to improve drainage and help it retain moisture. After planting, mulch to maintain even moisture and to keep the soil cool.

Care and Maintenance

Once lilies-of-the-valley become established, they require very little care. Provide water during hot, dry periods to prolong the life of the leaves. As the foliage ripens or dies back, you can either pull or rake out the old leaves to tidy up the area. If you plant lily-of-the-valley beneath trees, the plants will benefit from additional water and occasional fertilizer (5-10-5) to do their best. In autumn, topdress the plants with well-aged manure or compost. Since they grow and spread quickly, you can dig clumps and divide them every 3 to 5 years to share with friends. Plants should be dug in spring.

Additional Information

Lily-of-the-valley is a good cut flower; pick a bouquet of stems and enjoy these cute, fragrant blossoms indoors. *Please note: all parts of lily-of-the-valley are toxic, including the red-orange berries.*

Additional Species, Cultivars, or Varieties

There are a few cultivars available. 'Aureo-variegata' has bold leaves striped in cream. 'Fortin's Giant Bells' has larger leaves and flowers. 'Flore Pleno' has double flowers. 'Rosea' has soft lavender-pink flowers; it tends to be less invasive than the species.

Purple Iceplant

Delosperma cooperi

Height: 2 to 4 in. **Flowers:** Violet-purple **Bloom Period:** June to September **Zones:** 4, 5, 6	**Light Requirement:**

*E*ven though there have been years of numerous Rocky Mountain plant introductions, the appearance of a groundcover with succulent, grayish-green leaves and iridescent violet flowers is still a rare thing. Such a groundcover, purple iceplant, is a hardy soul and widely adaptable to Colorado conditions. Though iceplant is generally associated with the warmer climates of the west coast, this species is quite hardy in our region. Use it along pathways and sidewalks, and in borders, rock gardens, and mass plantings. Combine it with other perennials that have silver or gray foliage. When a touch of frost brushes the foliage of iceplant, the grayish-green color is transformed to a plum-purple; it remain that color throughout the winter. This is truly a well-adapted and useful plant for Colorado landscapes.

WHEN TO PLANT

The best time to plant iceplant is in early spring as soon as the soil can be worked. This will give the plants a long growing season, allowing them to establish a vigorous root system.

WHERE TO PLANT

Choose a sunny location that has some protection from winter sun and wind. This is one of our favorite groundcovers, and it can be used along driveways and sidewalks, on slopes to reduce erosion, and to fill in around other plants.

HOW TO PLANT

Loosen the soil in the area to be planted. Few groundcovers will grow vigorously in pure sand, and they will also have difficulty trying to establish in heavy clay soils that have poor drainage. The alternative is to add a high-quality soil amendment such as compost or sphagnum peat moss—to retain moisture in sandy soils or to improve drainage and porosity in clay soils. Prepare the soil with a volume of moisture-retentive compost equal to 30 to 40 percent of the volume of the native soil from the hole; mix uniformly together. Space plants 12 to 15 in. apart. Dig a hole wide enough to hold the root system. Position the plants at the same depth they were growing in their pots. Firm the soil around the roots and water-in well. Continue to water as needed, allowing the soil to dry out slightly between waterings.

CARE AND MAINTENANCE

If planted in a highly exposed site, purple iceplant can suffer injury from winter desiccation. Additional protection can be provided by covering the plants with evergreen boughs. If the plants become overcrowded, simply dig and divide clumps and transplant the sections to other areas. Iceplant is sensitive to heavy snowpack or excessive winter moisture. Unlike many other plants in our Colorado landscape that may need winter watering, it is best to leave iceplant alone. It prefers dry or exposed positions from fall to early spring.

ADDITIONAL INFORMATION

One of the desirable attributes of iceplant is that its succulent foliage is rarely browsed by deer. The plant is easy to propagate by taking stem cuttings and rooting them in the soil. Until the roots are established, keep the area where the cuttings are inserted moist.

ADDITIONAL SPECIES, CULTIVARS, OR VARIETIES

A more compact and lower-growing selection is *Delosperma nubigenum;* it forms a neatly packed mat of succulent lime-green foliage that turns purplish in fall and winter. Yellow blooms appear from early to midsummer.

Pussytoes

Antennaria parvifolia

Height: 2 to 6 in.
Flowers: White, buff, pink
Bloom Period: Early summer
Zones: 2, 3, 4, 5, 6

Light Requirement:

*P*ussytoes is one of the native plants in our plains landscape; it can be found growing contentedly in the grassy stretches alongside cacti, buffalograss, and blue grama. It is one of the few broadleaf groundcovers that remains evergreen year-round. It makes an ideal groundcover between red flagstones. Its silvery-gray leaves are made up of many tight small rosettes that grow into a handsome mat; its furry clusters of flowers are borne on shortened stalks and resemble the toes of a cat. This is a great groundcover for low-water zones, as it will reliably form an attractive ornamental carpet. Use it along pathways, sidewalks, and driveways, or tuck it among rocks on gritty soil. It is very appealing when planted between paving stones in a garden pathway. This water-thrifty groundcover is particularly good for rocky slopes when you want to control erosion. It combines well with hen-and-chicks, *Sempervivum* spp., or many of the *Sedum* spp.

WHEN TO PLANT

Container-grown plants can be planted in spring through fall. Pussytoes will self-sow readily. The seedlings can be transplanted in the spring as soon as the soil can be worked.

WHERE TO PLANT

Choose a sunny site and well-drained soil. Use as a border planting or mass planting, or plant it among rocks or on slight slopes. It works nicely when planted between flagstones or other paving stones. Pussytoes combines well with other groundcovers such as 'Dragon's Blood' *Sedum* and hen-and-chicks *Sempervivum*.

HOW TO PLANT

Loosen the soil in the area to be planted. Few groundcovers will grow vigorously in pure sand, and they have difficulty trying to establish in heavy clay soils that have poor drainage. The alternative is to add a high-quality soil amendment such as compost or sphagnum peat moss—to retain moisture in sandy soils, and to improve drainage and porosity in clay soils. Prepare the soil with a volume of moisture-retentive compost equal to 30 to 40 percent of the volume of the native soil from the hole; mix together uniformly. Space plants 10 to 12 in. apart. Set each in the hole at the same level the plant was growing in its container. Water-in well and lightly mulch with shredded bark or pine needles.

CARE AND MAINTENANCE

Antennaria is easy to grow and requires little care. As a native of the Rocky Mountains, it can survive on natural precipitation once it is established in your garden. No additional fertilizer is required. During long, hot spells, pussytoes may go dormant after it flowers. Dormancy can be prevented by supplying a little extra water and picking off the flowers.

ADDITIONAL INFORMATION

Pussytoes is a water-thrifty groundcover with foliage that stays close to the ground, protecting the plant from Colorado's wind. The blooms make nice cut flowers for drying. The plants will self-sow readily and spread into surrounding areas. If you don't want this to happen, harvest the flowers regularly.

ADDITIONAL SPECIES, CULTIVARS, OR VARIETIES

Antennaria dioca var. 'Rubra' has furry, pink flowers borne above a low carpet of small, woolly foliage resembling silvery spoons. *Antennaria plantaginifolia* has green leaves that are silvery beneath; it has a growth habit that forms neat, small turf-like patches. *Antennaria rosea* (4 to 12 in.) has flowers that are predominantly pink.

Snow-in-Summer

Cerastium tomentosum

Height: 6 to 12 in. **Flowers:** White **Bloom Period:** Spring **Zones:** 2, 3, 4, 5, 6	**Light Requirement:**

*T*he silvery carpet of snow-in-summer's foliage provides an attractive year-round mat. This groundcover is covered with an abundance of snowy-white flowers from late spring to early summer. It has become a favorite in the Green Thumb garden, simply because it has tolerated the heat and done so very well in our dry, infertile soils. After it finishes flowering, I've been known to take the lawnmower to it to shear it back and keep it neat. This has helped rejuvenate the plants so they produced fresh foliage and denser mat growth. Snow-in-summer is a good candidate for a difficult site in your landscape, and it works well in larger areas. It makes a good accent plant in rock gardens.

WHEN TO PLANT
Plant in spring to early fall. You can easily take divisions from older clumps in early spring and transplant them to new locations or to fill in spots that may have "run out." This plant reseeds; young seedlings can be transplanted in early spring or fall.

WHERE TO PLANT
Locate in full sun with plenty of space to spread; it prefers well-drained soil. This groundcover is an effective border plant along sidewalks, pathways, or driveways, and makes a good accent in a rock garden. I've seen it used effectively on rocky slopes, providing good erosion control.

HOW TO PLANT
Because snow-in-summer requires good drainage and aeration, loosen the soil of the area in which you will plant it. Few ground-covers will grow vigorously in pure sand, and they have difficulty trying to establish in heavy clay soils that have poor drainage. The alternative is to add a high-quality soil amendment such as compost

or sphagnum peat moss—to retain moisture in sandy soils, and to improve drainage and porosity in clay soils. Prepare the soil with a volume of moisture-retentive compost equal to 30 to 40 percent of the volume of the native soil from the hole; mix together uniformly. Dig the planting hole twice as wide as the rootball. Space plants 18 in. apart. Water-in well and mulch with compost or other suitable organic material.

CARE AND MAINTENANCE

Snow-in-summer is easy to grow and will spread rapidly. It requires pruning or shearing to keep it tidy and to promote new growth and dense mat growth. Water as the soil becomes dry to maintain vigor, but allow the soil to dry out slightly between waterings. Apply an all-purpose 5-10-5 fertilizer in early spring. Broadcast the fertilizer around the plants and water-in well. Avoid the use of high-nitrogen plant foods; this practice encourages weak, spindly growth and fewer flowers.

ADDITIONAL INFORMATION

Cerastium tomentosum is a rapid grower and can be aggressive. The less-invasive cultivars are suggested for a rock garden or perennial border. Shear off the faded flowers; this will keep snow-in-summer growing with a neat mat of fuzzy, silvery-white leaves for the rest of the growing season.

ADDITIONAL SPECIES, CULTIVARS, OR VARIETIES

Cerastium biebersteinii is more compact, growing 4 in. tall and producing larger flowers arranged in cymes of three to five. *C. tomentosum* 'Columnae' has a more refined growth habit for accent planting; it forms 4-in. mounds of silver-white foliage.

Spotted Dead Nettle

Lamium maculatum

Height: 8 to 12 in.
Flowers: Pink, rose-pink
Bloom Period: Late spring
Zones: 3, 4, 5, 6

Light Requirement:

*S*potted dead nettle produces a mat of variegated foliage that will enhance a shade garden. Each leaf is marked with a stroke, a splash, or an almost-complete coat of silver, bringing light to dim parts of the garden. In part shade and moist, well-drained soils, spotted dead nettle will grow quickly and fill in open spots. It roots readily at its leaf joints to form a tidy groundcover. The short spikes of hooded flowers, although not the main attraction, also create an attractive display. Blooms appear in May to early June on short spikes; they are typically pink, but there are cultivars with rose-pink and white flowers. Use *Lamium* as a groundcover under trees and shrubs, on shaded slopes, in shade gardens, and as a cover for bulb gardens. The foliage variegation creates movement in the garden, giving an effect of dappled light. Use it in containers and hanging baskets to accent annual flowers.

WHEN TO PLANT

Plant container-grown plants of spotted dead nettle in spring through fall. Be sure to provide adequate moisture if the plants are set out in the heat of summer.

WHERE TO PLANT

Spotted dead nettle does best in moist, well-drained soils. Partial shade to full shade will suit this groundcover just fine. The variegated foliage brings life to shade gardens. It can become straggly in dry shade where tree roots compete for moisture. Use as an edging in front of perennials, plant over bulbs, or use as accent plants in containers and hanging baskets.

HOW TO PLANT

Plant spotted dead nettle 12 to 18 in. apart. Dig the planting holes large enough to accommodate the root system. Position the plant so that the soil level is the same as it was in the container. Gently firm the soil around the roots and water-in well. In partial shade, the plants will fill in rather quickly.

CARE AND MAINTENANCE

Lamium does not usually need extra fertilizer when planted in average soils or in shade gardens. Provide regular watering during dry spells, especially if the plants have been located under trees where there is competition from tree roots. The plants can be sheared back after flowering to keep them compact and neat-looking. They can be dug and divided in spring or early summer. Lift sections and separate the plants; replant. Keep the new divisions moist until they become established in their new location. Mulch open soil to conserve moisture.

ADDITIONAL INFORMATION

If spotted dead nettle becomes leggy and sparse, it doesn't mind being sheared to keep it growing dense and compact. It combines well with shade-loving *Astilbe* and the coarse heart-shaped leaves of Siberian bugloss. The silver-streaked foliage is a good accent for white-flowering bulbs.

ADDITIONAL SPECIES, CULTIVARS, OR VARIETIES

Cultivars of *Lamium* have various amounts of variegation and different flower colors; some are more compact and have a spreading growth habit. 'White Nancy' has handsome silver-gray leaves edged in greenish gray; they look fresh for most of the summer. Pure-white flowers appear in June, bringing out the sheen of the foliage. 'Beacon Silver' has rose-purple flowers and a center stripe of silver. 'Shell Pink' and 'Pink Pewter' have pale-pink flowers. 'Aureum' has yellowish-green foliage with a creamy stripe.

Stonecrop

Sedum spp.

Height: 2 to 30 in.	**Light Requirement:**
Flowers: White, yellow, red, pink	
Bloom Period: May to October	
Zones: 3, 4, 5, 6	

Sedums comprise a diverse group of groundcovers that tolerate poor soil conditions to reward the gardener with an abundance of blooms and attractive foliage. The fleshy, succulent leaves remain attractive for months; if planted in a somewhat protected site, the foliage may remain evergreen, adding winter interest. *Sedum acre* (gold moss stonecrop) has a creeping growth habit and tiny, bright, evergreen leaves that form a dense mat over the ground. The flowers are borne in terminal clusters of shortened spikes or flattened heads. Colors come in yellow, white, pink, rose, purple, and red. Their bloom period can range from May through October, depending on the weather. Use them in rock gardens and mass plantings, or for filling in between stepping stones and terracing. They are well adapted to sunny exposures and thrive in heat.

WHEN TO PLANT

Plant from spring through early fall. Sedums are easy to start from cuttings almost any time of the year.

WHERE TO PLANT

Choose locations with full sun and well-drained soils. Stonecrop is heat and drought tolerant. Use it in perennial borders and dry gardens, and for mass plantings. If the soil is too fertile, the plants will tend to grow weaker and more prone to breakage. Plant between flagstones or other paving stones, on rocky slopes, and in corner plantings. Sedums are particularly effective planted around rocks or along pathways, or tucked into rock walls.

HOW TO PLANT

Few groundcovers will grow vigorously in pure sand, and they have difficulty trying to establish in heavy clay soils that have poor drainage. The alternative is to add a high-quality soil amendment such as compost or sphagnum peat moss—to retain moisture in sandy soils, and to improve drainage and porosity in clay soils. Prepare the soil with a volume of moisture-retentive compost equal to 30 to 40 percent of the volume of the native soil from the hole; mix together uniformly. Dig the hole twice as wide as the container. Position the plant so that the soil level is the same as it was in the container. Gently firm soil around the roots and water well. Space plants 12 to 15 in. apart.

CARE AND MAINTENANCE

The stonecrops need very little input from the gardener; they quickly spread to form a dense groundcover. An occasional watering when the soil gets dry will sustain the plants. Avoid fertilizing with high nitrogen, as this will make the plants weak and prone to rot.

ADDITIONAL INFORMATION

Stonecrops can be propagated by dividing the plants in spring, early summer, or early fall. Transplant divisions to open spaces and water-in well.

ADDITIONAL SPECIES, CULTIVARS, OR VARIETIES

There are many species and cultivars of sedum for landscape use. King's crown roseroot, *Sedum rosea* ssp. *integrifolium*, is a Colorado native with attractive green columns that elongate to produce a flat head of 2-in.-deep red blooms from May through June. *Sedum spurium*, two-row sedum, is a creeping species that has round, coarsely toothed leaves ranging from green and bronze to red; its pink or red flowers are borne in flat clusters. 'Dragon's Blood' has pink blooms and bright-red leaves throughout the growing season. 'Red Carpet' has reddish flowers and fruit, and red foliage. White-flowering cultivars are available. Orange stonecrop, *Sedum kamtschaticum*, is a more upright, shrubby plant with scalloped leaves; bright-yellow star-shaped flowers cover the plant from May to mid-June.

Strawberry

Fragaria spp.

Height: 4 to 10 in.
Flowers: White, pink
Bloom Period: Spring through fall
Zones: 2, 3, 4, 5, 6

Light Requirement:

*T*hough strawberries are not considered groundcover, there is great groundcover potential because of the nature of this plant's growth habit. Mother plants can send a half-dozen or more runner plants away from the central crown of the plant. As each of these runners root down, they form a dense groundcover rather quickly, then more runners are produced by the new plants. The wild strawberry, *Fragaria americana*, is among the most adaptable types for Colorado soils and climatic conditions. Its bright-green foliage hugs the ground, and the plants spread quickly to create an attractive carpet. Wild strawberry is sprinkled with fragrant white flowers and golden centers in spring, but the berries are small and tart. It is very tolerant of dry situations. One of the most attractive groundcover strawberries is 'Pink Panda', which has a multitude of bright-pink blooms in late spring through early fall.

WHEN TO PLANT

Plant container-grown plants in early spring through early fall. If you purchase bare-root plants from a mail-order nursery, get them planted in early spring as soon as the soil can be worked. This will allow for good establishment before the heat of summer.

WHERE TO PLANT

Strawberries perform well in full sun to part shade. The soil should be well drained. Plant this groundcover strawberry in shrub borders, along pathways, and on slopes to control erosion.

HOW TO PLANT

Loosen the soil in the area to be planted. Add a moisture-retentive compost to sandy, granite-based soils or to heavy clay soil to improve drainage. Few groundcovers will grow vigorously in pure sand, and they have difficulty trying to establish in heavy clay soils that have poor drainage. The alternative is to add a high-quality soil amendment such as compost or sphagnum peat moss—to retain moisture in sandy soils, and to improve drainage and porosity in clay soils. Prepare the soil with a volume of moisture-retentive compost equal to 30 to 40 percent of the volume of the native soil from the hole; mix together uniformly. Dig the planting hole twice as wide as the rootball and set the plants 1 to 2 ft. apart. Water-in well and mulch with compost or shredded cedar. Water weekly to get the plants established.

CARE AND MAINTENANCE
Strawberries will root and spread wherever soil and other conditions are favorable. Keep the soil evenly moist at the beginning and the plants will spread rapidly. Use an all-purpose fertilizer such as 5-10-5 or 10-10-10 in early spring and summer. Broadcast the fertilizer around the plants and water-in well. Be sure to water the area thoroughly each week if you are growing the plants in sandy soils that dry out fast. Plants can be kept in bounds by digging out runner plants as needed.

ADDITIONAL INFORMATION
Once the runner plants have rooted near the original plant, they can be separated from the mother and transplanted to other parts of the bed or shared with friends.

ADDITIONAL SPECIES, CULTIVARS, OR VARIETIES
Fragaria frel 'Pink Panda' forms a dense, spreading mound with handsome green leaves that are blanketed by rich-pink flowers from late spring to early fall. If you are looking for a less-aggressive type of strawberry that has a refined growth habit, try *Fragaria vesca* var. *semperflorens* (Alpine runnerless strawberry); it grows a compact tuft of green foliage, spreads to 12 in., and produces fragrant white flowers.

Sweet Woodruff

Galium odoratum

<table>
<tr><td>

Height: 6 to 8 in.
Flowers: White
Bloom Period: Late spring
Zones: 3, 4, 5, 6

</td><td>

Light Requirement:

</td></tr>
</table>

*S*weet woodruff is an adaptable groundcover that has fragrant white blossoms rising above bright green foliage. Its tiny, pure-white, star-shaped flowers cluster into loosely branched cymes. Though it prefers damp, slightly acid conditions, woodruff is tolerant of Colorado soils that have been enriched with humus. After it becomes established, it will make a nice groundcover for dry, shady locations, such as the areas beneath pines and junipers and around deciduous shrubs and hedges. In the semi-protected locations in our Green Thumb garden, it has retained its foliage year-round. Once you get sweet woodruff started, it can really spread; keep a shovel handy to dig it out of unwanted areas and put it to use in other spots.

WHEN TO PLANT

Plant container-grown plants from early spring through early fall.

WHERE TO PLANT

Plants will grow more rapidly if planted in full sun, but they are very well adapted to part shade. The soil should be well-drained and amended with compost or sphagnum peat before planting. Plant this groundcover underneath trees and shrubs; it will adapt to the shade quite well. The white, star-shaped flowers provide a nice contrast with evergreen foliage. Use it on slopes to control erosion and in areas where it doesn't need to be confined.

HOW TO PLANT

Loosen the soil in the area in which you will plant this groundcover. Few groundcovers will grow vigorously in pure sand, and they have difficulty trying to establish in heavy clay soils with poor drainage as well. The alternative is to add a high-quality soil amendment such as compost or sphagnum peat moss to retain moisture in sandy soils, and to improve drainage and porosity in clay soils. Prepare the soil with a volume of moisture-retentive compost equal to 30 to 40 percent of the volume of native soil. Work the organic amendment and soil uniformly together. Space plants 12 to 15 in. apart; water-in thoroughly and mulch with pine needles or coarse compost. Keep the area moist the first growing season to establish the plants.

CARE AND MAINTENANCE

Sweet woodruff is a durable groundcover; it will tolerate dry shade once it is established. Water as the soil becomes dry. A light application of organic fertilizer in spring will help maintain soil fertility. If the foliage should be damaged by winter desiccation or winter sunburn, shear back the plants in spring; new growth will eagerly return.

ADDITIONAL INFORMATION

Sweet woodruff is a very good groundcover to plant under trees and shrubs. It spreads rather quickly and provides a nice mass grouping. Its leaves have a mild, pleasant fragrance and can be used for making potpourris.

ADDITIONAL SPECIES, CULTIVARS, OR VARIETIES

The most common selection of sweet woodruff is *Galium odoratum*. Once you get it started, it will offer you plenty of small plant divisions to share with friends.

Woolly Thyme

Thymus pseudolanuginosus

Height: 1 to 4 in.
Flowers: Pink
Bloom Period: June to September
Zones: 3, 4, 5, 6

Light Requirement:

Woolly thyme is one of the most useful creeping evergreen groundcovers. Its leathery gray-green leaves form a dense, aromatic mat. Because it is tolerant of being walked on, this plant works well when planted among stepping stones. When the plant leaves are brushed or trod upon, an invigorating fragrance is released into the air. We have it planted between wooden pavers; when our Sheltie walks the pathway, the thyme is not at all damaged by the light paw traffic. His tiptoeing through this area leaves a pleasant scent on his paws. As a groundcover, woolly thyme will tolerate being mowed to keep it neat. The rose-pink to magenta flowers rise above the foliage in late spring and are much loved by bees. For a dramatic spring display, underplant thyme with pasqueflower, botanical tulips, dwarf iris, or other spring-flowering bulbs.

WHEN TO PLANT

Container-grown plants can be planted in early spring to early fall. Thyme also grows readily from seed, plant divisions, or cuttings.

WHERE TO PLANT

Full sun and well-drained soil are the prime requirements for this plant. Thyme is great for bordering walks and patios, and for use on top of and in crevices of rock walls where it can spill downward. Use it to fill in between flagstones and stepping stones.

HOW TO PLANT

Few groundcovers will grow vigorously in pure sand, and most are difficult to establish in heavy clay soils that have poor drainage. Add a high-quality soil amendment such as compost or sphagnum peat moss to retain moisture in sandy soils, and to improve drainage and porosity in clay soils. Prepare the soil with a volume of moisture-retentive compost equal to 30 to 40 percent of the volume of native soil; mix the compost uniformly with the native soil. Dig the planting hole twice as wide as the rootball and position the plant so that the soil level is the same as it was in the container. Gently firm the soil around the roots and water-in well. Keep the soil evenly moist until the plants are established. Space plants 12 to 15 in. apart, depending on how fast you want the plants to cover an area.

CARE AND MAINTENANCE

Thyme is easy to establish, as long as you don't overwater and cause the plants to rot. Water only when the soil becomes dry. The plants will eventually develop semi-woody stems, but this problem can be remedied by cutting them back in spring. Prune back to live wood to promote more compact growth. As the plants become old, they may start to die out in the center. This is a good sign that it will be time to lift the clumps and divide them when early spring arrives. Discard the center section and keep the healthy divisions from the outer section of the clump. Transplant new divisions at the same depth they were growing, gently firm the soil around the roots, and water-in well. The divisions will start growing quickly to fill in bare spots.

ADDITIONAL INFORMATION

Thyme is easy to propagate by division in early spring. Dig older clumps and gently pull apart the sections for replanting.

ADDITIONAL SPECIES, CULTIVARS, OR VARIETIES

Lemon thyme, *Thymus* × *citriodorus*, has a bushy upright habit, lavender flowers, and leaves that have a strong lemon scent. Mother-of-thyme, *Thymus serphyllum*, produces pink or lavender blossoms and nicely scented foliage.

CHAPTER FIVE

Hardy Bulbs

HETHER YOU'RE A NOVICE OR A WELL-SEASONED GARDENER, growing flowers from bulbs is a simple and rewarding experience. The mention of bulbs usually brings to mind colorful *spring* flowers—bouquets of tulips, bunches of bright-yellow daffodils, and carpets of crocuses—but there are bulbs that bloom in summer, autumn, and winter as well.

In the autumn garden, pink and lavender colchicum bloom atop naked stems. Many bulbs can be coaxed (some call it "forcing") to bloom ahead of their normal flowering season, providing weeks of color, fragrance, and pleasure during the cold winter months.

Summer gardens can be graced with gorgeous blooms of spiking gladiolus, dahlia blooms as big as dinnerplates, and the beautiful arching stems of lilies. The bright blossoms of begonias create pools of brilliant color that can awaken shady gardens.

Most gardeners have come to use the word bulb as a catch-all term for a variety of plants including corms, rhizomes, and tubers. A bulb is a living bud, and it is usually round. It is subterranean, growing roots below the ground and producing a stem that grows to the surface; from the stem emerges its foliage and blooms. Some examples of true bulbs are tulips, hyacinth, and daffodil. These are truly miracles of nature. Hidden within the bulbs are embryos which contain all the ingredients for next year's flowers, surrounded by fleshy layers of stored food energy.

The other plants sometimes referred to as bulbs are generally solid masses of storage tissue. Gladiolus and crocuses are corms; dahlias are tubers; and cannas grow from rhizomes. Whatever term you choose to use, these plant structures are all living buds that have a reserve of stored food.

Because each bulb contains within itself the nutrients necessary for one full season of growth and miraculous bloom, it is easy to grow bulbs successfully. All you have to do is provide the proper

Chapter Five

light, water, and soil. Some bulbs, such as paper-whites and hyacinths, don't even need the soil, and colchicum can be forced to bloom without soil *or* water.

Hardy bulbs are those classified by their ability to survive the minimum temperatures that occur during Colorado's winter. They can be left in the ground year-round and thus are treated as perennials. These hardy bulbs need a period of cold during their dormancy or they will not flower reliably. Planting in autumn will ensure proper chilling and reward you with colorful blossoms each spring.

Non-hardy or "tender" bulbs, corms, and tubers are unable to withstand cold temperatures, so they are generally dug from the garden and stored inside during the winter. They are treated as annuals and are planted anew each spring. This group includes dahlias, gladiolus, and cannas.

Our *Green Thumb rule of thumb* for landscaping with bulbs is to plant the same types together and don't be stingy or line bulbs up in rows like soldiers. Plant bulbs in clumps of a dozen or more to create uniformity of color and foliage texture. Massing bulbs will provide enough flowers to cut for indoor bouquets.

Place tall bulbs such as late tulips, lilies, and crown imperial in the background of a border or among similarly sized shrubs or perennial flowers. Crocuses, snowdrops, chionodoxa, scilla, and colchicum can be used as carpets in shrub borders or perennial beds, or naturalized in lawns and meadow gardens.

When you purchase your bulbs, make sure they are firm and large for their type. Larger bulbs generally bloom the first season, and they will have bigger blooms than smaller bulbs. To encourage the best growth and root development, plant spring-flowering bulbs when the ground temperatures are below 60 degrees Fahrenheit. In Colorado, this is usually in late September or later. If you don't get the bulbs planted right away, store them in a cool, dry place—but don't forget about them. Even if you plant them in December, they will generally bloom the following spring; if they don't, they will be back on schedule the following year.

Botanical Tulip

Tulipa tarda

Height: 4 to 6 in. **Flowers:** Yellow with white-tipped petals **Bloom Period:** Spring **Zones:** 4, 5, 6	**Light Requirement:**

These bright-yellow tulips with white-tipped petals may not be as showy as the large hybrid tulips, but they are prized in the rock garden as they bloom in late spring. Narrow, strap-like leaves are produced in a rosette at ground level; up to five of the rosettes will eventually appear on each stem. The flowers open widely to two inches in diameter and are stars of the garden in late April and May. Plant them in full sun and these heat- and drought-enduring tulips will naturalize and return in the garden year after year, long after the fancy hybrids have disappeared. Their clumps multiply rapidly to form a carpet of spring blooms. They make a nice combination in bulb plantings with grape hyacinth or Siberian squill. Try combining *Tulipa tarda* with woolly thyme groundcover and the downy nodding purple flowers of pasqueflower (*Anemone pulsatilla*); these three together make a spectacular spring display.

WHEN TO PLANT
Plant botanical tulip bulbs in October through November. Species tulips can be the last to be planted in the fall.

WHERE TO PLANT
Botanical tulips do best in well-drained soils and full sun. Good drainage is a must for growing tulips successfully in our Colorado soils. *Tulipa tarda* likes it warm and dry in the summer, so plant the bulbs where you won't have to do a lot of watering. Use them in the front of perennial beds, along pathways, driveways, and sidewalks, and by sunny patios and decks. Some of the best locations are rock gardens that have excellent drainage.

HOW TO PLANT
Amend clay soils with compost to improve drainage. Loosen the soil deeply and mix the compost uniformly. Plant the bulbs 5 to 6 in.

below the soil surface, spacing them 3 in. apart to create a natural effect. Mix bonemeal or a bulb fertilizer into the bottom of the planting hole, but try to keep the fertilizer from coming in contact with the bulb (this can encourage bulb rot). Water the area well after planting.

CARE AND MAINTENANCE
Botanical tulips will self-seed and spread if planted in well-drained locations. They should require little, if any, care throughout the year. Avoid overwatering in garden soils that are primarily clay (a lawn sprinkler system set for every third day will be certain death for these tulips).

ADDITIONAL INFORMATION
For the most dramatic and eye-catching effect, plant botanical tulips in groups of a dozen or more. They can be naturalized in a buffalo-grass lawn. Throw a handful of bulbs over the lawn and use a bulb planter to plant them where they fall. Botanical tulips do not leave behind much foliage when they have finished flowering.

ADDITIONAL SPECIES, CULTIVARS, OR VARIETIES
Tulipa batalinii, which grows 4 to 6 in. tall, sports fragrant creamy-yellow flowers; it blooms for a month, longer than most other tulips. Try 'Bronze Charm', 'Apricot Jewel', and 'Bright Gem'. *T. kolpakowskiana* reaches 6 to 8 in. and will often produce two flowers per stem in bright yellow; the interior of the petals are flushed red. *T. hageri* is a charming little (6 to 8 in.) species whose stems support two or more flowers in brick red. *T. humilis* is a dwarf species (4 in.) that comes in hot pink to deep purple. At the base of the petals, blotches of purple, yellow, and blue accent the blooms.

Crocus

Crocus spp. and hybrids

Height: 3 to 6 in.
Flowers: Yellow, white, purple, lavender, blue, stripes
Bloom Period: Late winter through spring
Zones: 3, 4, 5, 6

Light Requirement:

Though the first day of spring doesn't arrive until late March, you can tell this season is just around the corner when the bright-yellow and lavender chalices of crocus blooms unfurl in Colorado's sunshine. If you make the right plant selections, the crocus season can span several weeks. The petite snow crocus, *Crocus chrysanthus*, blooms about two weeks earlier than the larger-flowered Dutch hybrids. Even though its flowers are smaller, its blooms are most welcome in the landscape at the first stirrings of spring, when honeybees visit the flowers. Crocuses can be naturalized in lawns as long as you're willing to wait to mow the areas until the narrow leaves die back on their own. Plant them generously along garden paths, sidewalks, and driveways, in flower beds, and near the doorway. Autumn-flowering crocuses provide a colorful display for the gardener—and for the last of the foraging honeybees.

WHEN TO PLANT

Plant crocus corms in the fall.

WHERE TO PLANT

Crocuses prefer full sun and well-drained soil. They are particularly effective when mass-planted in drifts, near rocks, under shrubbery, and when used for edging borders. You can naturalize these flowers in lawn areas or under trees since the crocus foliage generally ripens before the deciduous trees leaf out. Crocuses are quite tolerant of dry shade. They look best when planted in groups of 24 or more. Their thin leaves ripen relatively fast and are not bothersome when planted among other perennials.

HOW TO PLANT

Plant the species crocus generously and densely, about 3 in. deep and 2 in. apart. In a few years, the plants will have multiplied from seed and from their new cormlets. The larger-flowered Dutch crocuses should be planted 4 in. deep and 4 in. apart. You can also follow the general rule by planting the corms 3 times as deep as the bulbs measure in diameter. Amend clay, sandy, and crushed granite soils with compost before planting. This will help retain moisture and improve drainage.

CARE AND MAINTENANCE

Crocus plants are long-lived. They require very little attention, though you should be careful not to dig the corms up when cultivating and planting in the perennial garden. They can be fertilized in autumn with a bulb food or fortified bonemeal. Field mice, squirrels, and voles find crocuses irresistible. You can prevent rodent damage by covering newly planted areas with rabbit or chicken wire—or enlist a hungry cat or dog to stand on patrol.

ADDITIONAL INFORMATION

Allow the foliage of crocuses to mature or ripen before removing it. When the leaves can be pulled with the slightest tug, the foliage can be removed with no danger of harming the corms.

ADDITIONAL SPECIES, CULTIVARS, OR VARIETIES

Dutch crocus selections include white 'Joan of Arc'; 'Pickwick', a striped form in white and lavender; 'Yellow Mammoth', which has large yellow flowers; and the blue-violet 'Remembrance'. Our favorite, which has proven most reliable, is *Crocus chrysanthus*, with brilliant golden anthers and orange stigmas that invite early honeybees to the garden. Many other colors are available: 'Goldilocks' is yellow with bronze feathering, 'Eye-catcher' has a purple base, and 'Blue Pearl' is a beautiful lavender-blue. *Crocus tommasinianus* 'Barr's Purple' and 'Whitewall Purple' are both ideal for naturalizing under shrubs and ornamental trees, and they provide an early carpet of rich purple to reddish-purple flowers in early spring. Autumn crocuses are similar in appearance to their spring cousins, but they send up blossoms as the chill of winter is in the air. They include *Crocus speciosus*, which has violet flowers, and *C. kotschyanus*, in lavender-blue. A highly prized plant is saffron crocus, *C. sativus*, with its bright orange-red stigmas; the stigmas are valued for imparting flavor and a golden glow to fine cuisine.

Daffodil

Narcissus spp. and hybrids

Height: 6 to 18 in. **Flowers:** Yellow, peach, pink, white **Bloom Period:** Spring **Zones:** 3, 4, 5, 6	**Light Requirement:**

Whether you call them jonquils, narcissus, or daffodils, no landscape can have too many of these flowers. While tulips herald spring with a bold fanfare of upright stems, daffodils are the quintessential spring flowers, with their graceful nodding heads in yellow, peach, pink, and white. They differ from other bulbs in that they prefer the cooler, moister areas of the garden, and they tolerate Colorado clay soils. Among the thousands of cultivars are those that provide ruffled flowers, those that offer double-flowered forms, some with split cups, some that have flowers with coronas, and even some with peachy-pink blossoms. It has been my experience that these hybrids don't last long, as the original bulb will divide into many smaller ones that crowd each other out, resulting in fewer flowers. This can be avoided if you take the time to dig and divide the bulbs every 5 years or so. The smaller types of daffodils, close to the species and wild forms, bloom reliably without a lot of maintenance.

WHEN TO PLANT
Plant daffodil bulbs in October through November. They will grow roots and become well established before the ground freezes.

WHERE TO PLANT
Plant *Narcissus* in drifts or naturalized in grassy areas. Make sure the soil is moisture-retentive yet well drained. These plants prefer a sunny location, but they will tolerate some shade from deciduous trees. They do best in soils that remain moist from the time they are planted until their leaves have died down in early summer. They tolerate drier conditions in summer.

HOW TO PLANT
Plant the large trumpet daffodils 6 to 8 in. deep and 4 to 6 in. apart. The smaller cultivars can be planted 4 to 6 in. deep and 3 to 4 in.

apart. Improve the soil by adding compost or well-aged manure before planting. This will improve moisture retention and drainage. Loosen the soil to a depth of 8 in. or more. If you use a bulb fertilizer, be sure to work it into the soil before planting.

CARE AND MAINTENANCE

Once planted, daffodils should be left undisturbed for years, except for those plants that are losing vigor and producing fewer blooms. Lift these bulbs, taking care not to damage them, divide the smaller ones, and replant them at the proper depth. The smallest bulbs will usually take 2 to 3 years to reach flowering size. One of the most frequently asked questions on our Green Thumb radio show is: "Should the leaves be cut off after the daffodils are done flowering?" The answer is: "No!" You can remove the spent flower heads, but leave the foliage intact until it has naturally ripened. With daffodils, this may take a month or more. And don't waste your time braiding or tying up the leaves; this will only impair the plant's ability to make and store the food which is needed for next year's flowering. Every 5 to 7 years, daffodil bulbs can be dug and divided to increase stock and reduce crowding.

ADDITIONAL INFORMATION

Daffodils are among the hardiest of perennials in the landscape. They are disliked by insects and four-legged critters, including squirrels, rabbits, deer, and elk, because the bulbs and other parts are toxic. They make excellent cut flowers.

ADDITIONAL SPECIES, CULTIVARS, OR VARIETIES

Trumpet daffodils, traditional favorites, bloom in early to mid-spring and have large center coronas (trumpets) that are as long as the petals. 'King Alfred', 'Golden Harvest', 'Dutch Master', and 'Mount Hood' are excellent choices. Large-cupped daffodils are similar but they have shorter trumpets; among them are 'Carlton', 'Ice Follies', 'Flower Record', and 'Professor Einstein'. One of our old-time favorites is 'Barrett Browning', which has white petals and an orange corona. *Narcissus poeticus*, pheasant's eye daffodil, is among the latest blooming and is good for naturalizing.

Dwarf Bulbous Iris

Iris reticulata

Height: 6 to 8 in.
Flowers: Purple, blue, violet
Bloom Period: Spring
Zones: 3, 4, 5, 6

Light Requirement:

The fragrant petite flowers of *Iris reticulata*, are a welcome sight in the spring garden. Along with crocuses and snowdrops, they are among the earliest flowers to bloom in spring. Given a proper home with good drainage, snow irises will thrive year after year. These diminutive beauties (6 to 8 in. tall) like to be grown hot and dry, so avoid frequent watering from the sprinkler system. The characteristic flowers have upright standards and downward falls in shades of purple, blue, and violet. The falls have a golden-orange beard bordered in white. Because they bloom so early, plant them in areas where they will be appreciated, not in an out-of-the-way location. One of our favorite places to plant *Iris reticulata* bulbs is in the buffalograss lawn. Our youngest son, Jonathan, really enjoys "hiding" the tiny bulbs in holes made by Dad. Come spring, the early flowers brighten the landscape. Later the leaves die back discreetly before it's time to mow the grass.

WHEN TO PLANT
Plant the bulbs of dwarf iris from October through November.

WHERE TO PLANT
Iris reticulata does best in well-drained soil and full sun. Avoid heavy clay soils that do not drain. Overwatering is sure doom for this diminutive flowering bulb. Its preference for sharp drainage makes it a good choice for rock gardens, near a front walk, on top of a rock wall, in front of a perennial border, or wherever good drainage can be provided. Use the plants in the perennial bed only if the soil drains well. These little bulbs are excellent for naturalizing in buffalograss lawns and rock gardens. Plant them freely—your children will probably want to help!

How to Plant

Dwarf iris does best in any good garden soil. Loosen the soil thoroughly and augment it with compost (to improve drainage in clay soils and retain moisture in sandy or gravelly free-draining soils). Plant the bulbs 4 in. deep and 3 to 6 in. apart. They can be grown in containers and in ordinary potting soil. For the best effect, plant in groups of 12 or more.

Care and Maintenance

Iris reticulata are generally reliable in Colorado if we grow them hot and dry. Poor drainage will doom these tiny bulbs, so it is best to avoid heavy wet clay soils. They require very little care and will multiply if conditions are ideal. Dwarf iris have no significant pest or disease problems.

Additional Information

Dwarf iris plants are ideal for rocky areas with sharp drainage. They do well on rocky slopes or when underplanted with *Juniperus horizontalis*, and can be naturalized in buffalograss lawns or prairie settings.

Additional Species, Cultivars, or Varieties

Different selections of *Iris reticulata* have different colors and markings. 'Cantab' is pale blue with an orange blotch on the blade of its falls. 'Purple Gem' is deep purple with a white blotch. 'Harmony' is an old cultivar, sky blue with a yellow beard on the blade of its falls. The yellow form is *Iris reticulata danfordiae* (4 in. tall), which has bright yellow and brown spots. It is very fragrant and forms flowers early in the spring, competing with snowdrops and crocuses to arrive first.

Glory of the Snow

Chionodoxa luciliae

Height: 4 to 5 in.	**Light Requirement:**
Flowers: Blue	
Bloom Period: Early spring	
Zones: 4, 5, 6	

The sky-blue blossoms of *Chionodoxa* are a cheerful sight in the early spring, and true to their name, they are often caught by a spring snow (a common occurrence in Colorado). The star-shaped flowers are about 1 in. wide, with 10 or more per spray or stem. Each flower has a starry white center and faces skyward, distinguishing this plant from *Scilla*, the Siberian squill, which nods its head and has deeper-blue flowers. This bulb will naturalize nicely and is well adapted to Colorado soils. It multiplies by means of both seeds and offsets to form a carpet of blue. It is effective near the front entry, along walkways, or in spots where it can be viewed from your windows. Glory-of-the-snow can be planted with early tulips and daffodils, but it is often planted by itself in large groupings and allowed to naturalize in meadow gardens or in front of shrub or perennial beds.

WHEN TO PLANT

Plant the small bulbs of glory-of-the-snow in fall.

WHERE TO PLANT

Plant in well-drained soil in a sunny location, though glory-of-the-snow will tolerate light shade from deciduous shade trees. Amend heavy clay soils with compost, and loosen deeply to help improve drainage. *Chionodoxa* will grow in short grasses, through groundcovers, and under shrubs and ornamental trees. Large groupings are particularly effective.

HOW TO PLANT

Amend the soil with compost if it is poorly drained, and loosen the soil well. Plant the small bulbs 3 to 4 in. deep and space them 3 in. apart. Bold plantings of 50 to 100 bulbs will produce the best displays. You can dig out an entire bed, plant the bulbs as suggested, then cover them with the backfill soil. If you prefer, use a strong bulb-planting trowel marked at the proper depth to plant glory-in-the-snow in lawn areas for naturalizing. Water-in well.

CARE AND MAINTENANCE
Chionodoxa needs very little attention. You don't even need to use fertilizer if you are planting many individual bulbs. When planting in a large prepared bed, you can work bulb fertilizer into the soil before planting. If you plant the bulbs in lawns, allow the *Chionodoxa* foliage to mature or ripen before mowing the grass.

ADDITIONAL INFORMATION
While it makes a bold display on its own, glory-of-the-snow also combines well with other early-flowering bulbs and perennials. Try it with with Lenten rose, *Helleborus orientalis*, daffodils, and early tulips.

ADDITIONAL SPECIES, CULTIVARS, OR VARIETIES
Chionodoxa luciliae is by far the best species, and it comes in various colors. It will produce as many as 10 flowers on 6- to 8-in. stems. 'Alba' is white, 'Blue Giant' is sky blue with a white center, and 'Pink Giant' is bright pink with a white center. *Chionodoxa gigantea* has large 1- to 2-in. flowers that face skyward. *C. sardensis* flowers somewhat later than the others and is shorter (4 to 6 in.). It naturalizes freely and creates a bold display. Some selections are 'Deep Blue' and 'Gentian Blue'.

Grape Hyacinth

Muscari armeniacum and *Muscari botryoides*

Height: 6 to 8 in. **Flowers:** Purple-blue, white **Bloom Period:** Mid-spring **Zones:** 3, 4, 5, 6	**Light Requirement:**

Grape hyacinths are reliable and easy-to-grow bulbs. Like bunches of little grapes in appearance, they create a striking combination of purple-blue and white for the early spring garden. Use them to provide a contrast for yellow daffodils; red, pink, and white tulips; or pansies. Grape hyacinths are very hardy across the state, and they will endure for years. As ours have multiplied by means of both seeds and offsets, they have spread rapidly in just a couple of years. Plant them in groups of 50 or more to make a bold display that will last for weeks. *Muscari* will frequently send up its grass-like foliage in the late summer and fall. In spring, the spikes of fragrant blue flowers appear and the leaves continue to grow. Eventually, the foliage dies down, the bulbs enter a dormant state, and they then start their growth cycle over again, producing many more plants. Grape hyacinths are excellent for naturalizing.

WHEN TO PLANT
Plant grape hyacinths in the fall. They should be planted as soon as possible because their foliage begins to grow in early fall.

WHERE TO PLANT
Grape hyacinths prefer sun and will grow in a wide range of soils. Well-drained soils are best, so loosen the soil deeply and amend with compost if needed. Use generous quantities of these bulbs to make an impact in your garden or along walkways. Plant them in drifts under shrubs and trees where they can remain and spread undisturbed. They are great for rock gardens, make good companions for daffodils, and set off the flaming hues of tulips. Grape hyacinths can be used for bordering bulb beds to mark the boundaries—in fall, when it is time to plant more bulbs or to work the flower bed, the grape hyacinth leaves mark the location of existing beds and reduce the chance of damaging established bulbs.

How to Plant

Bulbs should be planted 3 in. deep and 3 to 4 in. apart. If the soil is clay and compacted, amend with compost. Work the compost uniformly into the soil to a depth of 6 in. or so. Add a bulb fertilizer into the soil before planting. After planting the groups of bulbs, water-in well. If you notice squirrels watching as you plant, you may want to protect the plantings by covering the beds with rabbit or chicken wire.

Care and Maintenance

Water grape hyacinths thoroughly after planting and during the dry periods of fall and winter. Once established, they need very little care and are among the easiest bulbs to grow. If you want to control their spread, you can deadhead the flowers as they fade. If you want these little gems to spread rapidly and establish into large drifts, however, just leave them alone. They will self-sow from seeds and spawn numerous bulblets.

Additional Information

Muscari are great little bulbs to grow in containers. Crowd the bulbs together in a compost-based potting soil and place them in an unheated garage or garden shed to get the roots started. When the shoots appear, bring them indoors so you will be able to enjoy early-spring blossoms.

Additional Species, Cultivars, or Varieties

The most widely distributed species is *Muscari armeniacum,* whose deep-purple to purple-blue flowers (6 to 8 in.) are rimmed in white. Each flower cluster consists of 20 to 30 flowers. 'Blue Spike' has fluffy, soft-blue double flowers. *Muscari botryoides* is regarded as the true grape hyacinth with its sky-blue flowers rimmed in white. 'Album' is pure white and 'Carneum' has rosy flowers. *Muscari latifolium* and *M. comosum* are taller-growing species (10 in.) that produce 2 tiers of flowers.

Lily

Lilium hybrids

Height: 18 in. to 6 ft.
Flowers: White, pink, gold, yellow, orange, peach, red
Bloom Period: Summer
Zones: 3, 4, 5, 6, depending upon species

Light Requirement:

The true lilies are wonderful plants in the garden. Once you've grown a few, you'll surely want to plant more. With a little planning, you can have lilies in bloom throughout the year. Lilies are readily available, fresh and ready to plant in early spring. Their exotic, eye-catching flowers, sometimes ruffled or spotted, can be erect, pendant trumpets or upward-facing stars. Fertile, well-drained soil is essential for growing both Asiatic hybrids and trumpet lilies. The Oriental lilies prefer light shade in the afternoon and slightly acidic soil. You might try growing them in large pots or containers filled to the brim with humus-enriched potting soil. Many of our Oriental lilies have survived in pots for years. This growing technique works well with Asiatic hybrids as well, especially if your garden soil is heavy clay. Breeders have introduced improved varieties of lilies that are well adapted to garden culture. There are lilies for sun and shade, and there are tall-growing as well as dwarf selections.

WHEN TO PLANT

Plant lily bulbs in the spring as soon as the soil can be worked. Lily bulbs don't have a protective covering like tulips; they should be planted immediately so they won't dry out.

WHERE TO PLANT

These aristocrats of the garden are a bit fussy about location. Lilies don't like to compete with aggressive perennials or groundcovers. Plant them in gaps between clumping perennials or combine with low-growing annuals. Good drainage is essential for successful lilies. Most prefer moist, well-drained, humus-rich soil and full sun to part shade. You can grow many in containers or raised beds if your soil has too much clay.

How to Plant

Plant lily bulbs 6 to 8 in. deep, depending upon the size of the bulbs. Madonna lily, *Lilium candidum*, is the exception and should be planted so that the top of the bulb is at soil level. Work a generous amount of compost into the planting area and toss a handful of bulb fertilizer into the planting hole; incorporate it into the bottom of the hole. For dramatic displays, plant lilies of the same variety in groups of 3, spaced from 12 to 18 in. apart.

Care and Maintenance

Lilies that grow in well-drained soils are long-lived. When shoots emerge in the spring, apply a fertilizer such as 5-10-5 or 10-10-10. Be sure to provide adequate moisture during the active growth cycle. As the flowers begin to fade, deadhead spent blooms to prevent seed formation (unless you are hybridizing a lily). Leave as much foliage as possible to store food energy for next year's blooms. You can divide clumps if they become overcrowded and lose vigor, usually every 5 years or so. Perform this division in fall when the leaves have died back. Lift the bulbs with a spading fork, separate, and replant.

Additional Information

Be sure to buy only healthy bulbs. Avoid bulbs that look moldy or those that have dried out and have no roots. Some of the tall-growing lilies may need staking when grown in partial shade. Be careful not to pierce the lily bulb when inserting the stake in the ground.

Additional Species, Cultivars, or Varieties

There are so many cultivars of lilies that it is impossible to mention all of our favorites. Some excellent lilies for beginners are Asiatic hybrids such as 'Enchantment', a magnificent orange red; 'Montreux', with rose-pink blooms; 'Roma', a soft white with few spots; 'Rosefire', a tricolor; and 'Vulcan', a lily that goes where no lily has gone before, with black-red blooms. A few Oriental hybrids are 'Casa Blanca', a pure white; 'Star Gazer', with crimson-red flowers spotted in darker maroon; and the 'Elegance' series. A nice trumpet lily is 'Bright Star', which has white flowers with orange-yellow centers.

Meadow Saffron

Colchicum spp. and hybrids

Height: 6 to 12 in. **Flowers:** Pink, lavender, mauve, white **Bloom Period:** Late summer and fall **Zones:** 4, 5, 6	**Light Requirement:**

*T*he autumn garden can hold many surprises, though some of them may require planning! Just as sure as daffodils and tulips emerge in spring, the late summer and fall garden can come alive with *Colchicum autumnale*, meadow saffron. Meadow saffron is perhaps the showiest of fall bloomers. Its luminous pink blossoms are at their best when planted with a groundcover such as santolina or dusty miller. The wispy, goblet-shaped flowers are borne on 6- to 8-in. stems in late summer and fall. Colchicum is often mistaken for crocus, which is actually a relative to iris. A single colchicum bulb may produce up to ten flowers in bunches that add dimension to the perennial garden or border. The double-flowered hybrid colchicum 'Waterlily' resembles a waterlily and is an eye-catcher in the garden. Plant meadow saffron close to garden pathways and walkways where the emerging flowers will invite passersby to stop and admire. Meadow saffron eagerly pokes its way through low-growing groundcovers such as Turkish veronica or sweet woodruff.

WHEN TO PLANT
Colchicum bulbs are available in late summer to early fall. Plant them immediately. These plants have their own schedule and will bloom regardless of whether the bulbs are stashed on a shelf or planted in the ground.

WHERE TO PLANT
Plant meadow saffron in well-drained, moisture-retentive soil in full sun to part shade. In a woodland garden, plant colchicum bulbs near the front edge where they will receive more sunlight. Use this plant in rock gardens, under perennials, and among various silver-leaved groundcovers such as santolina, lamb's ears, and dusty miller. Pink colchicum combined with *Ajuga reptans* 'Burgundy Glow', or white colchicum combined with *Lamium maculatum*

(spotted dead nettle), will make the blossoms come alive. Some of the prettiest displays occur when you plant at the base of a shrub such as *Euonymus alatus* (burning bush), which has bright-red autumn foliage.

How to Plant
Place colchicum bulbs in the ground and cover their tops with 4 in. of soil. Space bulbs 6 to 9 in. apart. When planted in clusters, the flowers make a bold statement. Meadow saffron is not fussy about soil as long as it is well-drained. Colchicum is somewhat drought tolerant. Water well after planting. Though plants will tolerate dry periods and heat, they require adequate moisture in spring when the foliage is growing and the bulbs are storing food energy for the autumn display.

Care and Maintenance
After planting, colchicum sends up its flowers in just a few weeks. Plants will slowly form colonies if you leave them alone; be sure not to disturb the bulbs when working in the perennial border. Meadow saffron requires very little care. You need only provide adequate moisture when the foliage is growing in spring. The vegetative cycle can present a challenge to gardeners as the foliage turns yellow in late spring or early summer, but it must be left in place until the leaves die back or ripen naturally. Removing the leaves too early will rob the plant of nutrients needed for the flowering cycle. Plant among perennials and groundcovers to hide the unsightly ripening foliage.

Additional Information
If you grow meadow saffron in a naturalized setting such as a lawn or meadow garden, don't cut the grass in those areas until colchicum's foliage has died down. Though colchicums are often referred to as "autumn crocuses," they are botanically unrelated to the crocus.

Additional Species, Cultivars, or Varieties
Colchicum autumnale produces glowing pink flowers on stems that grow to 8 in. tall. The cultivar 'Alba' has small white flowers on 4-in. stems. *C. speciosum* has larger flowers of luminous lavender or rosy pink. Many of the showy colchicums are hybrids; these include 'Waterlily', 'Lilac Wonder', and 'The Giant'.

Ornamental Onion

Allium s p p .

	Light Requirement:
Height: 6 in. to 5 ft. **Flowers:** Purple, lavender, blue, pink, white **Bloom Period:** Late spring **Zones:** 4, 5, 6	

*A*llium is the genus that contains garlic, onions, leeks, chives, and shallots. There are many species of ornamental onions that are prized for their handsome foliage and spherical flowers. *Allium aflatunense* is one such ornamental which shows off dense, rounded 3- to 4-in. flower heads held high on strong straight stems (2 to 3 ft.). 'Purple Sensation' is a popular selection. The lilac-purple to rose-purple blossoms that appear in May and June provide a strong accent in the perennial garden. Each flower bursts from the bud to form a near-perfect globe which lasts for several weeks. Even after bloom, the spent flower heads are attractive for months until broken apart by the wind. Plant groups of *Allium aflatunense* at regular intervals to create an interesting accent and unifying rhythm to the perennial garden. There are many species of *Allium* that can be grown successfully, including dwarf selections such as *A. cernuum* (12 in. tall) and the tallest species, *Allium giganteum* (4 to 5 ft. tall). Ornamental onions make a nice addition to the landscape.

WHEN TO PLANT

Plant *Allium* bulbs in late September through mid-November. The plump, white-skinned bulbs can be found at local garden stores and are available from mail-order sources.

WHERE TO PLANT

Ornamental onions prefer full sun, but they will tolerate some light shade. They will prosper in average to rich, well-drained soils. Feel free to use them in perennial beds, as background or accent, and in mixed plantings.

HOW TO PLANT

Loosen the soil to a depth of 6 in. or more. Add moisture-retentive compost if the soil is extremely sandy or gravelly, or if it is primarily clay. Dig each planting hole deep enough so that the base of the bulb is 5 in. below the soil surface. A bulb fertilizer can be added to the bottom of the planting hole before planting. Don't leave any air pockets beneath the bulb. Use at least three to a grouping and space taller-growing types 12 in. apart, dwarf species 4 to 6 in. apart. Water-in well after planting.

CARE AND MAINTENANCE

Ornamental onions are perfectly happy on their own once they are established. Provide moisture during the growing season. The globular heads of ornamental onions will self-seed readily. If you don't want this to happen, deadhead the spent flower heads before they scatter seed. The foliage is attractive when young, but by flowering time can become ragged, so grow them among other plants that will hide the leaves. Our children find these plants fascinating when they bloom because they reach "so high to the sky."

ADDITIONAL INFORMATION

The dried flower heads of *Allium*, especially those of the taller-growing species, are handsome in floral arrangements. The characteristic onion odor of *Allium* is noticeable only when the leaves are crushed.

ADDITIONAL SPECIES, CULTIVARS, OR VARIETIES

There are many species of *Allium* to try in your garden, if you have the space to experiment. Drumstick allium, *A. sphaerocephalum*, is easy to grow and produces purple-crimson flowers atop stems that reach up to 3 ft. It is beloved by bees. *Allium karataviense*, one of our favorites, is worth growing for its foliage alone, producing two bluish green leaves, each up to 5 in. wide and 9 in. long. In early summer, globes of white flowers with a hint of pink grow up on 6 in. stems. *A. moly* is a very nice species with brilliant-yellow flowers carried on 12-in. stems above handsome bluish foliage that hugs the ground. It is good for naturalizing.

Siberian Squill

Scilla siberica

Height: 4 to 6 in.
Flowers: Blue
Bloom Period: Early spring
Zones: 3, 4, 5, 6

Light Requirement:

The beautiful blue blossoms of Siberian squill enhance the Green Thumb garden in early spring. You can't miss this little gem. The six-petaled nodding flowers, usually arranged five or six to a stem, are particularly effective along pathways, in rock gardens, or scattered in lawns. Like many of the other minor bulbs, squills will seed themselves throughout the garden and quickly form a carpet of electric blue to complement other spring flowers. Their pendant star-shaped flowers are among the earliest to open, after snowdrops open. Their deep-green foliage and bright floral color, sometimes Prussian blue, are bold contrasts for yellow and white daffodils. Squills make pretty companions for the smaller narcissus such as 'Jetfire', 'Peeping Tom', 'February Gold', and 'Jenny'. For a big splash of color in spring, plant squills by the hundreds.

WHEN TO PLANT

Plant squill bulbs in October through November, the same time you plant other minor or small bulbs.

WHERE TO PLANT

All squill are easy to grow and will thrive in well-drained soils in full sun to part shade. If the soil is compacted, be sure to loosen it thoroughly and augment it with compost to aid in moisture retention and to improve drainage. Avoid planting in "heat traps," or the flowers won't last as long. Squills prefer some shade, especially during the warmest part of the day. Use them generously at the edge of shrubs or ornamental trees, in rock gardens or lawns, and along pathways.

HOW TO PLANT

Plant the small squill bulbs 3 in. deep and space them 4 to 6 in. apart. You can mix a bulb fertilizer into the soil before planting.

After planting, lightly firm the soil over the bulbs and water the area well. All species do best if they have moisture while actively growing, followed by a drier resting period.

CARE AND MAINTENANCE

Siberian squills are easy to grow and will thrive in any well-drained soil. Be sure to provide adequate moisture while they are growing, but when they are in their rest period, keep them on the dry side. Once squills are established, they will endure for years if left undisturbed. Those that are planted in lawns should be allowed to grow until their foliage has ripened and turned brown; after that you may mow or cut the foliage.

ADDITIONAL INFORMATION

These little plants are wonderful when crowded together and should be planted in bold clumps. Squills will immediately brighten the spring garden before other bulbs or other perennials begin to open.

ADDITIONAL SPECIES, CULTIVARS, OR VARIETIES

One of the most popular squills is 'Spring Beauty' with its vivid blue flowers. The flowers appear before the leaves make much growth, and the blooms tend to last well. There is a white form listed as 'Alba', but it is not nearly as bold as are the blue types. *Scilla bifolia* is regarded as one of the best squills; it produces 2 leaves, as its name suggests, and flowers very early in spring. Six to 8 in. tall, it will produce up to 8 true-blue flowers per stem. It is great for naturalizing, and looks good planted in shrub borders or a woodland garden. *Scilla tubergeniana*, also known as *S. mischtschenkoana*, is a dwarf species (4 to 5 in.). Each bulb sends up 3 to 4 spikes with lighter-blue flowers and a darker stripe in each petal.

Snowdrop

Galanthus nivalis

Height: 6 in.
Flowers: White
Bloom Period: Early spring
Zones: 3, 4, 5, 6

Light Requirement:

*S*nowdrops are among the earliest heralds of spring. These petite gems have popped up in our garden as early as mid-February, often while there is still snow on the ground. The distinctive translucent flowers are composed of 3 green-tipped petals surrounded by 3 longer pure-white outer petals. The leaves are smooth and about 6 in. long. These little bulbs can be planted in part to full shade under shrubs, trees, and evergreens, or in a shady woodland garden. Like squills and grape hyacinths, snowdrops are most effective when planted in drifts or bold clumps in the landscape. Snowdrops are not unlike snowflakes (*Leucojum vernum*). The difference between these two flowers is that the segments of snowdrops are not of equal length, while those of snowflakes are. *Galanthus* flowers have inner segments that are shorter and notched at the tips, with green tips around each notch.

WHEN TO PLANT
Plant snowdrops with other minor bulbs in autumn.

WHERE TO PLANT
Snowdrops prefer some sunlight for part of the day and will appreciate partial shade in the very hottest exposures. While tolerant of most garden soils, *Galanthus* does best in well-drained soils with lots of humus. You may need to add compost before planting. Plant snowdrops in bold groupings under shrubs and trees, in rock gardens, in a woodland setting, in the front of a shady border, or in the lawn. If growing snowdrops in the lawn, don't mow them until their foliage has ripened or turned brown.

HOW TO PLANT
Snowdrop bulbs should be planted 3 to 4 in. deep and spaced 4 in. apart. If you desire, work bulb fertilizer into the soil of a prepared

bed before planting. Plant bulbs, gently firm the soil, and water-in well. They may be left undisturbed for years.

CARE AND MAINTENANCE

Snowdrops prefer conditions that are similar to those in the forest—shade with moist, fertile soil rich in humus and the nutrients that come from the continuous decay of organic materials. Moisture will be needed until the leaves mature and die down. If left undisturbed, snowdrops will thrive and form colonies. Topdress the bulb area each autumn with a $1/2$- to 1-in. layer of pulverized compost or leaf mold.

ADDITIONAL INFORMATION

Snowdrops make a great show when naturalized in lawns. Just remember to adjust your mowing routine to allow the foliage to ripen or mature before you cut the grass short.

ADDITIONAL SPECIES, CULTIVARS, OR VARIETIES

The common snowdrop is *Galanthus nivalis* (4 to 5 in.) It will generally open in mid- to late February and continue blooming into April. It is named for its ability to withstand late snowfalls or freezing temperatures. There are a number of varieties available, including 'Flore Pleno', with double flowers; 'Viridapics', with more prominent green markings on its flower petals; and 'Simplex', a type that produces larger flowers. 'Sam Arnott' is one of the best cultivars, with large flowers on stout stems.

Windflower

Anemone blanda

Height: 2 to 8 in.
Flowers: Blue, pink, red, white
Bloom Period: Early spring
Zones: 4, 5, 6

Light Requirement:

The daisy-like flowers of windflower are a welcome sight in early spring. These flowers are more closely related to buttercups than they are to daisies. A border of these little gems in front of daffodils, tulips, and other bulbs is quite eye-catching. There are several colors available. The selection known as 'Charmer', with deep-pink blossoms, is my favorite in the Green Thumb garden. It thrives in the sandy loam soil. The flowers are set off by the ground-hugging, deep-green, dissected foliage. Windflowers are impressive when planted in large groupings, so don't be stingy. When spring arrives, you won't be disappointed.

WHEN TO PLANT
Plant the brown fibrous tubers from late September through November.

WHERE TO PLANT
Anemone blanda does best in moist but well-drained soil that is rich in organic matter. Choose a sunny to partly shady location such as a woodland garden, perennial borders, under high trees, or at the edges of shrubs. Windflowers can withstand full sun if given enough moisture and if combined with other bulbs for protection from the afternoon heat. Some of the best displays can be created in a woodland setting.

HOW TO PLANT
Plant the tubers 2 to 3 in. below the soil surface and 4 to 6 in. apart. Locate the buds, or "eyes," and plant them facing upward. If you can't determine which way is up, don't worry. Simply set the tubers sideways and gently push them into the soil to the proper depth. We prefer to prepare a special area for windflowers and to plant them all at once. Then gently firm the soil over the tubers and water well.

You can also plant them individually with a bulb planter or trowel marked with the proper planting depth. Make sure you plant enough, though, not just one or two *here* and one or two *there*. For the most effective displays, be bold and plant them in groups of 30 or more.

CARE AND MAINTENANCE

Because they are shallow-rooted, windflowers can be a bit temperamental in colder zones, but they will survive if a mulch is applied over the growing area. A winter mulch of evergreen boughs, pine needles, or shredded cedar will prevent heaving and maintain soil moisture. Watering is essential during dry periods.

ADDITIONAL INFORMATION

Windflowers are fussy about soil conditions—good drainage is essential. Compost, scoria (crushed volcanic rock), perlite, or pea gravel can be used to improve soil structure and to improve the drainage in heavy clay soils. We have found that windflowers do quite well in sandy loam soil as well.

ADDITIONAL SPECIES, CULTIVARS, OR VARIETIES

There are several named strains available. Choose some of the more reliable ones such as 'Charmer', mentioned above; 'Radar', with reddish flowers that have white centers; and 'White Splendor', with pure-white flowers. Mixes of blue, white, and pink are also commonly available. 'Blue Shades' is a lovely mix of blue hues.

CHAPTER SIX

Lawns

$\mathcal{C}$OLORADO RESIDENTS TAKE GREAT PRIDE IN THEIR LAWNS. A healthy carpet of green lawn is attractive and functional. A lawn is a soft, cool area on which to throw out a blanket, enjoy a picnic, read a book, or just relax and appreciate the beauty of the world around you.

Lawns do much more than consume water and grow. Grasses contribute to the quality of our Colorado lifestyle. A well-planned and maintained lawn—unlike gravel, concrete, or plain dirt—will cool its surrounding area. Temperatures will be ten to fifteen degrees cooler around a lawn, and this helps reduce the water consumption of surrounding landscape plants. A lawn that is 2500 square feet will provide enough oxygen for a family of four—every day. Turf areas reduce noise, air, and water pollution and provide excellent dust control. Well-established turf areas with their extensive root systems provide erosion control. And the properly selected lawn is one of the safest and softest natural playing surfaces for children, adults, and pets.

There are several factors that need to be considered when selecting a turfgrass species for your Colorado lawn. Consider how much time you want to give the lawn and the type of maintenance you're willing to provide. You may prefer pulling weeds from flower beds, deadheading, and removing faded flowers to watering, fertilizing, and mowing a lawn.

With proper planning, you can have your grass and enjoy it, too! The Rocky Mountain Sod Growers Association has put together some helpful questions for you to answer when choosing the right turf for your landscape.

1. How will the turf be used? For recreation? Aesthetics? Groundcover? Near a house or heavily used building? For outlying areas?

2. How much water do you want to consume? What is the cost of water in your area?
3. How much traffic will the lawn bear, and what kind of wear tolerance do you need?
4. What are the mowing requirements?
5. How long do you want it to stay green?
6. What are the fertilizer requirements?
7. Will the grass grow in shaded or sunny areas—or both?
8. What is the soil like? Clay? Sandy? Salty?
9. How much time do you want to spend on lawn maintenance?

SITE PREPARATION

Proper soil preparation is especially important when growing lawns in Colorado. Subsoil from basement excavation or "contractor dirt" that has been spread out around a home and then compacted by heavy equipment is not suitable for lawn establishment. A soil test will determine the nutrients that are needed in the soil before you start a new lawn. Colorado State University's soil-testing laboratory or a local soil-testing lab can help you take a soil sample for analysis. Organic matter will improve the soil's ability to drain as well as its capacity to retain moisture. If the organic content of the soil is less than five percent, incorporate three to six cubic yards of well-aged manure or compost per 1,000 square feet, depending on the grass selection. Mix the organic amendment into the existing soil to a depth of eight to ten inches. Rake the surface smooth before seeding or sodding.

PLANTING AND CARING FOR YOUR LAWN

The best time to start a new lawn from seed is in late summer to late September. By this time, the nighttime temperatures are cooling down, the days are still warm, and weeds are less competitive. These conditions are ideal for the germination of grass seed and its eventual establishment. If you are unable to do seeding at this time, the second-best time to sow grass is in early spring. Buffalograss should be sown in May or June because it is a warm-season grass that needs warm soils for successful germination.

Chapter Six

Starting a lawn from seed is economical, but it requires more-frequent watering and it will take longer to achieve good results. Sod, while initially more costly, provides an "instant lawn." You can install sod from spring through late fall as long as the soil has been properly prepared and depending upon the availability of the sod from the sod farm. Whether you choose to seed or sod your new lawn, the key to success is proper soil preparation.

Before planting a lawn from seed or installing sod, it's a good idea to eliminate any weeds, especially the difficult perennial weeds such as Canada thistle, bindweed, quackgrass, and Bermudagrass. The best way to do this is by spraying the actively growing weeds with a herbicide that has no soil residual such as glyphosate, and to allow the herbicide to fully translocate and kill the weeds before cultivating the soil. Read and follow label directions.

After the organic matter has been thoroughly incorporated into the soil, it will be a good time to install an in-ground automatic sprinkler system if your budget allows. This is the most efficient way to water larger lawn areas and will save you time. Plan your automatic sprinkler system so that turf zones are separate from the watering zones for flowers, shrubs, and trees. Remember that shaded areas will generally need less watering than will full-sun exposures.

Seeding a New Lawn

Prepare the area with high-quality organic matter as previously discussed, and rake the surface smooth in preparation for seed or sod. Apply five pounds of a starter fertilizer such as diammonium phosphate (18-46-0) per 1,000 square feet of lawn by raking it into the soil surface. The soil should be left firm but not packed. If walking over the prepared soil leaves footprints more than one inch deep, the soil can be firmed with a roller. Spread grass seed in two directions at right angles, distributing half the seed in each direction. After planting, lightly rake or roll the area to make sure the seed gets in contact with the soil. Water and then cover the surface with a light mulch such as clean wheat straw or pulverized compost to conserve moisture. Water lightly and frequently to keep the soil surface moist during the germination process. This may mean watering three to five times daily until the seeds have germinated (here's where an automatic sprinkler is most effective and efficient).

Once the grass seed has germinated and the seedlings begin to develop a deeper root system, you can begin to water the lawn less frequently—but increase the amount of water applied each time you water. The deeper, less-frequent watering will encourage the development of a deeper root system, which makes lawn grasses more drought tolerant during the heat of summer.

Young, tender grass seedlings can be easily damaged by weed-killers. Although it is frustrating to watch weeds pop up in a newly seeded lawn, this event is common and should not discourage you. If you performed the proper pre-plant weed control, most of the weeds that sprout in a new lawn will be eliminated after the grass is mowed several times and the lawn thickens. Mow your newly seeded lawn when it grows to a height of three inches. Cut the grass to remove no more than one-half inch of the new grass plants.

Mow cool-season grasses high—two, two-and-a-half, or even three inches tall. With more surface area, the grass plants will be able to manufacture more food energy to nourish the roots and stems. Longer grass blades will also shade the soil surface, making it harder for annual weed seeds to germinate.

Lawns should be mowed frequently enough so that no more than a third of the grass blade is clipped off each time. This may mean mowing every four or five days when the lawn is growing fast in the spring. The lawn will look better and undergo less stress, and the volume of clippings will be smaller and will therefore drop back into the lawn more easily.

When clippings are returned to the lawn, you are recycling nitrogen and other nutrients in an organic, slow-release form that promotes a healthier lawn. It is a myth that grass clippings cause thatch. Thatch is actually the compacted, brown, spongy, organic layer of living and dead grass stems and roots that accumulate above the soil surface. It is usually a result of poor lawn-management practices. As thatch layers thicken, the lawn becomes predisposed to drought stress and insect, disease, and weed problems.

Chapter Six

WATERING ESTABLISHED LAWNS

Colorado soils, weather conditions, turfgrass species, and the desired quality of lawn will all influence how much water to apply and how often you will irrigate your lawn. Turf-type fescue lawns require as much or more water as the typical bluegrass lawn. Buffalograss and blue grama lawns will survive and look good for weeks without watering.

When you water, thoroughly wet the soil to the depth of the lawn's root system. Don't water again until it becomes dry at that depth. Deeper, infrequent watering promotes a deeper root system and drought endurance, and it conserves water. Colorado soils will vary in how they accept water. Sandy soils require less water more often than loam and clay soils. Grass growing in shade generally requires less water, but it will require more water in those places where tree roots compete with the lawn. Rather than applying water all at one time, try "interval watering." Water each section of the lawn for twenty to thirty minutes, then repeat the procedure for each section an hour or so later. This will allow water to percolate more deeply into clay soils. Core aeration can aid in water infiltration by reducing compaction and breaking through thatch.

CORE AERATION

One of the best ways to reduce soil compaction while controlling thatch accumulation is core aeration. Plugs or cores of soil and thatch, two to three inches long, are removed by a mechanical aerating machine and deposited on the lawn's surface. The holes left from aeration permit water, air, and nutrients to enter the soil and create a healthier root zone environment. You can either rake the plugs off the lawn after aeration, or leave them to disintegrate and filter back down into the lawn. Depending upon soil type, it may take several days to weeks before the plugs dissolve. Mowing over the plugs with a rotary lawn mower can break them down more rapidly, but this will dull the mower blade. The cores of thatch and soil can be collected and put into the compost pile.

Chapter Six

FERTILIZING THE HOME LAWN

One of the most frequently asked questions on our Green Thumb radio show is how often to fertilize a lawn. This gets us back to determining the kind of lawn you want. A low-maintenance or utility lawn won't look as uniform or as deeply green as a higher-maintenance lawn, but it won't need as much fertilizing, watering, or mowing, either.

Nitrogen is the most important nutrient for maintaining growth and good color; but in Colorado, do not overstimulate your lawn with excessive nitrogen, particularly during spring and summer. This can contribute to thatch accumulation and disease problems and will certainly increase mowing frequency.

Cool-season grasses such as Kentucky bluegrass, turf-type fescues, and perennial ryegrass need nitrogen fertilizer to produce an attractive, dense turf. Apply lawn fertilizer to provide one pound of available nitrogen per 1,000 square feet per application every six weeks, depending upon desired quality of lawn. Three to four applications are usually sufficient. Time your fertilizer applications around the following holidays: Memorial Day, Fourth of July, Labor Day, and Halloween.

Iron chlorosis, or yellowing of the grass blades, is a common problem in Colorado lawns. Our alkaline soils are the reason for this chlorosis because iron, while present in the soil, is not in a form available to turf. An appropriate lawn fertilizer with iron or a separate iron supplement can be applied to keep the lawn green. Most out-of-state or national lawn fertilizers contain little or no iron or sulfur, so it is best to choose a product formulated for our area.

HOW DO LAWN FERTILIZERS STACK UP?

The type of fertilizer you decide to use is a matter of personal choice. Remember that nitrogen is the most important nutrient in lawn fertilizers. Organic fertilizers, which are composed of natural products such as animal manures or plant components, are not as concentrated, so more fertilizer will be needed to apply the recommended rate of nitrogen. The content of nitrogen is usually five to

Chapter Six

fifteen percent by weight. The lower concentration means there will be less danger of pollution from runoff and there will be a lower potential to "burn" the grass if overapplied or applied under warm conditions. Organic and organic-based lawn fertilizers release nutrients slowly in conjunction with soil microorganisms. This reduces the growth surge that can occur when a straight chemical fertilizer is used, and provides long-term green color without stimulating excessive top growth.

Nonorganic or so-called chemical fertilizers can be categorized as two types: synthetic organic fertilizers and inorganic types. Synthetic organic fertilizers contain carbon; inorganic types are nutrients that are mined from the earth, but they contain no carbon. Synthetic organic fertilizers include urea, sulfur-coated urea, ureaform, and IBDU. These fertilizers are broken down by soil microbes to release nitrogen, carbon dioxide, and water. Most of the potassium, phosphorus, sulfur, and iron components are mined from the earth. Some fertilizers contain phosphorus derived from bonemeal.

WEEDS IN THE HOME LAWN

Weed control in your lawn begins with the proper identification of a weed. Lawn weeds are classified as grassy types (i.e., crabgrass, tall fescue, quackgrass) or broadleaf (i.e., dandelion, plantain, spurge). Once you've determined the type, you'll need to know if the weed is an annual that grows from seed each year or a perennial that grows back from its roots year after year. Knowing the kinds of weeds you are dealing with will help you determine the correct way to control them. You can decide whether you want to use a chemical weed-killer or just pull or dig the weeds by hand—"the cowboy way."

Before applying weed-killers over an entire lawn, analyze the extent of the weed problem. It may be possible to deal with weeds on a spot basis rather than by treating the whole lawn, which may not need it. If perennial weeds such as dandelions are a concern, dig them out with a long dandelion digger, pull by hand, or if desired, spot-treat them individually with an appropriate herbicide.

Chapter Six

The easiest way to control annual weeds is with pre-emergent herbicides that prevent weed seed germination and rooting. Of course, timing is important—these materials need to be applied before the seeds are allowed to germinate. To control annual weeds that begin to grow in late spring or early summer (crabgrass, spurge, purslane), a pre-emergent should be applied in mid- to late April, before warm weather causes the seeds to germinate. Some annual weeds will also germinate in late summer (annual bluegrass, cheatgrass, chickweed) and a pre-emergent should be applied in late August. Read product labels carefully to make sure a product will control the weeds you want to battle.

Perennial weeds like Canada thistle, bindweed, plantain, and buckhorn grow from their roots each year and spread from both seeds and underground roots. To control them, use a post-emergent herbicide after the weed leaves have emerged. You will need to know whether the weed is a grassy or broadleaf plant. Certain herbicides which kill broadleaf weeds are ineffective on grassy weeds, and vice-versa. Read the product label to determine if it will do the job you desire.

Blue Grama

Bouteloua gracilis

Type: Warm-season **Texture:** Fine leaf **Mowing Height:** 3 in. **Zones:** 4, 5, 6	**Light Requirement:**

*B*lue grama is a native warm-season bunchgrass that endures drought quite well. It goes dormant during extended hot, dry periods, then recovers when moisture returns. It has been used for erosion control and in pastures for many years. When grown under favorable conditions, blue grama will root at the stem nodes to form new plants which, together with short rhizomes, grow into a comparatively dense sod. Blue grama has an attractive grayish green to bluish purple cast and produces interesting seedheads in late summer. This grass does well in Colorado's alkaline soils and tolerates soil variations from clay to sand. It a warm-season grass that is often mixed with buffalograss for diversity and to reduce seed costs. Blue grama turf areas can be mowed to a height of 3 in., or left unmowed to naturalize (they will have a feathery appearance). The seedheads that form are quite ornamental and resemble short curved combs.

When to Plant

Sow seed in late spring when soil temperatures have warmed. This is a warm-season grass whose seeds will germinate in 10 to 15 days.

Where to Plant

Blue grama performs best in well-drained soils and full sun. It is tolerant of various soil types from sand to clay, as well as saline soils. Plant for erosion control, in parking strips, and on non-irrigated turf sites.

How to Plant

Refer to the instructions on site preparation in the introduction to this chapter. Make a light application of diammonium phosphate (18-46-0). Apply 1 to 3 lb. of seed per 1,000 sq. ft. of lawn. Mulch with clean straw or pulverized compost to retain moisture and protect the seed from washing away. Water and keep the seedbed moist daily, or as needed, for about 2 to 3 weeks while the seed germinates and gets established. It is normal to have weeds appear in a newly seeded lawn area. Annual weeds can be controlled by subsequent mowing and will be killed by a hard frost in autumn. The persistent perennial weeds can be effectively controlled by hand-pulling or digging. Spot treatments with an appropriate herbicide may be needed once the grass is established.

CARE AND MAINTENANCE

Blue grama is a drought-tolerant grass that can be left unirrigated once the lawn is established. To keep the grass looking good, however, water regularly during hot, dry spells; this will maintain the bluish green color of the grass and increase its density. Blue grama will turn brown and go dormant during prolonged drought conditions. Very little fertilizer is needed to maintain this native grass. If you desire, an application of $1/2$ to 1 lb. of nitrogen per 1,000 sq. ft. in mid- to late spring will give it a boost. Water deeply and infrequently, for its roots can grow quite deep (which is what makes it so drought tolerant). Blue grama can be mowed to a height of 3 in. to encourage a dense sod, or left unmowed to naturalize and produce ornamental seedheads.

ADDITIONAL INFORMATION

Blue grama is often combined with buffalograss for diversity and to reduce seed costs. Because blue grama is a bunchgrass, areas may become thinned out from foot traffic or hard play, and you will need to replace the grass by overseeding on the bare spots.

ADDITIONAL SPECIES, CULTIVARS, OR VARIETIES

Some good cultivars of blue grama are 'Lovington', 'Alma', and 'Hachita'. Check with your local seed supplier for the latest developments and seed availability.

Buffalograss

Buchloe dactyloides

Type: Warm-season **Texture:** Fine blade **Mowing Height:** 1 to 2 in. **Zones:** 4, 5, 6	**Light Requirement:**

*B*uffalo once roamed and grazed on it, and now Colorado home owners grow it as a lawn. Native buffalograss, *Buchloe dactyloides*, makes a durable, easy-to-care-for lawn. It is a warm-season grass that has excellent characteristics for heat and drought resistance. It is naturally low growing and does not require much mowing to keep it looking great. Because buffalograss is a warm-season species, it turns brown with autumn's first frost and greens up again around mid-May with the return of warm weather. Some home owners may not like the brown just at the time when cool-season grasses are looking their best! Buffalograss is not a grass for planting high in the Colorado Rockies; it does not do well above 7,000 ft. We planted several thousand square feet of buffalograss as part of our Green Thumb landscape and had to mow it only twice during the summer. It is an attractive grayish green and is perfectly happy if left to naturalize. Buffalograss is a vigorous sod-former that spreads by means of runners or stolons. It will require periodic edging along driveways, sidewalks, and shrub and flower beds to keep these persistent runners in check. All in all, this is one of our favorite low-maintenance, water-thrifty grasses.

WHEN TO PLANT

The preferred time to seed buffalograss in Colorado is May and June, when soil temperatures have warmed. With proper watering on a daily basis, seedlings should appear 7 to 10 days after planting. Buffalograss sod is available from various sod growers in the summer.

WHERE TO PLANT

Buffalograss performs best in full sun and is adapted to most well-drained soils. You don't have to amend the soil as extensively for buffalograss as you do for the cool-season grasses. Plant this warm-season grass along driveways, in median strips, on hard-to-mow banks, in parking strips, and in recreational areas.

How to Plant

Buffalograss will grow in Colorado clay soils, but it is easier to start and maintain on deeper, loamy soils. Compacted clay soils should be improved by spreading a 2-in. layer of high-quality organic matter (compost or aged manure) over the surface. With a disk or rototiller, incorporate the compost into the soil to a depth of 4 to 6 in. The planting area should be leveled, raked, and smoothed prior to planting. Broadcast 3 to 5 lb. of seed per 1,000 sq. ft. of lawn. Following seeding, rake the area to cover the seeds lightly. For better moisture retention, you can cover the seeded area with a layer of straw. Water daily to keep the seedbed moist. A few weeks after germination, watering intervals can be lengthened to every 2 or 3 days. Weeds can be a problem in a new stand and should be pulled out by hand. Do not use herbicides.

Care and Maintenance

Once buffalograss is established, it will thrive without supplemental watering. If you want a more attractive turf, however, deep-water the buffalograss every 10 days or so during the summer months. You can help get the lawn off to a vigorous start with a good soaking about the time the grass is greening up. Avoid excessive watering in early spring to discourage the germination of cool-season weeds. If weeds should appear, they can be treated with glyphosate herbicide *before* the buffalograss starts to grow. Since buffalograss is naturally low growing, little mowing is required. For a more uniform appearance, mow with a sharp mower at a height of 1 to 2 in. Mow once a month, or not at all if your goal is to naturalize this grass. It has low fertilizer requirements: $1/2$ to 2 lb. nitrogen per 1,000 sq. ft. per year. Apply fertilizer around mid-June.

Additional Information

Buffalograss lawns can be naturalized by underplanting with crocuses, *Iris reticulata*, and species tulips. The bulbs' foliage usually dies back before it's time to mow the lawn in June.

Additional Species, Cultivars, or Varieties

A few improved cultivars available as treated seed are 'Texoka', 'Sharp's Improved', 'Comanche', 'Plains', and 'Topgun'. Vegetative types that are sold as sod (sold in squares) or plugs include 'Prairie' and '609'.

Crested Wheatgrass

Agropyron cristatum

Type: Cool-season
Texture: Coarse blade
Mowing Height: 3 to 5 in.
Zones: 3, 4, 5, 6

Light Requirement:

heatgrasses have coarse-textured leaves and a bunch-type growth habit. There are several wheatgrasses that have admirable potential for lawn use. They have been adapted to tolerate precipitation as low as 10 in. per year, which makes them well suited for a water-thrifty Colorado landscape as well as for unirrigated sites. (If wheatgrass is watered too much, in fact, it will begin to thin out.) It adapts to hot, dry spells by going dormant, but it makes a rapid recovery when moisture returns. When wheatgrass is actively growing, it has an attractive bluish green color; it is often used as a bluegrass "look-alike." 'Fairway' crested wheatgrass is a selection from the crested wheat complex. It has the desirable qualities of being leafier and shorter in height, making it a good variety for landscape use. This cool-season bunchgrass comes highly recommended for dryland lawn situations.

WHEN TO PLANT

Sow seed in late April to mid-May, when the soil temperatures are still somewhat cool and rain is generally more plentiful. Crested wheatgrass can also be planted in late summer to early fall, when night temperatures are beginning to cool down and there is less competition from weeds.

WHERE TO PLANT

Crested wheatgrass performs best in sunny sites on well-drained soils of average fertility. This cool-season bunchgrass is best used for dryland lawns, for erosion control on embankments, and on parking strips.

HOW TO PLANT

Refer to the instructions on site preparation in the introduction to this chapter. Crested wheatgrasses are adapted to a wide range of

Colorado soil conditions. Make a light application of diammonium phosphate (18-46-0—$1/2$ to 1 lb. per 1,000 sq. ft. of lawn area) at planting time. Apply 5 lb. of crested wheatgrass seed per 1,000 sq. ft. of lawn. Mulch with clean straw to help hold in moisture and to keep the seed from washing away. Crested wheatgrass will not germinate if the soil is dry. Water daily for 2 to 3 weeks, until the seed begins to germinate. Then begin tapering off the watering in order to discourage the growth of weed seeds (stopping watering too suddenly will stress the new seedlings). It is normal to have some weeds; most annual weeds can be controlled by subsequent mowing. The persistent perennial weeds can be controlled by hand-pulling or digging—"the cowboy way"—or by spot treating with an appropriate herbicide.

CARE AND MAINTENANCE

Crested wheatgrass is a low-maintenance grass for dryland uses. It requires very little maintenance indeed and can survive without irrigation once it is established. Wheatgrass has the ability to go dormant or rest during severe drought conditions. Keep watering to a minimum, as too much water will make the grass thin out and will also invite the invasion of opportunist weeds. If you desire, you can mow wheatgrass to a height of 3 to 5 in., or allow it to grow naturally for a meadow effect (12 to 18 in.). It will respond to fertilization, but use minimal amounts. Apply 1 to 2 lb. nitrogen per 1,000 sq. ft in mid- to late spring each year.

ADDITIONAL INFORMATION

Western wheatgrass, *Agropyron smithii*, is a native sod-forming grass whose rhizomes grow aggressively when moisture and soil conditions are favorable. The leaves have a bluish green tinge, providing an extra visual feature to the landscape.

ADDITIONAL SPECIES, CULTIVARS, OR VARIETIES

Some cultivars with improved cold and drought tolerance are 'Fairway', 'Ephraim', and 'Hycrest'. Check with your local seed supplier for availability.

Fine Fescue

Festuca spp.

Type: Cool-season
Texture: Fine blade
Mowing Height: $2^1/2$ to 3 in.
Zones: 3, 4, 5, 6

Light Requirement:

Fine fescues are best adapted to the shady conditions of many older Colorado landscapes. In areas where trees mature and cast shade over lawn areas, fine fescues are mixed with other cool-season grasses to increase lawn density and to maintain a lawn that can stand up to tree competition. Fine fescues are drought resistant and cold tolerant, and they will grow in soils of poor-to-average fertility. In extreme heat and drought conditions, fine fescues go dormant and rest until moisture becomes available. Their fine leaf texture is what makes fine fescues so well adapted to shade. They perform best in well-drained soils and should not be watered excessively. Over-watering will make fescue grasses more prone to fungus diseases such as leaf spot or melting out. Fine fescues that are often combined with Kentucky bluegrass include chewings fescue, creeping red fescue, and hard fescue. Fescue grasses have minimal fertilization requirements.

WHEN TO PLANT

The preferred time to seed fine fescue is late August to mid-September, when night temperatures have begun to cool down. At this time there is less competition from weeds than at other times of the year. Seed can also be sown in spring from April to mid-May.

WHERE TO PLANT

Fine fescues have a fine leaf texture and are especially well suited for shady areas. Well-drained soils are preferred to ensure best performance. Avoid soggy sites.

HOW TO PLANT

Please refer to instructions on soil preparation in the introduction to this chapter. Sow fine fescue grass seed at the rate of 3 to 5 lb. per 1,000 sq. ft of lawn area. It is often mixed with other cool-season grasses such as Kentucky bluegrass or perennial ryegrass for increased density and shade tolerance. Be patient; fine fescue takes time to fill in. After sowing the seed, mulch with clean straw to hold in moisture and prevent the seed from washing away. Water 3 to 4 times daily to keep the soil moistened; this will allow for good germination. It is normal for weeds to pop up in a new planting. Most annual weeds will be controlled by subsequent mowing. Perennial weeds can be pulled or killed with a spot treatment of an appropriate herbicide. Do not use the herbicide until the lawn has been mowed 3 to 4 times.

CARE AND MAINTENANCE

Fine fescues require less fertilizer than other cool-season grasses. An application of 1 to 2 lb. of nitrogen per 1,000 sq. ft per growing season is adequate. The first fertilizer application ($1/2$ to 1 lb.) can be made around Memorial Day; make the second application around Labor Day. Mow fine fescue as high as possible ($2^1/2$ to 3 in.), and mow often to remove no more than a third of the blade at any one time.

ADDITIONAL INFORMATION

If watered too much or grown under stress conditions, this shade-tolerant grass will become susceptible to fungus diseases including red thread, leaf spot, and dollarspot. Follow good management practices to prevent disease outbreaks.

ADDITIONAL SPECIES, CULTIVARS, OR VARIETIES

There are many improved cultivars of fine fescue for lawn use. Chewings fescue (*Festuca rubra* spp. *commutata*), hard fescue (*Festuca longifolia*), creeping red fescue (*Festuca rubra* spp. *rubra*), and sheep fescue (*Festuca ovina*) are all available from local seed suppliers.

Kentucky Bluegrass

Poa pratensis

Type: Cool-season **Texture:** Fine to medium blade **Mowing Height:** 2¹/₂ to 3 in. **Zones:** 3, 4, 5, 6	**Light Requirement:**

*B*luegrass is the most popular and widely used lawn grass planted in Colorado, and rightfully so. It is a cool-season grass with very good durability. Home owners appreciate its rich appearance, deep green color, and texture. Kentucky bluegrass reproduces from rhizomes, forming a dense, carpetlike turf. Given time, it will recover from almost any physical abuse, disease, or insect invasion. Bluegrass is the standard when comparing the growth characteristics such as leaf texture and plant tolerances of lawngrasses. It has amazing drought endurance. If left unwatered, bluegrass will go dormant and turn brown, but it will resprout from the rhizomes when favorable conditions return. This grass is best suited for areas with full sun or part shade and generally requires more upkeep—watering and fertilizing—than do warm-season grasses. If that doesn't concern you and your goal is to have a beautiful, durable lawn, a blend of Kentucky bluegrasses is the right choice. As a cool-season grass, it grows best when the temperatures are between 60 and 85 degrees Fahrenheit. When the weather turns hot and dry, it is perfectly normal for bluegrass to go dormant unless you continue to water and fertilize it. Dormancy is a natural resting period a grass uses for survival. The miracle of this grass is its ability to green up again when cooler, wetter conditions return. To keep a Kentucky bluegrass lawn looking its best, however, supplemental irrigation is essential.

WHEN TO PLANT

Kentucky bluegrass sod can be planted any time from spring through late fall. As long as the soil has been properly prepared, bluegrass sod can even be installed in winter. Watering is essential during the heat of summer to keep the underlying soil moist. Seed bluegrass from mid- to late August through mid-September. At this time, temperatures are cooler and there is less competition from weeds than at other times of the year.

WHERE TO PLANT

The majority of bluegrass varieties perform best if planted in full sun. Some varieties such as 'Glade', 'Bristol', 'Eclipse', and 'Touchdown' are moderately shade tolerant. Bluegrass grows best in amended, well-drained soils. See instructions on soil preparation in the introduction to this chapter.

HOW TO PLANT

If you are seeding, sow at the rate of 1 1/2 to 3 lb. of high-quality seed per 1,000 sq. ft. of lawn area. Divide the seed into 2 equal parts and sow half by going across the area from north to south. The other half should be planted by going across the area from east to west. Rake lightly to bring the seed into contact with the soil and to protect the new seedlings from drying out. Frequent light waterings, as many as 3 to 5 a day, will be necessary until the seed has germinated. It may take 2 weeks or longer for germination, depending upon weather conditions. After the grass is up and growing well, reduce watering frequency while increasing the volume of water to encourage a deep root system.

CARE AND MAINTENANCE

A vigorous, healthy bluegrass lawn may require 1 1/2 to 2 1/4 in. of water per week during hot, dry, and windy conditions, but it requires much less when the weather is cooler. In most Colorado clay soils, you should not try to apply the water all at one time in a short period. Instead, run the sprinkler for 20 to 30 minutes in one area, then repeat again an hour later. This allows the water to percolate more deeply instead of running off. For information on fertilizing, see the beginning of this chapter. If you allow your lawn to go dormant during the hottest part of summer, do not apply a high-nitrogen fertilizer. Mow the lawn high, with the mower blade set between 2 1/2 and 3 in. This will improve overall quality, keep the soil cool, and conserve water. Mow often enough to remove no more than 1/3 of the blade height at any one time. A thick lawn will resist weed invasion.

ADDITIONAL INFORMATION

Improved cultivars of bluegrass have excellent drought endurance and cold hardiness.

ADDITIONAL SPECIES, CULTIVARS, OR VARIETIES

There are many cultivars of bluegrass available. Check with your local sod grower or seed supplier for specific varieties and blends.

Perennial Ryegrass

Lolium perenne

Type: Cool-season
Texture: Fine blade
Mowing Height: 2¹/₂ to 3 in.
Zones: 3, 4, 5, 6

Light Requirement:

*A*nother cool-season grass for Colorado is perennial ryegrass. Though it is not available as pure sod, it germinates and grows quickly from seed. The leaf texture and color of perennial ryegrass is very compatible with bluegrass. When combined, perennial ryegrass and Kentucky bluegrass form a tough, carpet-like sod perfect for high-traffic areas. The watering-and-fertilizing regime for perennial ryegrass is similar to the regime for Kentucky bluegrass. Perennial ryegrass has good heat and wear tolerance and if planted in deep, well-prepared soil, it is drought resistant. Without supplemental irrigation, perennial ryegrass will go dormant in extreme heat and during long periods of drought. We have planted a large expanse of perennial ryegrass on sandy loam soil and it has withstood the heat, wind, and drier conditions of summer extremely well. It is important to have a sharp mower blade when mowing perennial ryegrass; a dull blade will result in a ragged look. The presence of endophytic fungi in ryegrass improves the grass's ability to resist some insect species such as billbugs, cutworms, sod webworms, and possibly white grubs.

WHEN TO PLANT

Perennial ryegrass tends to form bunches if not seeded densely. The best time to sow seed is in late summer to late September; at this time night temperatures have begun to cool and there will be less competition from weeds. The second-best time for sowing is mid-April to mid-May.

WHERE TO PLANT

Perennial ryegrass performs best in deep, well-prepared soils of average fertility. Both full sun and part shade are acceptable. Plant perennial ryegrass in play areas and in places that need erosion control.

How to Plant

Instructions for site preparation and methods of seeding can be found in the introduction to this chapter. Apply at the rate of 4 to 5 lb. of seed per 1,000 sq. ft. of lawn. After seeding, mulch with clean wheat straw or pulverized compost. Mulch will maintain moisture and help prevent the seed from washing away. Keep the seedbed moist by watering 3 to 4 times daily for about 2 to 3 weeks while the seed germinates and becomes established. Any weeds that appear will be controlled by subsequent mowing. Tough, persistent weeds can be pulled or dug—"the cowboy way"—or killed with a spot treatment of the appropriate herbicide. Caution: If using a herbicide, wait until after the new lawn has been mowed 3 or 4 times. Read and follow label directions exactly.

Care and Maintenance

Perennial ryegrass should be fertilized with 1 lb. nitrogen per 1,000 sq. ft. per application. Three to 4 fertilizer applications can be made during the year—around Memorial Day, Fourth of July, Labor Day, and Halloween. Skip the July application if desired. Mow often with a sharp mower blade, to a height of $2^1/2$ to 3 in. The growth characteristics of perennial ryegrass make it necessary to keep your lawn mower blades sharp, or tearing of the leaf blades will result. This will give the lawn a tan to brownish cast after mowing.

Additional Information

For a more durable lawn, combine perennial ryegrass with bluegrass.

Additional Species, Cultivars, or Varieties

Some cultivars of perennial ryegrass contain moderate to high levels of endophytic fungi. Some of these cultivars are 'AllStar', 'Assure', 'Birdie II', 'Citation II', 'Commander', 'Cowboy', 'Dandy', 'Dasher II', 'Pennant', 'Pelude', 'Regal', 'Saturn', 'Sunrye', and 'Vintage'. Ask your local seed supplier for information on the latest cultivars.

Turf-type Tall Fescue

Festuca arundinacea

Type: Cool-season	**Light Requirement:**
Texture: Coarse blade	
Mowing Height: $2^1/2$ to 3 in.	
Zones: 3, 4, 5, 6	

*U*nlike bluegrass, which spreads by means of rhizomes, the turf-type tall fescues are cool-season bunchgrasses that grow in clumps. They are easy to establish, either planted alone or as the main grass in a mixture. Because turf-type tall fescue is a clump-type grass, you will need to seed the lawn generously to ensure dense growth and to form an acceptable sod. When it gets thin from foot traffic and play, it has the tendency to become coarse-bladed and develops bare spots where weeds can easily invade. Fescue, like bluegrass, needs irrigation to survive and stay green; tall fescue, in fact, requires more water than bluegrass. Its drought tolerance is due to its deep root system, which enables fescue to tap into a larger soil volume for moisture. Colorado clay soils must be properly and deeply prepared to encourage deep root development. Establishing tall fescue without extensive soil preparation will mean little water savings. Tall fescue is more tolerant of shade than bluegrass and exhibits fewer problems with insects and disease. Some turf-type tall fescue grasses are enhanced with endophytic fungi that improve the lawn's ability to resist sod webworms and billbugs. The newer cultivars of fescue offer a good range of color throughout the season.

WHEN TO PLANT

Sow seed from mid- to late August through September, when there is less competition from weeds and temperatures are generally cooler. Turf-type fescue sod is available from local sod growers and can be planted any time from spring through fall. Check with your local grower for more details.

WHERE TO PLANT

Tall fescues can be planted in sun or part shade. They will adapt to a wide range of soil types as long as the soil is deeply prepared. Use this grass as a durable groundcover on banks to reduce erosion or use it in playing areas, dog runs, or other utility applications.

How to Plant

Please see the instructions on site preparation and seeding procedures in the introduction to this chapter. If seeding, you will need 7 to 8 lb. of seed per 1,000 sq. ft. of lawn. If fescue is not planted at the proper density, the resulting plants will become "clumpy" and develop coarser leaf blades. Areas that are damaged will not fill in and must be reseeded or resodded. Many sod growers mix 5 to 10 percent bluegrass seed (a sod-forming grass) to produce turf-type fescue sod that will hold together. In this situation, however, bluegrass may take over and become the dominant grass in the lawn. To be a water-saving lawn grass, fescue must be grown in soils that have been improved with organic matter, mixed to a depth of 10 in. or more. Rake the surface smooth and remove debris to prepare for seeding or sodding.

Care and Maintenance

On deep, well-prepared soils, the newer varieties of turf-type fescue are quite attractive. They will develop an extensive root system and will possibly help you economize on water use. Avoid applying too much nitrogen to fescue as this stimulates rapid growth and will require more frequent mowing. Fescue grass blades are coarse; sharpen the mower blade regularly to get a nice, clean cut. Mow to a height of $2^1/2$ to 3 in. Mow often to remove no more than $1/3$ of the blade height at any one time. Let the clippings remain on the lawn where they will decompose and return nutrients to the soil. Resod or reseed bare spots to prevent unwanted weed invasion.

Additional Information

Tall fescues can withstand drought conditions, but they will brown out under severe stress. It takes time for the grass to recover. Avoid the older varieties of tall fescue, which are much coarser in appearance and texture.

Additional Species, Cultivars, or Varieties

There are many new and improved cultivars of tall fescue available. Check with your local sod grower or seed supplier.

*Gardening
in Colorado
presents
tremendous
opportunities
and Colorado
gardeners are a
resourceful lot.*

The Colorado Gardener's Guide
Photographic Gallery of Featured Plants

Cleome
Cleome hassleriana

Cosmos
Cosmos bipinnatus

Dusty Miller
Senecio cineraria

Flowering Cabbage
Brassica oleracea

Geranium
Pelargonium × *hortorum*

Impatiens
Impatiens wallerana

Love-in-a-Mist
Nigella damascena

Marigold
Tagetes spp.

Morning Glory
Ipomoea purpurea

Moss Rose
Portulaca grandiflora

Pansy
Viola × *wittrockiana*

Petunia
Petunia × *hybrida*

Pot Marigold
Calendula officinalis

Snapdragon
Antirrhinum majus

Zinnia
Zinnia elegans

Amur Maple
Acer ginnala

Eastern Redbud
Cercis canadensis

Flowering Crab Apple
Malus spp.

Goldenrain Tree
Koelreuteria paniculata

Green Ash
Fraxinus pennsylvanica

Hawthorn
Crataegus spp.

Hedge Maple
Acer campestre

Kentucky Coffee Tree
Gymnocladus dioica

Linden
Tilia spp.

Norway Maple
Acer platanoides

Oak
Quercus spp.

Ohio Buckeye
Aesculus glabra

Poplar
Populus spp.

Quaking Aspen
Populus tremuloides

River Birch
Betula nigra

Serviceberry
Amelanchier alnifolia

Thornless Honeylocust
Gleditsia triacanthos var. *inermis*

Western Catalpa
Catalpa speciosa

Western Hackberry
Celtis occidentalis

White Ash
Fraxinus americana

Willow
Salix spp.

American Arborvitae
Thuja occidentalis

Bristlecone Pine
Pinus aristata

Colorado Blue Spruce
Picea pungens

Creeping Juniper
Juniperus horizontalis

Douglas Fir
Pseudotsuga menziesii

European Larch
Larix decidua

Japanese Yew
Taxus cuspidata

Pine
Pinus spp.

Rocky Mountain Juniper
Juniperus scopulorum

White Fir
Abies concolor

Bigroot Geranium
Geranium macrorrhizum

Carpet Bugleweed
Ajuga reptans

Creeping Phlox
Phlox subulata

False Rockcress
Aubrieta deltoidea

Heart-leafed Bergenia
Bergenia cordifolia

Kinnikinick
Arctostaphylos uva-ursi

Lily-of-the-Valley
Convallaria majalis

Mother-of-Thyme
Thymus praecox var. 'Coccineus'

Purple Iceplant
Delosperma cooperi

Pussytoes
Antennaria parvifolia

Snow-in-Summer
Cerastium tomentosum

Spotted Dead Nettle
Lamium maculatum

Stonecrop
Sedum spp.

Strawberry
Fragaria spp.

Sweet Woodruff
Galium odoratum

Woolly Thyme
Thymus pseudolanuginosus

Botanical Tulip
Tulipa tarda

Crocus
Crocus spp.

Daffodil
Narcissus spp.

Dwarf Bulbous Iris
Iris reticulata

Glory of the Snow
Chionodoxa luciliae

Grape Hyacinth
Muscari armeniacum

Lily
Lilium hybrids

Meadow Saffron
Colchicum spp.

Ornamental Onion
Allium spp.

Siberian Squill
Scilla siberica

HARDY BULBS

Snowdrop
Galanthus nivalis

Windflower
Anemone blanda

Blue Fescue
Festuca ovina

ORNAMENTAL GRASSES

Blue Oat Grass
Helictotrichon sempervirens

Feather Reed Grass
Calamagrostis acutiflora

Fountain Grass
Pennisetum alopecuroides

Japanese Silver Grass
Miscanthus sinensis

Little Bluestem
Schizachyrium scoparium

Northern Sea Oats
Chasmanthium latifolium

PERENNIALS

Switchgrass
Panicum virgatum

Artemisia
Artemisia ludoviciana

Blanket Flower
Gaillardia × grandiflora

Bleeding Heart
Dicentra spectabilis

Bloody Cranesbill
Geranium sanguineum

Butterfly Weed
Asclepias tuberosa

Chiming Bells
Mertensia ciliata

Coneflower
Rudbeckia spp.

Coral Bells
Heuchera sanguinea

Daylily
Hemerocallis hybrids

False Indigo
Baptisia australis

False Spirea
Astilbe × *arendsii*

Gayfeather
Liatris spicata

Goldenrod
Solidago spp. and hybrids

Hardy Chrysanthemum
Chrysanthemum × *morifolium*

Hosta
Hosta spp. and hybrids

Japanese Anemone
Anemone × hybrida

Joe-Pye Weed
Eupatorium purpureum

Lamb's Ears
Stachys byzantina

Lenten Rose
Helleborus orientalis

Lupine
Lupinus hybrids

New England Aster
Aster novae-angliae

Peony
Paeonia lactiflora and hybrids

Perennial Flax
Linum perenne

Perennial Salvia
Salvia × superba

Purple Coneflower
Echinacea purpurea

Rocky Mountain Columbine
Aquilegia caerulea

Russian Sage
Perovskia atriplicifolia

Scarlet Bugler
Penstemon barbatus

Showy Stonecrop
Sedum × 'Autumn Joy'

Siberian Iris
Iris sibirica

Sneezeweed
Helenium autumnale

Sweet William
Dianthus barbatus

Thread-Leaf Coreopsis
Coreopsis verticillata

Veronica
Veronica spicata

Climbing Rose
Rosa × *hybrida*

Floribunda
Rosa × *hybrida*

Grandiflora
Rosa × *hybrida*

Hybrid Tea Rose
Rosa × *hybrida*

Miniature Rose
Rosa × hybrida

Old Garden Rose
Rosa

Polyantha
Rosa × hybrida

Species Roses
Rosa spp.

Alpine Currant
Ribes alpinum

American Plum
Prunus americana

Apache Plume
Fallugia paradoxa

Barberry
Berberis spp.

Beauty Bush
Kolkwitzia amabilis

Blue Mist Spirea
Caryopteris × clandonensis

Burning Bush
Euonymus alatus

Butterfly Bush
Buddleia spp.

Cinquefoil
Potentilla fruticosa

Common Ninebark
Physocarpus opulifolius

Coralberry
Symphoricarpos spp.

Daphne
Daphne spp.

Dwarf Arctic Willow
Salix purpurea

Firethorn
Pyracantha coccinea

Forsythia
Forsythia × *intermedia*

Glossy Buckthorn
Rhamnus frangula

Golden St. Johnswort
Hypericum frondosum

Hedge Cotoneaster
Cotoneaster lucidus

Leadplant
Amorpha canescens

Lilac
Syringa spp.

Mockorange
Philadelphus spp.

Mountain Mahogany
Cercocarpus montanus

Oregon Grape
Mahonia aquifolium

Redtwig Dogwood
Cornus sericea

Rocky Mountain Sumac
Rhus glabra var. *cismontana*

Rose-of-Sharon
Hibiscus syriacus

Scotch Broom
Cytisus scoparis

Sea Buckthorn
Hippophae rhamnoides

Serviceberry
Amelanchier alnifolia

Siberian Pea Shrub
Caragana arborescens

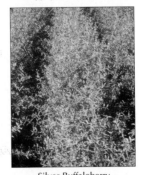

Silver Buffaloberry
Shepherdia argentea

Spirea
Spiraea spp.

Tatarian Honeysuckle
Lonicera tatarica

Viburnum
Viburnum spp.

American Bittersweet
Celastrus scandens

Clematis
Clematis spp.

Climbing Hydrangea
Hydrangea petiolaris

Common Hops
Humulus lupulus

English Ivy
Hedera helix

Honeysuckle
Lonicera spp.

Perennial Pea
Lathyrus latifolius

Porcelain Vine
Ampelopsis brevipendunculata

Silver Lace Vine
Polygonum aubertii

Trumpet Vine
Campsis radicans

VINES

Virginia Creeper
Parthenocissus quinquefolia

Wintercreeper
Euonymus fortunei

USDA HARDINESS ZONE MAP

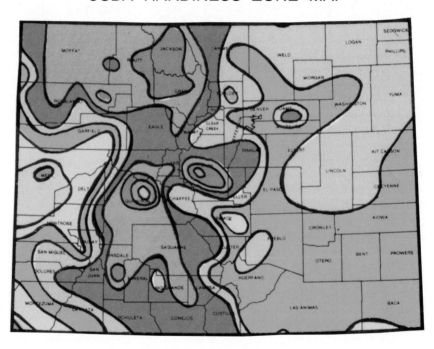

Average Annual Minimum Temperature

Temperature (°C)		Temperature (°F)	Temperature (°C)		Temperature (°F)
-42.8 to -45.5	2a	-45 to -50	-26.2 to -28.8	5a	-15 to -20
-40.0 to -42.7	2b	-40 to -45	-23.4 to -26.1	5b	-10 to -15
-37.3 to -40.0	3a	-35 to -40	-20.6 to -23.3	6a	-5 to -10
-34.5 to -37.2	3b	-30 to -35	-17.8 to -20.5	6b	0 to -5
-31.7 to -34.4	4a	-25 to -30	-15.0 to -17.7	7a	5 to 0
-28.9 to -31.6	4b	-20 to -25			

The Kiss of the
Sun for Pardon,
the Song of the
Birds for Myrth;
One is Nearer
God's Heart in a
Garden Than
Anywhere Else on
Earth.

CHAPTER SEVEN

Ornamental Grasses

*O*RNAMENTAL GRASSES HAVE INCREASED IN
POPULARITY and are becoming an important part of
Colorado landscapes. Their beauty is natural, never contrived,
and they provide a unique textural contrast to other plants. When
selected and sited correctly, ornamental grasses add beauty and
grace to the garden. They are worth growing if only for the sounds
they make when the slightest breeze blows; the gentle rustling of
the leaves and seedheads evoke sounds of the prairie. Plant ornamental grasses in drifts or swathes or as accent plants in the shrub
or perennial flower garden, where their fine textures will create
dramatic contrasts.

When planted in groups throughout the landscape, ornamental
grasses help unify flower beds and borders. Specimen grasses combine well with asters, rudbeckia, coneflower, liatris, Joe-Pye weed,
helianthus, and goldenrod. The larger dramatic grasses such as big
bluestem look good with flowers that grow on long stems (such as
daylilies, hibiscus, and cannas). Russian sage and yarrows make natural grass companions. The beauty of ornamental grasses in the fall
garden can be accented with *Sedum* 'Autumn Joy', *Zauschneria ari-
zonica* (hummingbird trumpet), obedient plant, and agastache.

When selecting the right kind of grass for your garden, understand the grass's growth habit. Most ornamental grasses are
perennials and grow in two different ways. Those classified as running grasses will generally spread quickly by means of vigorous
underground stems or rhizomes. These are the ones that will have to
be contained so they won't become invasive in the flower garden.
Others are clump-formers; they increase in size more slowly. They
grow in bunches and produce new buds at the base of the clump
near the crown. Their growing buds are close to ground level, protected from Colorado's fluctuating climate; their dense, fibrous root
systems are quick to rejuvenate.

Chapter Seven

Most ornamental grasses do best in full sun, but there are some that will do just fine in light shade. They are available at garden retailers and from mail-order sources. Plant them in the spring or early summer. If you wait to plant them in the fall, remember that grasses can be damaged and heaved out of the soil by alternate freezes and thaws. Take precautions by applying a winter mulch over fall-planted grasses after the soil freezes.

If you plant ornamental grasses close together in mass plantings, you will create a sea of grass. Spacing them farther apart will emphasize the individual plant's form. You may space ornamental grasses as far apart as their height at maturity.

Ornamental grasses are not maintenance-free, but they come pretty close to it. They will grow in poorer soils than many other plants, and once established, they rarely need watering. Cutting back the foliage is the most important maintenance activity, but because ornamental grasses transcend each season, don't be too hasty to cut them back right away. Instead, leave the foliage to dry and ripen in the winter sun. You will have another season of pleasure as you view the layers of frost and snow on the stems and seedheads that are silhouetted against the snow.

Cut back the faded stalks in March or April when spring fever demands that you get outdoors and exercise that itching green thumb. To give new shoots more light and room to grow, remove the dead foliage close to the ground as soon as the shoots start emerging.

Spring is a good time to rejuvenate old clumps, too. Dig up the clump with a spading fork and divide by cutting or tearing out rooted sections. This technique will also renew an occasional clump of grass that is "running out" or dying back in the center. Keep the most vigorous divisions and discard the old center portion. Replant the new clumps and water well. Continue to provide ample moisture as needed until they show new growth.

Blue Fescue

Festuca ovina

Height: 6 to 18 in.
Flowers: Light green
Bloom Period: Summer
Zones: 4, 5, 6

Light Requirement:

The blue fescue grasses are among the most tame and attractive ornamental grasses for Colorado landscapes. When grown in groups, they resemble an army of symmetrical bluish gray hedgehogs. Dwarf blue fescue is valued for its delicate, light silvery-blue foliage which retains good color year-round. Fescue is ideal for Colorado landscapes, as it prefers cool conditions. We especially like to plant it in groups in well-drained soils on rocky slopes, and as accent plants in rock gardens. In heavy Colorado clay soils, the plants are more short-lived, more prone to dying out in the center. *Festuca glauca* 'Sea Urchin' is a clump-forming ornamental grass with light-blue foliage. It grows to a height of 12 to 15 in., and an individual clump can be 12 to 15 in. wide. It holds its blue foliage longer than the species, and is one of our favorites. Whether you choose to plant blue fescue as a specimen plant or in groups for groundcover, this is an excellent and hardy ornamental grass.

When to Plant

Blue fescue can be planted from spring through fall as long as container-grown plants are available. Planting early in the spring when temperatures are cooler will allow the plants to become well established before the heat of summer.

Where to Plant

This ornamental fescue will tolerate a wide range of soils, but good drainage is essential. Rocky slopes, sandy loam, or well-loosened clay soils that have been amended with compost will create favorable conditions for growth. Do not plant in heavily shaded areas or the colors will appear faded. These plants are excellent for rock gardens, in the foreground of perennial beds, as specimen plantings, and as groundcover.

How to Plant

Heavy Colorado clay soil must be prepared before planting. Till or dig 2 in. of high-quality compost into the top 6 in. of soil. Dig the planting holes wide enough to accommodate the root system without crowding. Space the plants 12 to 15 in. apart. Position the plants so they are growing at the same level they were in their containers. Lightly firm the soil around the roots and water-in thoroughly. Mulch around the plants with pine needles or shredded cedar to conserve moisture.

Care and Maintenance

Blue fescue is relatively free of insect pests and diseases. If grown in full sun, it will thrive and reward you with its handsome foliage. Water only as needed when the soil dries out. Avoid watering too often in clay soils; this will cause the plants to die out in the center, making them short-lived. In early spring, a light fertilization of 10-10-10 can be applied around the plants and watered in. This will give them a boost to begin the season. A second fertilizer application can be made in early fall if you desire.

Additional Information

Blue fescue is a delightful ornamental grass that can be grown successfully in large containers. It will create a special effect on a deck or patio.

Additional Species, Cultivars, or Varieties

In addition to the standard species blue fescue, look for the cultivars 'Glauca', 'Elijah Blue', and the sea urchin clone, 'Sea Urchin'.

ORNAMENTAL GRASSES

Blue Oat Grass

Helictotrichon sempervirens

Height: 2 to 3 ft.	**Light Requirement:**
Flowers: Beige	
Bloom Period: Late spring to early summer	
Zones: 4, 5, 6	

With its blue metallic leaves and beige flowers which rise 1 to 2 ft. above the foliage on arching, silvery-gray stems, blue oat grass is one of my favorites in the landscape. As a cool-season grass, *Helictotrichon sempervirens* gets a head start on the season, producing its handsome foliage in early spring. Blue oat grass flowers arrive early to wave in the spring breezes. The spiky, 18- to 24.-in. tall tufts of steel-blue leaf blades augment the pink, purple, and magenta flowers of late spring and early summer. The clumps of foliage are persistent in the winter. Blue oat grass can be planted in groups or used alone as an accent grass among perennials or shrubs.

WHEN TO PLANT
Plant blue oat grass in the spring or fall.

WHERE TO PLANT
Choose a full-sun location with well-drained soil. Blue oat grass is tolerant of a wide range of soils, but avoid heavy, wet soil conditions. Plants will grow in light shade for a portion of the day. When planted in the foreground of a flower bed, the tall flowering stems add height to the garden, but their delicacy allows you to see through the plant. Try blue oat grass with Russian sage or smokebush. Other good companions are the spring-flowering bulbs such as *Allium aflatunense*, ornamental onion with its giant purple globes, and white or lavender tulips.

HOW TO PLANT
Space blue oat grass 2^1/$_2$ to 3 ft. apart. Plants that are planted too close together won't be able to display their dramatic form. Dig the planting hole wide enough to accommodate the roots without crowding. Position the plant so that the soil level is the same as it was in the container. If the plants you purchased are rootbound,

loosen the roots gently. Add backfill soil to the planting hole and lightly firm some soil around the roots. Water the plants thoroughly and keep them moist until established; mulch to maintain and conserve moisture.

CARE AND MAINTENANCE

Blue oat grass does require some grooming, but not the severe pruning sometimes given other ornamental grasses. You don't have to cut it back to the ground. Cut only the top of the clump in early winter. You may keep the plants tidy by cleaning out the dead foliage—do this by lightly tugging on it during the spring. Remove the flowering stems when they are no longer appealing (usually by mid- to late summer). Plants will perform much better if they are watered during dry spells.

ADDITIONAL INFORMATION

As plants mature, they may need an occasional division. Do this in spring. Lift the clump out with a heavy-duty spading fork and divide it into sections with a sharp spade or knife. New divisions may take several years to develop their characteristic tufted form.

ADDITIONAL SPECIES, CULTIVARS, OR VARIETIES

Some similar but smaller ornamental grasses with blue coloration are the blue fescues, including *Festuca cinerea*, *F. glauca*, and *F. ovina*, which grow to a height of 6 to 18 in. and remain evergreen in Zone 5. *F. ovina* 'Elijah Blue' (10 in.) is one of the better choices. Blue fescues generally require division every 2 years. They suffer from "brownout" in the heat of summer.

ORNAMENTAL GRASSES

Feather Reed Grass

Calamagrostis × acutiflora

Height: 3 to 4 ft. **Flowers:** Purple-green changing to gold **Bloom Period:** Early summer **Zones:** 4, 5, 6	**Light Requirement:**

*I*f you are uncertain about growing ornamental grasses in your landscape, try feather reed grass. Its wheat-like look makes this grass one of the showiest and most popular ornamental grasses for home garden use. Feather reed grass creates an attractive, changing display for almost 10 months out of the year. It is a cool-season grass and quickly forms a fresh green clump in spring that matures to about 3 ft. In late spring and early summer, when other ornamental grasses are just getting started, feather reed grass sends out its greenish flower spikes tinged with purple. Later, the plumes turn to a golden wheat color and stiffen into a handsome vertical form. Add a breeze and these upright plumes are just like amber waves. As late fall arrives, the foliage turns orange to yellow. The beautiful foliage persists into winter. Feather reed grass is considered a well-behaved ornamental grass; it is sterile and does not self-seed. When grown in full sun, this grass will not require staking. Use feather reed grass with perennials of all types. It makes an attractive background grass where a stately effect is desired, or you can grow single specimen plants for a vertical accent in the landscape.

When to Plant

Plant feather reed grass in spring so it will have time to establish roots before the heat of summer ensues. You can plant this grass at a later time, but be sure to provide ample moisture to help it establish in hot weather.

Where to Plant

Though a sunny location is best, feather reed grass will tolerate some shade. Too much shade will cause the clumps to flop over. This plant prefers moderately moist to medium-dry soil conditions. Colorado soils can be amended with compost to improve drainage and retain moisture. Plant this vertical grass as an accent for perennials, in drifts as a screen, with shrubs, or in meadow-like mass plantings with other grasses and perennials.

How to Plant
Plant feather reed grass specimens $2^1/2$ to 3 ft. apart. Dig the planting hole wide enough to accommodate the roots without crowding. Position the plant so that the soil level is the same as it was in the container. If the plants you purchased are rootbound, gently loosen the roots. Add backfill soil to the planting hole and lightly firm soil around the roots. Water the plants thoroughly and keep moist until established. Mulch to maintain and conserve moisture.

Care and Maintenance
Because it requires little care, feather reed grass is one of the easier ornamental grasses to introduce into the landscape. Cut the clumps back to within 6 in. from the ground in mid- to late winter. Feather reed grass starts to grow earlier than warm-season grasses. It does not require frequent division, but clumps can be split to increase your collection. Make divisions in the spring. Lift the older clumps with a heavy-duty spading fork and split them apart. A sharp shovel or pruning saw will make it easy to separate the clumps. Discard the woody unproductive center and replant the vigorous, healthy sections. Replant divisions at the same level they were growing. Keep plants watered until they are established.

Additional Information
The attractive foliage and flowers of feather reed grass are outstanding for dried arrangements.

Additional Species, Cultivars, or Varieties
The cultivar 'Karl Foerster' is one of the best selections. If you have limited garden space, we suggest *Calamagrostis × acutiflora* 'Overdam'. It reaches 3 to 4 ft. when in flower and has all the attributes of feather reed grass. The handsome, cream-striped foliage forms an 18-in. clump. 'Overdam' prefers partial shade.

Fountain Grass

Pennisetum alopecuroides

Height: 3 to 4 ft.	**Light Requirement:**
Flowers: Pinkish green or whitish tan	
Bloom Period: Midsummer	
Zones: 5, 6	

When backlit by the Colorado sun, fountain grass resembles a sparkling fountain in the garden. Its glossy, narrow leaves and pinkish foxtail flowers create a pleasing loose-cascade effect. Fountain grass is a warm-season grass that may freeze in the coldest Colorado winters, but it is worth trying in your landscape. Plant it at 2- to 3-ft. intervals for a meadow-like groundcover, or use it in flower beds. Specimen plants will soften a corner or accent pathways. It starts to grow when the tulips are emerging; the graceful green clumps are a nice contrast to other plants in the garden. The buff-colored flower heads with their pink, maroon, or magenta cast appear in midsummer. The flowers are held close to the clump, creating the same cascading effect produced by the foliage. In autumn, when fountain grass begins to fade, it continues to add garden interest with foliage in shades of gold, apricot, or rose. The leaves bleach to tan by late fall; they persist to catch the snow and add more volume to the winter scene.

WHEN TO PLANT

Fountain grass should be planted in spring so that its roots will have a chance to develop before the heat of summer.

WHERE TO PLANT

Choose a sunny location with well-drained soil. Fountain grass is adapted to a wide range of soil types, but Colorado soil should be amended with a moisture-retentive compost to ensure healthy root development. Plant fountain grass to show off its full, cascading growth habit. Use it to provide contrast with the coarser-looking plants such as tall sedums and 'Goldsturm' black-eyed Susan. In many metropolitan parks, fountain grass is combined with annuals.

HOW TO PLANT

Space fountain grass at least 3 to 4 ft. apart. Closer spacing is suggested for a meadow-like effect, and dwarf cultivars such as

'Hameln' can be spaced closer together as well. Dig the planting hole wide enough to accommodate the roots without crowding. Position the plant so that the soil level is the same as it was in the container. If the plants you purchased are rootbound, gently loosen the roots. Water the plants thoroughly and keep them moist until they are established. Mulch to maintain and conserve moisture.

CARE AND MAINTENANCE

Fountain grass will thrive in full sun. Cut it back in early spring to several inches from the ground. For larger mass plantings, this can be easily accomplished with a hedge trimmer. Mature clumps will eventually die out in the center and split open. When this happens (every 5 years or so), lift and divide the old clumps in spring. Let the new foliage emerge so you can determine which parts of the clump are alive. Dig the clump with a heavy-duty spading fork and split with an ax or pruning saw. Remove and discard the woody center portion. Divide and keep the remaining vigorous healthy sections. Replant the new divisions and keep them well watered until established.

ADDITIONAL INFORMATION

Fountain grass is not completely hardy in many Colorado gardens. In unusually cold and fluctuating winter conditions, and in exposed locations, portions of the clump may perish; the entire clump may die if conditions are severe. Winter mulching after the ground freezes offers some protection. This grass is known to self-sow; volunteer seedlings can be thinned out and relocated.

ADDITIONAL SPECIES, CULTIVARS, OR VARIETIES

There are dwarf cultivars like 'Hameln', 'Little Bunny', and 'Moudry' ($2^1/2$ to 3 ft.); these are excellent choices for limited spaces. They are not as dramatic as the species but are hardier for our area. Their fine-textured foliage and smaller white plumes appear earlier than those of other cultivars. Purple fountain grass, *Pennisetum setaceum* 'Rubrum' (2 to 3 ft.), is a tender annual grass with burgundy foliage and purplish-red plumes. It works well in containers and as a backdrop for annuals or perennials.

Japanese Silver Grass

Miscanthus sinensis

Other Names: Maiden Grass, Eulalia
Height: 4 to 8 ft.
Flowers: Pinkish bronze, turning to silver white
Bloom Period: Late summer to early fall
Zones: 4, 5, 6

Light Requirement:

apanese silver grass, with its long, fine, arching leaves, has the noble bearing of a garden aristocrat. Cultivated in Japan for centuries and used in American gardens at the turn of the century, *Miscanthus* is now back in vogue. It is well adapted to Colorado landscapes; its handsome growth habit, adaptability, fall color, silvery plumes, and winter presence are just a few of the reasons to grow this ornamental grass. There are many cultivars available, so be sure to choose those that are hardy for your area. Many selections will survive in Zone 5, although they may not survive the fluctuating temperatures of winter. "Silver grass" refers to the attractive silver plumes, which can be awesome against a blue Colorado sky. Selections that flower earlier in the season are recommended for Colorado landscapes. The cultivar 'Purpurascens', often called "flame grass," is one good selection. It grows more compact (to 5 ft.), flowers in August, and has striking reddish-orange fall color beginning as early as September. Its smaller growth habit makes it easy to use. You can find cultivars with variegated, banded, fine-textured, or coarse-textured foliage. The fluffy plumes catch the snow and the plant remains attractive until spring.

WHEN TO PLANT

Plant Japanese silver grass in spring. Plants are available from local garden retailers and mail-order catalogs.

WHERE TO PLANT

Japanese silver grass prefers full sun but will take some light shade. In too much shade, the clumps will sprawl open and they may need to be staked. Moist, average-to-rich soil is ideal for making this grass grow taller and wider in less time, but it will tolerate a wide range of soil types from moist to dry. Use it as a specimen plant near evergreens, or plant it near a water feature.

How to Plant

Space Japanese silver grass 3 to 6 ft. apart, depending on the culti-var. *A Green Thumb tip: Space plants as far apart as they will become tall*—if a particular grass grows to 4 ft. tall, space it 4 ft. apart. But if you want the area to fill in faster and provide more cover, you should space plants more closely. Dig the planting hole wide enough to accommodate the roots without cramping and position the plant at the same level it was growing in its container. Gently firm the soil around the roots and water thoroughly. Keep the soil moist until the plant is established. Mulch to conserve water.

Care and Maintenance

Provide water during dry periods. The leaf blades will roll, indicat-ing stress, when the grass needs watering. In early spring, cut the clumps to several inches from ground level. Use hedge trimmers or pruning loppers to make this task easier. Wear long sleeves and gloves because *Miscanthus* leaves are sharp and can scratch and irritate your skin. Do not use high-nitrogen fertilizer; this will makes the plants weak, and they will blow over. If you wish to fertilize, use a slow-release or organic type that is low in nitrogen.

Additional Information

Older clumps may need rejuvenation every 5 to 7 years. Divide the clumps in the spring when emerging foliage allows you to tell what parts of the clump are alive. Use a pruning saw or ax to divide them. Remove and discard the old, woody center portion. Divide the remaining healthy sections into pieces and replant. Keep new transplants well watered to get them established.

Additional Species, Cultivars, or Varieties

Miscanthus sinensis 'Gracillimus', maiden grass, has been widely grown for its elegant fine texture. 'Morning Light' (5 to 6 ft.) has finely variegated leaves which appear silvery. 'Variegatus' (5 to 7 ft.) has wider variegated foliage and an almost white effect in the land-scape. *M. oligostachys*, small Japanese silver grass, has wide leaves resembing bamboo. It flowers early and is good for limited space. *M. floridulus*, giant Chinese silver grass, grows tall (8 ft.) and has 10 in. fluffy silver plumes. It may not flower every year in Colorado.

Little Bluestem

Schizachyrium scoparium

Other Name: *Andropogon scoparius*
Height: 2 to 3 ft.
Flowers: White, light beige
Bloom Period: Midsummer
Zones: 3, 4, 5

Light Requirement:

ittle bluestem is a native American prairie grass that is well suited to Colorado landscapes. It has outstanding drought and cold tolerance in our region. Its common name comes from the bluish green coloration at the base of the clump. In winter, the fiery orange to russet-red foliage accents the otherwise colorless landscape. This grass has a handsome growth habit, good adaptability, beautiful autumn color, fluffy white plumes, and a fine winter presence. Little bluestem will grow in almost any soil, especially dry and rocky sites, and it prefers full sun. It is particularly attractive in a naturalized garden as its fluffy white seed plumes wave in the breeze. The leaves are medium-textured and range from green to blue-green to blue. The upright clumps create a nice contrast when planted with spring-flowering bulbs and help to draw attention away from the slowly maturing foliage of the bulbs. Little bluestem is a good companion to irises, poppies, and other taller perennials.

WHEN TO PLANT
Plant little bluestem in the spring. Container-grown plants will have plenty of time to establish before the heat of summer.

WHERE TO PLANT
Little bluestem prefers full sun and dry soil conditions. Avoid soils that are wet or mucky. This ornamental grass evokes the prairie when it ripples in the wind. Plant in groups throughout the garden to provide a unifying element in beds and borders. Color and texture will also tie together different flower colors.

HOW TO PLANT
Space little bluestem grass plants 1¹/₂ to 2 ft. apart in the landscape, depending on the effect you want to create. *A Green Thumb tip: Space*

the plants as far apart as they will become tall—if a grass grows to 2 ft. tall, space it 2 ft. apart. If you want to have the grasses fill in faster and provide more cover, space them more closely. Dig the planting hole wide enough to hold the root system without crowding it. If the plants you purchased are rootbound, gently loosen the roots before setting the plant in the hole. Position the plant so that the soil level is the same as it was in the container. Add backfill soil to the planting hole and lightly firm the soil around the roots. Water the plant thoroughly and keep it moist until established. Mulch to maintain and conserve moisture.

CARE AND MAINTENANCE
Little bluestem is a native prairie grass that thrives in heat and in drier soils. Water periodically during dry, hot spells, but avoid overwatering. Cut back clumps in early spring before the new growth expands. It is much easier and less time-consuming to cut straight across the old blades than around and among new shoots. For larger mass plantings, use hedge or weed trimmers to cut the grasses back to within a few inches of the ground.

ADDITIONAL INFORMATION
Little bluestem is often used in soil conservation to reduce erosion and stabilize roadbanks. It is useful for dry, sunny slopes and will add interesting appeal with its reddish-bronze fall foliage and flower heads.

ADDITIONAL SPECIES, CULTIVARS, OR VARIETIES
Another species that is adapted to Colorado landscapes is *Andropogon gerardi*, big bluestem (4 to 6 ft.), with bluish foliage that turns to shades of bronze. It is easy to establish and combines well with tall perennial flowers.

Northern Sea Oats

Chasmanthium latifolium

Other Name: Wild Oats
Height: 2 to 3 ft.
Flowers: Green changing to copper-tan
Bloom Period: Midsummer
Zones: 5, 6

Light Requirement:

The wide green leaf blades of northern sea oats are held roughly perpendicular to its stems. It resembles a small 2- to 3-ft. bamboo and gives the garden a somewhat tropical appearance. It is native to the rich woodlands and riverbanks of the eastern United States, but is right at home in many parts of Colorado. Its native woodland origin makes it one of the few ornamental grasses that prefer partial shade. Wild oats is a warm-season grass and begins its growth cycle when warm temperatures return in spring. By early summer, the flower stalks arise; as they mature, their thread-like wire stems barely support their 1-in. flattened spikelets, creating a nodding habit. The flowers start out green and are gradually transformed to a coppery-tan color. This grass offers natural beauty and graceful movement in the land-scape as its dangling spikelets sway in even the slightest breeze. The effect is particularly striking when the copper-tan spikelets are backlit by sunshine. Northern sea oats offers diversity and accent in the shade garden.

WHEN TO PLANT

Plant northern sea oats in spring to allow for good root growth before the heat of summer. If you plant it later, be sure to provide adequate moisture for proper establishment.

WHERE TO PLANT

This ornamental grass prefers moist, well-drained soils in partially shady sites. The soil should be amended with compost prior to planting. Spread a 2- to 3-in. layer of compost in the planting area and mix uniformly to a depth of 6 in. or more. With adequate mois-ture, northern sea oats will grow in sun, but the foliage may be lighter green. Plant it in moisture-retentive or shady perennial beds, by streams, ponds, or water features, as an accent grass, and in woodland settings.

How to Plant

Space wild oats in the landscape $1^1/2$ to $2^1/2$ ft. apart. Dig the planting hole wide enough to hold the root system without crowding it. If the plants you purchased are rootbound, gently loosen the roots before setting the plant in the hole. Position the plant so that the soil level is the same as it was in the container. Add backfill soil to the planting hole and lightly firm the soil around the roots. Water the plant thoroughly and keep it moist until established. Mulch to maintain and conserve moisture.

Care and Maintenance

Northern sea oats prefers partial shade and the moist conditions associated with shade gardens. If it is located in full sun, be sure to provide regular watering during hot, dry periods. The clumps of grass should be cut back to the ground in spring as new growth begins to emerge; older clumps can be divided in the spring. Dig the clumps with a strong spading fork and split apart with a sharp shovel or knife. Remove the old woody portions and replant vigorous, healthy sections at the same level the plant was originally growing. Water regularly to allow the transplants to develop new roots.

Additional Information

Northern sea oats makes a wonderful cut ornamental grass for dried arrangements. The drooping spikelets create an elegant outline in a large vase. If the stems are cut while still young, they keep a greenish cast and later turn coppery-brown. Sea oats will self-sow. Volunteer plants can be transplanted to expand your planting or shared with friends.

Additional Species, Cultivars, or Varieties

There are no listings of cultivars.

Switchgrass

Panicum virgatum

Height: 4 to 6 ft. **Flowers:** Pinkish green **Bloom Period:** Midsummer **Zones:** 4, 5, 6	**Light Requirement:**

*S*witchgrass is native to the tallgrass prairie and is tolerant of various soil extremes. Full sun is essential to grow this plant, but it is not particular about soil or drainage. Since it is a warm-season grass, it starts out slow in spring and eventually forms clumps of leaves about 3 to 4 ft. tall. By late summer, a hazy cloud of flowers rises another foot or two over the foliage. The growth habit is subtle, but when the foliage begins to color, this grass takes on a fiery beauty of its own, especially when it is backlit with Colorado sunshine. The species varies in height, habit, and fall color, and it is best used for wildlife cover in prairie-style gardens or naturescapes. The early fall color—yellow, orange, and purplish-red—adds an incendiary glow to the landscape. In winter, the bleached leaves become straw colored and the sturdy stems provide a striking visual silhouette. Look for cultivated selections (cultivars) which offer compact growth habits, upright forms, and attractive autumn colors.

When to Plant

Plant switchgrass in spring so that the roots will have time to develop before the heat of summer. If planting in summer, mulch to maintain and conserve moisture.

Where to Plant

Switchgrass is very adaptable and will tolerate soil extremes. It grows most rapidly in full sun and moist, fertile soils, but it will also do well in dry sites. In extremely dry areas, however, the grass will be stunted. Use it in combination with a fall-blooming perennials like *Anemone* × *hybrida* 'Honorine Jobert', whose simple white flowers make a nice contrast. Russian sage is another good companion. Plant switchgrass in small groups or in large sweeps. It is well suited to meadow gardens and massing with prairie plants.

How to Plant

Space switchgrass 3 to 4 ft. apart. Dig the planting hole wide enough to accommodate the roots without crowding. Position the plant so that the soil level is the same as it was in the container. If the plants you purchased are rootbound, gently loosen the roots. Add backfill soil to the planting hole and lightly firm the soil around the roots. Water the plants thoroughly and keep them moist until established. Mulch to maintain and conserve moisture.

Care and Maintenance

Cut back switchgrass in late winter or early spring; it can be cut down to within 4 in. of the ground. If the plants begin to split open in late summer, the clump should be divided. Divide clumps in spring as the leaves begin to emerge. Lift them out of the ground and split apart with a sharp knife or pruning saw. Discard the spent center and replant vigorous, healthy sections taken from the outside of the clump. Replant at the same level at which they were growing. Keep moist until well established.

Additional Information

The delicate flowers and colorful foliage of switchgrass are excellent for drying. To create a prairie-style garden, use switchgrass with yellow coneflower, purple coneflower, blazing star, and Culver's root.

Additional Species, Cultivars, or Varieties

There are many cultivars on the market. One favorite is 'Rotstralbusch' (4 ft.). It has burgundy foliage in late summer. 'Strictum' (4 to 5 ft.) grows more upright and has orange to purplish red fall color. 'Haense Herms' (4 to 4$^{1}/_{2}$ ft.) has fiery fall color and a compact growth habit. 'Heavy Metal' (4 to 5 ft.) is upright with steel-blue foliage. It goes well with pale-pink anemones and the lavender-blue dwarf aster, 'Professor Kippenburg'. 'Cloud Nine' (6 to 8 ft.) makes a nice accent grass.

CHAPTER EIGHT

Perennials

*G*ROWING PERENNIALS IN THE COLORADO LANDSCAPE is a pleasure. With some thoughtful planning, a perennial garden can provide glowing patterns of color and beauty from early spring to late autumn. Unlike annual flowers, which must be replaced each year, most perennials will grow and bloom in the same location year after year (that is, unless your perennial acts like a "perannual" and refuses to survive our cold winters and fluctuating climatic conditions).

A true hardy perennial is a plant that does not die after a season's growth, but renews itself every year. In this chapter you will be introduced to a group of perennials that are "herbaceous," which means that their stems are green and soft and will die back in the fall; the crown and roots will begin growth again in the spring. Signs of life all over the perennial garden will awaken your spirits as little green shoots and buds emerge from the earth. There are some perennials that may remain evergreen all year long. Some, like the hellebores, will brave the cold days of winter with shows of unique blooms.

Perennials are a hardy bunch and will grow in a wide range of conditions. It's a good thing that perennials are so adaptive, because we have quite diverse conditions, from the High Plains to the High Country. We are blessed with quality sunshine and low humidity in our state, and we can grow perennials without the high incidence of plant diseases that is common in the more humid parts of the country.

The plants I've chosen for this chapter have proved to be dependable plants in Colorado gardens. They are generally long-lived and adapt to our various soil types. They suffer few, if any, insect pests and diseases when they are planted in the right location and properly maintained. As is true of all plants, the secret to growing perennials successfully is having the right soil for the right plant. Soil preparation is especially important for perennials since they are meant to remain in one location for many years. They may outlive

Chapter Eight

the gardener who plants them! Before planting, get to know a little about each plant and amend the soil as needed.

SELECTING PERENNIALS

When choosing perennials for your landscape, consider what they will look like when they're not blooming. Many bloom for a week or a few weeks, but their foliage can be an important element in the garden all season long. Hostas, for example, are grown more for their leaves than for their flowers. You are not limited to growing perennials in sunny borders, since there are many perennials that will thrive in partial to full shade. With so many new and interesting plants coming into our region all the time, it's tempting to try to grow one of each. Certain qualities can help you determine which ones will be hardy and reliable in your garden. If you're looking for plants that require the least amount of maintenance, be sure to choose varieties that don't require staking, or site the plants so that other plants will help support them.

Some of us grow perennials for sheer pleasure, and we don't really care about the low maintenance. We're looking for plants that will offer a wide range of diversity and opportunities for experimentation. It's fun, and in many ways relaxing, to embark on the adventure of growing the more unusual varieties—that is, if the pocket gophers don't get them first!

Either way you go with growing perennials, make your garden a reflection of your personality. Grow what you like, experiment, and follow the 4-H motto: "Learn by doing."

We don't have a staff of gardeners who maintain our perennials. The perennials in Colorado's Green Thumb garden pretty much take care of themselves. When and if they need our attention, we make it a family affair. Everyone takes part in the mulching, the fertilizing, and if we remember, the dividing, the weeding, and the soil cultivation. If we can grow perennials and still enjoy the other diversions Colorado has to offer, you can too!

Artemisia

Artemisia ludoviciana

Height: 2 to 3 ft.
Flowers: Whitish flower heads (but grown primarily for its silvery foliage)
Zones: 4, 5, 6

Light Requirement:

With distinctive silver foliage that calms bright colors, this perennial is a favorite in the Green Thumb garden. Artemisia provides textural interest, and its spreading habit creates a silver backdrop that helps tie other plantings together. Two popular cultivars, 'Silver Queen' and 'Silver King', are commonly available. 'Silver King' grows to about 3 ft. tall and has slender stems with narrow, fine-textured silver leaves. 'Silver Queen' grows to 2 ft. tall and has wider leaves with jagged edges. These plants can withstand drought and they grow well in light, sandy soils. In heavier clay soils, their growth is somewhat more controlled; it is easy to keep them in check by digging out unwanted portions each spring. If you have room, plant them in drifts as part of a large, sweeping display. Artemisias make good companion plants for yellow yarrow and violet-blue salvia.

WHEN TO PLANT

Artemisias are available as container-grown plants and can be planted from spring through early fall.

WHERE TO PLANT

Locate artemisias in full sun for the best growth and display. They are tolerant of a wide variety of soil types, but will spread more rapidly in sandy loam soils. Plant in informal areas where artemisia's spreading growth habit will be welcome.

HOW TO PLANT

Plant 2 to 3 ft. apart to allow for artemisia's spreading growth habit. Dig the planting hole twice as wide as the container in which the plant was growing. Position the plant so that the soil level is the same as it was in the container. Fill the planting hole about halfway with soil, gently firm, and water well. After the water has soaked in, add more soil to completely fill the hole. Water regularly until the plants are established.

CARE AND MAINTENANCE

Artemisias are water-thrifty plants and should not be overwatered or overfertilized. Doing so will make the plants grow soft and cause them to sprawl. They do quite well without additional plant fertilizer. It's a good idea to evaluate the plantings each spring and to tidy up the garden by removing unwanted sections. Underground roots will spread several feet from the main plant, so you will need to cut down with a sharp spade to sever all roots. Pull and remove plants. As the older clumps begin to die out in the center, dig them up and replant with vigorous sections from the outside edges.

ADDITIONAL INFORMATION

If you want to control the spread of the plant, grow it in a bottomless 5-gallon bucket (much as mint is often grown) to prevent it from spreading its underground root system. Artemisia is good for cutting and drying. It can be used as filler for arrangements and in herbal wreaths.

ADDITIONAL SPECIES, CULTIVARS, OR VARIETIES

Common Wormwood, *Artemisia absinthium,* is an upright, well-branched subshrub whose stems and leaves are coated with silky hairs. 'Lambrook Silver' is one of the best silver fern-like plants for the perennial garden and is readily available. *Artemisia schmidtiana* 'Silver Mound' grows into a rounded mound of silvery silky-haired foliage about 8 to 10 in. tall. It is best grown in lean soil as it may split open in soils that are too rich. Cut it back hard to force new growth.

Blanket Flower

Gaillardia × *grandiflora*

Height: 2 to 3 ft.
Flowers: Red and yellow
Bloom Period: Summer to fall
Zones: 4, 5, 6

Light Requirement:

*Y*our summer garden will never be boring if you plant blanket
flowers. The bright, dazzling, daisy-like flowers offer a mixture
of red and yellow that is sure to generate summer cheer. *Gaillardia*
is a hardy soul that can really stand up to the heat and dryness of
Colorado summers. Cutting back leggy growth and spent flowers
enables the plants to provide another, later display of blooms. In
Colorado's heavy clay soils, blanket flower is a short-lived perennial,
but it reseeds itself so freely that new plants invariably grow to replace
those that don't make it through the winter. Blanket flowers make
good cut flowers. They are excellent when planted in a meadow
garden and make good border plantings.

WHEN TO PLANT
Plant in spring through fall. Seedlings started indoors in late
winter should be ready to transplant into the garden in 8 weeks.
Container-grown plants are readily available at local garden stores.
Root cuttings can be taken from older plants in early spring and
transplanted.

WHERE TO PLANT
For best growth and flowering, plant blanket flowers in a sunny
location. Soils should be well drained. In hard, compact clay soil,
plants tend to be short-lived perennials. Sandy soils yield compact
plants with lots of blooms. *Gaillardia* is a great border plant and will
provide near-constant bloom from early summer to fall.

HOW TO PLANT
Dig the planting hole twice as wide as the spread of the root system,
or twice the width of the container in which the plant was growing.
Position the plant so that the soil level is the same as it was in the
container. Fill the planting hole about halfway up with soil, gently

firm, then water-in well. After the water has soaked in, add more soil to completely fill the hole. Water regularly until the plants are established.

CARE AND MAINTENANCE

Once blanket flowers are established, they need very little care. They are tough, and they thrive in heat. An annual application of 5-10-5 fertilizer in spring will give the plants an early boost of energy for the flowers they will produce later in the season. Deadhead spent flowers and the plants will produce flowers well into autumn.

ADDITIONAL INFORMATION

Gaillardia is a self-sowing plant that distributes seed freely. These seed-grown plants are variable, but they do produce some interesting color combinations. Cultivars remain true only when asexually propagated, as when you take root cuttings or divide the plants in spring.

ADDITIONAL SPECIES, CULTIVARS, OR VARIETIES

There are several cultivars available. One of the most popular is 'Goblin', a compact plant (12 in.) that produces large, dark-red flowers with wide, irregular, yellow borders. 'Burgundy' grows 2 to 3 ft. tall and has large 3-in. wine-red flowers. A dwarf cultivar is 'Baby Cole', which grows 6 to 8 in. tall and sports red flowers with yellow tips. If you're looking for a sprawling growth habit for a meadow garden, *Gaillardia aristata* will work quite nicely. It produces colorful 3- to 4-in. yellow flowers that are purple at the base. This species grows 2 to 3 ft. tall and is exceptionally drought tolerant.

Bleeding Heart

Dicentra spectabilis

Height: 2 to 3 ft.
Flowers: Pink-and-white, white
Bloom Period: Mid-spring through June
Zones: 3, 4, 5, 6

Light Requirement:

The bleeding heart is one of our favorite old-fashioned perennials that can be used in the shade garden or a naturalized woodland setting. Its graceful arching growth habit and handsome, fern-like leaves add a special touch to the perennial border. Its distinctive heart-shaped flowers hang individually from stalks that are 6 or more in. long. The flowers' outer petals are rose-red, while the inner petals are white. Cultivars that produce all-white flowers are also available. These long-lived plants thrive when a few simple requirements are met: soil enriched with humus, moist conditions, and partial shade. Plant bleeding heart with shade-loving ferns, astilbe, or hosta to make up for its lack of foliage in late summer.

WHEN TO PLANT

Container-grown plants can be planted from spring through early fall. Bare-root plants should be planted in early spring to allow for good establishment before the heat of summer.

WHERE TO PLANT

Choose a partially shaded location where the soil has been enriched with compost. Soil should be well drained. Avoid locations that are hot, dry, or windy. Bleeding heart will tolerate some sun as long as you provide adequate moisture. Too much sun, however, will shorten the blooming season and make the foliage die back prematurely.

HOW TO PLANT

Plant bleeding heart plants 18 to 24 in. apart. Dig the planting hole twice as wide as the container in which the plant was growing, or wide enough to accommodate bare roots without cramping them. Position the plant so that the soil level is the same as it was in the container. Fill the planting hole about halfway up with soil and water well. After the water has soaked in, add more soil to complete the planting. Water regularly until the plants are established. Apply a mulch to maintain even moisture and conserve water.

CARE AND MAINTENANCE

Bleeding hearts grow best in evenly moist soil with relatively high organic content. Use organic mulches to maintain soil moisture; you may need to add humus over the years as the mulches break down. A winter mulch protects plants at higher elevations from frost heave. Older plants can be divided to yield more plants in early spring. Lift the clump before the stems elongate, as they are quite brittle and easy to break. Transplant to prepared soil and water-in well.

ADDITIONAL INFORMATION

Bleeding hearts tend to die back in summer, leaving a gap in the perennial garden. You can interplant other shade-loving plants around bleeding heart to overcome this situation. Use ferns, hostas, astilbe, bigroot geraniums, forget-me-nots, and tulips.

ADDITIONAL SPECIES, CULTIVARS, OR VARIETIES

There is a white-flowering cultivar called 'Alba' that is often called "Lady-in-the-bath" due to the flower's appearance when it is held upside-down. Combine it with the green-yellow of cushion spurge for a dramatic effect. The fringed bleeding heart, *Dicentra eximia*, has a more compact growth habit (10 to 18 in.) and produces blue-gray mounds of finely dissected leaves. Flowers are pink or white with an elongated heart shape. The foliage of this plant does not go dormant. Fringed bleeding heart is not as showy or as tall as the common bleeding heart, but it has a longer blooming period, making it desirable in the shady or woodland garden. A few bleeding heart hybrids are available; these include 'Luxuriant' and 'Bountiful', both with carmine-red blossoms, and 'Zestful', with rosy-pink flowers. Most hybrids are more tolerant of sunny locations.

Bloody Cranesbill

Geranium sanguineum

Height: 10 to 12 in.
Flowers: Magenta, reddish purple, white
Bloom Period: Late spring through summer
Zones: 2, 3, 4, 5, 6

Light Requirement:

*B*loody cranesbill, a hardy geranium, has stunning bright magenta flowers that glow like embers in the perennial garden. The deeply lobed foliage makes this plant attractive even when not in bloom. Low mounds of spreading foliage add texture to the garden; leaves mature to a darker red in the fall. Bloody cranesbill is a good filler plant for other perennials, including Rocky Mountain columbine, the yellow-green blooms of lady's mantle, and the blues of Siberian iris. Its weaving growth habit makes it an effective groundcover; it also makes an excellent accent plant around taller perennials. Like other hardy geraniums, bloody cranesbill is easy to grow.

WHEN TO PLANT
Plant in spring to early summer. Bloody cranesbill can be planted later in the season if adequate moisture is provided during hot weather.

WHERE TO PLANT
Cranesbill thrives best in moist, well-drained soils. Improve soil conditions before planting by adding a moisture-retentive compost. Full sun with adequate moisture is ideal, but this perennial will tolerate partial shade. Its growth will be more open in a shady environment. Bloody cranesbill's fleshy root system makes it drought tolerant. Use this plant as a groundcover or for edging, and in rock gardens, cottage gardens, and perennial beds.

HOW TO PLANT
Space plants 1¹/₂ to 2 ft. apart. Dig the planting hole twice as wide as the container in which the plant was growing. Position the plant so that the soil level is the same as it was in the container. Fill the planting hole halfway with soil and water well. After the water has soaked in, add more soil to complete the planting. Water regularly until the plants are established.

CARE AND MAINTENANCE

Bloody cranesbill is easy to grow. Be sure to provide adequate water in the heat of summer or during drought conditions. If plants are deadheaded after the flowers fade, additional blooms will develop in late summer. This hardy geranium rarely needs division, but in tight situations, lifting a crowded plant in spring and dividing it will curtail its spread. Separate clumps into smaller sections and replant. Add a layer of mulch to maintain and conserve moisture.

ADDITIONAL INFORMATION

Cranesbills get their name from the long, narrow fruit capsule that splits open when dry. Seeds are dispersed far and wide. If the plant becomes too scraggly and shabby after flowering, cut it back to promote a new flush of growth.

ADDITIONAL SPECIES, CULTIVARS, OR VARIETIES

There are many species of cranesbill that deserve a place in the perennial border. Most are of low to medium height, but there are tall varieties available, such as *Geranium psilostemon* (4 ft.), which has tall, brilliant magenta flowers that can be staked or allowed to weave in and out of other plants. *G. sanguineum* var. *striatum* or *lancastriense* has a low-growing habit and fern-like foliage. Its pale-pink flowers are etched with darker-rose veins. Use this hardy geranium as a groundcover or edging plant around shrubs or roses. 'Album' produces pure-white flowers and has a loose growth habit. *Geranium pratense* 'Plenum Violaceum' has deeply divided leaves and perfect double, deep-violet flowers tinged with purple. It grows 2 to 3 ft. tall and makes an excellent specimen plant. With its compact growth habit, *Geranium wallichianum* 'Buxton's Blue' (12 in.) is a superior species for groundcover use. It blooms profusely with China-blue flowers that have large white centers.

Butterfly Weed

Asclepias tuberosa

Height: 18 in. to 2 ft.
Flowers: Orange
Bloom Period: Summer through August
Zones: 4, 5, 6

Light Requirement:

When butterfly weed makes its display in summer, the splash of bright orange lights up the perennial garden. Once established, butterfly weed is easy to care for, although it make take a season or two for it to bloom freely. Butterfly weed's deep taproot makes it sensitive to disturbance, so handle the plant carefully. Because it emerges late in spring, extra effort must be made not to disturb the area in which butterfly weed is growing. The name of this plant comes from its attractiveness to butterflies. When in bloom, it draws them in profusion. Although a milkweed, butterfly weed does not produce a milky sap. The orange flowers grow in clusters on upright stems with handsome linear leaves. Later in the season, tapered seedpods (4 to 6 in.) appear and open to release typical milkweed seeds with their fun, fluffy parachutes. Butterfly weed is great when interplanted with lavenders, with the rosy-purple spires of verbena, or with ornamental grasses. One plant will certainly create an eye-catching focal point.

WHEN TO PLANT

Plant butterfly weed in spring through early fall. These plants are temperamental about their roots, so handle them carefully to prevent transplant shock and slow establishment. Planting container-grown stock is preferred to dividing old clumps.

WHERE TO PLANT

Butterfly weed should be planted in full sun. Soil should be well drained with lean-to-average fertility. A sandy loam is ideal, but clay soils are fine if drainage is good. These plants are very drought tolerant and thrive in a meadow garden or naturescape.

HOW TO PLANT

Space plants 1 1/2 to 2 ft. apart. Dig the planting hole at least twice as wide as the container in which the plant was growing. Position the plant so that the soil level is the same as it was in the container. Be extra careful with the brittle tuberous roots. Fill the planting hole halfway with soil and water well. Add more soil after the water has soaked in to complete the planting. Water regularly as the soil dries out until the plants are well established.

Care and Maintenance
Once established, butterfly weed needs very little care. As previously mentioned, the deep tuberous roots resent disturbance, so allow the plants to develop into mature clumps for several years. Division is seldom needed. Plants will self-sow if seedheads are allowed to disperse. Deadheading will help to encourage an additional flush of blooms later in the season.

Additional Information
Because butterfly weed emerges in late spring, it is easy to damage the plant when weeding or overplanting annuals earlier in the season. Mark the plant with a label or leave 6 in. of stem when cutting it back to help you remember its location. Stem or root cuttings are sometimes successful. Cautiously dig the whole root, being careful not to slice through it. Split the clump into sections with a sharp knife, ensuring that each piece contains at least one bud. Plant buds 1 in. below the soil surface and keep the soil moist. It will take several years for transplants to reach their full potential.

Additional Species, Cultivars, or Varieties
Asclepias incarnata has bright rose-pink flowers and prefers heavier, wet soils. It grows to 4 ft. tall. A white-flowering selection, 'Ice Ballet', makes an unusual addition to the garden. The 'Gay Butterflies' strain includes plants with flowers of red, pink, or yellow. These all make fine cut flowers. The ornamental seedheads can be used in dried arrangements.

Chiming Bells

Mertensia ciliata

Other Name: Mountain Bluebell	**Light Requirement:**
Height: 12 to 24 in.	
Flowers: Blue	
Bloom Period: Late spring to summer	
Zones: 3, 4, 5	

*I*f you've never seen our native mountain chiming bells before, get one glimpse of the pinkish-blue nodding clusters opening to dainty blue flowers and you will want to include this perennial in your shade garden. These mountain bluebells spring up from the forest floor at subalpine and montane zones in early spring to form bluish green clumps of foliage. Taller stems emerge bearing smaller leaves and a hanging cluster of pink buds at the end that open to light blue. These sweet blue nodding flowers are a welcome addition to the shade or woodland garden. Blossoms will remain attractive for several weeks, taking on a pinkish blush as they fade. If you live in an older neighborhood with lots of shade trees, plant chiming bluebells beneath deciduous trees where they will receive sun at the beginning of the season and shade after the trees leaf out. As is true of many of our native forest plants, mountain bluebells thrive in a shady site with well-drained, but moist and fertile soils. Take a lesson from the forest floor, where you will find these plants growing happily amid decaying leaves and other organic materials in Colorado's high country. Provide those conditions in your shade garden, and mountain bluebell will thrive and spread. *Mertensia virginica*, Virginia bluebell, is more widely grown in perennial gardens, but our native species is well worth the effort.

WHEN TO PLANT
The best time to plant mountain bluebells is as soon as the soil can be worked in early spring. Avoid the heat of summer as this perennial takes a rest period when the weather gets dry and hot. Keeping the soil moist will delay summer dieback.

WHERE TO PLANT
Mountain bluebells prefer shade to part shade in moist, well-drained soil. The soil needs to be rich in humus, like the forest floor. If this

does not describe the area where you want to plant your bluebells, amend the soil with compost or leaf mold. Combine these plants with other shade-loving perennials such as bleeding heart, bloodroot, hosta, bergenia, and woodland ferns.

How to Plant
Make sure the soil has been prepared in advance with a generous supply of organic matter such as well-rotted manure, compost, or leaf mold. A combination of these amendments will simulate natural growing conditions. Add a volume equal to 30 to 40 percent of the soil in a new planting site. Work the organic materials deeply and uniformly into the planting area. Space plants 15 to 18 in. apart. Dig the planting hole at the same depth as the container in which the plant was growing previously. Add backfill soil around the roots, gently firm with your hands, and water slowly. Apply a mulch of shredded leaves or shredded wood chips to maintain uniform moisture and to discourage weed seed germination.

Care and Maintenance
Try to mimic the native habitat where mountain bluebells thrive; they perform best in moist conditions. Keep the plants mulched to maintain even moisture. Mulch with chopped leaves; these will eventually break down and release nutrients that contribute to healthy plant growth. If you need to rejuvenate an older plant that has lost vigor, dig the clump as the foliage dies down in late summer and divide into sections. Transplant divisions at the same level the plant was growing, water-in well, and mulch.

Additional Information
The foliage of bluebells must remain on the plant after flowering. It is when the foliage turns yellow and tan that the plant is storing nutrients.

Additional Species, Cultivars, or Varieties
Mertensia virginica (Virginia bluebells) produces nodding clusters of fragrant, trumpet-shaped flowers (1 in.) that are pink when in bud, then open to a porcelain blue. *M. sibirica* has deeper-blue flowers.

Coneflower

Rudbeckia spp.

Height: 2 to 3 ft.	**Light Requirement:**
Flowers: Orange-yellow	
Bloom Period: Mid- to late summer	
Zones: 3, 4, 5, 6	

The yellow-and-orange daisies and chocolate brown centers of *Rudbeckia* provide flamboyant color in the perennial garden from summer till frost. These easy-care perennials are long-lived if planted in well-drained soils. The familiar black-eyed Susan, *R. hirta*, is a short-lived perennial, but there are many other cultivars available that bloom for weeks and last for years. *Rudbeckia fulgida* var. *sullivantii* 'Goldsturm' is one of the most popular coneflowers. From midsummer until frost, it produces masses of 2- to 3-in. yellow-orange flowers with dark centers over coarse, deep-green foliage. When in full bloom, it offers a sunny meadow feeling to the landscape. Flowers continue to proliferate for 2 to 3 months. The brown center cones remain attractive even into the winter. Gardeners often combine 'Goldsturm' with *Sedum* × 'Autumn Joy' and ornamental grasses; they do this so often, in fact, that it is becoming a cliché. Try combining coneflowers with blue asters softened by the wispy stems of switch grass.

WHEN TO PLANT

Plant container-grown rudbeckia in spring through early fall. To ensure good plant establishment, provide ample water if planting in the heat of summer.

WHERE TO PLANT

Rudbeckia are at their best in open, sunny locations. They prefer soil of average fertility; too rich a soil results in soft, floppy growth. Good drainage is essential and though the plants are tolerant of heat, they need water during extended dry periods.

HOW TO PLANT

Space rudbeckia 18 in. to 2 ft. apart. Dig the planting hole twice as wide as the container and position the plant so that the soil level is the same as it was in the container. Fill in with soil around the root system about halfway up, gently firm, and water-in well. After the water has soaked in, add more soil to completely fill the hole. Water regularly until the plants are established.

CARE AND MAINTENANCE
Keep rudbeckia well watered during hot, dry spells. While additional fertilizer is not necessary, a light application of 5/10/5 in spring will give the plants a boost. Most are vigorous growers, and clumps can be divided every 3 to 4 years as the centers die out. Lift the old clumps and use compost or rotted manure to amend the soil in which the plants were growing. Separate the clumps with a sharp knife and discard the spent center sections. Replant the new divisions at the same level they were growing and water in well. New transplants will usually bloom the first season.

ADDITIONAL INFORMATION
Blooming can be extended by regular deadheading of the spent flowers, although the raised brown cones in the centers of the flowers do provide winter interest.

ADDITIONAL SPECIES, CULTIVARS, OR VARIETIES
There are many other garden-worthy rudbeckias to add to your perennial garden. One of our favorites in the Green Thumb garden is *Rudbeckia laciniata*, cutleaf coneflower, with its deeply cut, dark-green leaves. The smooth, branched stems support large flower heads with raised olive-green disks and drooping, golden-yellow 1- to 2-in. rays.

Coral Bells

Heuchera sanguinea

Height: 1 to 2 ft.	**Light Requirement:**
Flowers: Red, pink	
Bloom Period: June through August	
Zones: 3, 4, 5, 6	

Sprays of dainty bell-shaped flowers held high above handsome foliage make coral bells a beautiful addition to the shade garden. The foliage—dark green with scalloped, lobed, or wavy edges—remains evergreen for most of the year. In early June, slender stalks support a profusion of flowers that form a cloud of brilliant red. Coral bells will invite hummingbirds to your garden as the hovering jewels migrate from the high country. They make good cut flowers, too. Plant drifts of coral bells with columbine and hardy geraniums. Coral bells are old-fashioned favorites that many of us remember from our parents' and grandparents' gardens.

WHEN TO PLANT

Plant coral bells in spring or late summer. Their roots are shallow and subject to frost heaving in winter. Spring planting will allow enough time for plants to develop a strong root system.

WHERE TO PLANT

Coral bells will grow in full sun or partial shade. They will flower more abundantly in sun, though they will need ample moisture. They prefer moist, well-drained soils that have been enriched with moisture-retentive compost. Avoid locations that are heat traps and poorly drained. Plant in perennial beds or drifts in the lightly shaded woodland garden. They are effective for edging pathways and flower beds.

HOW TO PLANT

Plant coral bells 12 to 15 in. apart. Dig the planting hole twice as wide as the container or root system. Position the plant so that the soil level is the same as it was in the container or at the same depth the plants were originally growing. Fill in with soil around the roots about halfway, gently firm the soil, and water well. After the water has soaked in, finish filling in the hole with soil. Water regularly as the soil dries out. Mulch to conserve water and to keep the soil cooler.

CARE AND MAINTENANCE

Coral bells need additional water during dry spells to perform at their best. Deadheading the spent flowers will ensure continued bloom. Let the leaves remain in the autumn, as this plant will usually stay evergreen all winter. As plants become old (4 to 5 years), flowering may diminish and the plants will develop woody crowns. This is the signal to divide. Dig up the old clumps and gently pull them apart. Discard the old, woody portions and replant the young, vigorous pieces. Each new section should have a rosette of foliage, woody roots, and healthy fibrous roots. Replant the piece to the level of the foliage, gently firm the soil, and water-in well. Augment the soil with additional compost before replanting.

ADDITIONAL INFORMATION

Coral bells are shallow-rooted and can be damaged by alternate freezing and thawing during the winter. These conditions will lift the plants out of the ground (called "heaving") and expose the roots to desiccation and dehydration. A winter mulch of evergreen boughs or pine needles can be applied after the ground freezes to prevent heaving; a thick cover of snow also provides excellent insulation.

ADDITIONAL SPECIES, CULTIVARS, OR VARIETIES

There are several cultivars of coral bells that are hybrids of *H. sanguinea*, *H. micrantha*, and *H. americana*. The Bressingham hybrids (20 in.) are mixed colors in pink, red, coral and white. *Heuchera micrantha* var. *diversifolia* 'Palace Purple' has maple-like leaves that are bronze-red above and beet red beneath. It makes a superior groundcover in a lightly shaded garden.

Daylily

Hemerocallis hybrids

Height: 12 to 48 in.	**Light Requirement:**
Flowers: Orange, yellow, red, pink, lavender	
Bloom Period: Early to late summer	
Zones: 3, 4, 5, 6	

*D*aylilies are among the most popular easy-to-grow perennials throughout the nation. Such popularity has triggered both amateur and professional breeders to develop thousands of varieties from which to choose. Even when planted in Colorado's alkaline clay soils, daylilies will adapt and thrive. They grow so rapidly and propagate so easily that within a few years the thick foliage will be crowding out any competing weeds. A display of daylilies is as close as you will ever come to a "plant-it-and-forget-it" garden. The only frustration connected with growing daylilies is choosing which varieties to grow. The strong flower stalks, called "scapes," produce several flowers that bloom for only 24 hours, a trait that Carolus Linnaeus took into account when he named this genus *Hemerocallis* (translated from Greek, it means "beautiful for a day"). The plant will produce many flowers over a period of several weeks. Daylilies are attractive when teamed with finer textured plants such as Russian sage and 'Moonbeam' coreopsis.

WHEN TO PLANT
Daylilies can be planted any time from spring through fall. Container-grown plants are readily available, and bare-root plants are offered by many mail-order nurseries. If planting in hot weather, just be sure to provide ample water.

WHERE TO PLANT
For the best flowering, plant daylilies in full sun to light shade. Intense afternoon sun can cause "scorching" of the flowers. The ideal soil is well drained and has average fertility. Loosen the soil in the areas that are to be planted and add a moisture-retentive compost. Daylilies are an attractive foil for other perennials. Plant them in drifts of three or more. On steep or erosion-prone areas of the landscape, the tough root system of daylilies will effectively hold the soil in place.

HOW TO PLANT

Space daylilies 2 to 3 ft. apart. Dig the planting hole twice as wide as the root system and position the plant so the soil level is the same as it was in the container. Bare-root plants should be set no deeper than 1 to 1^1/$_2$ in. below the soil surface. An all-purpose 5-10-5 or 10-10-10 fertilizer can be worked into the soil at the time of planting. Fill in with soil around the roots about halfway up, firm gently, and water-in well. Add more soil to completely fill in the hole. Water regularly until plants are well established. Mulch with more compost or shredded cedar to conserve moisture.

CARE AND MAINTENANCE

Daylilies are tough, long-lived plants that can prosper even if neglected. To maintain healthy foliage and encourage flowering, supply the plants with plenty of water during dry spells. A single application of slow-release fertilizer in spring will carry the plants through the growing season. In about 3 to 5 years, a daylily clump can become so overcrowded that it produces fewer flowers. This is the time to rejuvenate the plant. Dig an overgrown plant with a spading fork and shake the soil off the clump. Separate the clump into smaller sections. Each division should have a stem with at least two fans and plenty of healthy roots. Replant in prepared garden soil and water-in well. Deadhead old flowers to keep the plants neat.

ADDITIONAL INFORMATION

There are several pests and diseases that may attack daylilies. Crown rot can cause the plant to turn into mush. Remove infected plants to prevent spread of the disease. Be on the watch for aphids, mites, and slugs. Early detection and control will prevent severe damage.

ADDITIONAL SPECIES, CULTIVARS, OR VARIETIES

There are so many cultivars of daylilies it is hard to make specific recommendations. Take into consideration color, flower size, stem height, bloom times, and the amount of money you want to invest. If you select early, mid-season, and late cultivars, your flowering season may last for several months. 'Stella de Oro', 'Condilla', 'Happy Returns', 'Hyperion', 'Jason Salter', and 'Jolyene Nichole' are a few excellent choices.

False Indigo

Baptisia australis

Height: 3 to 4 ft.
Flowers: Blue-violet, white
Bloom Period: Summer
Zones: 3, 4, 5, 6

Light Requirement:

*B*lue false indigo, with its tall spires of pea-like blue-violet flowers, adds grace to the late-spring and summer garden. This multi-talented plant has mounds of soft, gray-green foliage in addition to its gorgeous flowers. When used in the landscape, it is a fine addition to a flower border, native plantings, meadow gardens, and the transitional areas between a perennial bed and open space. Allow plenty of space for this plant to grow and develop. It grows thick, deep roots; as the plant matures, large clumps, up to 3 ft. tall and equally as wide, may appear. Stems grow rapidly in spring; in June, the intense blue flowers open on tall stalks. For the remainder of the season, the three-lobed clover-like leaves add a soft textural form to the garden. The inflated, almost blackish-purple seedpods can be used in dried arrangements. Use false indigo for the back of a flower bed, as its blue-green foliage remains attractive throughout the growing season. Plant drifts of hybrid anemones and red switch grass for late-season interest.

WHEN TO PLANT

Plant false indigo in spring through early fall. Newly planted transplants should be protected with a winter mulch for the first year. As is true of other members of the pea family, baptisia doesn't like root disturbance.

WHERE TO PLANT

Choose sites that receive full sun and have moist, well-drained soil; average to fertile soil will do. In compacted soils, loosen and work in a moisture-retentive organic amendment such as compost or well-aged manure. Too much shade will cause the plants to grow open and flop over. Allow for plenty of room. Use as a backdrop for a perennial flower garden or in transition areas.

How to Plant

Space false indigo 3 to 4 ft. apart. Dig the planting hole twice as wide as the container. Position the plant so that the soil level is the same as it was in the container. Fill in with soil around the root system about halfway up, firm gently, and water-in well. After the water has soaked in, add more soil to completely fill the hole. Water regularly until the plants are established.

Care and Maintenance

Though false indigo is a bit slow to start, it will live a long time and does not become invasive. It requires little care once established and is a water-thrifty perennial. The deep taproot of this species makes it a poor candidate to transplant. If it should need dividing, do so in early spring before growth begins. Keep at least 3 eyes per plant division and cut the roots back to 4 in. Replant at the same depth the plants were originally growing and water-in well.

Additional Information

Be patient after planting false indigo. It will take several years for the plant to reach maturity, but it is worth the wait. The plant is toxic, so avoid planting it where grazing animals might get to it.

Additional Species, Cultivars, or Varieties

Baptisia alba, white false indigo (2 to 3 ft.), has creamy-white pealike flowers on dark-green stems, and handsome blue-gray foliage. *Baptisia lactea* (3 to 5 ft.), also called white or prairie false indigo, has a shrubby growth habit and produces white flowers tinged with purple.

False Spirea

Astilbe × arendsii

Other Name: Astilbe **Height:** 1¹/₂ to 4 ft. **Flowers:** White, red, pink **Bloom Period:** Late spring to summer **Zones:** 4, 5, 6	**Light Requirement:**

A stilbe is highly regarded for use in the shade garden. It has excellent green foliage and showy, feathery sprays of flowers held high above its leaves. The plants do best in shade and moist soils; they can be grown in part sun and dry soil, though the plants may bake and leaves may scorch. Just be prepared to provide adequate moisture and use mulches in more exposed sites. Astilbe's shiny leaves persist throughout the growing season; it is quite handsome in a woodland garden setting when other plants are dormant. Its clump-forming habit makes this perennial a great choice for formal flower gardens, borders, and informal settings. Dramatic effects can be achieved when astilbes are planted in large sweeps; specimen plants can also be very attractive.

WHEN TO PLANT

The best time to plant is in early spring so the root system will become established before summer's heat. Container-grown plants are readily available, and bare-root plants can be obtained through various mail-order sources.

WHERE TO PLANT

Astilbes prefer a humus-enriched soil with plentiful moisture in part-shade locations. They can tolerate sun, but only if constant moisture is available. Some ideal locations for this showy shade-loving perennial are north and northeast exposures, woodland gardens, and near water gardens.

HOW TO PLANT

Plant astilbes 1¹/₂ to 2 ft. apart. Dig the planting hole twice as wide as the container or root system. Place the plant in the hole so that the soil level is the same as it was in the container. Fill in with soil around the roots about halfway up, firm gently, and water well. After the water has soaked in, add more soil to complete the planting. Water regularly to allow for good plant establishment. A layer of organic mulch will conserve and maintain uniform soil moisture.

CARE AND MAINTENANCE

The secret to success in growing astilbes is to provide a deep, humus-rich soil that drains well but never gets bone dry. Apply a complete all-purpose fertilizer such as 5-10-5 or 10-10-10 in early spring to help the plants get started. A summer mulch of shredded cedar or compost will keep the soil temperature cool and provide moisture that is more even. During dry spells, it is important to water the plants regularly to prevent wilt and scorch. Once the plants have finished flowering, you can deadhead the spent flower plumes or leave them for fall and winter interest. As growth resumes in the spring, old flower stalks can be removed.

ADDITIONAL INFORMATION

After 3 to 5 years, astilbes may start to lose vigor; they will benefit from division. Lift and divide the older plants in spring as soon as you see the foliage emerge. Clumps can be split apart with a sharp knife. Leave 3 to 5 "eyes" in each division and replant so that the eyes are about 1/2 inch below the soil. Be sure to enrich the soil with compost to hold moisture and increase fertility. Replant new divisions, water-in well, and apply a mulch to keep them moist.

ADDITIONAL SPECIES, CULTIVARS, OR VARIETIES

There are many cultivars of astilbe, and you can find them in various nursery catalogs. 'Avalanche' and 'Bridal Veil' bloom midseason and have white flowers. 'Fanal' is a nice red that blooms early and has deep-red young leaves. 'Cattleya' has rosy-pink blooms. To extend the blooming season, try *Astilbe chinensis* 'Pumila'; it is more drought-tolerant and has a low growth habit that makes it good for a dry shade garden. The deep magenta-pink flowers appear later in summer.

Gayfeather

Liatris spicata

Other Name: Blazing Star
Height: 2 to 4 ft.
Flowers: Purple, rosy-purple
Bloom Period: Early to late summer
Zones: 4, 5, 6

Light Requirement:

iatris is also known as "blazing star." It is truly spectacular, with long, plump spikes of rosy-purple flowers above handsome narrow foliage. You may often see it used in florist's arrangements, but it is more at home on the prairie. This perennial is a good addition to the formal perennial garden and borders, as well to a meadow or wildflower garden. The flowers open from top to bottom and will attract butterflies to the garden. Blazing star is at its best in prairie and meadow plantings where its tall stems (up to 3 1/2 ft.) are supported by the grasses and other meadow flowers. In the open garden, the tall spires may need to be staked, especially in windy areas. A cultivar 'Kobold' (15 to 18 in.), also called 'Gnome', has a compact growth habit, which eliminates the need for staking. Bright red-violet flower spikes stand out in the garden; these are good cut flowers, with strong stems and spikes that continue to open from the top down, making a long-lasting display.

WHEN TO PLANT
Plant *Liatris* in spring through early fall. Be sure to keep the new plants moist during hot, dry weather. Plants are available in containers, or can be obtained as bare-root early in the spring.

WHERE TO PLANT
Blazing star does best in a sunny location. To get vigorous plants, plant in humus-enriched, well-drained soil. Amend the soil with compost prior to planting to make sure the soil retains moisture during the heat of summer. Some good companions are Russian sage, purple coneflower, and ornamental grasses.

HOW TO PLANT
Plant blazing star 18 to 24 in. apart. Dig the planting hole twice as wide as the container. Position the plant so that the soil level is the

same as it was in the container. Fill in with soil around the root system about halfway up, gently firm, and water-in well. After the water has soaked in, add more soil to completely fill the hole. Water regularly until the plants are established. Bare-root plants should be planted so that their pinkish buds are 1 to 2 in. below the soil surface. Firm the soil gently and water-in well.

CARE AND MAINTENANCE
Blazing star is an easy-grow perennial. Water occasionally during the summer, especially during extended dry, hot periods. Although the plants will endure drought, they prefer moist soils. Moisture-retentive organic amendments at the initial planting are crucial for growing the plants successfully. To increase your collection, lift established plants in the spring and divide the corms. You can dead-head flower spikes as they fade to keep the garden neat; in a naturalized setting leave the seedheads for the wild birds.

ADDITIONAL INFORMATION
Don't forget to use the tall spikes for flower bouquets. They make excellent and long-lasting cut flowers, both fresh and dried. Tall varieties may need to be staked in windy sites, or you can plant shorter cultivars to avoid this inconvenience.

ADDITIONAL SPECIES, CULTIVARS, OR VARIETIES
There are several cultivars available. 'Silver Tip' (2 to 3 ft.) has lavender flower spikes. 'Floristan White' ($2^1/2$ to 3 ft.) is a good white-flowering cultivar. Its buddy 'Floristan Violet' (3 ft.) is a tall rose-purple selection. 'Kobold' is a compact plant with dark-purple spikes on 12- to 18-in. stems. The rough blazing star, *Liatris aspera* (4 to 5 ft.), is particularly drought tolerant and prefers dry, sandy soils. It is a excellent choice for a prairie or meadow garden.

Goldenrod

Solidago spp. and hybrids

Height: 2 to 5 ft.
Flowers: Golden yellow
Bloom Period: Late summer to fall
Zones: 3, 4, 5, 6

Light Requirement:

oldenrod has suffered from an unjustified bad rap. It is thought to cause hay fever, when in fact, its pollen is much too heavy and waxy to float in the wind. This plant relies on bees and butterflies to pollinate it, not wind-borne pollen. Goldenrod still gets the blame, although the primary cause of sneezing and runny noses is another plant. Ragweed is blooming inconspicuously at the same time golden-rod blooms, and ragweed releases clouds of tiny airborne pollen grains. Goldenrod is tolerant of clay or sandy soils and will thrive in sun or part shade. It can be grown as the Europeans do in formal perennial beds; or better yet, use it in naturalized settings with asters and grasses. There are compact forms with showy plumed clusters of golden yellow from late summer into autumn. The taller types are good for cut flowers. Beware of planting the aggressive species in rich soil as the plants may take over!

WHEN TO PLANT
Plant goldenrod in spring through fall. Container-grown plants are easy to get started.

WHERE TO PLANT
Choose a sunny site with average, well-drained soil; sandy or loamy soils are preferred. Soils that are too rich will result in floppy growth. Once established, goldenrods are drought-enduring peren-nials. Use them in perennial borders, meadow or prairie gardens, naturalized areas, or areas with ornamental grasses. Lavender-blue *Aster frikartii* makes an ideal foil for goldenrod. Burgundy, orange, and red mums and black-eyed Susans are good companion plants.

HOW TO PLANT
Plant goldenrod 18 to 36 in. apart, depending on the species or culti-var. Dig the planting hole twice as wide as the container. Position

the plant so that the soil level is the same as it was in the container. Fill in with soil around the root system about halfway up, gently firm, and water-in well. After the water has soaked in, add more soil to completely fill the hole. Water regularly until the plants are established.

CARE AND MAINTENANCE

Once goldenrod is well established it will need no special care. Avoid excessive watering and fertilizing; this will result in soft, weak growth, and the plants will require staking to stay upright. Additional watering is suggested during extended hot, dry periods. Many goldenrods produce self-sown seedlings which can be weeded out in the spring. Deadheading after blooming will reduce some of this seed dispersal. New plants can be started by division in the spring or early fall. Lift the clump and split it into pieces with a sharp knife. Replant the vigorous pieces from the outside of the clumps and toss out the unproductive middles. Keep new transplants well watered to help them establish.

ADDITIONAL INFORMATION

Powdery mildew can become a problem on the foliage of goldenrod. To reduce the problem, grow plants where there is good air circulation. The homemade remedy of baking soda and water (1 teaspoon baking soda per quart of water) sprayed on the leaves can help prevent a severe disease outbreak.

ADDITIONAL SPECIES, CULTIVARS, OR VARIETIES

Solidago sphacelata 'Golden Fleece' (18 in.) is a highly ornamental variety that produces compact, horizontal trusses of bright-yellow flowers. Stiff goldenrod, *S. rigida*, grows 4 to 6 ft. tall and has gray-green leaves and straight stems that support tight, rounded clusters of golden flowers. Another tall species is seaside goldenrod, *S. sempervirens*, which has graceful sprays of flowers on arching stems. On the shorter end of the spectrum, dwarf goldenrod, *S. nana* (18 to 24 in.), resembles its larger cousins. Other compact forms are 'Peter Pan', 'Baby Gold', and 'Golden Showers'.

Hardy Chrysanthemum

Chrysanthemum × morifolium

Height: 1 to 3 ft.
Flowers: White, yellow, red, pink, bronze, lavender
Bloom Period: Late summer until frost
Zones: 4, 5, 6

Light Requirement:

*A*s summer days shorten, hardy chrysanthemums burst into bloom to brighten the fall garden when other flowers have faded. In warm shades of russet, deep red, purple, soft pink and lavender, or glowing gold, hardy garden mums complement the changing foliage of autumn. The National Chrysanthemum Society has divided this vast and varied group of plants into 13 classifications according to flower types. It can be a challenge to find plants that are dependable for Colorado, especially when considering varieties that will overwinter in our colder regions. Visit with garden friends and local horticulturists to find out which ones have been reliable over the years. Some attractive companions for soft-pink mums are *Coreopsis* 'Moonbeam' and *Aster frikartii*, either 'Monch' or 'Wonder of Staffa'. White and pink mum cultivars look especially nice when combined with *Sedum* 'Autumn Joy'.

WHEN TO PLANT

Plant in spring, whether container-grown, bare-root, or divided. Spring-planted mums have a better survival rate when it comes to overwintering. Plants sold in late summer and early fall can be successfully planted then, and should be protected with a winter mulch after the ground freezes. This will prevent repeated cycles of freezing and thawing.

WHERE TO PLANT

Hardy mums do best in humus-enriched, well-drained soils. They prefer full sun but will tolerate partial shade. Too much shade causes leggy growth and fewer flowers. Group mums, 3 to 5 of the same cultivar, for a more dramatic impact in the garden.

HOW TO PLANT

Space mums 18 to 24 in. apart. Dig in compost or well-rotted manure, for moisture retention and to improve drainage. Incorporate an all-purpose granular fertilizer into the soil at planting time. Dig the planting hole twice as wide as the container or root system. Position the plant so that the soil level is the same as it was in the container or at the same depth the plants were originally growing. Fill in with soil around the roots about halfway, gently firm the soil, and water well. After the water has soaked in, complete filling in the hole with soil. Water regularly as the soil dries out. Mulch to conserve water and to keep the soil cooler.

CARE AND MAINTENANCE

You don't need to cut down the plants in the fall. Apply a winter mulch around Thanksgiving. The dried stems offer winter interest and catch snow to provide additional protection. Fertilize hardy mums in early spring, mid-spring, and summer. Apply an all-purpose 5-10-5 or 10-10-10 granular fertilizer around the plants according to directions, and water-in well. To achieve the best flowering, mums should be pinched back during the spring and summer to encourage lateral branching and a sturdier, more compact plant. Unpinched mums will flower, but the plants tend to be more open and have fewer flowers. Pinch as soon as the new shoots are 4 in. long. Grasp the growing tip and the first set of leaves between your thumb and forefinger and nip them off, removing about 1 in. of the shoot. Pinch again when the stems reach 4 in. Finish this pinching process around mid-July.

ADDITIONAL INFORMATION

Hardy mums should be lifted and divided every 3 years to maintain vigor. Discard the old, woody portion in the center of each clump. Divide and transplant in early spring. Aphids and spider mites may visit the plants. Inspect plants periodically; if pests are detected, wash them off with a strong stream of water or use a homemade soap spray.

ADDITIONAL SPECIES, CULTIVARS, OR VARIETIES

Some of the most dependable hardy mums for Colorado gardens are 'Clara Curtis' (pink flowers), 'Mary Stoker' (buff-yellow daisy flowers), 'Sheffield Pink' (salmon-pink blooms), and 'Grenadine' (coppery-pink, plus a red selection). There are many more chrysanthemums on the market, but not all may be hardy in your area. Experiment and grow your favorites.

Hosta

Hosta spp. and hybrids

Height: 8 to 48 in.
Flowers: White, lavender
Bloom Period: Midsummer to late summer
Zones: 3, 4, 5, 6

Light Requirement:

*H*ostas are dependable perennials for shade gardens in Colorado. Although they produce attractive, sometimes fragrant flowers on taller stems, hostas are prized for their colorful foliage. The plants add textural interest and color to shady areas of the landscape. Leaves vary in color from green to chartreuse, blues to variegated. Some leaves have interesting textures, including a puckered appearance; some are veined, looking as if they have been quilted. Leaf edges may be smooth or wavy. They will make a bold statement in the perennial garden. Hostas will form clumps ranging from several inches to several feet wide. Use them under trees, along a shady pathway, or around a patio or deck. Plants are hardy and handsome from late spring through fall, often turning golden in autumn. To bring light to the shade garden, select variegated forms. Even though hostas are attractive on their own, they can be used as a contrast to other shade perennials such as ferns, bleeding heart, and astilbe. If you need a groundcover under a specimen tree or shrub, consider hostas.

When to Plant

Container-grown plants can be planted from spring through early fall. Bare-root plants should be planted in spring as soon as the soil can be worked.

Where to Plant

Hostas thrive in moist, well-drained soils in partial shade to full shade. The soil should be amended with moisture-retentive compost to add fertility and improve drainage. Hostas are excellent additions to shady perennial gardens, edges of ponds, foundation beds, and woodland gardens. Use them as groundcovers or use a large hosta as a specimen plant for a dramatic accent.

How to Plant

Smaller hostas can be spaced 1¹/₂ to 2 ft. apart, larger specimens
2 to 3 ft. apart, depending on the variety. Avoid planting them too
close together, as the plants will spread. Dig the planting hole twice
as wide as the container. Position the plant so that the soil level is
the same as it was in the container. Fill in with soil around the roots
about halfway up, firm gently, and water well. After the water has
soaked in, add more soil to complete the planting. Water regularly
as the soil dries out until the plants are well established. Use an
organic mulch to conserve moisture.

Care and Maintenance

Once hostas are established, they require little care. During hot, dry
weather be sure to provide ample water. Start new plants by dividing older plants in spring before the leaves are fully expanded.
Dig out the clump and separate it into pieces with a sharp knife.
Replant new divisions at the same level at which they were growing. Water as needed.

Additional Information

Slugs can present a problem in moist, shaded areas. You can apply
the usual remedies for slugs, or hunt them down at dusk and
destroy these pests before they shred the foliage.

Additional Species, Cultivars, or Varieties

Hosta sieboldiana 'Elegans' is a classic shade plant with large bluish
green leaves. It forms clumps 2 to 3 ft. across and grows 18 to 24
in. tall. 'Gold Standard' (18 to 22 in.) has golden leaves with green
edges. It grows in partial shade as well as in full shade. For an edging hosta, try 'Gingko Craig' (6 to 10 in.), with its green lance-shaped
leaves with white margins. A good groundcover hosta is 'Janet'
(16 in.), with variegated leaves and pale-lavender blossoms. One
of the taller hostas for background is 'Mira' (24 to 36 in.) with large
greenish-blue leaves and whitish-lavender flowers.

Japanese Anemone

Anemone × hybrida

Height: 4 to 4¹/₂ ft.	Light Requirement:
Flowers: Pink, white	
Bloom Period: Late summer to early fall	
Zones: 4, 5, 6	

The Japanese anemone is one of the most prized perennials that bloom in late summer and autumn. It adds an element of surprise to the garden. For most of the growing season, this plant will grow as a low clump of handsome foliage; then, as the garden begins to slow down, hybrid anemones burst forth onto the scene with a multitude of delicate spring-like flowers in shades of rose, pink, and white. The divided leaves, which reach a height of 1 to 1¹/₂ ft., are attractive and durable and bring a nice texture to the garden. By late summer, the plant is 3 to 4 ft. tall and its branching stems push upward, topped with round, silvery, furry buds. The buds open to reveal simple yet delicate flowers with pink or white petals surrounding a green button and yellow stamens. These blooms sway in the breeze from late summer until frost. Combine this plant with other late flowers, such as asters, and with ornamental grasses.

WHEN TO PLANT

Plant anemones in spring to early summer. Container-grown plants are readily available. Older plants can be easily lifted and divided in spring.

WHERE TO PLANT

Japanese anemones prefer a location in sun or light shade. They do not do well in hot, dry sites. The planting area should be enriched with a moisture-retentive compost mixed into the native soil. Anemones will tolerate heavier soils if the soil is amended to improve drainage. They work well as a groundcover with other spreading perennials.

HOW TO PLANT

Plant Japanese anemones 2 ft. apart. Dig the planting hole twice as wide as the clump of roots or twice the width of the container in which the plant was growing previously. Position the plant so that the soil level is the same as it was in the container. Fill the planting hole halfway with soil, gently firm, and water well. Once the water has soaked in, add more soil to complete the planting. Water regularly until the plants are established. Apply an organic mulch to maintain and conserve moisture.

CARE AND MAINTENANCE

To get the most from your Japanese anemones, be sure to provide ample water during dry spells. A light application of all-purpose fertilizer such as 5-10-5 or 10-10-10 in spring will help the plants get started. Spring is also a good time to control any plants that may have spread into areas where they are not wanted. Dig the clumps and make divisions for transplanting or for giving to gardening friends.

ADDITIONAL INFORMATION

Apply a winter mulch to help protect the plants in colder areas. The late blooming period of some cultivars can be troublesome, as an early frost may curtail the magnificent flower display.

ADDITIONAL SPECIES, CULTIVARS, OR VARIETIES

Anemone tomentosa 'Robustissima' is a tall-growing species with grape-like foliage. It blooms earlier than most anemones, starting in late July and blooming through August. The pale-pink flowers grow to about 2 in. across, and cottony seedheads remain into autumn. *Pulsatilla vulgaris*, the pasqueflower, has a short growth habit (12 in.) and blooms from April through May. The purple or red-purple blossoms are 2 to $2^1/2$ in. across and glisten in the morning sun. Pasqueflower makes an excellent spring plant; its feathery seedheads persist into summer.

Joe-Pye Weed

Eupatorium purpureum

Height: 4 to 6 ft.
Flowers: Rose-pink to purplish
Bloom Period: Summer to fall
Zones: 3, 4, 5, 6

Light Requirement:

*I*f you want to make a bold architectural statement in a perennial garden, try Joe-Pye weed. It can grow to 6 ft. tall and 4 ft. wide. Its large, lanceolate leaves are produced in whorls, usually with three to five leaves at each node. Strong, hollow, cane-like green stems are often marked with purple where the leaves attach. The large (up to 18 in. across), showy rose-pink to purplish flower heads bloom for weeks beginning in late summer. Where water is plentiful, use this tall perennial for naturalizing in the landscape. It can be used as a backdrop for perennial borders or as a focal point in the fall garden. As the plants sway in the breeze, Joe-Pye weed's masses of flowers attract numerous butterflies and bees.

WHEN TO PLANT

Plant Joe-Pye weed from spring through early summer so that the plant will have time to establish a strong root system. Older plants will benefit from division every 3 to 4 years.

WHERE TO PLANT

This plant grows tall and wide. It is not meant for a small garden; give it plenty of space. Use it as a background accent or in a naturalized planting near a stream or water source. Locate in full sun and in a relatively moist area. Joe-Pye weed will tolerate partial shade. Fountain grass makes a good companion for this plant.

HOW TO PLANT

Space Joe-Pye weed 2^1/$_2$ to 4 ft. apart. Dig the planting hole twice as wide as the root system, or twice the width of the container in which the plant was growing previously. Position the plant so that the soil level is the same as it was in the container. Fill the planting hole halfway with soil, gently firm in place, and water well. After the water has soaked in, fill in the rest of the hole with soil. Water regularly as the soil dries out. Once the plant has become established, it can endure drought with only periodic watering.

CARE AND MAINTENANCE
Joe-Pye weed is a classic American native that prefers moist sites along streams and roadsides. It performs admirably in Colorado's cooler nights but requires a constant supply of water in our bright sunlight. If the plant gets too dry, its foliage will become scorched and wilted in the heat of summer. A summer mulch will help conserve soil moisture and prevent severe stress. Old stalks can be cut back in late spring to achieve a more compact plant.

ADDITIONAL INFORMATION
Joe-Pye weed spreads quickly in moist soils, but it is less aggressive under drier conditions. It may need staking in windy areas.

ADDITIONAL SPECIES, CULTIVARS, OR VARIETIES
Similar plants that also prefer moist locations are *Eupatorium maculatum*, whose stems are speckled with purple; *E. fistulosum*, which has purple, hollow stems; and 'Gateway', a smaller cultivar that grows to 5 ft. and has large, mauve-pink blooms above reddish stems. Blue mist flower, or hardy ageratum (*Eupatorium coelestinum*), produces a profusion of 4-in.-wide fluffy, tubular, compact purple-blue flower clusters in late summer and autumn. A white cultivar is also available. This hardy ageratum is a late grower, so take care not to injure the plant while cleaning and cultivating the garden in spring.

Lamb's Ears

Stachys byzantina

Height: 12 to 15 in.
Flowers: Purple-red
Bloom Period: Late spring to early summer
Zones: 4, 5, 6

Light Requirement:

*O*ur children can't resist petting the fuzzy silver leaves of lamb's ears. This perennial forms dense mats of woolly silvery-white leaves that make it ideal for use as an edging and a groundcover. Lamb's ears spread by means of creeping fibrous-rooted rhizomes that help hold the soil on slopes and terraces. The foliage remains attractive all season, though it is brightest in spring. As summer approaches, flowering stalks bear rosy-purple flowers in furry clusters. Tall stems may become floppy and can be pruned off if you desire. Some cultivars do not produce flowering stems. Use lamb's ears with other perennials such as Russian sage, salvia, creeping thyme, hybrid yarrows, and catnip, and with ornamental grasses.

WHEN TO PLANT

Plant container-grown plants in spring to early fall. Plant divisions can be transplanted in spring when the old clumps are lifted and separated.

WHERE TO PLANT

Lamb's ears do best in sunny exposures. Well-drained soil with average-to-low fertility is best; excess fertilizer and water will promote soft, weak growth that rots.

HOW TO PLANT

Space lamb's ears 18 to 24 in. apart. Dig the planting hole twice as wide as the root system, or twice the width of the container in which the plant was growing previously. Position the plant so that the soil level is the same as it was in the container. Fill the planting hole halfway with soil, gently firm in place, and water well. After the water has soaked in, fill the rest of the hole with soil. Water regularly as the soil dries out.

Care and Maintenance

Lamb's ears are drought tolerant and should not be overwatered. Avoid getting water on the leaves; constant moisture on the foliage tends to promote foliar diseases and crown rot. Deadhead old flower stalks to prevent self-seeding. Older plants will eventually die out in the center and should be divided in spring. Dig up the old clumps and separate them into pieces. Replant the vigorous outer portions of the plant and discard the spent centers. Set at the same level at which the plants were growing previously and water well.

Additional Information

The plants will benefit from a bit of grooming in spring. Gently remove any brown or dead leaves. How quickly the plants grow and spread will determine how often you need to divide them. It is generally recommended that they be divided every 3 to 4 years.

Additional Species, Cultivars, or Varieties

'Silver Carpet' is a nonflowering cultivar which forms a dense, silver, felt-like carpet. 'Sheila MacQueen' produces flowerless silver spikes good for cutting and drying. *Stachys macrantha*, big Betony (1 to 2 ft.), has upright spikes with whorls of purple, pink, or white flowers offset by rough, dark-green foliage.

Lenten Rose

Helleborus orientalis

Height: 15 to 18 in.
Flowers: White, purple, maroon
Bloom Period: Late winter to spring
Zones: 4, 5, 6

Light Requirement:

Colorado gardeners wait and watch for signs of spring in late winter; one of the first plants to greet us is the Lenten rose. In February and early March, you can brush the snow from this plant's evergreen leaves to reveal thick flower buds patiently waiting for warmer temperatures. The flowers emerge as nodding waxy blooms pushing their way up from the crown. They range in color from soft-white to rose to purple and are often stippled with maroon. Lenten rose, or hellebore, blooms for an extended period, and it remains attractive even after its petals and stamens have dropped. Cool spring air prolongs the blooming time. The plants are somewhat slow to establish. Hellebores are good companions for other herbaceous shade plants. They are valued not only for their flowers, but for their shiny evergreen leaves as well.

WHEN TO PLANT

Plant container-grown plants in early spring or early fall. Plants that are 3 years old will often produce seedlings around the base of the mother plant; these can be easily dug and transplanted in spring. Starting Lenten rose from seed requires patience. Sow fresh seed about 1/4 in. deep in a shady spot and mulch with a light layer of compost or shredded leaves. Germination may occur during the next year or two.

WHERE TO PLANT

Plant Lenten roses in partial to full shade in well-drained soil that is rich in organic matter. Use these plants in shady borders, wood-land gardens, shade gardens, and as foundation plantings. Tuck them where they will be noticed under shrubs and small flowering trees. Combine Lenten roses with forget-me-nots to create a delightful display.

How to Plant

Space plants 1¹/₂ to 2 ft. apart. Dig the planting hole twice as wide as the container in which the plant was growing. Position the plant so that the soil level is the same as it was in the container. Fill the planting hole halfway with soil, gently firm, and water well. Add more soil after the water has soaked in to completely fill the hole. Water regularly until the plants are established. Lenten rose roots resent disturbance, so don't skimp on the initial soil preparation.

Care and Maintenance

During extended dry periods it is important to supply hellebores with ample water. Fertilize in spring with a 5-10-5 all-purpose plant food to give them a boost. Remove any brown leaves in early spring to allow for the development of new growth. Avoid damaging the flower buds that rest close to the ground. It will take the plant 2 to 3 years to develop an impressive clump of evergreen foliage, but the wait is worth it. An annual topdressing of compost, well-aged manure, or shredded leaves each fall will help keep the soil rich.

Additional Information

Lenten roses growing in ideal sites with plenty of moisture and rich organic soil will readily produce new seedlings. Seedlings form at the base of the clump and can be lifted and transplanted in spring. *A word of caution: All parts of this plant are poisonous to humans and animals.*

Additional Species, Cultivars, or Varieties

The Christmas rose, *Helleborus niger*, is somewhat temperamental but can be grown successfully. *H. foetidus*, stinking hellebore, has pale-green flowers edged in maroon; it is tolerant of most growing conditions. *H. argutifolius*, Corsican hellebore, has coarse, holly-like leaves and chartreuse flowers streaked with purple.

Lupine

Lupinus hybrids

Height: 2 to 3 ft. **Flowers:** Blue, purple, pink, bicolors **Bloom Period:** May to July **Zones:** 3, 4, 5, 6	**Light Requirement:**

 *L*upines prefer cooler conditions. They are among the most dependable plants in the higher elevations of Colorado; if sited properly, they can also be grown successfully in the High Plains. The Russell hybrids are among the showiest for the perennial garden, but they require a rich soil that is well drained. Some of our native species are more drought tolerant and thrive under less-than-average soil conditions, though they are not as showy as the hybrids. Lupines form large mounds of palmately compound leaves, adding exceptional interest and contrast to the perennial bed. The showy pea-like flowers are borne on columnar racemes in a great variety of solid and bicolors including white, cream, yellow, orange, pink, red, blue, dark-blue, and purple. 'Minarette' and 'Little Lulu' are dwarf strains that grow from 12 to 18 in. tall.

WHEN TO PLANT

Plant container-grown lupines in the spring. Seeds can be started indoors in winter and transplanted outside in spring.

WHERE TO PLANT

Lupines prefer a sunny location, but they will benefit from after-noon shade. Good air circulation and well-drained soils are essential for vigorous and disease-free plants. The soil can be amended by adding compost to retain moisture and improve drainage. Use in flower borders and mass plantings.

HOW TO PLANT

Space lupines 18 to 24 in. apart. Dig the planting hole twice as wide as the root system or twice the width of the container in which the plant was growing previously. Position the plant so that the soil level is the same as it was in the container or at the same depth the plants were originally growing. Fill the planting hole halfway with soil, gently firm in place, and water well. After the water has soaked in, fill in the rest of the hole with the remaining soil. Water regularly as the soil dries out. Mulch to conserve water and to keep the soil cool.

CARE AND MAINTENANCE

Water plants deeply in hot weather. It's a good idea to mulch lupines to maintain and conserve moisture. Deadhead the spent flower spikes to encourage more blooms later into the season. This will also reduce prolific self-seeding. Hybrid lupines produce rather large, heavy blooms; these plants may need staking. Provide winter protection by mulching with shredded leaves or cedar shavings in late fall or early winter.

ADDITIONAL INFORMATION

Lupines make excellent cut flowers. The hybrid strains tend to be short-lived and will have to be replaced periodically. Aphids love lupines, so be prepared for war when these pests begin to invade. Gently washing off the flower buds with a stream of water can reduce aphid populations.

ADDITIONAL SPECIES, CULTIVARS, OR VARIETIES

The 'Russell' hybrids form clumps of upright stems and have a bushy growth habit and long stalks of palmately compound leaves. Above this handsome foliage appear spikes of flowers in shades of blue, purple, pink, red, cream, yellow, and orange, as well as bicolors. 'Dwarf Lulu' and 'Minarette' are compact strains growing only 18 in. tall. Unlike the species, which can thrive under poorer soil conditions, these hybrids perform best in rich, well-drained soils. *Lupinus pusillus*, our native low lupine, grows in the sandy plains along the eastern slope of Colorado. In July through August, pale blue-lavender flowers combine with the prairie grasses. *Lupinus argenteus*, the silvery lupine, is another native with light bluish lavender-to-purple blossoms (12 to 30 in. tall). It can be seen growing from the foothills to subalpine level in open meadows and forests, and along roadsides.

New England Aster

Aster novae-angliae

Height: 18 in. to 4 ft. **Flowers:** Lavender-blue, pink, white **Bloom Period:** Late summer to fall **Zones:** 3, 4, 5, 6	**Light Requirement:**

The *Aster* genus represents a large group of plants that can be found growing wild in open fields and along roadsides. They are adapted to a wide range of soils from moist to dry, but they prefer lean soils that are low in fertility. Some varieties are only a few inches tall, while others tower above neighboring perennials, reaching 4 ft. or more. One of our favorites in the Green Thumb garden is New England aster, *Aster novae-angliae*, which livens the garden with a bold profusion of bright-purple daisy-like flowers from late summer to frost. These are not care-free plants; the taller types may flop over without staking or frequent pinching. Powdery mildew can become a problem, but it can be reduced by thinning overcrowded plants in the spring or spraying with a fungicide as necessary. Plants perform best when they are divided every 3 to 4 years in spring. To prolong the blooming season and keep the plants tidy, deadhead asters when the flowers begin to fade.

WHEN TO PLANT

Plant container-grown plants in spring or early summer. Older plants should be divided every 3 years to keep them vigorous. Lift and divide clumps in spring.

WHERE TO PLANT

Asters require full sun. Be sure to plant them in well-drained soils that can be kept moderately moist. Asters are excellent perennials for the back of a border, in mixed plantings, and in meadow or prairie-style gardens. They make valuable additions to rock gardens and cutting gardens. Combine asters with ornamental grasses, goldenrod, coneflowers, and Joe-Pye weed for a spectacular autumn display.

How to Plant

Plant New England asters 2 to 3 ft. apart. Avoid overcrowding; asters do best with good air circulation. Dig the planting hole twice as wide as the root system or twice the width of the container in which the plant was growing previously. Position the plant in the hole so that the soil level is the same as it was in the container. Fill the planting hole halfway with soil, gently firm in place, and water-in well. Add more soil after the water has soaked in and fill in the rest of the hole with the remaining soil. Until the plants are established, water them regularly when the soil begins to dry out.

Care and Maintenance

Asters are drought-enduring, but they do best in moderately moist locations. Water regularly during dry periods. Wet foliage creates a more favorable environment for leaf diseases, so be sure to apply the water at the base of the plant. These perennials benefit from frequent division in spring to maintain vigor. When the center of the clump begins to thin out or die, it's time to divide and conquer. Dig up the clump and separate sections with a sharp knife. Discard the unproductive center portion. Replant the new divisions at the suggested spacing and water well until established. A summer mulch of shredded cedar or coarse compost will help conserve and maintain moisture.

Additional Information

To keep asters from becoming too tall and flopping over, pinch in late spring to encourage bushier, more compact growth. Taller varieties may need to be staked. Mildew can be a recurring problem, so keep plants thinned to prevent overcrowding and to improve air circulation.

Additional Species, Cultivars, or Varieties

Alma Potschke has beautiful warm-pink blooms on a more compact (3 ft.) plant. Combine it with Russian sage or ornamental grasses. 'Purple Dome' produces a profusion of purple on compact plants; it works well in smaller gardens. *Aster novi-belgii*, the New York aster and its many cultivars, are similar to New England asters, but they are more prone to mildew problems and need more frequent division. Frikart's aster, *Aster × frikartii*, has a long blooming season with an abundance of large lavender flowers; it is less prone to mildew. Combine it with *Sedum ×* 'Autumn Joy' to support the plant and create a stunning effect. The alpine aster, *Aster alpinus*, is one of our favorites; it has a compact growth habit (6 to 12 in.), an early bloom period from May to June, and beautiful flowers in white, blue, lavender, purple, and pink.

Peony

Paeonia lactiflora and hybrids

Height: 18 in. to 3 ft.
Flowers: White, pink, red; single or double
Bloom Period: Late spring to early summer
Zones: 3, 4, 5, 6

Light Requirement:

While other perennial flowers may come and go, peonies last a lifetime. Also known as the "Queen of Garden Flowers," the peony is beloved by gardeners and nongardeners alike. When I was a child, my family and I brought bouquets of fragrant peony blooms to the cemetery on Memorial Day. Flowers can range from 3 in. to 10 in. wide and may be single, double, or semi-double. As herbaceous perennials, peonies die back to the ground each winter. Tree peonies are somewhat different; even after herbaceous peonies have finished blooming, the tree peony's glossy green leaves remain attractive into late fall. The vigorous, woody plants grow into mounds that are 18 to 36 in. tall and equally as wide. Use peonies as specimens or as an informal herbaceous hedge; or integrate them into the perennial flower bed. Some of the new cultivars, as well as the single peonies, tend to bloom earlier and stand up to Colorado's wind better than do the older double types of the common peony, *Paeonia lactiflora*.

WHEN TO PLANT

Plant container-grown plants in spring through fall. Established plants can be divided in late fall, if needed. Bare-root plants are available from mail-order sources and can be set out in early spring.

WHERE TO PLANT

Peonies should be planted in well-drained, deeply cultivated, humus-enriched soils. The soil can be improved by adding a generous supply of moisture-retentive compost or well-aged manure. Be sure the site is sunny; at least a half-day of sun is necessary for good blooming. Avoid shady locations on the north side of buildings or shade from towering trees. Because peonies are so long-lived, good soil preparation at the beginning will pay off for decades.

HOW TO PLANT

Dig the planting hole about the size of a standard bushel basket or

3 times the width of the rootball. With the soil removed from the hole, scatter and work in a handful of high-phosphorus 5-10-5 fertilizer. Gently firm the soil in the hole so that the peony plant won't settle too deep when planted. Place the crown of the plant so that the buds or "eyes" are pointing upward. Planting at the correct depth is one of the secrets to success with peonies. The buds should be at just barely below to 1 in. below the soil's surface. If peonies are planted too deeply or if they settle too deep, they will not flower. Continue to fill the planting hole with amended soil and water-in well. You can space peonies 2 to 3 ft. apart.

CARE AND MAINTENANCE

To keep the plant tidy, remove faded flowers. To avoid exposure to dry winds and extreme temperature fluctuations, spread an organic mulch around the plants in late fall or early winter. Remove this mulch in early spring, taking care not to damage the new bud growth. Water deeply and regularly; plants may use up to an inch of water each week during the growing season. In spring, apply a general 10-10-10 granular fertilizer. Avoid high-nitrogen fertilizers, which stimulate foliage but not flower production. Peony cages or an inconspicuous tomato cage turned upside down should be placed around the plants in spring as the peonies begin to grow. Remove mature or ripened foliage in late fall or early winter.

ADDITIONAL INFORMATION

Peonies may fail to bloom for several reasons. A lack of adequate moisture during plant development, unusually cool spring weather, too much shade, lack of nutrients, and plants that have settled too deeply are common causes. Don't worry about the ants that visit peonies. They are attracted by the sweet secretions of nectar on peony buds; they have also been known to "farm" the aphids that gather there.

ADDITIONAL SPECIES, CULTIVARS, OR VARIETIES

If you make the right selections, it is possible to stretch the season of peony bloom to up to 4 weeks. The fernleaf peony, *Paeonia tenuifolia*, has finely dissected leaves and bright-red flowers; it is the earliest to bloom. A late peony is 'Elsa Sass', with fragrant double-white flowers. *Paeonia suffruticosa*, the tree or "shrub" peonies, don't die back to the ground in winter and will thrive in partial shade. They are truly elegant in the garden. If you have room, consider growing one or two of these plants. They can grow 4 to 5 ft. tall and will display dozens of large flowers that open earlier than the old-fashioned double peonies.

Perennial Flax

Linum perenne

Height: 1 to 2 ft. **Flowers:** Blue, white **Bloom Period:** Late spring through summer **Zones:** 3, 4, 5, 6	**Light Requirement:**

*P*erennial flax is one of our favorites in the Green Thumb garden. Its narrow bluish green leaves provide an airy appearance among the foliage of other perennials. Its wiry, often arching stems support a profusion of delicate, simple blue flowers. White and dwarf cultivars are available. Individual flowers open on sunny days, but they generally close and drop to the ground by late afternoon. New flowers are produced every day so you won't even notice this natural thinning. Perennial flax will self-sow in abundance and can fill in a large area within a few years. We allow seedlings to grow every year; this keeps the planting vigorous. You can transplant seedlings in spring to share with friends. Plants are very drought resistant, good for a water-thrifty garden.

When to Plant

Plant container-grown perennial flax in spring through early fall. Seedling plants can be lifted and replanted in early spring.

Where to Plant

Perennial flax prefers full sun, but it will tolerate some light shade. Too much shade will cause the plants to grow leggy and produce fewer flowers. Perennial flax will tolerate Colorado clay soils that are well drained. Use it in perennial borders, informal flower beds, or meadow gardens. Allow enough space for plants to self-sow and fill in bare spots.

How to Plant

Space perennial flax 15 to 18 in. apart. Dig the planting hole twice as wide as the root system or twice the width of the container in which the plant was growing previously. Position the plant so that the soil level is the same as it was in the container or at the same depth the plants were originally growing. Fill the planting hole halfway with soil, gently firm in place, and water well. After the water has soaked in, fill in the rest of the hole with soil. Water regularly as the soil dries out. Mulch to conserve water and to keep the soil cooler.

CARE AND MAINTENANCE

Perennial flax needs little care. It does well in soils of poor-to-average fertility. Avoid fertilizing with high-nitrogen plant food; this will result in tall, weak growth and significantly fewer flowers. A light application of a 5-10-5 in early spring is all that is needed. Mulch plants in winter after the ground freezes to prevent frost heave. We have found that deadheading the developing seedheads encourages flax to bloom again in late summer. Cut the plants back by half to tidy up the garden and induce new growth. Leave some seeds if you want new seedling plants to grow and fill in open areas.

ADDITIONAL INFORMATION

Perennials that are planted in fall will benefit from a light mulch to protect them from Colorado's drying winds. Winter mulch will also help to keep the soil cold, preventing the cycle of freezing and thawing that is common throughout the winter and that can damage delicate new roots.

ADDITIONAL SPECIES, CULTIVARS, OR VARIETIES

The cultivar 'Alba' has dainty white flowers. 'Nanum Sapphire' produces gorgeous sapphire-blue flowers on 10- to 12-in. stems. *Linum alpinum* has more compact growth (8 to 10 in.), small heather-like leaves, and clear-blue 3/4-in. flowers. Prairie flax, *Linum lewisii* (2 to 3 ft.), is a western native with sky-blue flowers; it tolerates partial shade.

Perennial Salvia

Salvia × superba

Height: 18 to 24 in.
Flowers: Violet-blue
Bloom Period: Late spring to midsummer
Zones: 4, 5, 6

Light Requirement:

*P*erennial hybrid salvia, or violet sage, will provide months of cooling purple-blue color on sturdy upright spikes. It is outstanding when combined with *Achillea* 'Moonshine', 'Coronation Gold' yarrow, or *Coreopsis* 'Moonbeam'. Like these other perennials, salvia performs best in full sun. It produces numerous dense, slender spikes above mounds of grayish-green foliage. The spikes are attractive even after the flowers drop, their reddish-purple bracts providing contrast to the foliage. Combine with a silver-foliaged plant such as lamb's ears or *Artemisia* 'Silver King' for a calming effect. Salvia's rich violet-purple is also a good companion for magenta, pink, and lavender flowers.

When to Plant

Plant in spring through summer. The earlier you plant, the more time there will be before winter for strong root establishment.

Where to Plant

Locate a site in full sun for optimum growth and flowering. Too much shade will result in sprawling plants with few flowers. The soil should be well drained. Hybrid salvia can endure drought conditions, but it should be provided with adequate moisture during a normal growing season. Use in formal garden settings or as informal perennial border plantings.

How to Plant

Plant perennial salvia $1^1/2$ to 2 ft. apart. Dig the planting hole at least twice as wide as the container in which the plant was growing previously. Set the plant in the hole so that the soil level is the same as it was in the container. Fill the planting hole halfway with soil, gently firm in place, and water-in well. After the water has soaked in, fill in the rest of the hole with the remaining soil. Water regularly until the plants are well established. Plants are quick to grow and generally bloom well in the first growing season.

CARE AND MAINTENANCE

Plants that are properly located will need a minimum of care. Remove spent flower stalks to keep the planting tidy and prolong the bloom period. You can cut the plants back hard to the basal leaves for a second flush of bloom. For best results, water regularly during the growing season. Older plantings can be rejuvenated by dividing clumps in the spring. Carefully split the clumps with a spading fork or sharp knife. Mulch the plants in late fall or early winter with pine needles or evergreen boughs. This will prevent severe desiccation and possible "winter kill."

ADDITIONAL INFORMATION

Hybrid salvias are sold under many names, including *Salvia nemorosa*, *S. sylvestris*, *S. virgata*, and *S. virgata nemorosa*.

ADDITIONAL SPECIES, CULTIVARS, OR VARIETIES

'East Friesland' has purple flowers and grows to 2 ft. 'May Night' has darker violet-blue flowers. For a lower-growing growth habit, look for 'Lubeca'. It grows 15 to 18 in. and has purple flowers; pink- and white-flowering forms are available but may be hard to find. *Salvia officinalis*, the culinary sage, works well in herb gardens and container plantings, or as an accent in the perennial bed. It is an evergreen plant that grows into a shrub-like mound. In spring, cut back to live wood to shape the plant.

Purple Coneflower

Echinacea purpurea

Height: 2 to 4 ft.
Flowers: Bright rosy-pink, white
Bloom Period: Early to late summer
Zones: 3, 4, 5, 6

Light Requirement:

The purple coneflower is a favorite of butterflies who seek its nectar and of flower arrangers who love its long-lasting blooms and dried coneheads; it is also a favorite in the Green Thumb garden. It is an easy-to-care-for perennial that will thrive in a sunny border or meadow garden. Native Americans have long used the purple coneflower and its relatives for medicine; today *Echinacea* has gained renewed popularity as a preventative of the common cold. If you've ever touched the cone of one of these flowers, it will come as no surprise that the name *Echinacea* is from the Greek *echinos*, which means "hedgehog." Purple coneflower's common name is "hedgehog coneflower." Coneflower is a bright, dependable addition to the perennial garden.

When to Plant

Plant container-grown plants in early spring through early fall. You can purchase bare-root plants through mail-order catalogs. These should be planted as soon as the soil can be worked in the spring.

Where to Plant

This hardy perennial will tolerate a wide range of soils, including heavy clay, crushed granite, and sand, though it prefers moderately moist, well-drained soils. Full sun is best, but the coneflower will tolerate part shade in late afternoon. Use purple coneflower in the perennial flower bed, the cutting garden, the meadow garden, or in mixed plantings. It is especially effective in a naturescape setting.

How to Plant

Dig the planting hole twice as wide as the spread of the root system or twice the width of the container in which the plant was growing previously. Position the plant so that the soil level is the same as it was in the container. Fill the planting hole halfway with soil, gently firm in place, and water-in well. Add more soil to complete the planting. Water regularly as the soil dries out until the plants are established. Space coneflowers $1^1/_2$ to 2 ft. apart.

CARE AND MAINTENANCE

This easy-to-grow plant is generally an undemanding perennial favorite. Coneflower will withstand heat and drought and needs water only occasionally. Early fertilization in spring with an all-purpose 5-10-5 will help the plants get off to a healthy, vigorous start. Deadhead or remove spent flowers to prolong the blooming season. As late summer approaches, you may wish to leave some flowers to form seedheads, providing a source of fall and winter food for wild birds.

ADDITIONAL INFORMATION

Purple coneflower self-sows or distributes seeds that will germinate throughout the garden. These seedlings will be large enough to bloom the second or third year, but may not be identical to the parent plant. This works well for a naturescape or meadow garden. If you desire a more formal garden, weed out the seedlings as needed.

ADDITIONAL SPECIES, CULTIVARS, OR SPECIES

More cultivars are becoming readily available. 'Bright star' has rosy-pink flower rays with maroon disks; the petals tend to be more horizontal than the species. 'White Swan' is a compact white form (24 to 36 in.) with copper-orange cones. Our native coneflower, *Ratibida pinnata*, has shuttlecock-like flowers with yellow petals that droop from a prominent central cone. This is truly a prairie plant and works well in the High Plains of Colorado.

PERENNIALS

Rocky Mountain Columbine

Aquilegia caerulea

Height: 2 to 4 ft.
Flowers: Bluish-purple to lavender
Bloom Period: Mid-May to August
Zones: 2, 3, 4, 5, 6

Light Requirement:

ocky Mountain columbine, the Colorado state flower, is an old-fashioned favorite and the parent of many hybrids. It produces an abundance of long-spurred flowers from mid-May through June and will bloom again in August if deadheaded soon after flowering. The delicate 2^1/$_2$-in. flowers have bluish purple sepals and white petals. Columbine plants are charming additions to the perennial garden, and some of the new hybrids are especially nice. Our state flower is a bit more fussy about its growing conditions. It prefers cool, moist locations, and gardens in the High Plains are often too hot; but it is a perfect choice in the foothills and high country. The secret to success with columbines is to keep in mind that the plants are short-lived perennials. They should be replanted every 3 to 4 years if you desire to keep the original varieties. Allow them to go to seed and they will sow themselves in a multitude of colors. They thrive with regular watering and produce the best color if given some afternoon shade. Flower colors will fade if the plants are grown in full sun, which may account for frequent questions about transplanted columbines that lose their true color. Rocky Mountain columbine is excellent for mountain communities, and many hybrids are adapted across the state.

When to Plant

Plant container-grown plants from spring through fall. The small jet-black seeds may be collected and scattered while still fresh in late summer to early fall. These seed-grown plants will generally flower the following year. Seedling plants grown from hybrids will vary considerably in flower color, and the color will be more muted than that of the parents.

Where to Plant

The ideal conditions for columbine are light, well-drained, humus-enriched soils. It also grows well in sandy or rocky spots. Clay soils should be improved with compost or aged manure. Good drainage is essential to growing columbines successfully. Companion plants for columbine include cranesbill, coral bells, and lady's mantle. The foliage of columbine makes a nice addition to the perennial garden.

How to Plant

Position container-grown plants at the same depth they were growing in their containers. Space the plants 12 to 15 in. apart. Mulch after transplanting to maintain and conserve moisture, keep the roots cool, and discourage weeds from germinating.

Care and Maintenance

When established in well-drained soils with sufficient humus, columbines will thrive for several years. Good drainage is essential. Since individual columbines are short-lived, allow them to reseed in order to keep the population stocked with new plants. Hybrid columbines should be dug when they begin to lose their vigor and replaced with new plants to maintain the original varieties.

Additional Information

Leaf miners can become a nuisance. The damage created as they tunnel through the leaves in irregular trails is unattractive, but it does not kill the plant. Infested leaves should be removed and destroyed. The plant will send out new growth to sustain itself through the season. Powdery mildew can appear in late summer and early fall. Snip off infected leaves and discard.

Additional Species, Cultivars, or Varieties

There are many columbine hybrids including the series 'Song Bird', which was developed in Colorado and adapts very well to sunny exposures. Another hybrid is 'Blue Jay', which is similar to Rocky Mountain columbine. 'Pretty Bird' and 'Tanager' have red-and-yellow blooms. 'Cardinal' is very handsome, with deep-red-and-white flowers; 'Mockingbird' produces plum-and-white flowers; and 'Dove' has beautiful white blossoms. The European *Aquilegia vulgaris* has nodding 1- to 2-in. deep-purple flowers that resemble a flock of plump doves.

Russian Sage

Perovskia atriplicifolia

Height: 3 to 5 ft.
Flowers: Lavender-blue
Bloom Period: Early summer to fall
Zones: 4, 5, 6

Light Requirement:

*R*ussian sage is a graceful, aromatic perennial clothed in silvery, grayish-green foliage and topped with beautiful lavender-blue blossoms. Bees love it. Its flowers last for months and make an elegant statement in the landscape when combined with ornamental grasses in late summer. With its light and airy appearance, Russian sage works nicely as a backdrop for daylilies and 'Autumn Joy' sedum, and it combines well with purple coneflower. It makes a nice cut flower and can be included in the cutting garden. The foliage when crushed has a distinctive odor that is similar to culinary sage; Russian sage, however, is not used in the kitchen. It is classified as a subshrub and, unlike many perennials, it doesn't die back completely in winter. The silvery-white stems add winter interest to the landscape. Cut Russian sage back each spring before new growth starts and you will be rewarded with a vigorous plant with lots of colorful blossoms.

WHEN TO PLANT

Russian sage can be planted from container-grown stock in spring through early fall. Don't wait too long to plant, because the roots need time to establish before winter. Bare-root plants are available from mail-order sources and can be planted in early spring.

WHERE TO PLANT

Plant in full sun for optimum growth and flowering. Some shade can be tolerated, but the plant will lean toward the light and sprawl. Use Russian sage as a backdrop and in perennial borders, shrub borders, mixed plantings, and cutflower gardens.

HOW TO PLANT

Russian sage can be spaced $1^1/2$ to 2 ft. apart. Dig the planting hole at least twice as wide as the root system or twice the width of the container in which it was previously growing. Position the plant so that the soil level is the same as it was in the container. Fill the planting hole halfway with soil, gently firm in place, and water well. Add more soil to complete the planting. Water regularly as the soil dries out. Once it has become established, this perennial is quite drought tolerant.

CARE AND MAINTENANCE

Plants prefer soil on the lean side, so don't fertilize too often. Avoid high-nitrogen plant fertilizer. A light application of all-purpose 5-10-5 in early spring will be sufficient. Good drainage is essential; avoid overwatering. Don't cut the plants back in autumn—their silvery stems add interest to the winter garden. Wait until spring to prune Russian sage as new growth appears. At this time you can cut the plant down to the ground; or remove dead, weak branches and cut back the remaining branches, leaving 5 to 7 vigorous buds.

ADDITIONAL INFORMATION

Russian sage has an unprecedented blooming period that is among the longest of any perennial. This makes it available for use in many plant combinations. It is especially effective when used with daylilies and purple coneflowers in midsummer. In late summer, it makes a nice companion for black-eyed Susan and gaillardia. Pink asters with a backdrop of Russian sage are quite effective in the fall. This is a tough, long-lived perennial that has no serious insect pests or disease problems.

ADDITIONAL SPECIES, CULTIVARS, OR VARIETIES

Look for some outstanding cultivars such as 'Blue Spire', which has finely dissected leaves and bluer flowers; it grows to 3 ft. 'Longin' is a very upright selection with silvery leaves that are not as divided as those of the species; it tends to be a bit more formal and not as graceful. 'Blue Haze' has paler-blue flowers with nearly entire leaves.

Scarlet Bugler

Penstemon barbatus

Height: 2 to 3 ft.
Flowers: Scarlet-red
Bloom Period: Late spring to July
Zones: 3, 4, 5, 6

Light Requirement:

*P*lant scarlet bugler in your perennial garden, and if it's hummingbirds you want, it's hummingbirds you'll get! The panicles of bright scarlet trumpet flowers rise up on 2- to 3-ft. stems, attracting hummingbirds, butterflies, and sphinx moths from miles away. *Penstemon barbatus* is native to the hot, dry plains and is right at home in Colorado landscapes. It makes a great addition to a water-thrifty garden or naturalized setting. The plants will be short-lived if you overwater them. Scarlet bugler will not tolerate soggy conditions; good drainage is essential. Because it is so long-lived, this species is popular for hybridization and has been crossed with other penstemons to create some exceptional varieties. One such cultivar is 'Prairie Dusk', which has rich rose-purple flowers on 12- to 18-in. stems. 'Prairie Fire' has vermilion blossoms on 2-ft.-tall stems. Another gorgeous cultivar is 'Elfin Pink', with bright salmon-pink flowers on 18-in. stems. Plant scarlet bugler in masses for a grand summer display.

When to Plant

Plant in spring through early fall. Container-grown plants are readily available, as are transplants from mail-order sources.

Where to Plant

Scarlet bugler does best in full sun. Well-drained soils are a must. Plant in soil of low-to-average fertility. Too much organic amendment can encourage crown rot. Penstemons are subject to rot if they become too wet in winter, so they are often planted on slopes or in raised flower beds. Combine scarlet bugler with the low-growing silver creeper *Artemisia frigida* for a nice effect.

How to Plant

Space plants 18 to 24 in. apart. The soil should be loosened in areas that are to be planted, but do not over-enrich the soil with too much organic matter. Dig the planting hole twice as wide as the root system or twice the width of the container in which the plant was growing previously. Position the plant so that the soil level is the same as it was in the container or at the same depth the plants were originally growing. Fill the planting hole halfway with soil, gently firm in place, and water well. After the water has soaked in, add more soil to complete the planting. Until the plants are established, water them regularly as the soil dries out.

Care and Maintenance

Scarlet bugler and other penstemons are drought-tolerant perennials that resent soggy conditions. Once they are established, it is best to leave them alone. Resist the urge to fertilize penstemons. You will find that with less water and little care, the plants will bloom longer than those placed in more formal watered flower beds.

Additional Information

Most of the tall-growing penstemons make excellent cut flowers. Many are temperamental about heavy soils and grow best in those that are sandy or gravelly.

Additional Species, Cultivars, or Varieties

Rocky Mountain penstemon, *P. strictus* (2 to 3 ft.), is a striking plant with shiny foliage and deep-blue to purple flowers. It thrives in hot, dry sites and is an excellent plant for a naturescape. *P. perfoliatus* (3 ft.) is a tall, handsome plant with white flowers. One of our favorites for use in the rock garden and as edging is pineleaf penstemon, *P. pinifolius*. It has compact growth (1 ft.) with shrubby needle-like foliage and small but bright scarlet flowers. Its remarkably long bloom period lasts from June to early September. Dwarf hairy beard-tongue, *P. hirsutus* (1 to 2 ft.), is a dwarf plant with sticky, hairy foliage and lavender flowers. Blossoms appear from late May through early July. *P. procerus* (8 to 12 in.) has delightful blossoms of lavender-blue and narrow, glossy dark-green leaves which make a nice groundcover.

Showy Stonecrop

Sedum × 'Autumn Joy'

Height: 1 to 2 ft. **Flowers:** Vivid-pink maturing to red-pink **Bloom Period:** August to frost **Zones:** 3, 4, 5, 6	**Light Requirement:**

*I*f you're looking for a dependable perennial for Colorado, you will find that *Sedum* 'Autumn Joy' is one of the best. The attractive, fleshy, light-green leaves add texture to the flower garden from spring through fall. The chunky flower bud heads resemble broccoli. As the flowers open, the tight clusters reveal a vivid, near-iridescent pink color that beckons honeybees, bumblebees, and a variety of butterflies. In late summer to early fall, the pink flowers become a mellow deep-rose and open wider, finally maturing to a richer mahogany color. The plants remain upright throughout the fall and winter unless they are buried by an early wet, heavy snow. Its adaptability has made *Sedum* 'Autumn Joy' a widely used plant in commercial landscaping. It is especially useful in rock gardens and water-thrifty landscapes.

WHEN TO PLANT
Plant *Sedum* × 'Autumn Joy' from spring through late fall. It is available as a container-grown plant in sizes ranging from small 2$^{1}/_{4}$-in. pots to larger gallon-sized containers. It can also be obtained from various mail-order sources.

WHERE TO PLANT
To get the best growth and lots of blooms, locate in a site that gets full sun and has average, well-drained soil. Avoid soils that are too rich, or the plant will grow leggy and the weight of the large flower heads will require support. Stonecrop is highly tolerant of heat and drought. You will find it useful in border plantings, dryland gardens, and "hell strips" (those areas between the sidewalk and the street), and it makes a good accent plant in the rock garden.

HOW TO PLANT
Plants can be spaced from 1$^{1}/_{2}$ to 2 ft. apart. Dig the planting hole twice as wide as the pot in which the plant was growing previously. Position the plant so that the soil level is the same as it was in the

container. Fill the planting hole halfway with soil and lightly firm, then water-in. Once the water has soaked in, add more soil to completely fill the hole. Water regularly as the soil becomes dry until the plants are well established.

CARE AND MAINTENANCE

Sedum × 'Autumn Joy' will grow with almost no input from the gardener. A light application of all-purpose 5-10-5 fertilizer in early spring will get the plant off to a hardy start. Avoid high-nitrogen fertilizer, which promotes leafy growth and weak stems. When the older clumps become crowded and begin to split open in the center, this is a signal to divide the plant. In April or early May, lift the clumps with a spading fork and remove the unproductive center. Replant healthy, vigorous divisions from the outside of the clump. Reset the pieces at the same depth, gently firming them into the soil, and water-in well. Water plants thoroughly during the heat of summer, but not too frequently. Allow the soil to dry out between waterings.

ADDITIONAL INFORMATION

It is not uncommon for tiny pests known as aphids to be attracted to this plant. Their presence does not usually create a significant problem, but you can keep them in check by washing them off with a spray of water from the garden hose. To tidy up the garden in spring, cut back the dried seedheads to make way for a burst of fresh new growth.

ADDITIONAL SPECIES, CULTIVARS, OR VARIETIES

The showy stonecrops offer you a wide range of easy-to-grow perennials, from the lower-growing *Sedum kamtschaticum* 'Variegatum' with its creamy-white-banded leaves and cymes of dark-yellow flowers, to the more upright *Sedum spectabile* with tall stems that support showy flowers from summer to late fall. Other outstanding varieties are 'Star Dust', which has near-white to very pale-pink blossoms; 'Meteor', with more vivid-pink blooms; and 'Variegatum', which has stunning variegated foliage. *Sedum maximum* 'Atropurpureum' has lightly toothed purple-to-maroon leaves with clusters of small pink flowers. If you need a groundcover for a slope or difficult site, *Sedum kamtschaticum* is an excellent choice. Its dark-green toothed leaves are topped with golden yellow flowers from late spring to midsummer. *Sedum spurium*, or two-row sedum, is another great groundcover; its flowers are a deep rose-pink. 'Dragon's Blood' is a familiar purple-bronze form. Several variegated varieties are also available.

Siberian Iris

Iris sibirica

Height: 20 in. to 4 ft.
Flowers: Blue, purple, red-violet, white
Bloom Period: Late spring to early summer
Zones: 3, 4, 5, 6

Light Requirement:

Siberian irises are hardy perennials for Colorado gardens. Their flowers have the same elements of bearded irises—three spreading outer petals called falls and three upright petals called standards—but they are smaller and more open, and their beards lack the furry strips or beards of bearded irises. The falls on Siberian irises often have intricate veining and a marking called a "blaze." The light, airy flowers dance like butterflies atop slender, upright stalks of grass-like leaves. The elegant blooms, which come in blue, purple, red-violet, and white, are truly beautiful under a blue Colorado sky. Siberian iris's handsome arching foliage adds vertical lift to the perennial garden all summer long. Use Siberian irises as accent plants or plant them in masses or combinations. The foliage makes a graceful screen and the blooms paint a cloud of color. They are dependable and easy to grow. As its name suggests, the Siberian iris is very cold hardy and can survive even the coldest Colorado winters.

WHEN TO PLANT

Container-grown Siberian irises can be planted from spring through early fall. If you purchase by mail order, plant the rhizomes in spring to ensure good establishment.

WHERE TO PLANT

Siberian irises do best in well-drained soils that are rich in humus. Choose a site with full sun to part shade. These plants prefer soils that retain moisture; they don't like to dry out. In sandy soils, be sure to add a generous supply of compost before planting. Try planting as a screen among other perennials such as campanulas, poppies, and coreopsis.

HOW TO PLANT

If the soil has not been previously prepared, add 3 to 4 in. of compost to retain moisture and improve drainage. Space plants 1 1/2 to

2 ft. apart. Set rhizomes 2 in. deep and water-in well. Provide ample water for the first month or so, until the leaves emerge. Container-grown plants should be planted in a hole that is twice as wide as the container in which they were growing. Position the plant so that the soil level is the same as it was in the container. Fill the planting hole halfway with soil, gently firm in place, and water-in. After the water has soaked in, add more soil to complete the planting and water again. Apply a mulch around the plants to maintain and conserve moisture.

CARE AND MAINTENANCE

Water Siberian irises regularly during the summer months. They can be lightly fertilized in spring with a low-nitrogen plant food such as 5-10-5. Sprinkle the fertilizer granules over the soil and water-in. Deadhead, or remove the spent flower stalks, after flowering is finished. Though they don't need frequent division, if clumps of Siberian iris die out in the center and produce fewer flowers, this is a sign to lift and divide the clump. Use a heavy-duty spading fork to lift an old clump in spring. Split the clump in pieces with a pruning saw or sharp knife. Discard the woody center and replant the vigor-ous portions from the outside of the clump. Add more compost to the soil if needed and replant the new divisions. Keep transplants well watered and add mulch. New divisions may take 2 years to put on a show.

ADDITIONAL INFORMATION

Dead foliage can be cut back in the late fall after it has died back. Foliage left standing will flop over and can provide a haven for rodents who love to forage on the roots.

ADDITIONAL SPECIES, CULTIVARS, OR VARIETIES

There are hundreds of cultivars of Siberian iris; many are hybrids and come in a wide range of colors. 'Butter and Sugar' is yellow; 'Caesar's Brother' is a deep purple; 'Ego' is medium-blue; and 'Super Ego' is pale blue. 'Ruffled Velvet' has velvety, reddish-purple flow-ers with falls that roll under at the edges. A new class of tetraploids, which have double the number of chromosomes, is also available. 'Marshmallow Frosting' has white flowers, and 'Reddy Maid' produces blossoms in deep wine-red.

Sneezeweed

Helenium autumnale

Height: 3 to 5 ft.
Flowers: Orange-red, yellow
Bloom Period: Late summer to fall
Zones: 3, 4, 5, 6

Light Requirement:

Sneezeweed, an indispensable perennial in the summer and early-fall garden, lights up the flower border. Each daisy-like flower has a prominent raised, rounded knob of disk florets, surrounded by wedge-shaped, notched, reflexed petals. It has become a favored plant because of its heat tolerance and long blooming season. Among the best-known are 'Butterpat', with long-blooming yellow flowers and 'Bruno', which has reddish-bronze flowers. With a name like sneezeweed, it's easy to see why this plant has a hard time achieving fame. Many years ago, its leaves were dried and ground up to produce a type of snuff. Today this perennial is among the best for intense summer colors and ease of care. You will find it listed as Helen's flower in catalogs and at nurseries. It seldom needs staking and will fill in an area quickly. Since the colors are so bright, combine it with 'Coronation Gold' yarrow or threadleaf coreopsis for a nice effect. It works well with butterfly bush, perennial sages, and verbena.

WHEN TO PLANT
Container-grown plants can be planted from spring through fall. Divide the plants every 3 to 4 years in spring to retain vigor.

WHERE TO PLANT
Pick a spot with full sun and well-drained soil. A deep soil enriched with moisture-retentive compost will keep the plants from drying out in summer's heat. Use sneezeweed in sunny perennial beds, borders, moist areas, and naturalized plantings.

HOW TO PLANT
Space plants 18 to 24 in. apart. Dig the planting hole twice as wide as the container. Position the plant so that the soil level is the same as it was in the container. Fill in with soil around the root system

about halfway up, gently firm, and water-in well. After the water has soaked in, add more soil to completely fill the hole. Water regularly until the plants are established. Mulch to maintain and conserve moisture.

CARE AND MAINTENANCE

If sited properly, sneezeweed will thrive and bloom profusely. Be sure to provide ample water during dry, hot spells. To encourage more flowers, deadhead old flowering stems after the first flush of blooms. The plants will mature and the clumps will die out, and it will be time to divide the plants the following spring. Dig old clumps and split the fibrous root system into several sections. Replant the most vigorous sections taken from the outside of the clump. Set at the same level the plant was originally growing and water-in well. Plants can go for 4 to 5 years before having to be divided.

ADDITIONAL INFORMATION

Sneezeweed makes an excellent cut flower, so don't be afraid to pick a few large bouquets in summer. If the plants start to get spindly, pinch them back by half to produce bushier (though later-blooming) plants. Tall leggy growth is usually a result of too-rich soil, overfertilizing, or too much shade.

ADDITIONAL SPECIES, CULTIVARS, OR VARIETIES

If you don't like staking taller species, choose from among the more-compact cultivars. 'Butterpat' (3 to 4 ft) produces beautiful sunny-yellow flowers. 'Moerheim Beauty' is an old favorite (3 ft. tall) with rich reddish-brown flowers that fade to burnt orange. 'Wyndley' (2 to 2^1/$_2$ ft.) has copper-orange flowers and 'The Bishop' (2 to 2^1/$_2$ ft.) has yellow flowers.

Sweet William

Dianthus barbatus

Height: 12 to 18 in.
Flowers: Red, pink, purple-red, multicolored
Bloom Period: Late spring to summer
Zones: 3, 4, 5, 6

Light Requirement:

---

*S*weet william is an old-fashioned beauty whose clove-scented flowers evoke memories of a parent's or grandparent's flower garden. It is a member of the *Dianthus* genus, which includes pinks and carnations. Unfortunately, many of the new cultivars have lost the intoxicating fragrance of times past. Sweet william is considered a biennial, but the plants self-sow so readily that they appear to persist almost indefinitely. Their flat-topped, multi-flowered, 3- to 4-in. cymes are dense and subtended by narrow green bracts. Colors range from white through pinks, reds to purplish red, some multicolored. Numerous cultivars are available, including dwarf, double-flowered ones, and mixed colors. Taller ones are excellent for long-lasting cut flowers. If you cut them back after flowering, the plants will bloom again in late summer. Once established, sweet williams are drought tolerant. Cottage pink, *Dianthus plumarius*, is an excellent mat-forming (6 to 12 in.) species with flowers 1/2 to 1 1/2 in. across in colors of red, pink, white, and bicolors. Its foliage is usually gray-green and often evergreen, providing a contrast to the foliage of other plants even in winter. Use it in front of borders, in rock gardens, and as accent plants.

WHEN TO PLANT

Plant in early spring through early fall. Container-grown plants and bare-root plants are available from mail-order sources. Bare-root stock is best planted in early spring.

WHERE TO PLANT

Dianthus grows best in sunny locations, but will tolerate some partial shade. It prefers well-drained, Colorado-alkaline soils. Heavy soils should be thoroughly loosened and amended with compost to improve drainage. Use in borders and rock gardens, and as specimen plants.

How to Plant

Space sweet williams 18 in. to 2 ft. apart. Dig the planting hole twice as wide as the container or the root system. Position the plant so that the soil level is the same as it was in the container. Fill in with soil around the roots about halfway, gently firm the soil, and water well. After the water has soaked in, finish filling in the hole with soil. Water regularly as the soil dries out. Apply an organic mulch to maintain and conserve moisture.

Care and Maintenance

Dianthus does best in cool weather, but it will tolerate drought if watered regularly during dry spells. Avoid overwatering, especially in winter, as the plants will rot if kept too wet. Do not use high-nitrogen fertilizers; they promote soft, weak growth that is susceptible to breakage and rot. Deadhead the plants when they have finished flowering. This will promote reblooming and keep the plants tidy.

Additional Information

Garden slugs are fond of dianthus, but they can be deterred by applying a collar of wood ashes around the plants.

Additional Species, Cultivars, or Varieties

In addition to the old-fashioned sweet william, there are many other species of *Dianthus* for the perennial garden. *D. deltoides* 'Brilliant', maiden pink, makes a nice groundcover (6 to 8 in.) with mat-forming, bright-green foliage. Double bright-crimson blossoms appear for several weeks in summer. Shear or cut back for neatness, vigor, and reblooming. *Dianthus × allwoodii*, cottage pink (12 to 18 in.), has kept its fragrance, grows in mats of grassy-green foliage, and is covered with a profusion flowers at blooming time. Many beautiful cultivars are available.

Thread-Leaf Coreopsis

Coreopsis verticillata

Height: 18 in. to 3 ft.
Flowers: Pale to bright yellow
Bloom Period: Early summer to fall
Zones: 3, 4, 5, 6

Light Requirement:

One of the best flowering perennials for Colorado gardens is *Coreopsis verticillata*. Its common name, thread-leaf coreopsis, describes its finely cut foliage, but one of its finest features is its long blooming season. 'Moonbeam' will bloom from early summer into autumn, with peak bloom in midsummer. The pale-yellow, daisy-like flowers blend so nicely with purple-, blue-, and white-flowering perennials, without distracting. Its finely textured foliage and growth habit gives the plant an attractive airy look. The scientific name, *Coreopsis*, comes from the Greek *koris*, meaning bug, and *opis*, which indicates the resemblance of the seeds to ticks. You can leave it uncut for fall and winter, and the small dark-brown button-like seed-heads will add landscape interest. Some good companions to pair with 'Moonbeam' are salvia 'May Night' and 'Butterfly Blue' pincushion flower.

WHEN TO PLANT

Plant container-grown plants in spring or early summer. Coreopsis can be divided in spring and the new divisions transplanted at the same level they were originally grown.

WHERE TO PLANT

Coreopsis does best in full sun and moderately moist, but well-drained soils. Once established, this plant is very drought-enduring. Use it for perennial borders, mass it as an edging or groundcover, or combine it with ornamental grasses.

HOW TO PLANT

Plant coreopsis 2 to 3 ft. apart. Dig the planting hole twice as wide as the container or the root system. Position the plant so that the soil level is the same as it was in the container. Fill in with soil around the roots about halfway up, gently firm, and water-in well. Once the water has soaked in, add more soil to completely fill the hole. Water regularly until the plants are established.

CARE AND MAINTENANCE
Thread-leaf coreopsis needs little care such as staking, pinching, or watering. In light soils and full sun, this perennial will spread quickly. After several years, older plants will begin to die out in the middle, flowering less profusely or spreading into areas where they are not wanted. This is the time to divide and conquer. In spring, lift the old clumps of spreading rhizomes and fibrous roots, and divide them into sections. Replant the most vigorous and healthy pieces. This is a great way to procure more plants. Water well until established. The variety 'Moonbeam' tends to be fairly tame. It spreads more slowly and is less likely to need division.

ADDITIONAL INFORMATION
When the flowering period begins to wane, you can deadhead the plants by shearing them back to encourage a new crop of leaves and to promote more blooms. If you don't have time, the plant need not be cut back and it will continue to bloom on and off with development of seedheads for fall and winter interest. Cut back the brittle stems in spring to ground level, and apply an all-purpose 5-10-5 granular fertilizer. Lightly cultivate into the soil and water-in well.

ADDITIONAL SPECIES, CULTIVARS, OR VARIETIES
For larger and louder yellow blooms, try 'Golden Showers' with its 2^1/$_2$-inch golden-yellow flowers. It can be somewhat more invasive and require more frequent division. 'Zagreb' has a shorter growth habit (12 to 18 in.) and is useful for edging. 'Moonbeam' is our favorite and forms a nice mound of dark-green foliage and pastel-yellow blossoms. Combine it with blues, purples, and whites in your perennial flower garden for a very special effect. *Coreopsis rosea*, pink coreopsis, is a pink-flowering form that is similar to 'Moonbeam'.

Veronica

Veronica spicata

Other Name: Spiked Speedwell
Height: 18 to 24 in.
Flowers: Blue, pink, white
Bloom Period: Early summer to late summer
Zones: 3, 4, 5, 6

Light Requirement:

*S*piked speedwell is a superior garden perennial that will provide vertical lift to the mounds and mats of the garden foreground and bring a spiky contrast to an abundance of rounded plants. Veronica's tapering spikes of light blue to lavender blossoms tower above the neat clumps of green foliage. Some cultivars such as 'Blue Fox' can be fairly tall at 24 in. and are suitable for the center of the perennial bed or border. The upward spires give visual relief from the flat-topped clusters of golden yarrow—a nice combination. 'Red Fox' sports 8 to 12 in. spikes of red-violet blooms from a low clump of foliage. 'Icicle' has clean white flowers with contrasting dark green foliage that blooms most of the summer. Veronicas are truly the elite of the perennial garden with their showy spikes and variety of growth habits. Some form tight mounds for a rock garden, others are easy-care groundcovers and the taller species are superior for the perennial bed or border. They are an excellent foil for both pastels or hot colors.

When to Plant

Plant container-grown plants of veronica in spring through early fall.

Where to Plant

Choose a location in full sun to partial shade and with average, well-drained soil. Good drainage is a must for this perennial. Loosen the soil well and augment with compost for moisture retention and to improve soil porosity. The soft yellow of 'Moonbeam' coreopsis makes an attractive pairing with light blue veronica 'Blue Peter'. Use it in mixed plantings of lady's mantle, cheddar pinks, and with hardy geraniums.

How to Plant

Space spiked speedwell 18 to 20 in. apart. Dig the planting hole twice as wide as the container or root system. Position the plant so that the soil level is the same as it was in the container or at the same depth the plants were originally growing. Fill in with soil around the roots about halfway, gently firm the soil and water well. After the water has soaked in, complete filling in the hole with soil. Water regularly as the soil dries out. Mulch to conserve water and to keep the soil cooler.

Care and Maintenance

When planted in full sun and well-drained soil, speedwell is durable and pest-resistant. It is important to provide ample water during hot, dry spells. Deadhead the spent flowering spikes to promote rebloom. Avoid too much fertilizer as it will cause the plants to flop over. Older plants can be divided for rejuvenation. This should be done in the spring. Dig the clumps and split them apart with a sharp knife. Replant the vigorous sections taken from the outside of the clumps. Keep new divisions well watered until established.

Additional Information

Taller species of speedwell make good cut flowers. Deadheading as soon as the first blossoms fade will encourage reblooming. Divide old plants every 3 to 4 years to keep the plants vigorous and compact.

Additional Species, Cultivars, or Varieties

Woolly veronica, *V. incana* (12 to 24 in.) is a wonderful plant with silvery foliage and an ocean of navy blue flowers. Use it to border a pathway or driveway. Turkish veronica, *V. liwanensis*, is a superior groundcover that makes a dense mat and thrives in the heat of summer and cold of winter. Foliage is covered with a carpet of cobalt blue flowers in April and June.

PERENNIALS

$\mathcal{C}$OLORADO GARDENERS INSTINCTIVELY LOVE ROSES.
But loving roses and knowing how to grow them are two different matters. As a child, I was always fascinated by the old shrub rose 'Harison's Yellow' that grew along our fence row. It bloomed every year without fail, filling the air with its unforgettable fragrance. Though this old rosebush would bloom only once, it offered hundreds of scented blooms over a three- to four-week period. Today's modern roses, particularly hybrid tea roses, are much more tame and will bloom from summer till a hard frost in autumn. Perhaps we have become spoiled: developing a long bloom period has become the driving force in modern rose breeding. We haven't come to expect this from the spring-blooming daffodils, tulips, and peonies because there are so many other flowering plants to enjoy in each different season.

Fortunately, there are roses for all tastes. Let us briefly explore the world of rose gardening as it pertains to Colorado.

To be a successful rose gardener in Colorado, one must not forget about the practicalities. Roses pose a particular challenge for Colorado gardeners, since many of the modern types cannot endure our cold and fluctuating winter conditions. How much coddling do you want to give to rosebushes in your landscape? It's not only disappointing to buy roses each spring, only to have them die after the first winter, but it's hard on the pocketbook. So if you stumble upon an old variety that is still around, it has stood the test of time, and it deserves consideration. Though that old shrub rose from yesteryear is remarkably water thrifty and adaptable, it roots deeply and demands deep digging prior to planting. Don't expect a rose to do well if you just dig a hole, stick in the bush, and water it now and then. It will take a bit of planning to find the logical location for specific rose varieties and it will take a bit of time to properly prepare the soil.

Chapter Nine

I admit to being a lazy gardener. With the size of our landscape and so many other things to grow, I don't have time to lavish a lot of winter care on needy rosebushes. If I could have it my way, none of our roses would receive special treatment. Over the years we have learned that roses are less demanding than many of the rose gardening books make them out to be. Roses don't need an inordinate amount of care, just a little care on a regular basis. Well-drained soil, adequate moisture, occasional fertilizing, and regular maintenance will make your roses thrive.

With so many roses to choose from, it's a good idea to gain a basic understanding of how roses are classified. The American Rose Society (ARS) lists over fifty categories. This can become quite confusing, even a bit intimidating. You will discover that rose aficionados are very serious about rose classification. That may be fine for them, but for us average gardeners, growing roses should be fun and rewarding. In this chapter, you will find brief descriptions of some of the more popular groups of roses that can be grown successfully in Colorado landscapes. You can even grow roses in pots if you don't have space anywhere else. Happy rose gardening and welcome to Colorado Rose Gardening 101!

LOCATING THE PLANTING SITE

Most roses perform best in full sun, but you can expect excellent results if they are planted in a spot where they receive at least six to eight hours of sun daily. The location should have good air circulation—it should not be a "heat trap" where afternoon sun will stress the plants. Too much shade will yield few flowers and early attacks from powdery mildew disease. Good soil drainage is essential for growing roses successfully. Poorly drained sites or locations where water accumulates will make rosebushes short-lived. To test your soil's drainage, dig several holes eighteen inches deep in scattered locations where you intend to plant. Fill each hole with water. After twelve to twenty-four hours, fill the holes with water again. If the water drains away in eight hours or less, it means your soil is adequately permeable to air and water and will support plant life. Soils that drain as fast as the water enters are too permeable (sandy); soils that do not drain in eight hours are not permeable enough (clay) and will result in oxygen starvation to plant roots. The solution to both problems is similar—add a high-quality organic material such as compost, sphagnum peat moss, or a combination of both. Organic matter will help hold moisture in sandy, fast-draining soils, and open up clay soils to improve drainage and add air.

SOIL PREPARATION

Roses will grow in the varied soils of Colorado, from heavy clay to crushed granite to sandy conditions. The time you invest into building a good soil, however, will produce more vigorous plants with more prolific blossoms. Even the ugliest soil can be improved by adding high-quality organic matter, plus all the loosening and aerating. If the planting location is new, infertile, compacted, and in need of improvement, dig the planting hole three feet wide and eighteen inches deep. The subsoil in the bottom of the hole should be thoroughly loosened. To your native soil, add one-third to one-half compost by volume and thoroughly blend the compost and soil. If your soil does not require such extensive treatment, it can be improved by spreading a two- to three-inch layer of compost over the soil surface and working it in to a depth of ten to twelve inches. Then proceed to dig the appropriate-sized planting hole.

SELECTING ROSES

Rosebushes are available bare-root, potted, and in packages. Mail-order nurseries usually send out bare-root dormant plants. Local garden and nursery retailers sell container-grown roses. Department and grocery stores may offer both packaged and potted roses. Our experience has shown that bare-root dormant plants are excellent choices for Colorado gardens. Planted early in the spring, they acclimate and adapt to local soil conditions very successfully. Potted roses are a good choice if the nursery has practiced good cultural practices in potting and growing the plants. Packaged roses should be purchased before they send out long shoots or before they have had a chance to dry out in storage.

PLANTING

The preferred time to plant roses in Colorado is spring, though container-grown plants can be planted successfully from spring through early fall. The earlier you can plant, the more time the plant will have to develop a strong, vigorous root system before the heat of summer or before the soil freezes. The planting location should be prepared in advance of receiving the roses. If bare-root roses and packaged roses have dry roots when they arrive, put them in a five-gallon bucket of tepid water to soak overnight. Avoid soaking the roots longer than twenty-four hours. Bring the rose to the planting hole and prepare it for planting. Prune away any damaged or broken roots. Position the bush in the hole so that the graft or bud union (swollen knot or knob) will be an inch below ground level. If needed, make a mound of backfill soil in the center of the hole to properly position the bush. Gently add the prepared backfill soil around the roots and firm it with your hands. When you have filled in the hole halfway, stop and water thoroughly. After the water has soaked in, add the remaining soil and water again.

When planting is complete, the top of the bush can be pruned. To keep the center of the bush open for light and air circulation, prune the canes to an outward-facing bud. Pruning cuts should be made at a 30- to 45-degree slant above a bud, leaving six to eight inches of the cane.

Next, cover the newly planted and pruned rosebush with a mound of the loose, prepared backfill soil. This prevents the canes from desiccation while the root system is becoming established. In early spring, this technique will protect the emerging shoots from frost damage. Be careful when removing the soil from around the stems to not damage the tender new growth.

Potted roses can be planted throughout the growing season. Dig the planting hole wide enough to accommodate the root system without crowding and deep enough to position the bud union one inch below ground level. If the roots have become rootbound, carefully loosen and spread them out into the planting hole. Fill in with backfill soil and water-in thoroughly.

WATERING
Roses growing in clay soils will require less watering than roses in sandy soils. To grow vigorously and produce lots of blooms, roses

need plenty of water. Dig down in the top two to four inches of soil—if the soil is dry, it's time to water. When you water, water thoroughly and deeply. To reduce leaf diseases, water roses from the bottom rather than sprinkling overhead. To maintain soil moisture and conserve water, mulch. Pine needles, coarse compost, shredded cedar, and pole peelings are some good choices for mulching roses.

With Colorado's fluctuating weather conditions in late fall and winter, dry air, and long periods without rain or snow, it is important to drag out the hose occasionally and water. Extended dry spells during fall and winter can result in the death of the root system. Watering should be done when air temperatures are above freezing and when the soil is not frozen solid. Apply water early in the day so it will have time to soak in before nightfall. Fall and winter watering may need to be done every five to six weeks, depending on weather and soil conditions.

FERTILIZING

Today's modern roses need several applications of fertilizer to keep blooming and growing vigorously. An appropriate rose fertilizer should be applied monthly, beginning in mid-May and ending in mid-August. Follow label directions on the rose fertilizer package. Pay no attention to the old saying: "If a little fertilizer is good, a bunch more will be even better." To reduce the chance of stressing the roots, water the soil the day before you apply rose food.

PRUNING

A rosebush needs to be pruned to maintain vigor and health, and in some cases to keep the bush in bounds. Depending on the effect you want, roses can be pruned in a variety of ways. In Colorado, don't prune roses back severely in the fall; they need all their stored food energy to withstand our fluctuating climate. Some general guidelines for pruning established roses: prune hybrid teas, grandifloras, floribundas, and polyanthas in the spring at budswell or right after bud-break; climbing roses should be pruned after flowering. Prune the non-productive, old heavy canes of climbing roses to ground level in early spring. Just remember that roses are resilient and will benefit from proper pruning.

Chapter Nine

WINTER CARE

Some of the most popular roses, including hybrid teas, grandifloras, floribundas, and many climbing types, cannot endure the cold, fluctuating Colorado weather conditions. After the first hard freeze, these types can be protected by applying a layer of loose soil at the base of each rose. Make a six- to twelve-inch cone-shaped mound around the base of the canes. For additional protection, you can add evergreen boughs or straw on top of these mounds to protect the upper portions of the canes. Some gardeners use an inverted tomato cage to hold the loose materials in place. Tie the loose canes with soft twine to prevent wind damage. Climbing roses can be laid on the ground and protected with shredded wood mulches or a covering of evergreen boughs. As mentioned in the section on watering, don't forget to water if the weather has been dry and windy.

Climbing Rose

Rosa × hybrida

Height: 10 to 20 ft.
Bloom Period: Late spring, summer
  (may repeat-bloom, depending
  on variety)
Zones: 3, 4, 5, 6

Light Requirement:

*N*o rose is a true climber (no rose has the tendrils necessary for attaching to supports), but members of the group classified as climbers produce long canes that can be tied or trained to a trellis or fence. When trained to a trellis, fence, wall, pillar, or arbor, climbing roses can raise your landscape to new heights. Often included in the group known as "ramblers," these roses generally bloom only once in late spring to early summer. They have mixed parentage and vary in color, growth rate, hardiness, and fragrance. The summer blossoms usually develop on "carryover canes" from the previous year. Climbing roses can grow up to 20 ft. or more if you properly train and guide the canes. In Colorado, it is wise to select the hardier cultivars, as fluctuating winter weather can readily kill exposed and unprotected canes. After a severe winter, climbers may produce few flowers. Most of the hybrid tea climbers are not hardy in Colorado, but the Canadian Explorer series offers hope to gardeners who wish to grow climbers that can withstand Colorado's extreme weather fluctuations. Climbing roses require different care from the care needed by most other roses, so be prepared to devote some extra time to growing these beauties in your landscape.

WHEN TO PLANT

Plant climbing roses in early spring. Bare-root plants can be planted as soon as the soil becomes workable; container-grown bushes can be planted at any time from spring through summer. To reduce transplant shock and stress, it is best to plant before the heat of summer.

WHERE TO PLANT

Plant in full sun in well-drained fertile soil. The location should have good air circulation to reduce the incidence of leaf diseases. If you don't want the rose to sprawl, train climbers on trellises, arbors, pillars, or fences.

How to Plant

First prepare the soil in the planting site by incorporating compost into the soil; this extra effort will ensure longer survival of the rose. Once the compost is blended in, dig the planting hole large enough to accommodate the rose's roots without crowding them. If you are planting a grafted rose, position the bud union about 1 in. below soil level. For bare-root roses, make a mound in the bottom of the planting hole. Prune off damaged or broken roots and spread the healthy roots over the mound to evenly anchor the tree. Fill in about 2/3 of the planting hole with soil, firm gently, and water-in. After the water has soaked in, add the remaining backfill soil and water again. Mulch with cedar shavings, pine needles, or other organic mulch to maintain and conserve moisture. For additional protection from wind desiccation, you can mound soil around the newly planted bare-root rose about 10 to 12 in. deep. After several weeks, when the rose is showing signs of new growth, carefully remove the soil. Regular watering during establishment is essential.

Care and Maintenance

Climbing roses need regular applications of water and fertilizer to grow vigorously and bloom. (Refer to the information at the beginning of this chapter.) Fertilizer should be applied monthly, starting around mid-May and continuing through to mid-August. In mid- to late spring, prune away any dead or "winter killed" canes. Loosely tie or guide the canes to the support structure with twine or fabric strips. Train the canes in any direction you desire.

Additional Information

The canes of climbers are more exposed to severe cold and wind and will often need additional protection to survive Colorado's weather extremes. You can wrap the canes in burlap or other insulating material. If you have the time, canes can be laid to the ground and mulched for winter protection.

Additional Species, Cultivars, or Varieties

Some varieties that grow well in Colorado are 'John Cabot', 'William Baffin', 'Blaze', 'Joseph's Coat', 'American Beauty', 'Dr. J. H. Nicolas', 'New Dawn', 'Don Juan', 'Dortmund', 'Altissimo', 'Golden Showers', 'Galway Bay', and 'Handel'.

Floribunda

Rosa × hybrida

Height: 2 to 5 ft. **Bloom Period:** Early summer to frost **Zones:** 4, 5, 6	**Light Requirement:**

Floribunda roses are the result of crossing hybrid teas with polyanthas. As their name implies, these rosebushes will produce flowers in abundance and have become widely used in commercial and home landscape plantings. Floribundas are versatile roses with a long season of bloom. Their blossoms are borne in clusters like those of polyanthas, but the flowers are larger—reminiscent of the hybrid teas. The floribunda rosebush is generally grows in the 2- to 3-ft. range, but that doesn't stop the bush from producing a continuous show of blooms from early summer through late autumn. This group of roses comes in a rainbow of colors and the blossoms have good fragrance. If you aren't sure if you can grow roses in your garden, start out with a floribunda and you can't go wrong. Floribundas are great for mass plantings, edging pathways or borders, or creating an informal low hedge.

WHEN TO PLANT
Bare-root floribundas should be planted in early spring, just as soon as the soil is workable. If the plants have arrived dry, soak the roots overnight in a bucket of water. Container-grown rosebushes can be planted from spring to early summer.

WHERE TO PLANT
Plant in a sunny location that receives at least 6 to 8 hours of full sun daily. The soil should be well drained and fertile.

HOW TO PLANT
Plant floribunda roses in a prepared garden bed or dig individual planting holes at least 18 in. deep and 2 ft. wide. You can put some of the prepared backfill soil into the hole to form a mound in the center. Position the plant at the proper depth and, if working with a bare-root plant, spread the roots over the mound. The bud or graft

union should be at least 1 in. below ground level. Container-grown plants can be set at the same level they were growing in their pots, but check for the graft union and position accordingly. Fill in about 2/3 of the planting hole with soil, and water-in. After the water has soaked in, add the remaining soil and water again. Apply a mulch to maintain and conserve moisture.

CARE AND MAINTENANCE

Watering roses properly requires careful observation of the plants to see what works best. Since soils differ, it is best to devise your own schedule for watering. Dig down into the soil (2 to 4 in.) and feel to check if it is is dry. Roses grow best in soil that is kept evenly moist but not soggy. Water the soil thoroughly as needed (perhaps once or twice a week). Fertilize floribundas starting in mid-May, and continue monthly through mid-August. Watch the bushes for insects and diseases. Prevention is the best medicine for rose problems.

ADDITIONAL INFORMATION

Floribundas are great roses for beginners. They don't need a lot of coddling, and even if they die back hard each winter, they return with vigorous growth each spring.

ADDITIONAL SPECIES, CULTIVARS, OR VARIETIES

Some reliable varieties to try are 'Betty Prior' (pink with white center), 'Europeana' (dark red), 'Fred Loads' (vermilion-orange), 'Angel Face' (lavender), 'Iceberg' (white), 'Gruss an Aachen' (salmon pink), 'Purple Tiger' (purple-and-white striped), 'Pinocchio' (salmon pink), 'Gene Boerner' (medium pink), 'Sunsprite' (deep yellow), 'Eutin' (carmine red), and 'Nearly Wild' (rosy pink).

Grandiflora

Rosa × hybrida

Height: 4 to 6 ft.	**Light Requirement:**
Bloom Period: Summer to frost	
Zones: 4, 5, 6	

*T*he grandiflora rose is a cross between the hybrid tea and floribunda. Grandiflora rosebushes have the best traits of their parents. The flowers are larger than those of floribundas and may be borne singly or in clusters. The blossoms and long stems come from the hybrid tea parent, while the vigor and abundant blooming come from the floribunda parent. This continuous abundant bloom and tall growth habit make grandiflora roses excellent background plants. Use them as hedges and screens, and as backdrops for other roses in a border. Care for grandiflora roses as you would for hybrid teas (refer to the information at the beginning of this chapter). Grandiflora rosebushes produce long-stemmed blooms that are excellent for cut flowers and floral arrangements.

WHEN TO PLANT

Plant bare-root grandiflora roses in early spring. Container-grown bushes can be planted from spring through fall. It is best to plant before the heat of summer.

WHERE TO PLANT

Grandiflora roses prefer sunny locations where they will receive at least 6 hours of full sun per day. Soil should be well drained and fertile. Read about soil preparation in this chapter's introduction.

HOW TO PLANT

Plant grandiflora roses in a prepared garden bed or dig individual planting holes as described at the beginning of this chapter. Position the graft or bud union about 1 in. below the ground level. Fill in about 2/3 of the hole around the roots with soil; water-in well. After the water has soaked in, add the remaining backfill soil and water again. Mulch with compost or shredded cedar to maintain moisture while the bush is becoming established.

CARE AND MAINTENANCE

As with hybrid tea roses, grandifloras need ample water and nutrients to grow vigorously and repeat-bloom. Water the rosebushes thoroughly when the soil begins to dry out a few inches below the surface. Check your soil conditions to determine the frequency of watering required in your garden. Sandy soils require more attention, while clay soils do not need to be watered as often. Use mulches around your roses to conserve and maintain moisture, and keep the roots cool. Fertilize grandifloras once a month, beginning in mid-May and continuing through mid-August. Prune in mid- to late spring as new growth is emerging. These roses thrive in Colorado's bright sunshine. Provide good air circulation with proper pruning, and disease problems should be minimal.

ADDITIONAL INFORMATION

Grandiflora roses make a nice addition to the Colorado landscape. They are versatile and can be used as screens, hedges, and backdrops, and they can be grown as specimen plants.

ADDITIONAL SPECIES, CULTIVARS, OR VARIETIES

Some popular varieties for Colorado are 'Cherry Vanilla' (pink blend), 'Love' (red with white reverse), 'Pink Parfait' (pink blend), 'Queen Elizabeth' (soft pink), 'Shreveport' (orange blend), 'Prima Donna' (fuchsia pink), 'Solitude' (coral orange), 'Aquarius' (pink blend), 'Arizona' (orange blend), 'Gold Medal' (deep-yellow-tipped orange-red), 'Scarlet Knight' (dark red), and 'Sundowner' (apricot blend).

Hybrid Tea Rose

Rosa × hybrida

Height: 3 to 5 ft. **Bloom Period:** Summer till frost **Zones:** 4, 5, 6	**Light Requirement:**

*P*erhaps the most popular of roses, hybrid teas feature the classic rose form with attractive buds and large flowers. Most of the flowers are produced one bloom to a long stem rather than in clusters. They can range in height from 3 to 5 ft. or more, depending on how the bushes are pruned and trained. Most blooms are composed of many petals; they are generally fragrant and will bloom throughout the entire growing season. One of my favorites, 'Dainty Bess', does not have multiple petals, but flat, single soft-pink blossoms. Hybrid tea roses come in a wide variety of colors, sizes, and shapes. The chosen hybrid tea variety is budded (grafted) onto a hardy rootstock. This practice makes the plant better adapted to a wide range of soils. The area on which the new stem sprouts is called the bud or graft union, and it appears as a swelling at the base of the bush. In Colorado, the bud union can be vulnerable to winter damage, particularly during fluctuating weather conditions. Intolerably cold, drying winds, long dry periods, and a roller coaster ride of temperature extremes can all damage or kill the graft union. Hybrid tea roses require some extra care in cold climates, but they can be successfully grown in many Colorado landscapes. Refer to this chapter's introduction for more details on planting and protecting.

WHEN TO PLANT
Plant bare-root rosebushes in early spring, as soon as the soil is workable. Container-grown plants can be planted as soon as they are available at garden outlets, but they are best planted before the heat of summer.

WHERE TO PLANT
Hybrid tea roses prefer full-sun locations that have good air circulation. The soil should be well drained and fertile. Heavy, compacted areas should be loosened deeply (18 in.) and enriched with compost

to improve drainage and increase fertility. See the section on soil at the beginning of this chapter.

How to Plant

Hybrid teas are notorious for suffering winter damage to the bud or graft union. Plant this swollen portion about 1 in. below the ground level. This area is easy to identify on bare-root plants, but you may not see it right away on container-grown bushes; gently dig around the base to find the origin of the graft union and position the plant in the planting hole accordingly. Dig the hole 18 in. to 2 ft. deep and at least 18 in. wide, wider if necessary, to spread out the roots without cramping. Position the rosebush and fill in about 2/3 of the hole with the prepared backfill soil; water well. After the water has soaked in, add the remaining soil and water again. Mulch with shredded cedar or compost to maintain moisture while the plant is becoming established.

Care and Maintenance

Hybrid tea roses need plenty of water and nutrients to grow vigorously and produce flowers throughout the growing season. They require less-frequent watering in clay soils than in sandy soils. Roses prefer soil that is evenly moist but not soggy. Apply water at the base of the bush, soaking the soil thoroughly, at least once a week. Organic mulches help conserve moisture and keep the roots cool. Add fertilizer once a month according to the manufacturer's recommendations.

Additional Information

When removing a bloom from a hybrid tea rose, make the cut above a five-leaflet leaf; this will promote a new flowering sprout. Monitor the plants for signs of insect pests or diseases and stop them before severe damage occurs. Homemade soap solutions and a forceful spray of water from the hose can keep aphids and mites at bay.

Additional Species, Cultivars, or Varieties

Here are some varieties to grow: 'La France' (silvery pink, reverse bright pink), 'Peace' (yellow flushed with pink), 'Double Delight' (white-yellow with red edges), 'Chicago Peace' (deep pink with yellow base), 'Dainty Bess' (pink, 5-petaled), 'Honor' (white), 'Mikado' (scarlet with gold base), 'Mister Lincoln' (deep red), 'Miss All-American Beauty' (medium pink), 'Olympiad' (medium red), 'Paradise' (lavender blend), 'Sutter's Gold' (orange-yellow), and 'Pascali' (white).

ROSES

Miniature Rose

Rosa × hybrida

Height: 6 to 24 in. **Bloom Period:** Summer until frost **Zones:** 3, 4, 5, 6	**Light Requirement:**

*M*iniature roses are the little jewels of a Colorado garden. They possess the same characteristics of many of the larger roses, only in miniature. A rainbow of colors is available with tiny pointed buds, fully formed blooms (some fragrant), delicate foliage, and a compact growth habit. They can be grown as tiny bushes, cascading from planters, and even as climbers. These close-to-the-ground roses are adapted to endure Colorado's climate. Miniatures are excellent for gardeners who have limited space; they can be grown in containers and brought indoors for the winter if you have a sunny, cool location. They are generally much hardier than other roses and don't need extensive winter protection. Light mulching will provide some winter protection and help retain moisture.

WHEN TO PLANT

Mini-roses in containers can be planted at any time from spring through fall. Bare-root plants should be planted in spring as soon as the soil becomes workable. It is best to plant them early enough to allow the roots to become established before the leaves emerge.

WHERE TO PLANT

Plant miniature roses where they will receive full sun. If this is not possible, the location should get at least 6 hours of sun daily. These smaller plants do not require intensive soil preparation, but the soil should be well drained. Use miniature roses for borders, around shrubs, in front of perennials, or in front of taller roses.

HOW TO PLANT

To get the best results from miniature roses, prepare the planting site in advance. Add 4 to 6 in. of compost and work it into the soil to a depth of 8 in. or more. Mark, then dig, the planting holes. This one-time preparation will reward you with healthy, vigorous, free-blooming plants. Dig the hole large enough to accommodate the root system. For a bare-root rose, spread the roots out on a small mound in the bottom of the planting hole. Hold the plant so that it will be planted at the same level it was growing in the nursery; plant container-grown plants at the same level they were growing in their original containers. If planting miniatures in pots, use a compost-based, well-drained potting soil. Keep the rootball intact and position it in the planting hole. Add soil around the bush about halfway, and water. After the water has soaked in, add the remaining soil to complete the planting, and water again. Apply a 2-in. layer of mulch to maintain and conserve moisture.

CARE AND MAINTENANCE

Because miniature roses generally have shallow root systems, it is necessary to maintain a moist soil. Fertilize monthly beginning in mid-May, and make a final fertilizer application around mid-August. A time-released plant fertilizer works nicely, saving time. This type of fertilizer can be used in container gardening as well. Maintain mulch around the plants to conserve moisture and keep the soil cool during summer. Prune miniatures in spring as new growth begins to break. Remove dead, broken, or weak stems. Deadhead, or remove faded blooms, to encourage repeat flowering.

ADDITIONAL INFORMATION

Miniature roses are propagated on their own root systems, so they are well adapted to Colorado's climate. Winter protection is usually not necessary, other than watering during long, dry spells. Winter mulching is easy because you can cover most, if not all, of the bush with loose soil after the ground has frozen. Snow is an excellent cover, too!

ADDITIONAL SPECIES, CULTIVARS, OR VARIETIES

There are hundreds of miniature roses from which to choose. The American Rose Society suggests the following, giving each one a rating of 8.5 or higher: 'Rainbow's End', 'Magic Carrousel', 'Jean Kenneally', 'Minnie Pearl', 'Winsome', 'Rise'n Shine', 'Cupcake', and 'Millie Walters'. Check with your area rose society and rose catalogs for a multitude of other varieties.

Old Garden Rose

Rosa × hybrida

Height: 3 to 9 ft.
Bloom Period: Summer and repeat to frost
Zones: 4, 5, 6

Light Requirement:

The old garden rose category consists of roses that were introduced before 1867. Their old-fashioned look is reminiscent of grandma's garden of rich fragrant blooms whose scents permeated the evening air. Many of these roses produce large hips that can be collected to make tea and homemade jellies. Old garden roses have been in cultivation for centuries; today these hardy plants are gaining popularity, and for good reason. Old garden roses, also known as heritage roses, are ideal candidates for Colorado landscapes. Unlike the modern-day hybrid tea roses, they are low-maintenance, hardy, and disease resistant. They do need room to grow, so take this into consideration when selecting your planting sites. Unlike contemporary roses, most of the old garden roses thrive without a lot of coddling and pruning. As you drive around Colorado's back roads and see roses blooming around long-abandoned homesites, you can bet that they are the result of gardeners who planted an old garden rose. Old garden roses form a large class that can be broken down into sub-classifications distinguished by their parentage. The sub-classifications include Alba, Centifolia, Damask, Gallica, Moss, Tea, Hybrid Perpetual, Bourbon, China, Noisette, and Portland. Old garden roses offer a range of scents from a light "tea scent" to a heavy musk-like scent.

WHEN TO PLANT

Get bare-root plants into the ground in spring as soon as the soil can be worked. Early planting allows the roots to get started before the canes break into leaf. Container-grown roses can be transplanted at any time from spring to fall.

WHERE TO PLANT

Plant in a location that receives full sunshine all day. If this is not possible, plant where they will receive a minimum of 6 hours bright sun daily. Morning sun is essential, and afternoon shade is acceptable. Good air circulation is important for reducing the incidence of disease. Old garden roses need plenty of room, so choose an appropriate location. They can be used as a backdrop or for specimen planting.

How to Plant

Loosen the soil deeply in the area you select to plant old garden roses. Add 2 to 4 in. of well-aged manure or compost and incorporate it into the soil to a depth of 12 to 18 in. Why so deep? Soil deeply enriched will grow vigorous, healthy, trouble-free, long-living roses. This will be your once-only chance to change the soil structure this deeply. After the amendments have been worked in, settle the soil by watering. Dig the planting hole 18 to 24 in. wide and 18 in. deep. The hole should be big enough so the roots won't be cramped. For bare-root roses, make a mound in the bottom of the planting hole. Prune off any damaged roots and broken canes, and position the rose on the mound, spreading out the roots. If the rose has been grafted, set the plant so that the bud union is 1 in. below the surrounding soil. Firm the soil gently to eliminate any air pockets underneath the roots. Fill in with backfill soil about 2/3 of the way, and water well. After the water has soaked in, add the remaining soil. Mulch with shredded cedar, pine needles, or other suitable mulch. For additional protection, mound soil around the bare-root rose about 10 to 12 in. deep. After several weeks, when the rose is showing signs of new growth, carefully remove the mound of soil.

Care and Maintenance

Water your newly planted roses regularly. Old garden roses are resistant to pests and diseases. They have low fertility requirements, but will benefit from a late-spring application of an all-purpose 5-10-5. They need little pruning other than that required to maintain shape and spread. Pruning is best done in spring to remove dead or damaged canes. Older woody branches can be removed periodically to rejuvenate an older bush and encourage young vigorous growth.

Additional Information

Although many of the old garden roses bloom only once with a spectacular showing, others will repeat-bloom throughout the season. Check descriptions for specific information.

Additional Species, Cultivars, or Varieties

A few old garden roses to grow are 'Maiden's Blush' (Alba), 'La Reine Vicotoria' (Bourbon), 'Boule de Neige' (Bourbon), 'Centifolia Variegata' (Centifolia), 'Petite Lisette' (Centifolia), 'Shailer's Provence' (Centifolia), 'Rouletii' (China), 'Blush Damask', 'Autumn Damask', 'Crested Jewel' (Moss), 'Gloire des Mousseuses' (Moss), and 'Marbree' (Portland).

Polyantha

Rosa × hybrida

Height: 2 to 3 ft. **Bloom Period:** Summer to frost **Zones:** 3, 4, 5, 6	**Light Requirement:**

olyanthas are generally low-growing, free-flowering roses. They are among the hardiest, at least more so than the hybrid teas. (That's a plus for us lazy gardeners!) The cultivar 'The Fairy' is one of the hardiest; it will thrive without winter coddling, down to a temperature of -25 degrees Fahrenheit. The name polyantha means "many flowers," and these roses will bloom continually throughout the growing season. The flowers are smaller than those of many roses, but they are produced in mass quantities from late early summer through the first hard frost in autumn. Polyantha roses have very small, narrow leaves that are somewhat delicate and finely textured; this foliage characteristic comes from their multiflora parentage. Because the plants have a compact growth habit, they make ideal bushes for mass planting and for use in borders and informal hedging, and the dwarf varieties are ideal candidates for containers. Blossoms may be single, double, or semi-double, and they come in a rainbow of colors. Some are fragrant. Polyanthas have neatly-formed flower buds; they make nice cut flowers in small bud vases.

WHEN TO PLANT

Plant polyantha roses in spring. Bare-root plants can be set out as soon as the soil can be worked. Container-grown bushes can be planted from spring through early summer. Try to beat the summer heat.

WHERE TO PLANT

As is true for most roses, you will get the best performance from polyanthas when they are planted in a full-sun site that has good air circulation. The soil should be well drained, and amended with compost as needed. See the information at the beginning of this chapter. Plant polyanthas in groups, for low shrub borders, and as edging for taller plants; the dwarf polyanthas can be grown in containers.

HOW TO PLANT

Have the planting site and soil prepared well in advance. It is much easier to dig the hole and plant if the organic material has had time to meld with the soil for a while. Dig the planting hole 18 in. to 2 ft. wide and at least 18 in. deep. Don't cramp the roots in the hole. For a bare-root plant, make a mound in the bottom of the planting hole. Prune off any damaged roots, position the rose on the soil mound, and spread out the roots. If the rose is grafted, the bud union should be set about 1 in. below soil grade. Fill in about $2/3$ of the hole with backfill soil, gently firm the soil, and water-in. After the water has soaked in, add the remaining backfill soil and water again. Mulch with shredded cedar shavings, pine needles, or other organic material to maintain and conserve moisture. For additional protection during establishment, mound the soil around the newly planted rose about 10 to 12 in. deep. After several weeks, as the rose is showing signs of growth, carefully remove the soil.

CARE AND MAINTENANCE

Keep roses well watered and mulched during early establishment, but don't let them get soggy. Fertilizer can be applied around mid-May; continue applications through mid-August. Roses need to begin a "hardening-off" process before winter arrives. Read and follow label directions on the fertilizer container, and don't go overboard with feeding. Prune in spring as signs of growth are starting to show. Keep an eye out for insect pests and diseases, and treat appropriately. Prevention is the best medicine if you want healthy, vigorous roses.

ADDITIONAL INFORMATION

The number of polyantha selections may be smaller than that of other roses, but those available are really worth growing. 'China Doll' is an excellent choice; it has soft-pink blossoms.

ADDITIONAL SPECIES, CULTIVARS, OR VARIETIES

Try growing some of these varieties: 'Cécile Brünner' (white-and-pink blend), 'Dick Koster' (deep pink), 'Mignonette' (rosy pink), 'Margo Koster' (salmon pink), 'The Fairy' (light pink), and 'China Doll' (soft pink).

Species Roses

Rosa spp.

Height: 4 to 12 ft. **Bloom Period:** Late spring and early summer **Zones:** 3, 4, 5, 6	**Light Requirement:**

$\mathcal{S}$pecies roses are tough, disease resistant, and quite winter hardy in Colorado. They will thrive in a wide range of soils and will adapt to higher elevations. Most of the species roses bloom once, early in the season. Although modest, the blossoms are beautiful, and most are very fragrant. After flowering, brightly colored seed hips develop; these add landscape interest and provide a source of food for wild birds. Species roses require a minimum of care and maintenance. Spraying chemicals, lots of pruning, and mounding with mulch in the chilly days of late fall are all chores that are unnecessary for these roses. Just be sure to allow plenty of room for the plants to grow. The flowers of species roses usually have single petals; some have edible fruits. One of our favorites in our landscape is the Austrian copper rose with its early show of blooms in orange-red and yellow, some-times on the same bush. *Rosa glauca*, which has single pink blossoms, has particularly attractive silvery foliage overlaid with hues of maroon. This rose works well in shrub and perennial borders. Many species roses have contributed to crosses with other roses, resulting in improved hybrids.

WHEN TO PLANT
Plant bare-root roses in spring as soon as the soil can be worked. Early planting will allow the roots to become established before the canes break into leaf. Container-grown bushes can be planted into the landscape any time from spring to fall. If planting in the heat of summer, be vigilant about watering so the rosebush will not be stressed by becoming parched.

WHERE TO PLANT
Species roses are adapted to a variety of conditions from full sun to partial shade. They do best with a minimum of 6 hours of full sun daily; afternoon shade is acceptable. Good air circulation is essential for discouraging leaf diseases. It is important that the soil be well

drained. A row of species roses can make an attractive backdrop for other roses or a perennial garden. They can be used for hedging, softening a fence, or lining a long driveway.

How to Plant

Dig the planting hole 18 to 24 in. wide and at least 18 in. deep. If the soil was not previously prepared, add compost to improve drainage and retain moisture. For a bare-root bush, make a mound in the bottom of the planting hole. Remove broken or damaged parts and broken canes. Position the rose on the mound and spread out the roots so they won't be cramped. Look for *rugosa* roses grown on their own roots. If the rose is grafted, it should be positioned so the bud union is 1 in. below the surrounding grade. Gently firm the soil to remove any air pockets underneath the roots. Fill in around the rose about 2/3 of the way with backfill soil and water. After the water has soaked in, add the remaining soil and water. Apply a 2- to 3-in. layer of mulch to maintain and conserve moisture.

Care and Maintenance

Keep the newly planted rose well watered during the time of establishment. Once species roses are established, they need only to be watered deeply and infrequently. They will not tolerate overwatering. It is best to allow them to become naturalized, which will cause them to be hardy. In spring, prune or thin out dead canes if needed. Firm, green canes will greet you for another season of growth and bloom. Fertilizer needs are minimal, but you can apply a 5-10-5 in late spring; that single application is all that's required.

Additional Information

Species roses generally need little pruning. Each bush will develop its own character, and you may wish to train the bush to your individual liking. Older wood can be removed to stimulate and encourage young vigorous growth.

Additional Species, Cultivars, or Varieties

There are several selections and named varieties derived from species roses that do well in Colorado. Some tough *rugosa* hybrids are 'Blanc Double de Coubert', a semi-double white; 'Mrs. Anthony Waterer', which has double magenta blooms; and 'Therese Bugnet', a semi-double pink. *Rosa xanthina* f. *hugonis*, Father Hugo rose, has single yellow flowers with showy stamens; its blooms are followed by small maroon rose hips and handsome orange-bronze fall foliage. Among the favorites in our garden are *Rosa* × *harisonii* (Harison's yellow), *Rosa foetida* bicolor (Austrian copper), and *Rosa spinosissima*, which has single white blooms and fern-like foliage.

Shrubs

AT ONE TIME SHRUBS WERE SIMPLY THE PLANTS THAT HOME OWNERS AUTOMATICALLY PLANTED AROUND THE FOUNDATION—just because every other house in the neighborhood used them that way. But you don't have to install shrubs in this antiquated fashion. They are as diverse as the gardeners who grow them, and they can serve several different functions. Shrubs provide a solid background for perennial and annual flower beds. Many have unique flowers and fruit that add color and texture to the landscape. These plants provide privacy, screen out unsightly views, or even serve as a windbreak to protect some of our more tender and vulnerable plant selections. They offer shelter and food to attract wild birds, an important asset for those of us who believe that the landscape should be heard as well as seen. The sweet fragrance of my grandmother Nonnita's lilacs at the front entranceway is a treasured memory for me. With the right planning, shrubs offer beauty and versatility to our Colorado landscapes in every season. The shrubs chosen for this chapter are among the best for Colorado, but there are many more that can be utilized. Feel free to experiment and discover some that may soon become your favorites.

WHAT IS A SHRUB?

Generally speaking, the classification "shrub" refers to that group of plants that are woody, like trees, but smaller in stature. Some are deciduous, losing their leaves in winter, while others are evergreen. Some evergreen shrubs have needles; these are often the shorter species of the evergreens that normally grow as trees. Some evergreen shrubs, like 'Berries Magic' holly, *Ilex × meserveae*, have broad leaves. Some shrubs are grown for their flowers, some for their berries, and some, like burning bush, are noted for their brilliant autumn color. Among the many pleasures of growing these plants is

Chapter Ten

discovering ways to combine the various shrubs so that they complement the other plants in our garden.

Many shrubs will live to a ripe old age, so allow them space in which to grow and spread their branches. Unless you're planting a hedge, keep in mind a shrub's mature landscape size when choosing its location.

Caring for Shrubs

Shrubs are among the most adaptable and easy-to-care-for landscape plants. Like trees, most shrubs develop root systems that help them endure periods of drought, yet their small size allows them to be moved if needed. Growing shrubs successfully in Colorado begins with making the right choices, being sure to select a shrub whose needs match the special growing conditions in your area. Most shrubs are relatively resistant to insects and diseases. If a problem should develop, it's generally the fault of the gardener, not of the shrub. If spider mites appear on a euonymus, that is probably an indication that the shrub's natural defense system is stressed from being planted too close the house or fence or other "heat-trap."

Soil

As with most plants, shrubs will thrive in well-drained soils that have been enriched with compost or other high-quality organic matter. Most soils in Colorado are both alkaline (high pH) and low in organic matter—but don't overamend the soil with too much organic matter. When it comes to supplementing the backfill soil, less is better. Adding excessive amounts of organic amendments or fertilizer to the planting hole will create a "bathtub" effect: the roots of a newly planted shrub may decide to remain within the planting hole and never explore the surrounding native soil. Roots will grow and move into soil that contains a balance of oxygen and moisture, so the best advice is to dig the planting hole wide rather than deep, loosening the soil thoroughly.

A Tip on Planting

Container-grown shrubs that have a tight mass of roots encircling the rootball and no soil visible are considered extremely rootbound. In these situations, use the "split ball" or "butterfly" technique. This method of root pruning is done by laying the plant on its side and slicing through the rootball vertically from the bottom about halfway to the top. Spread the two halves, like butterfly wings, over a mound of soil in the planting hole. Add the backfill soil and water slowly. A note of caution: don't use this technique on larger balled-and-burlapped shrubs, newly potted specimens, or containerized plants whose roots are not rootbound.

Pruning Shrubs

Many trees never need pruning after they reach a mature shape, but shrubs will benefit from regular pruning. Pruning is done to achieve specific results—to keep the shrub the proper size and shape, to help it produce more flowers, or to rejuvenate a tired, old shrub into youthful vigor. The pruning of shrubs can be a simple procedure which means removing three to five of the oldest stems each year almost to ground level (leaving stubs of only three to four inches). New buds on the stubs will become activated to grow into new, vigorous stems. This process is called "renewal" pruning. It will keep the shrub youthful with healthy stems that produce more flowers. Pruning to limit a shrub's size is generally reserved for those plants that have outgrown their space (this may occur if the wrong shrub was selected to fit the planting site). Try to make the pruning cuts just beyond a healthy bud or small branch you would like to preserve on the shrub. To enjoy the pruning process, use a sharp pair of by-pass hand pruners. If larger stems need to be cut off, a long-handled lopper will make this task a breeze. Forget about those electric hedge trimmers; the problems they cause usually outweigh their benefits. Shearing the tops of shrubs with trimmers and clippers will turn your favorite shrubs into "green meatballs." The resulting dense shell of green foliage on the top and outside of the shrub

Chapter Ten

causes the inside to become dark, dead, and lifeless. You will always get the best results and maintain the shrub's natural shape by using hand tools.

Prune flowering shrubs to promote more blooms. Those shrubs that bloom on last-season's growth, such as lilacs and forsythia, should be pruned right after they flower. If you prune any of these in fall or winter, you'll remove the flower buds for next spring!

Those that bloom on current-season's growth, such as butterfly bush, blue mist spirea, summer spirea, and potentilla, should be pruned in early spring. Many of these perform at their best if cut back to the ground in March.

Alpine Currant

Ribes alpinum

Height: 3 to 6 ft.	**Light Requirement:**
Spread: 3 to 6 ft.	
Flowers: Greenish-yellow	
Bloom Period: Early spring	
Zones: 2, 3, 4, 5, 6	

*I*t's easy to see why this old-fashioned shrub was beloved by our ancestors. It is hardy, is tolerant of most garden soils, and will thrive in sun or partial shade. Its compact growth habit makes it a good choice for small hedges, an informal shrub border, or a backdrop for the flower garden. It needs very little pruning to maintain its neat and tidy appearance. This is an excellent naturescape plant that will attract wildlife to your garden. The greenish-yellow flowers are inconspicuous; they are followed by juicy red berries that can be eaten by wildlife. If you live in the High Country, this shrub is a must.

WHEN TO PLANT
Plant container-grown shrubs in spring through early fall. Bare-root plants should be planted in spring as soon as the soil can be worked. These shrubs transplant easily.

WHERE TO PLANT
Locate in full sun to part shade. Currants do very well in almost any garden soil that is well drained. Use alpine currant for a shrub border, a background, or for mass plantings.

HOW TO PLANT
Dig the planting hole wide enough to accommodate the root system. Loosen the soil in the planting area and add compost if the soil is extremely sandy or rich in clay. Plant bare-root plants in early spring. Inspect the root system of shrubs grown in containers. If the roots form a tight mass that encircles the rootball, the shrub has been in the pot for awhile and is rootbound. As long as the plant is healthy, it is acceptable for purchase. To make sure it survives, use the "butterfly technique" to plant it. To do this, lay the plant and the rootball on their sides; with a knife or sharp shovel, cut through the

lower portion of the rootball. Insert the knife in line with the main trunk or stems and slice through the bottom of the rootball to a distance halfway up. This will allow you to spread the lower halves of the rootball apart. When positioning the shrub in the planting hole, you are bringing the roots, which have grown to the bottom of the container, nearer the surface where soil conditions are more favorable for vigorous root development. Add backfill soil to the planting hole and water slowly to eliminate any air pockets underneath the roots. Space plants 3 ft. apart to form hedges. Mulch with shredded wood chips or pine needles.

CARE AND MAINTENANCE
Currants are widely adaptable and easy to maintain. Water them when the soil dries out. Avoid overfertilizing since this will lead to lanky, weak growth. Trim out the oldest canes after flowering to keep a shrub growing vigorously. Prune in spring to shape and to keep the plant in bounds for hedge purposes.

ADDITIONAL INFORMATION
The alpine currant is easily transplanted. It is an excellent plant for higher elevations in the High Country. Wild birds love the fruit, so be sure to include it in a wildlife garden.

ADDITIONAL SPECIES, CULTIVARS, OR VARIETIES
Golden currant, *Ribes aureum*, is a native with spicy, clove-scented blooms followed by edible black berries in late summer. Its foliage is a striking scarlet red in autumn. *Ribes odoratum* is similar to *R. aureum*, but its young stems are pubescent. *Ribes cereum*, wax currant, is a low growing native (2 to 4 ft.) with grayish-green foliage and bright-red berries. It is useful for mass planting and for naturalized areas.

American Plum

Prunus americana

Height: 10 to 20 ft.
Spread: 8 to 12 ft.
Flowers: White
Bloom Period: Early spring
Zones: 3, 4, 5, 6

Light Requirement:

A common native plant, American plum is frequently seen growing along roadsides in the plains of Colorado. It is a harbinger of spring, blooming profusely before its leaves emerge. Many gardeners still use the fruit to make jam and jelly. American plum is a tough, widely adaptable shrub. It can be used as a background plant or as a single-trunk specimen. Unlike many other *Prunus* species, American plum is resistant to crown borers. It makes an excellent tall shrub for a naturescape.

WHEN TO PLANT

Plant American plum in spring. Bare-root plants can be transplanted in early spring. Container-grown specimens are available at many local nurseries.

WHERE TO PLANT

This shrub does best in well-drained soils in a site with full sun. Use it as a backdrop or informal hedge, or in a windbreak.

HOW TO PLANT

Dig the planting hole 2 to 3 times wider than the rootball. Add compost to the planting site (25 to 30 percent by volume) and loosen the soil thoroughly. Inspect the root system of shrubs grown in containers. If the roots form a tight mass that encircles the rootball, the shrub has been in the pot for a while and is rootbound. As long as the plant is healthy, it is acceptable for purchase. To ensure its survival, use the "butterfly technique" to plant a rootbound plant. Lay the plant and rootball on their sides. Using a knife or sharp shovel, cut through the lower portion of the rootball. Insert the knife in line with the main trunk or stems and slice through the bottom of the rootball halfway up its length. This will allow you to spread the lower halves of the rootball apart. When positioning the shrub in the planting hole, place the roots which were growing at the bottom of the container nearer the surface, where soil conditions are more favorable for vigorous root development; water-in thoroughly. Water regularly when the soil begins to dry out.

CARE AND MAINTENANCE

Once American plum becomes established in the landscape, it will be a permanent feature. It tends to sucker and spread, so prune periodically to help keep it in bounds. A complete fertilizer such as 10-10-10 can be applied in early to mid-spring according to package directions. Keep in mind, though, that too much fertilizer will make the plant leggy and weak. Avoid overwatering *Prunus*, as it can quickly succumb and will suffer in poorly drained soils.

ADDITIONAL INFORMATION

American plum is prone to leaf spot fungi, powdery mildew, and aphids. Early detection and control will prevent severe problems. Many *Prunus* are subject to crown borer. Another common summer pest is the pear slug. An infestation of this pest causes the leaves to become skeletonized. One of the safest ways to control pear slugs is by dusting the foliage with wood ashes. This will transform the pests into "crispy critters."

ADDITIONAL SPECIES, CULTIVARS, OR VARIETIES

There are many species of *Prunus* for Colorado landscapes, though some of them, such as purpleleaf plum, have been overused. One of the lesser-used yet more drought-resistant varieties is *Prunus besseyi*, western sandcherry. It is a low-growing shrub (about 3 ft. tall or more) that produces masses of white flowers in May. The glossy silver-green leaves are quite showy and turn burgundy-red in the fall. Western sandcherry is one of the few selections that will tolerate hot, dry conditions. The 3/4-inch black cherries are edible, but birds and other wildlife may beat you to them.

Apache Plume

Fallugia paradoxa

Height: 3 to 6 ft.	**Light Requirement:**
Spread: 3 to 6 ft.	
Flowers: White	
Bloom Period: Late spring	
Zones: 3, 4, 5, 6	

The Apache plume grows as a lacy, arching shrub with finely dissected leaves. Because it is drought-enduring and can be planted in dry, sunny locations, it is a good choice for Colorado landscapes. Attractive single white rose-like flowers appear in early summer and continue to bloom through late summer. As the flowers mature, rounded, feathery silver-pink seedheads develop. These seed plumes are quite decorative on the shrub, particularly when they are backlit by the sun. They add fall and winter interest to the garden. The Apache plume adds color to the landscape and is effective as a single specimen plant or when combined with perennials such as Russian sage (*Perovskia atriplicifolia*) for use as a shrub border. Its ability to survive Colorado's arid climate and hot, dry summers makes this shrub a must for water-thrifty landscapes.

When to Plant

Plant container-grown plants in spring. Though you may have to check with several local nurseries to find this shrub, Apache plume is well worth the effort. It may be available through some mail-order catalogs.

Where to Plant

Plant this shrub in a well-drained site. Choose a location that receives full sun. Apache plume is an excellent choice for dry, open, sunny locations; it combines well with our native soapweed, *Yucca glauca*. Compacted soils should be loosened and amended with scoria (crushed volcanic rock) or pea gravel to add porosity and improve drainage. A small amount of compost (20 to 25 percent by volume) can be mixed with the backfill soil. This shrub is useful for erosion control on rocky slopes. It is a great plant for mass plantings.

How to Plant

Dig the planting hole to accommodate the root system and loosen the soil well beyond the shrub. It may take two growing seasons for the plant to establish, so add a mulch of pine needles or pea gravel to conserve natural moisture and reduce soil compaction. Water deeply but infrequently.

Care and Maintenance

Shrubs that are planted in very hot, dry locations will need to be thoroughly and deeply watered several times during the spring and summer to sustain growth and flowering. Pruning is generally not recommended; Apache plume looks best when it is allowed to grow and cascade naturally. Once it is established, a few suckers may appear, but these can be dug and transplanted. Older stems can be periodically cut to ground level to encourage new growth. This is one shrub that will not tolerate "wet feet," so be careful not to overwater at any time of the year. Apache plume will often succumb in wet winter situations where drainage is poor.

Additional Information

Although this shrub is widely adaptable to Colorado soils, clay soils that are overwatered will cause the plant to succumb. Check soil conditions and amend as needed to improve drainage. Native Americans used the stems of Apache plume to make brooms and arrow shafts. The whitish exfoliating bark adds seasonal interest to the Colorado landscape.

Additional Species, Cultivars, or Varieties

This is the only species in cultivation. You may have to shop around or purchase the plant via a mail-order nursery catalog.

Barberry

Berberis spp.

Height: 3 to 5 ft.
Spread: 3 to 6 ft.
Flowers: Yellow
Bloom Period: Late spring
Zones: 4, 5, 6

Light Requirement:

*B*arberry is a popular upright-growing shrub that is used for hedging, in mass plantings, and as an accent plant. It is mainly deciduous, though some cultivars are semi-evergreen with foliage that persists into winter. Barberry's inner wood is yellow and its leaves grow in small clusters. The leaves turn a brilliant orange, red, or yellow in autumn. The foliage is dense and the bush produces a multitude of arching branches with thorns. Though barberry is not noted for its flowers, small yellow or red blooms appear each spring, followed by red berries in late summer. There are many selections available. Read through mail-order catalogs and check with your local garden retailer for some outstanding color variations.

WHEN TO PLANT

Plant in spring through fall. Container-grown plants are readily available.

WHERE TO PLANT

To get the most intense leaf color, plant in full sun. Some varieties will tolerate partial shade. Most are adapted to our Colorado soils, though 'Japanese Redleaf Barberry' is notorious for chlorosis (yellowing leaves) in highly alkaline soils. Use barberry as a barrier plant or plant it as an informal hedge.

HOW TO PLANT

Dig the planting hole 2 to 3 times wider than the rootball. In soils that are compacted and poorly drained, it is advisable to amend the soil with compost before planting. This will help maintain soil fertility and moisture. When planting a hedge, space plants 2 ft. apart; space them 5 to 6 ft. apart for mass plantings. Inspect the root system of shrubs grown in containers. If the roots form a tight mass that encircles the rootball, the shrub has been in the pot for a while and is rootbound. As long as the plant is healthy, it is acceptable for purchase. To ensure its survival, use the "butterfly technique" to plant a rootbound plant. Lay the plant and rootball on their sides. Using a knife or sharp shovel, cut through the lower portion of the rootball. Insert the knife in line with the main trunk or stems and slice through the bottom of the rootball halfway up its length. This will allow you to spread the lower halves of the rootball apart. When positioning the shrub in the planting hole, place the roots which were growing at the bottom of the container nearer the surface, where soil conditions are more favorable for vigorous root development.

CARE AND MAINTENANCE

Barberry takes a few years to establish. After establishment, it has good drought resistance. It is sensitive to excess moisture, so avoid frequent watering. As individual plants become ragged, cut the oldest canes down to ground level. This technique will rejuvenate the shrub with fresh, colorful stems and brightly colored leaves.

ADDITIONAL INFORMATION

Barberry's growth habit and thorns make it a good foundation plant for thwarting would-be burglars or stray animals. If this shrub should develop a problem with iron chlorosis due to a lack of available iron, apply a chelated iron nutrient in spring. This will provide essential iron for that growing season.

ADDITIONAL SPECIES, CULTIVARS, OR VARIETIES

'Crimson Pygmy' (Berberis thunbergii var. atropurpurea) is a low-growing form with deep-red foliage. At a height of 18 to 24 in., it makes a nice background plant or accent plant. Berberis × 'Tara', or emerald carousel barberry, is a good choice for our region. It grows 4 to 5 ft. in height with a comparable spread. The 'Japanese Redleaf Barberry' has showy reddish-purple leaves and good reddish-orange fall color. 'Cherrybomb' is an intermediate-sized plant that grows 3 to 4 ft. tall with an equal spread. Berberis thunbergi 'Kobold' has a compact growing habit (1 to 2 ft.) and will grow in sun or part shade. Berberis koreana, or Korean barberry, has spreading, thorny branches clothed by dark-green oval leaves that turn deep red in the fall.

Beauty Bush

Kolkwitzia amabilis

Height: 6 to 12 ft.
Spread: 8 to 12 ft.
Flowers: Pink
Bloom Period: Early summer
Zones: 3, 4, 5, 6

Light Requirement:

Beauty bush is a hardy, old-fashioned shrub that has withstood the test of time. It can survive years of utter neglect. The bright-pink, tubular, yellow-throated flowers are quite spectacular and appear in early June. Clusters of feathery brown seeds precede the flowers and persist into winter. On older canes, the gray-brown bark exfoliates, giving this shrub an interesting winter texture. Upright arching branches make it somewhat leggy, so give beauty bush plenty of room to grow. Plant it as a specimen plant or in an open area as part of a naturescape for wildlife. Its foliage takes on a nice reddish color in autumn. We have planted a few in our windbreak to provide contrast with the evergreens. Beauty bush is a shrub that deserves more attention in Colorado landscapes.

WHEN TO PLANT

Container-grown shrubs can be planted from spring through early fall. Bare-root plants should be planted in early spring as soon as the soil can be worked.

WHERE TO PLANT

Locate beauty bush in an open, sunny exposure with plenty of room to grow. It will tolerate a wide range of soils and is easily transplanted. Use as a backdrop for the perennial border or in a windbreak for contrast.

HOW TO PLANT

Dig the planting hole 3 times wider than the rootball. No soil amendment is necessary as long as the soil has been broken up and is not severely compacted. Sandy soils will benefit from some compost to help retain moisture. When planting bare-root plants, spread the roots out in the planting hole without crowding them. Inspect the root system of shrubs grown in containers. If the roots form a tight mass that encircles the rootball, the shrub has been in the pot for a while and is rootbound. As long as the plant is healthy, it is acceptable for purchase. To ensure its survival, use the "butterfly technique" to plant a rootbound plant. Lay the plant and rootball on their sides. Using a knife or sharp shovel, cut through the lower portion of the rootball. Insert the knife in line with the main trunk or stems and slice through the bottom of the rootball halfway up its length. This will allow you to spread the lower halves of the rootball apart. When positioning the shrub in the planting hole, place the roots which were growing at the bottom of the container nearer the surface, where soil conditions are more favorable for vigorous root development. Add backfill soil to the planting hole and water slowly to eliminate air pockets beneath the roots. Mulch with shredded wood chips or cedar shavings. Water deeply as needed.

CARE AND MAINTENANCE

Once established, this shrub will thrive with little care. You can renew older, overgrown plants by pruning them completely to the ground in spring. To keep beauty bush in bounds and to shape, prune the oldest stems down to the ground after flowering to maintain vigor. New growth will emerge from the base.

ADDITIONAL INFORMATION

The beauty bush is not used as much as it should be in Colorado landscapes, possibly because it is not widely available. It is a rugged plant with beautiful pink flowers and handsome blue-green foliage. If you can't find it locally, try ordering it through a mail-order nursery.

ADDITIONAL SPECIES, CULTIVARS, OR VARIETIES

There are a few selections that are improved for flower color. 'Pink Cloud' and 'Rosea' produce blossoms of a deeper pink than those of the species.

Blue Mist Spirea

Caryopteris × clandonensis

Other Name: Bluebeard
Height: 2 to 3 ft.
Spread: 2 to 3 ft.
Flowers: Light-blue, dark-blue
Bloom Period: Late summer
Zones: 4, 5, 6

Light Requirement:

*T*he blue mist spirea is not a true spirea, but its long arching branches give it a similar appearance. Leaves are bluish-green on top and silvery underneath. They have a spicy aroma when bruised. The light- to dark-blue blossoms emerge in late summer when few other shrubs are in bloom. The flowers are a favorite of bees, so it might be a good idea to avoid planting blue mist near entryways. This versatile shrub can be combined with perennial flowers or used as a single specimen plant for accent. It looks great with ornamental grasses. Its foliage and flowers make an attractive combination with fall-blooming magenta, pink asters, and *Sedum* 'Autumn Joy'.

WHEN TO PLANT
Container-grown plants can be planted from spring to early fall. Bare-root plants from mail-order sources should be planted in early spring as soon as the soil can be worked.

WHERE TO PLANT
Choose a sunny location for the best foliage and most prolific flowering. Blue mist spirea can be used in shrub or perennial borders. Its silvery gray foliage makes it a delightful foil for yellow- and white-flowering potentillas. Avoid wet or poorly drained sites where crown rot may result.

HOW TO PLANT
Plants are available in containers or as small potted plants from mail-order sources. Their fibrous root systems makes them very easy to transplant and establish. Avoid amending the soil with too much organic matter; this will cause rank growth with few flowers. Inspect the root system of a shrub grown in a container. If the roots

form a tight mass that encircles the rootball, the shrub has been in the pot for a while and is rootbound. As long as the plant is healthy, it is acceptable for purchase. To ensure its survival, use the "butterfly technique" to plant a rootbound plant. Lay the plant and rootball on their sides. Using a knife or sharp shovel, cut through the lower portion of the rootball. Insert the knife in line with the main trunk or stems and slice through the bottom of the rootball halfway up its length. This will allow you to spread the lower halves of the rootball apart. When positioning the shrub in the planting hole, place the roots which were growing at the bottom of the container nearer the surface, where soil conditions are more favorable for vigorous root development. After positioning the shrub in the hole, add backfill soil and water slowly to eliminate any air pockets under the roots. Mulch with shredded cedar or other organic material to maintain and conserve moisture during the heat of summer.

CARE AND MAINTENANCE
Though this shrub is adapted to dry conditions, it can still suffer severe wilt in the heat of summer. Mulch with compost or cedar mulch and water thoroughly, but infrequently. Blue mist generally does not need supplemental fertilizer. Each year, the branches die back to the woody center or crown of the plant. Cut the shrub back to near ground level in early spring before growth begins. Apply an all-purpose 5-10-5 fertilizer in spring as soon as growth appears. Broadcast the fertilizer around the shrub according to the manufacturer's recommendations and water-in well.

ADDITIONAL INFORMATION
Seedlings are very common and will sprout beneath the shrub as well as elsewhere in the garden. Remove or transplant them to other areas. Butterflies and bees love blue mist's late-season blooms.

ADDITIONAL SPECIES, CULTIVARS, OR VARIETIES
'Blue Mist' has striking powder-blue flowers. 'Dark Knight' has darker gray-green foliage and darker-blue flowers from late July through August.

Burning Bush

Euonymus alatus

Height: 8 to 15 ft.
Spread: 10 to 12 ft.
Flowers: Greenish-yellow
Bloom Period: Spring
Zones: 3, 4, 5, 6

Light Requirement:

*L*eaves that turn bright red in fall make this shrub appear to be on fire and give it its common name, "burning bush." Only our native sumac, *Rhus glabra*, comes close to matching the burning bush's brilliant fall color. This shrub is well adapted statewide and will tolerate a wide range of soil conditions. It can be used for screening, in shrub borders, or as a foundation planting. Its autumn display is so intense that a single specimen planting is effective. Plant a *euonymus* shrub near a water garden to reflect its brilliant scarlet colors on the water's surface. The dark-green foliage grows on unusual stems that have corky ridges, or wings, all along them. In winter, these winged stems collect snow, creating an interesting plant sculpture for the winter garden. Burning bush is Colorado-tough and will resist most plant diseases.

When to Plant
Plant container-grown shrubs from spring through fall. If planting in the heat of summer, be sure to protect *euonymus* from stress or it will become more susceptible to spider mites.

Where to Plant
Burning bush does well in part shade to full sun. Plants grown in locations that are too shady will not grow as thick or be as brightly colored in autumn. Plant in mass plantings, or as a background shrub or informal hedge.

How to Plant
These shrubs are easily transplanted as container-grown nursery plants. They do quite well in well-drained soils of any type. They do not like to have "wet feet." It is important that you amend the soil with compost to improve soil porosity and drainage. Dig the plant-

ing hole 3 times wider than the diameter of the rootball. Add up to 30 percent by volume of a high-quality homemade or commercial Colorado-made compost to the backfill soil. Set the plant in the planting hole; keep the top of the rootball level with the surrounding soil grade. Water-in thoroughly and apply a few inches of shredded pole peelings or cedar mulch around the base of the shrub.

CARE AND MAINTENANCE

The *Euonymus* grows in somewhat horizontal tiers, which gives it a flat-topped look. Pruning is generally not recommended. Frequent pruning or shearing may destroy this plant's natural shape. Burning bush is a workhorse of a shrub and is very adaptable to many landscape situations. Once the plant is established, water deeply and infrequently. Keep a layer of mulch around the bush to retain moisture and keep the soil cool in the heat of summer. A light application of an all-purpose 5-10-5 fertilizer in early spring as the leaves are expanding will help get the shrub off to a healthy start. Broadcast fertilizer around the dripline and water-in thoroughly.

ADDITIONAL INFORMATION

To get the best fall color, avoid full-shade locations. During the heat of summer, spider mites can become a nuisance. They can be controlled by washing them off with a strong stream of water from the garden hose; or set a "frog-eye" sprinkler under the shrub periodically to help eliminate these pests.

ADDITIONAL SPECIES, CULTIVARS, OR VARIETIES

Euonymus alatus 'Compacta' is a dwarf form (5 to 6 ft.). The corky wings on its stems are not as pronounced as those of the species; this gives the plant a finer texture in winter. *Euonymus europaeus*, European spindle tree, is a larger shrub that grows up to 18 ft tall. It produces attractive red-pink fruits in late summer or early fall. Autumn foliage is a handsome reddish purple.

Butterfly Bush

Buddleia spp.

Height: 4 to 6 ft.
Spread: 3 to 4 ft.
Flowers: White, pink, purple, lavender, red
Bloom Period: Summer
Zones: 4, 5, 6

Light Requirement:

*I*f you are thinking of creating a naturescape that will attract butterflies, choose *Buddleia* to make them feel right at home. Butterfly bush has arching branches with willow-like light-green to bluish-green leaves. The profuse white, pink, red, purple, or lavender flowers are borne on racemes. Their sweet, woodsy fragrance will draw the butterflies to your yard.

WHEN TO PLANT

Spring is the best time for planting, since winter often kills this plant to the ground. Container-grown plants are readily available. Order bare-root plants from mail-order catalogs in early spring.

WHERE TO PLANT

Plant in full sun to encourage vigorous growth and an abundance of blossoms. A butterfly bush growing in the shade will soon become leggy and have few, if any, flowers.

HOW TO PLANT

Dig the planting hole 2 to 3 times wider than the rootball of the plant. Inspect the root system of shrubs grown in containers. If the roots form a tight mass that encircles the rootball, the shrub has been in the pot for a while and is rootbound. As long as the plant is healthy, it is acceptable for purchase. To ensure its survival, use the "butterfly technique" to plant a rootbound plant. Lay the plant and rootball on their sides. Using a knife or sharp shovel, cut through the lower portion of the rootball. Insert the knife in line with the main trunk or stems and slice through the bottom of the rootball halfway up its length. This will allow you to spread the lower halves of the rootball apart. When positioning the shrub in the planting hole, place the roots which were growing at the bottom of the container nearer the surface, where soil conditions are more favorable for vigorous root development. Water thoroughly after planting and spread a mulch of compost or shredded cedar under the plant. Keep the soil evenly moist for several weeks to ensure good establishment.

CARE AND MAINTENANCE

Butterfly bushes are adapted to poor soil conditions and will bloom without extra fertilizer. If desired, an all-purpose 5-10-5 fertilizer at the rate of $1/4$ cup per foot of height can be applied in spring and early summer. Use a crowbar or metal rod to make a series of holes, 8 to 10 in. deep and 12 in. apart, around the dripline of the shrub. Broadcast fertilizer in the area where the holes were made and water-in thoroughly. Be sure to water this shrub in the heat of summer to encourage vigorous growth and an abundance of blossoms. During most winters, the plants will die back to the ground, but the roots will survive. Cut butterfly bush back to the ground and new growth will emerge.

ADDITIONAL INFORMATION

The foliage can be attacked by spider mites during hot, dry summers. Symptoms appear as mottled and twisted foliage. Hosing the bottom of the leaves with water can help reduce mite infestations; or use an appropriate miticide.

ADDITIONAL SPECIES, CULTIVARS, OR VARIETIES

Buddleia alternifolia, fountain butterfly bush, is one of the hardiest species. It has silvery foliage and bark; its arching stems and lavender flowers are delightful in early summer. Keep the plant vigorous by cutting half the stems to ground level after flowering. *Buddleia davidii* 'Black Knight' has dark-purple flowers; 'Pink Charming' has fragrant pink blossoms; 'Empire Blue' sports violet-blue flowers with orange eyes; and 'White Bouquet' produces white clusters with yellow eyes. *Buddleia davidii* var. *nanhoensis* has a more compact growing habit (3 to 5 ft.) with sprays of flowers in lavender, mauve, or white.

Cinquefoil

Potentilla fruticosa

Height: 2 to 4 ft.	Light Requirement:
Spread: 2 to 5 ft.	
Flowers: Yellow, white, red	
Bloom Period: Summer	
Zones: 2, 3, 4, 5, 6	

*P*otentillas are one of the mainstays of the Colorado landscape. Their bright yellow flowers grow from 1 to 1³/₈ inches wide and are set off by fine-textured greenish-gray leaves. Cinquefoil grows into a dense shrub with soft, slender, upright branches. A first flush of bloom generally occurs in late May; flowering continues until frost. This plant is tolerant of Colorado's alkaline soils and will endure drought conditions. It makes an excellent shrub for the lower elevations of the High Plains all the way up to the higher elevations of the High Country.

WHEN TO PLANT

Plant in early spring through fall. Container-grown plants are available at most local nurseries and garden stores.

WHERE TO PLANT

Find a sunny site with good air circulation where the soil is well drained. Use cinquefoil as an informal hedge, a specimen planting, or a backdrop.

HOW TO PLANT

When grown in containers, plants quickly develop strong fibrous root systems that make them easy to transplant. Dig the planting hole wider than the rootball to encourage continued growth of a strong, vigorous root system. Inspect the root system of a shrub grown in a container. If the roots form a tight mass that encircles the rootball, the shrub has been in the pot for a while and is rootbound. As long as the plant is healthy, it is acceptable for purchase. To ensure its survival, use the "butterfly technique" to plant a rootbound plant. Lay the plant and rootball on their sides. Using a knife or sharp shovel, cut through the lower portion of the rootball. Insert the knife in line with the main trunk or stems and slice through the bottom of the rootball halfway up its length. This will allow you to spread the lower halves of the rootball apart. When positioning the shrub in the planting hole, place the roots which were growing at the bottom of the container nearer the surface, where soil conditions are more favorable for vigorous root development.

CARE AND MAINTENANCE
These shrubs are very hardy and drought-enduring once they become established. Use an organic mulch to conserve water and keep the soil from baking. A cedar mulch will set off the clean, bluish-green foliage and brilliant flowers. If plants become unkempt, pruning will renew them. Remove $1/3$ of the oldest stems each year and new growth with fresh blooms will emerge. To rejuvenate older shrubs, cut the entire plant to ground level in late winter or early spring.

ADDITIONAL INFORMATION
Spider mites can become a problem in hot, dry exposures. Control by hosing off regularly with a strong stream of water. Chlorosis can be a problem in some areas and can be corrected with a chelated iron supplement in spring and midsummer.

ADDITIONAL SPECIES, CULTIVARS, OR VARIETIES
One of the toughest and longest-lived varieties is *Potentilla fruticosa* var. 'Davurica', or prairie snow potentilla. When in bloom, it is covered with a cloud of white flowers and bright-green leaves. 'Abbotswood' has blue-green leaves with large white blooms; 'Gold Drop' is a compact plant with bright-yellow flowers that bloom continually throughout the summer; 'Goldfinger' has an upright growth habit and sports golden-yellow blossoms; and 'Katherine Dykes' has a wider-spreading habit, greenish-gray foliage, and a heavy spring bloom of pale-yellow flowers. 'Pink Whisper' is a pink-flowering selection whose flowers fade to creamy white. It has an upright compact growth habit. 'Jackman' is a larger specimen shrub that grows up to 5 ft. tall and has large bright-golden blooms throughout the summer.

Common Ninebark

Physocarpus opulifolius

Height: 4 to 10 ft.
Spread: 3 to 6 ft.
Flowers: White
Bloom Period: Early summer
Zones: 2, 3, 4, 5, 6

Light Requirement:

---

ommon ninebark is a hardy deciduous shrub whose growth habit resembles that of spirea. It is upright and somewhat arching; the shrub becomes open and leggy as it matures. Common ninebark produces masses of white flowers in spring with toothed leaves that are usually three- to five-lobed. As the shrub's bark matures on the stems, it exfoliates in thin, coarse sheets that add winter interest to the landscape. Ninebark is a rugged, well-adapted shrub for Colorado. Some selections have golden to lime-green foliage. Mountain ninebark, *Physocarpus monogynus*, is especially useful for mass planting and as a low, informal hedge.

WHEN TO PLANT

Plant container-grown shrubs from spring through fall. If you purchase bare-root plants, plant them in early spring as soon as the soil can be worked.

WHERE TO PLANT

Ninebark can become leggy over time, so locate in full sun to part shade. Moderately fertile, well-drained soil is preferred, but the shrub will tolerate dry situations.

HOW TO PLANT

Dig the planting hole twice as wide as the rootball. Loosen the soil deeply and add 25 to 30 percent by volume of compost to the native soil. Inspect the root system of a shrub grown in a container. If the roots form a tight mass that encircles the rootball, the shrub has been in the pot for a while and is rootbound. As long as the plant is healthy, it is acceptable for purchase. To ensure its survival, use the "butterfly technique" to plant a rootbound plant. Lay the plant and rootball on their sides. Using a knife or sharp shovel, cut through the lower portion of the rootball. Insert the knife in line with the main trunk or stems and slice through the bottom of the rootball halfway up its length. This will allow you to spread the lower halves of the rootball apart. When positioning the shrub in the planting hole, place the roots which were growing at the bottom of the container nearer the surface, where soil conditions are more favorable for vigorous root development. Add backfill soil and water slowly to eliminate any air pockets under the roots. Mulch with pine needles or shredded wood chips.

CARE AND MAINTENANCE
Once established, ninebark requires only periodic watering. Prune when necessary to thin out branches which die back. Renew an older shrub by cutting it to the ground in late winter or early spring. After a hard pruning, apply with an all-purpose 5-10-5 granular fertilizer, following label directions. Punch a series of holes with a crowbar or metal rod, 8 to 10 in. deep and 12 in. apart, all around the shrub. Broadcast fertilizer in the area where the holes where made and water-in thoroughly.

ADDITIONAL INFORMATION
Ninebark is extremely hardy and resistant to pests and diseases. The common ninebark is a long-lived shrub that "dares to go where no shrub has gone before."

ADDITIONAL SPECIES, CULTIVARS, OR VARIETIES
Physocarpus opulifolius 'Dart's Gold' has attractive lime-green leaves and flowers that open in late spring. It is one of the better cultivars for alkaline soils; plant it against evergreens for a nice contrast. Dwarf ninebark, *Physocarpus opulifolius* 'Nanus', is a compact bush that works well for hedging.

Coralberry

Symphoricarpos spp.

The bright blue-green foliage of snowberry is quick to produce a bushy, rounded shrub in almost any type of Colorado soil. It is widely adapted to sunny exposures and will do quite well in semi-shaded conditions. Its tiny pink blossoms make a nice contrast against its leaves in early summer. Showy $3/4$-in. berries soon follow; they persist into winter, attracting birds and other wildlife. Coralberry is an excellent plant for a naturescape planting. It has a spreading growth habit and is excellent for planting on steep slopes or in other problem locations. Its tendency to sucker profusely makes it useful as a ground-cover for soil stabilization. The arching, spreading branches grow about 3 to 5 ft. high.

When to Plant

Plant container-grown plants in spring through early fall. If you purchase bare-root plants, plant them in early spring as soon as the soil can be worked.

Where to Plant

These shrubs are adaptable to the varied soil conditions throughout our state. They can grow in sites that get full sun or shade. Use in mass plantings, as informal edging, or as an accent shrub in a corner.

How to Plant

Dig the hole twice as wide as the rootball. Container-grown plants will transplant easily. If the soil is hard and compacted, add a quality homemade or Colorado-made compost to the planting area. Use $1/3$ by volume of soil conditioner to the planting site. Inspect the root system of shrubs grown in containers. If the roots form a tight mass that encircles the rootball, the shrub has been in the pot for a while and is rootbound. As long as the plant is healthy, it is acceptable for purchase. To ensure its survival, use the "butterfly technique" to plant a rootbound plant. Lay the plant and rootball on their sides. Using a knife or sharp shovel, cut through the lower portion of the rootball. Insert the knife in line with the main trunk or stems and slice through the bottom of the rootball halfway up its length. This will allow you to spread the lower halves of the rootball apart. When positioning the shrub in the planting hole, place the roots which were growing at the bottom of the container nearer the surface, where soil conditions are more favorable for vigorous root development. Once the plant is positioned in the planting hole, add backfill soil and water-in slowly. Mulch is helpful during establishment but will not be necessary when the plant matures, as the stems and branches will naturally cover the ground.

CARE AND MAINTENANCE
Once established, *Symphoricarpos* will grow and thrive. It benefits from a periodic pruning in early spring to keep the plant in bounds. If flowers are lacking, prune in spring to encourage the current season's growth to produce blossoms.

ADDITIONAL INFORMATION
In late summer and early fall, it is not uncommon to see powdery mildew on the foliage. You can prevent this disease by pruning to increase air circulation; or use the appropriate fungicide treatments in early summer.

ADDITIONAL SPECIES, CULTIVARS, OR VARIETIES
Chenault coralberry, *Symphoricarpos* × *chenaultii* 'Hancock', is an attractive low-growing shrub that makes an effective groundcover. Pink flowers are followed by fruit that is pink, or white tinged with pink. *Symphoricarpos orbiculatus* or red coralberry has handsome green leaves with clusters of 1/4-in. coral-red berries that last all winter. *Symphoricarpos albus* has blue-green leaves; it produces snowy-white berries that persist throughout winter.

Daphne

Daphne spp.

Height: 3 to 5 ft.
Spread: 2 to 5 ft.
Flowers: White, pink, rose
Bloom Period: Late spring
Zones: 4, 5, 6

Light Requirement:

*I*f you're looking for a highly fragrant shrub to plant beneath a window, be sure to include Daphne on your plant list. The sweet fragrance from its spring blossoms will permeate the air. Daphne is a beautiful small- to medium-sized shrub with dense clusters of white, pink, or lilac blossoms that appear in late May and early June. The flowers are star-shaped, about $1/2$ in. in diameter, and have a waxy, somewhat artificial appearance. In addition to its fragrant flowers, Daphne produces handsome foliage throughout the year. *Daphne ×burkwoodii* 'Carol Mackie' has rich-green leaves with creamy white or yellow margins. Pleasantly fragrant clusters of light-pink flowers bloom in late spring. While lilacs may be damaged by late spring frosts, Daphnes bloom later and will generally escape Colorado's fickle spring weather. Plants grow as densely branched semi-evergreen shrubs and work well as foundation plants or for specimen plantings. Combine with low-growing evergreens, plant in perennial flower gardens, or grow Daphne in a shrub border backed by evergreens.

WHEN TO PLANT
Plant container-grown plants in early spring through early fall.

WHERE TO PLANT
Choose a location that receives full sun to part shade. This shrub does best in well-drained soils; it will not tolerate wet feet. Avoid planting near roof lines where loads of snow and ice may fall on the fragile stems and branches.

HOW TO PLANT
Dig the planting hole 3 times wider than the diameter of the rootball and as deep as the container in which the plant is growing. Add a high-quality soil amendment such as compost or sphagnum peat

moss to the soil at the rate of $^1/_3$ by volume. Mix the amendment uniformly with the soil. Container-grown plants will transplant easily, but avoid disturbing the root system during planting. Place the plant in the center of the planting hole, setting it level with the ground. Add backfill soil halfway and water thoroughly. Once the water has soaked in, add the remaining soil and water again. Mulch with compost, shredded cedar, or wood mulch.

CARE AND MAINTENANCE

Avoid excessive use of high-nitrogen fertilizer; use an all-purpose 5-10-5 fertilizer instead, at the rate of 1 tablespoon per foot of the plant's height. Apply in spring and again in midsummer. Pruning is generally not required. It is important to keep the soil uniformly moist, so use a 2- to 3-inch layer of mulch around the plant. To reduce stem rot, pull the mulch 3 to 4 in. back from the stems and lower branches. Check soil moisture regularly during the summer season.

ADDITIONAL INFORMATION

Daphne can be somewhat slow to establish, so expect an occasional failure. Check exposure and soil conditions, but don't give up on this shrub; it is well worth your efforts. The weight of wet snow and ice can often cause Daphne's brittle branches to split and break; depending on the plant's location, winter protection may be necessary.

ADDITIONAL SPECIES, CULTIVARS, OR VARIETIES

Daphne × burkwoodii 'Carol Mackie' is a very adaptable shrub that has become one of our favorites. It grows up to 5 ft. tall and has green-and-white-striped leaves. It will endure somewhat drier conditions once it becomes established. 'Somerset' has dark-green foliage with deeper rosy-pink blossoms. *Daphne cneorum*, rose Daphne, is a good rock garden shrub that grows 6 to 12 in. tall and develops into an attractive groundcover. Its dark-green foliage is accented with a profusion of rosy-pink flowers in mid- to late spring.

Dwarf Arctic Willow

Salix purpurea

Height: 3 to 6 ft.	**Light Requirement:**
Spread: 3 to 5 ft.	
Flowers: Yellow-green catkins	
Bloom Period: Early spring	
Zones: 2, 3, 4, 5, 6	

*M*ost of us have a difficult wet site in our landscapes. Luckily, willows can come to the rescue. The dwarf arctic willow has a dense, compact growth habit and slender, gray-green leaves on handsome purplish branches. Its yellow-green catkins appear before the leaves emerge. Problem sites such as low-lying areas that stay moist are especially suitable for this willow. It will thrive when planted near the downspout of the house in a foundation planting.

WHEN TO PLANT

If you purchase bare-root plants, plant in early spring as soon as the soil can be worked. Container-grown willows can be planted from spring to early fall.

WHERE TO PLANT

Willow prefers moist soil, so amend with a moisture-retentive compost, sphagnum peat moss, or a combination of the two. Once established, the plants will endure drier conditions. Locate in sun to part shade. Plant willow in moist sites as an informal hedge or screen.

HOW TO PLANT

Dig the planting hole 2 to 3 times wider than the rootball. Bare-root plants should have the roots spread into the hole without cramping. Add a good organic soil amendment to heavy clay, sandy, or gravelly soils to help retain moisture. Inspect the root system of shrubs grown in containers. If the roots form a tight mass that encircles the rootball, the shrub has been in the pot for a while and is rootbound. As long as the plant is healthy, it is acceptable for purchase. To ensure its survival, use the "butterfly technique" to plant a rootbound plant. Lay the plant and rootball on their sides. Using a knife or sharp shovel, cut through the lower portion of the rootball. Insert the knife in line with the main trunk or stems and slice through the bottom of the rootball halfway up its length. This will allow you to spread the lower halves of the rootball apart. When positioning the shrub in the planting hole, place the roots which were growing at the bottom of the container nearer the surface, where soil conditions are more favorable for vigorous root development. Add backfill soil to the planting hole and water slowly. Mulch with pole peelings, cedar shavings, or compost after planting to maintain moisture and keep the soil cool.

CARE AND MAINTENANCE

These shrubs need proper moisture to grow and look good. Extreme periods of drought will kill them. Mulching around the plants can conserve and maintain moisture. Willows are fast growers, so don't be afraid to prune heavily in order to keep them growing vigorously with bright, insect-free stems.

ADDITIONAL INFORMATION

Like poplars, willows can be plagued by a variety of pests and diseases. Aphids, willow gall, oyster shell scale, and *Cytospora* canker can present problems. Keep the plants growing vigorously to reduce severe problems.

ADDITIONAL SPECIES, CULTIVARS, OR VARIETIES

A rather attractive selection is *Salix purpurea* 'Pendula', blue fountain willow. It has graceful arching branches and showy, pliable purplish-gray stems. Bluestem willow, *Salix irrorata*, is a more upright-growing shrub with handsome fuzzy gray catkins that emerge from jet-black calyxes in spring. Coyote willow, *Salix exigua*, is a taller-growing shrub (6 to 12 ft.) that has slender, golden-yellow branches that mature to ash-gray. The foliage is a handsome grayish-green. Where moisture is abundant, coyote willow will grow into a dense thicket.

Firethorn

Pyracantha coccinea

Height: 4 to 8 ft.
Spread: 4 to 6 ft.
Flowers: White
Bloom Period: Early summer
Zones: 4, 5, 6

Light Requirement:

The firethorn is a desirable broadleaf evergreen shrub with showy white blooms in spring and bright-red to orange fruit in autumn. Its lustrous dark-green leaves make it useful as a screen or an informal hedge. The stems are noted for their thorns; this is a good choice for a barrier plant. Birds use it for nesting and find the fruit a good food source. You can train firethorn on a trellis or for espaliers on walls. If you're looking for a shrub that tolerates hot, dry conditions and grows well in alkaline soils, this one fits the bill. It is adaptable to locations with full sun or part shade. There are many cultivars in the nursery trade; be sure to read the plant tags to ensure that the selection you choose is cold hardy for your particular location.

WHEN TO PLANT
Container-grown nursery plants can be planted from early spring to early fall.

WHERE TO PLANT
Plant in full sun to part shade in a site that allows for the growth and spread of this shrub. Firethorn is difficult to move once established, so choose your location carefully. Use this shrub as a barrier hedge or in mass plantings, or train it as an espalier.

HOW TO PLANT
Dig the planting hole 3 times wider than the rootball. Inspect the root system of shrubs grown in containers. If the roots form a tight mass that encircles the rootball, the shrub has been in the pot for a while and is rootbound. As long as the plant is healthy, it is acceptable for purchase. To ensure its survival, use the "butterfly technique" to plant a rootbound plant. Lay the plant and rootball on their sides. Using a knife or sharp shovel, cut through the lower portion of the

rootball. Insert the knife in line with the main trunk or stems and slice through the bottom of the rootball halfway up its length. This will allow you to spread the lower halves of the rootball apart. When positioning the shrub in the planting hole, place the roots which were growing at the bottom of the container nearer the surface, where soil conditions are more favorable for vigorous root development. Water thoroughly and mulch. Water again when the soil begins to dry out.

CARE AND MAINTENANCE

This shrub is very tolerant of dry conditions. It will succumb to root rot if watered too heavily in our clay soils. Water as the soil begins to dry out. Spread a mulch around the base of the plant to set off the glossy foliage and brightly colored berries. The thorns can make pruning somewhat difficult, but if it becomes necessary to do so, prune firethorn shortly after flowering.

ADDITIONAL INFORMATION

Pyracantha can be prone to fireblight, a bacterial disease that is difficult to control. Infected stems should be pruned out in late winter. Pests such as aphids, spider mites, and scale can become a problem. Early detection and control will prevent a severe problem.

ADDITIONAL SPECIES, CULTIVARS, OR VARIETIES

There are various cultivars available from the nursery trade. Make selections that have good cold tolerance. 'Fiery Cascade' is one of the hardier disease-resistant selections. It has small glossy leaves and abundant reddish-orange berries. 'Pauciflora' is a more rounded, compact-growing shrub with orange-red berries. 'Wyatti' grows more upright to a height of 6 ft. or more. *Pyracantha angustifolia* 'Gnome' is a globular shrub with dense, thorny branches and dark, narrow, evergreen leaves. Domed clusters of white flowers appear in late spring, followed by tight bunches of orange berries.

Forsythia

Forsythia × intermedia

Height: 5 to 8 ft.
Spread: 6 to 10 ft.
Flowers: Yellow, golden
Bloom Period: Early spring
Zones: 3, 4, 5, 6

Light Requirement:

*S*tanding tall above the flowering spring bulbs, forsythia's bright-yellow blossoms are eager harbingers of spring. For the impatient gardener who just can't wait, branches can easily be coaxed into bloom indoors in late January and February. This shrub's growth habit is upright and it has a multitude of spreading, arching branches. Left unpruned, it can become unruly. It is a good idea to thin out the older stems and renew forsythia every three years to encourage healthy stems and more prolific blooming. Masses of bell-shaped flowers grace the arching, tannish-gray branches in early spring. While it may lose its appeal in summer, forsythia has attractive bright-green foliage and works well as a foundation planting or screening. Plant it on banks for soil stabilization or as a shrub border. Forsythia is long-lived and will grow in most Colorado soil types.

WHEN TO PLANT

Container-grown plants can be planted from spring to early fall. Bare-root plants should be planted in early spring as soon as the soil can be worked.

WHERE TO PLANT

Choose a site that will allow plenty of room for forsythia's arching branches. For a screen or hedge, plant 2 to 3 ft. apart. In mass plantings, space 9 to 12 ft. apart to allow the arching branches to spread naturally. Locate in full sun for the best, most prolific blossoms. The brilliant yellow flowers show up well against a backdrop of dark evergreens.

HOW TO PLANT

Prepare the planting hole 3 times as large as the rootball. If the soil is compacted in the planting site, add $1/3$ compost to the planting area. Container-grown plants that have become rootbound will benefit from having the roots lightly scored, or you can unwind the longest ones and spread them in the planting hole. Add the backfill soil around the plant and water-in thoroughly. Water as needed to establish the shrub. A few inches of mulch can be applied at the time of planting. As forsythia matures, its arching branches will cover the ground and make additional mulching unnecessary.

CARE AND MAINTENANCE
Once established, forsythia grows vigorously. As it matures, the plant should be pruned every few years to maintain general health and to ensure prolific blossoms. Avoid shearing the top of the shrub in order to make a formal shape; this will destroy the natural arching growth habit and cause flowering only on the top portion of the plant. It is easiest to selectively remove older stems, cutting them back to ground level. New young stems will arise and flower within a few years. Water deeply and thoroughly in summer to avoid severe drought stress and leaf scorch. Fertilize with an all-purpose 5-10-5 fertilizer in early spring and midsummer.

ADDITIONAL INFORMATION
This shrub has endured the test of time in Colorado landscapes, but the flower buds can be killed when temperatures drop below -15 degrees Fahrenheit. It is not unusual to lose blooms everywhere but on the portion of the shrub protected by snowcover. Look for varieties that have a greater flower-bud hardiness. Prune some branches in late winter when the buds are swollen. Cut branches 18 to 24 in. long, set them in a vase of water indoors, and enjoy a preview of spring's coming attractions.

ADDITIONAL SPECIES, CULTIVARS, OR VARIETIES
A hardy cultivar with superior flower bud hardiness is *Forsythia* × 'Meadowlark' with flower buds hardy to -35 degrees Fahrenheit. Bright-yellow flowers appear in early April before the leaves emerge. 'Northern Gold' is a smaller shrub (6 to 8 ft.) that has outstanding yellow blossoms with excellent flower-bud hardiness. 'Arnold Dwarf' is a low-growing, drought-tolerant plant with good pest resistance. Its deep-green foliage is more impressive than its pale-yellow flowers, making it effective as a groundcover.

Glossy Buckthorn

Rhamnus frangula

Height: 8 to 12 ft.
Spread: 3 to 5 ft.
Flowers: Greenish-white (not showy)
Bloom Period: Spring
Zones: 2, 3, 4, 5, 6

Light Requirement:

*B*uckthorn is one of the most attractive fast-growing screen or hedge plants in Colorado landscapes. Its lustrous foliage grows densely from near ground level to the top of the plant. Buckthorn is strongly columnar, which makes it an excellent choice for landscapes with limited space. *Rhamnus frangula* 'Columnaris', or tallhedge, has a dense growth habit; it works well as a screen for privacy. It thrives in both sun and part shade. The glossy, dark-green leaves make this shrub a nice background plant for perennials or low-growing evergreens. Creamy-white flower clusters are preceded by red berries that turn black as they mature; the berries attract wildlife. We have found buckthorn to be a very useful plant for landscapes with limited space.

WHEN TO PLANT

Plant container-grown shrubs from spring through early fall. Bareroot plants are available in early spring. Container-grown plants are sold at nurseries year-round.

WHERE TO PLANT

Buckthorn prefers a well-drained, moderately rich organic soil. It needs plenty of water to become established. Locate in full sun or part shade. Plant as a narrow privacy screen or hedge, or use in a windbreak.

HOW TO PLANT

This shrub transplants readily. Dig the planting hole twice as wide as the rootball. Inspect the root system of shrubs grown in containers. If the roots form a tight mass that encircles the rootball, the shrub has been in the pot for a while and is rootbound. As long as the plant is healthy, it is acceptable for purchase. To ensure its survival, use the "butterfly technique" to plant a rootbound plant. Lay the plant and rootball on their sides. Using a knife or sharp shovel, cut through the lower portion of the rootball. Insert the knife in line with the main trunk or stems and slice through the bottom of the rootball halfway up its length. This will allow you to spread the lower halves of the rootball apart. When positioning the shrub in the planting hole, place the roots which were growing at the bottom of the container nearer the surface, where soil conditions are more favorable for vigorous root development. Add backfill soil into the planting hole and water slowly to eliminate any air pockets under the roots. Spread a 2-in. layer of organic mulch beneath the plant to conserve moisture. Apply water regularly during the first year to ensure good establishment.

CARE AND MAINTENANCE

Once buckthorn is established, it requires a minimum of care. Though it tolerates a wide range of soils, this shrub does not do well in heavily compacted soils. Water deeply and thoroughly once a week during the summer to maintain vigorous growth and to prevent leaf scorch. Apply an all-purpose 5-10-5 granular fertilizer in early spring according to package directions. Punch a series of holes 8 to 10 in. deep and 12 in. apart around the dripline with a crowbar or old ski pole. Broadcast fertilizer in the area where the holes have been punched and water-in well.

ADDITIONAL INFORMATION

The growth habit of this shrub makes it very useful for screening in landscapes where space is limited.

ADDITIONAL SPECIES, CULTIVARS, OR VARIETIES

The selection *Rhamnus frangula* 'Asplenifolia' has a finer texture with narrow, irregularly margined leaves that give it a fern-like appearance. *Rhamnus smithii* develops a more rounded form, spreading outward to 6 ft. or more. The common buckthorn, *Rhamnus catharticus*, will grow to 20 ft. with comparable spread and makes a good, dense background shrub. Birds love the berries and help to spread the seeds.

Golden St. Johnswort

Hypericum frondosum

Height: 3 to 4 ft.	**Light Requirement:**
Spread: 3 to 4 ft.	
Flowers: Yellow	
Bloom Period: Summer	
Zones: 4, 5, 6	

*S*t. Johnswort is a highly desirable shrub with attractive bluish green foliage and glistening yellow flowers in summer. The showy stamens form a dense brush that shimmers in the sunlight. Brownish-red exfoliating bark makes a nice foil for the leaves. Use this shrub as a foundation plant, in a shrub border, for mass planting, or as an accent plant. It is tolerant of poor soil conditions, dry areas, and infertile soils, and it will adapt to partial shade. With this kind of adaptability, St. Johnswort is right for almost any Colorado landscape.

WHEN TO PLANT
Plant St. Johnswort in spring to allow for good establishment.

WHERE TO PLANT
This adaptable shrub will grow in full sun or filtered shade. It thrives in sandy or clay soils and is tolerant of alkaline conditions. Use it for mass plantings or for an accent shrub in a perennial bed or rock garden.

HOW TO PLANT
Container-grown plants are easy to transplant. Dig the planting hole 2 to 3 times wider than the rootball. Inspect the root systems of shrubs grown in containers. If the roots form a tight mass that encircles the rootball, the shrub has been in the pot for a while and is rootbound. As long as the plant is healthy, it is acceptable for purchase. To ensure its survival, use the "butterfly technique" to plant a rootbound plant. Lay the plant and rootball on their sides. Using a knife or sharp shovel, cut through the lower portion of the rootball. Insert the knife in line with the main trunk or stems and slice through the bottom of the rootball halfway up its length. This will allow you to spread the lower halves of the rootball apart. When

positioning the shrub in the planting hole, place the roots which were growing at the bottom of the container nearer the surface, where soil conditions are more favorable for vigorous root development. Add backfill soil to the planting hole and water slowly to eliminate any air pockets under the roots. Water well when the soil dries out to a depth of 4 to 6 in. Mulch with shredded cedar or pine needles to maintain uniform moisture.

CARE AND MAINTENANCE

Once established, St. Johnswort will require a minimum of care. Avoid overwatering and, if needed, apply fertilizer sparingly. Pruning may be necessary to maintain the shrub's shape. The best time to prune and to thin out older wood is late spring after new growth has hardened off. St. Johnswort will prove itself a durable, easy-to-care-for, pest-free shrub. Flowering occurs on new growth. You can apply an all-purpose 5-10-5 fertilizer in mid- to late spring. Broadcast the fertilizer around the dripline of the shrub and water-in well. This will provide some additional nutrients early in the season. Water deeply but infrequently.

ADDITIONAL INFORMATION

Some of the more-tender varieties of St. Johnswort will benefit from winter protection. Mulch with shredded wood chips or cedar mulch after the ground has frozen.

ADDITIONAL SPECIES, CULTIVARS, OR VARIETIES

There are many hybrid cultivars available in the nursery trade. *Hypericum ascyron* is one of the hardier species. It grows 3 to 4 ft. tall with large 2-in. golden blossoms. *Hypericum* 'Hidcote' has handsome blue-green foliage with golden flowers. 'Kalm' has narrower blue-green leaves and is hardier in most areas of Colorado. *Hypericum kouytchense* is a species that grows 2 to 4 ft. tall and is ideal for borders or a rock garden setting. The large 2-in.-wide blossoms are a beautiful golden-yellow.

Hedge Cotoneaster

Cotoneaster lucidus

Height: 6 to 10 ft.
Spread: 4 to 6 ft.
Flowers: Pink
Bloom Period: Spring
Zones: 2, 3, 4, 5, 6

Light Requirement:

---

*T*he lustrous dark-green foliage of cotoneaster makes it a versatile shrub in the landscape. The hedge cotoneaster is ideal for pruning into topiaries or formal hedges. In my opinion, this shrub is best when left unpruned and allowed to grow and spread naturally. Its upright growth habit makes it useful as a screen or as a privacy hedge. It also works well in background or mass plantings. Small pinkish-white flowers appear in late spring, followed by black berries that persist into winter. The fruit is a source of food for wild birds. Hedge cotoneaster's red-orange foliage provides a beautiful display in autumn.

WHEN TO PLANT

If you purchase bare-root specimens, plant them as soon as the soil can be worked in early spring. Container-grown plants can be planted any time and are available at your local garden retailer.

WHERE TO PLANT

Hedge cotoneaster thrives in full sun to part shade. It will grow in almost any garden soil that is well drained. Plant it as an informal or formal hedge, as a screen, or as a background shrub.

HOW TO PLANT

Dig the planting hole 2 to 3 times wider than the rootball. When planting bare-root plants, spread the roots in the planting hole without cramping them. Inspect the root systems of shrubs grown in containers. If the roots form a tight mass that encircles the rootball, the shrub has been in the pot for a while and is rootbound; as long as the plant is healthy, it is acceptable for purchase. To ensure its survival, use the "butterfly technique" to plant a rootbound plant. Lay the plant and rootball on their sides. Using a knife or sharp shovel, cut through the lower portion of the rootball. Insert the knife in line with the main trunk or stems and slice through the bottom of the rootball halfway up its length. This will allow you to spread the lower halves of the rootball apart. When positioning the shrub in the planting hole, place the roots that were growing at the bottom of the container nearer the surface, where soil conditions are more favorable for vigorous root development. Water-in thoroughly. Add a 2-in. layer of mulch around the plants and water as needed when the soil dries out.

CARE AND MAINTENANCE

Hedge cotoneaster is widely adaptable to our region. It grows well despite Colorado's frequent weather fluctuations. Deep-soak plants in the heat of summer to maintain vigor and plant health. Overcrowded shrubs can be thinned out in spring to tidy up the plants and increase air circulation.

ADDITIONAL INFORMATION

Cotoneaster is often attacked by pear slugs, who skeletonize the leaves. This damage is merely cosmetic and does not harm the plant. Control infestations by hosing the pests off; or dust the infested leaves with wood ashes to turn the slugs into "crispy critters."

ADDITIONAL SPECIES, CULTIVARS, OR VARIETIES

Cotoneaster has many forms, including tall-to-medium shrubs and groundcovers. *Cotoneaster apiculatus,* or cranberry cotoneaster, is an attractive 2-to-3-ft.-tall shrub with glossy green leaves. Its large red berries are borne on cascading branches. It is good for mass planting or as a specimen plant. *Cotoneaster dammeri* 'Coral Beauty' and 'Lowfast' grow as low-spreading semi-evergreen shrubs (1 to 2 ft. tall with a spread to 6 ft. or more). Plant them where they will cascade over retaining walls or rocks. *Cotoneaster horizontalis,* or rock cotoneaster, has stiff, fanning branches that grow in a herringbone pattern. Its pink flowers in spring are followed by bright-red berries. It is a good choice for the rock garden. *Cotoneaster divaricatus,* or spreading cotoneaster, is a great choice for a large informal hedge or screen. The arching branches produce small bright-red berries in September which persist into winter. Autumn foliage color may be orange, red, or yellow.

Leadplant

Amorpha canescens

Height: 2 to 4 ft.	**Light Requirement:**
Spread: 3 to 4 ft.	
Flowers: Purple	
Bloom Period: Summer	
Zones: 3, 4, 5, 6	

This native of the mixed-grass and tallgrass prairies is truly a drought-resistant plant. Its broad, flat-topped growth habit and arching stems make it an attractive, fine-textured landscape shrub. The foliage is composed of 15 to 45 grayish, 1-in.-long leaflets that give leadplant an airy texture. Silvery gray hairs on the leaves color this shrub a grayish-green that is quite attractive in the summer landscape. Spikes of purple flowers appear in summer on dense 6-inch terminal racemes and contrast nicely with the silvery foliage. Its small stature helps leadplant fit well into the perennial garden. It is also effective in group plantings or as an accent plant in a mixed-shrub planting. Leadplant thrives despite hot, dry conditions; it is an ideal water-thrifty shrub for Colorado landscapes.

WHEN TO PLANT

Plant from spring through fall. Bare-root stock is available and should be planted in early spring; container-grown plants can be planted anytime.

WHERE TO PLANT

Leadplant prefers full sun and well-drained soils. Dry conditions are best, as this shrub will suffer if kept too wet. It is very tolerant of Colorado's alkaline soils. Plant leadplant in dry, sandy soils and it will live long and prosper with minimal care.

HOW TO PLANT

Space plants 2 to 3 ft. apart. Dig the planting hole twice as wide as the root system. Heavy clay soils may require some soil amendment. Mix 25 to 30 percent by volume of compost into the native soil and blend it in uniformly. Inspect the root systems of shrubs grown in containers. If the roots form a tight mass that encircles the rootball, the shrub has been in the pot for a while and is rootbound. As long as the plant is healthy, it is acceptable for purchase. To ensure its survival, use the "butterfly technique" to plant a rootbound plant. Lay the plant and rootball on their sides. Using a knife or sharp shovel, cut through the lower portion of the rootball. Insert the knife in line with the main trunk or stems and slice through the bottom of the rootball halfway up its length. This will allow you to spread the lower halves of the rootball apart. When positioning the shrub in the planting hole, place the roots that were growing at the bottom of the container nearer the surface, where soil conditions are more favorable for vigorous root development.

CARE AND MAINTENANCE

Once leadplant is established, it requires little maintenance other than a periodic pruning in late winter to clean up the garden. Water thoroughly but infrequently. Leadplant fixes nitrogen from the atmosphere and does not need to be fertilized often. A light application of an all-purpose 5-10-5 fertilizer in late spring will provide supplemental nutrients to start the growing season. This plant is drought-enduring and tolerates hot, windy conditions. Before summer begins to heat things up, apply a layer of shredded cedar shavings or pine needles at the base of the plant to conserve moisture.

ADDITIONAL INFORMATION

Leadplant may die back from a harsh winter or from being browsed on by deer, but it can be cut to ground level in early spring to tidy up the plant. It will grow back readily.

ADDITIONAL SPECIES, CULTIVARS, OR VARIETIES

Amorpha fruticosa, or indigobush, has a taller growth habit (6 to 12 ft. with a spread of up to 10 ft.) and bright-green foliage. It grows well in poor soils and is very drought resistant. *Amorpha nana* is the dwarf leadplant (2 ft.). It has dark-green leaves and pink flowers. Use it for erosion control on sunny, dry slopes.

Lilac

Syringa spp.

Height: 6 to 15 ft.
Spread: 5 to 12 ft.
Flowers: Purple, lilac, pink, white
Bloom Period: Spring to late spring
Zones: 2, 3, 4, 5, 6

Light Requirement:

ilacs are undeniably one of the most enduring flowering shrubs throughout Colorado. The sweet smell of this familiar shrub in spring often brings back memories of grandma's house. The common lilac species has purple flowers borne on 4-to-8-in. terminal panicles. Today there are many species, hybrids, and cultivars available that range in size from the compact shrub 'Miss Kim' to larger shrub forms. Flowers come in white, blue, violet, lilac, magenta, pink, reddish purple, and deep purple. In a good growing season, you can use multiple species to produce a bloom period that lasts for up to 8 weeks.

WHEN TO PLANT
Plant lilacs in spring through early fall.

WHERE TO PLANT
Plant lilacs in full sun or part shade with plenty of space for good air circulation. This will help reduce the development of powdery mildew, a disease which thrives in shady, wind-protected locations. Soil should be well-drained, with a good complement of compost worked into the planting area. Once established, lilacs are quite drought tolerant. They can be used for an informal hedge or planted as a privacy screen. Single specimen plantings can grow into large shrubs and produce spectacular displays when in bloom.

HOW TO PLANT
Dig the hole wide enough so that the root system of bare-root plants can be spread out fully. Plants are available as bare-root nursery stock in early spring; container-grown or larger shrubs are sold as balled-and-burlapped specimens. When planting rootbound container-grown plants, untangle the roots and spread them into the planting hole. Add backfill soil to complete the planting and water-

in thoroughly. Mulch with pine needles, compost, or other organic material.

CARE AND MAINTENANCE

Lilacs can take up to 3 years to become established. Once established, however, they are easily maintained. Deep-soak the soil periodically during hot, dry weather. Avoid overwatering, as this may encourage more disease problems. Apply an all-purpose 5-10-5 fertilizer each spring according to directions. It is not necessary to remove spent flowers unless you find them unattractive. The seeds that remain will provide a food source for wild birds. If you do decide to deadhead old flowers, be careful not to remove next year's flower buds, which develop on the same branch just below the dead flower heads. Older plants that have become thick with old stems can be rejuvenated by removing the old stems to ground level. New growth will come from the base of the plant.

ADDITIONAL INFORMATION

To grow and flower prolifically, lilacs need a minimum of 6 hours of full sunlight daily. Because they are so popular, lilacs have been overused in certain instances and as a result have been plagued by a variety of insect pests and diseases. The proper selection of varieties, as well as careful planting and maintenance, will help keep these problems in check.

ADDITIONAL SPECIES, CULTIVARS, OR VARIETIES

Some of our favorites in the Green Thumb landscape are *Syringa vulgaris* 'Charles Joly', with double reddish-purple flowers; 'Sensation', with large purple florets edged in white; 'Wedgewood Blue', with sweetly fragrant lilac-pink buds that open to blue; and 'President Lincoln', with long panicles of single blue florets. 'President Grevy' has double blue flowers; 'Congo' has very fragrant single deep purple-red blooms; 'Beauty of Moscow' has lavender-pink buds which open to double white flowers; their pointed petals give the blooms a star-shaped appearance. *Syringa × hyacinthiflora* are hardy early-blooming crosses between *S. oblata* and *S. vulgaris*. They bloom and grow foliage all the way to their lower branches. These cultivars are adapted to thrive at higher elevations. The late-blooming lilacs, *Syringa × prestoniae*, are prolific bloomers; flowers open a week to 10 days later than *S. vulgaris*. Colors range from pink to lavender-magenta and they are smaller, trumpet-shaped florets with a spicy fragrance. *Syringa patula* 'Miss Kim' is very hardy and late-blooming, and has fragrant, icy-blue flowers.

Mockorange

Philadelphus spp.

Height: 6 to 10 ft. **Spread:** 3 to 5 ft. **Flowers:** White **Bloom Period:** Early summer **Zones:** 4, 5, 6	**Light Requirement:**

The sweet mockorange is one of our favorite fragrant shrubs. *Philadelphus coronarius* is the common mockorange; you'll fall in love with the fragrance of its pure white blossoms. It is also known for its ability to withstand drought and poor soil conditions. The 'Lewis Mockorange' (*Philadelphus lewisii*) is one of the only mockorange shrubs that continues to thrive and bloom at the Cheyenne Research Station in Wyoming. It is native to the western United States. It can be grown at higher elevations and will develop into a rounded, upright shrub. Once established, it will produce an abundance of 1- to 1¹/₄-inch pure-white flowers in early summer. Plant these sweetly fragrant blossoms beneath a window or near a pathway where the scent can be enjoyed.

WHEN TO PLANT
Plant container-grown nursery plants from spring through fall. If you purchase bare-root plants from mail-order nurseries, plant in early spring as soon as the soil can be worked.

WHERE TO PLANT
Choose a site with full sun for best growth and prolific flowering. This shrub needs plenty of space to grow and spread. Though it is tolerant of a wide range of soils, mockorange performs best in well-drained locations. Use as a background shrub or as a specimen planting.

HOW TO PLANT
Dig the planting hole 2 to 3 times wider than the rootball. If the soil is a heavy clay, amend it with a good portion of compost (30 percent by volume) to increase porosity and improve soil drainage. Set the plant so that the top of the rootball is level with the surrounding

grade. Inspect the root systems of shrubs grown in containers. If the roots form a tight mass that encircles the rootball, the shrub has been in the pot for a while and is rootbound. As long as the plant is healthy, it is acceptable for purchase. To ensure its survival, use the "butterfly technique" to plant a rootbound plant. Lay the plant and rootball on their sides. Using a knife or sharp shovel, cut through the lower portion of the rootball. Insert the knife in line with the main trunk or stems and slice through the bottom of the rootball halfway up its length. This will allow you to spread the lower halves of the rootball apart. When positioning the shrub in the planting hole, place the roots that were growing at the bottom of the container nearer the surface, where soil conditions are more favorable for vigorous root development. Add backfill soil to complete the planting and water-in thoroughly. Mulch with shredded cedar or pine needles.

CARE AND MAINTENANCE
Once established (usually 3 to 5 years after planting), mockorange is a dependable drought-tolerant shrub that will provide years of fragrant blossoms. If the plant becomes overcrowded, prune out the oldest stems to rejuvenate the shrub and induce new growth from the base. This will ensure a continuous supply of flowering wood for future blooms. Remove as much as 30 percent of the older wood every two to three years.

ADDITIONAL INFORMATION
These shrubs are seldom bothered by insects or disease problems. If grasshoppers feed on the foliage, employ a duck or goose to control them, or use an appropriate insecticide.

ADDITIONAL SPECIES, CULTIVARS, OR VARIETIES
The littleleaf mockorange *Philadelphus microphyllus* is a slower-growing species that can reach a height of up to 6 ft. Its star-shaped pure-white flowers bloom in June and are pleasantly fragrant. *Philadelphus* × 'Miniature Snowflake' is a more compact shrub. It sports double white flowers in early summer with contrasting dark-green leaves. It makes a good foundation plant beneath a window, but keep it away from hot, reflective surfaces on a west or south exposure. *P.* × 'Buckley's Quill' is another more compact shrub; it produces many clusters of fragrant double flowers with narrow petals that have pointed tips and resemble quills.

Mountain Mahogany

Cercocarpus montanus

Height: 3 to 10 ft.
Spread: 4 to 6 ft.
Flowers: Yellow
Bloom Period: Early spring
Zones: 2, 3, 4, 5, 6

Light Requirement:

One of the most drought-resistant shrubs for a water-wise landscape is mountain mahogany. The wedge-shaped leaves are an adaptation that reduces the plant's exposure to Colorado's hot sun and drying winds. This allows the plant to survive dry, arid conditions. Even the curled seeds are especially adapted to continue the species. Once the seed falls to the ground, damp conditions make it coil up, but when weather becomes dry, the seed straightens out again. This adaptation helps work the seed into the ground so that it germinates successfully. Though sparse, mountain mahogany's foliage is a handsome gray-green. Tiny yellow flowers in mid-spring are followed by fuzzy, twisted seed tails that add an interesting texture. This shrub has an open, spreading growth habit that makes it a good choice for use as a screen or informal hedge. It is also effective as a background for perennials.

WHEN TO PLANT
Plant mountain mahogany in spring to allow for good root development. Container-grown plants are becoming more widely available.

WHERE TO PLANT
Choose a sunny site with well-drained soil. Its resistance to drought makes mountain mahogany very useful as a foundation plant. It also makes an excellent specimen plant or informal hedge.

HOW TO PLANT
Though soil preparation is generally not required, it is a good idea to break up compacted areas where you intend to plant. Set the rootball at the same level the plant was growing previously and water-in thoroughly. Mountain mahogany needs regular watering to establish, but be sure to avoid overwatering. Water only as needed when

the soil dries out. Apply a mulch of pine needles, shredded leaves, or shredded wood chips around the plants to conserve moisture. Mountain mahogany is a slow-growing shrub, so be patient.

CARE AND MAINTENANCE

Once established, mountain mahogany requires little care. It can survive without supplemental irrigation except during a long, hot, dry period. At such a time, water the shrub deeply every 10 to 14 days or as needed. An occasional pruning to keep the plant in bounds can be done in late winter or early spring. A mulch of pea gravel or shredded bark will help set off the interesting foliage and seed tails.

ADDITIONAL INFORMATION

One of mountain mahogany's best features is its evergreen nature in winter. The foliage adds winter interest to the landscape. In summer, the white feathery plumes are quite attractive.

ADDITIONAL SPECIES, CULTIVARS, OR VARIETIES

Cercocarpus ledifolius, or curl-leaf mahogany, is a larger shrub or small tree (10 to 20 ft. tall with a spread of 8 to 12 ft.). The dark-green lance-shaped leaves are leathery, with edges that curl under and give the plant its common name. This is a good drought-resistant shrub that holds its leaves through fall and winter with fuzzy seed tails for winter interest. The dwarf mountain mahogany, *Cercocarpus intricatus* (4 ft.), has a dense growth habit with finer-textured foliage.

Oregon Grape

Mahonia aquifolium

Height: 3 to 6 ft.
Spread: 3 to 5 ft.
Flowers: Yellow
Bloom Period: Early spring
Zones: 3, 4, 5, 6

Light Requirement:

The Oregon grape is one of the few broadleaf evergreens for Colorado landscapes. It is especially useful as a foundation plant in a north or east exposure; or it can be planted as a shrub border or specimen plant. The glossy, leathery leaves are highlighted by bright, yellow flowers in May, followed by clusters of deep-blue berries in late summer. The holly-like leaves are spiny and remain evergreen throughout the year, turning a purplish-bronze with the onset of cold weather. If they are exposed to persistent wind and sun, expect the leaves to develop scorch and turn tannish brown. Oregon grape is a somewhat aggressive grower that spreads by underground stems. Over time it will form irregular colonies. Its foliage has nice color variation in autumn, turning dull red, orange, and yellow.

When to Plant

Plant container-grown plants in early spring. If you have to plant during the summer months, be sure you provide ample moisture for good root establishment.

Where to Plant

Oregon grape does best in locations with shade to part shade. It will need protection from winter wind and sun in order to avoid leaf scorch. Soil should be moderately fertile, well-drained, and slightly acidic.

How to Plant

Dig the planting hole 2 to 3 times wider than the rootball. It is best to prepare the soil with compost or sphagnum peat moss before planting to improve water retention and bring down the pH. Add up to 50 percent by volume of soil amendment, and mix uniformly with the native soil. Work the soil conditioner into the planting hole

as well. Set transplants level with the ground. Inspect the root systems of shrubs grown in containers. If the roots form a tight mass that encircles the rootball, the shrub has been in the pot for a while and is rootbound; as long as the plant is healthy, it is acceptable for purchase. To ensure its survival, use the "butterfly technique" to plant a rootbound plant. Lay the plant and rootball on their sides. Using a knife or sharp shovel, cut through the lower portion of the rootball. Insert the knife in line with the main trunk or stems and slice through the bottom of the rootball halfway up its length. This will allow you to spread the lower halves of the rootball apart. When positioning the shrub in the planting hole, place the roots which were growing at the bottom of the container nearer the surface, where soil conditions are more favorable for vigorous root development. Mulch with pine needles and water-in thoroughly.

CARE AND MAINTENANCE
Oregon grape prefers evenly moist conditions and should not be overwatered. Because it spreads by underground roots, over time the shrub will create its own natural living mulch. If the plant becomes straggly, prune to renew it after flowering. This will help maintain the desired height and spread. Protect Oregon grape from intense winter sun and wind by constructing a screen of burlap on the windward exposures.

ADDITIONAL INFORMATION
Oregon grape is an excellent shrub for shady locations on the north and northeast side of buildings. You will enjoy the glossy new foliage in spring and the bluish-purple fruit in late summer and fall.

ADDITIONAL SPECIES, CULTIVARS, OR VARIETIES
Our Rocky Mountain native, *Mahonia repens* or creeping mahonia, is a useful woody groundcover with handsome foliage, flowers, and fruit. It is drought-resistant, has excellent red fall foliage, and does well when planted beneath evergreens. *Mahonia aquifolium* 'Compactum' has a compact growth habit (2 to 3 ft.) and works well as a foundation plant in shady locations.

Redtwig Dogwood

Cornus sericea

	Light Requirement:
Height: 6 to 8 ft.	
Spread: 8 to 10 ft.	
Flowers: White	
Bloom Period: Late spring	
Zones: 2, 3, 4, 5, 6	

*T*he redtwig dogwood is widely adaptable to Colorado's diverse climate and soil conditions. Though it prefers a moist climate, it will grow successfully in a moderately dry environment. This shrub bears clusters of small creamy-white flowers in spring, followed by bunches of white fruit in late summer. The dark-green leaves turn burgundy-red in autumn. One of the redtwig dogwood's most striking features is its glossy red stems, which are especially attractive when framed in winter snow.

WHEN TO PLANT

Container-grown dogwood shrubs can be planted from spring through early fall. Bare-root stock, if available, is best planted in early spring as soon as the soil can be worked.

WHERE TO PLANT

Redtwig dogwood thrives in full sun or part shade. Too much shade will cause the plant to grow leggy and will decrease flowering. Plant this shrub for an informal hedge or as a screen for privacy. It is especially attractive as a backdrop for the perennial bed.

HOW TO PLANT

Dig the planting hole much wider than the width of the rootball. When planting bare-root plants, spread the roots into the planting hole. Be sure they are not cramped. If roots are given adequate space, the plant will be quick to establish. Inspect the root systems of container-grown shrubs. If the roots form a tight mass that encircles the rootball, the shrub has been in the pot for a while and is rootbound. As long as the plant is healthy, it is acceptable for purchase. To ensure its survival, use the "butterfly technique" to plant a rootbound plant. Lay the plant and rootball on their sides. Using a knife or sharp shovel, cut through the lower portion of the rootball. Insert the knife in line with the main trunk or stems and slice through the bottom of the rootball halfway up its length. This will allow you to spread the lower halves of the rootball apart. When positioning the shrub in the planting hole, place the roots which were growing at the bottom of the container nearer the surface, where soil conditions are more favorable for vigorous root development. Water-in thoroughly. Water every 5 to 7 days for the first month to ensure good establishment. Dogwood shrubs will perform and thrive best if mulched with shredded cedar shavings or other organic material. This will help conserve soil moisture and keep the soil cool.

CARE AND MAINTENANCE
Though native dogwood does best in moist soils, it will tolerate dry conditions if properly mulched. Water thoroughly and deeply during the heat of summer to prevent severe leaf scorch. A complete all-purpose 5-10-5 fertilizer should be applied in early spring. To keep the shrub vigorous and promote brightly colored stems, prune out 1/4 to 1/3 of the oldest canes each year. Remove these canes to ground level; new growth will emerge from the base.

ADDITIONAL INFORMATION
An insect pest known as "oystershell scale" can become a problem on older stems; prune out infested canes to ground level. Older shrubs can be renewed in early spring by removing the shrub to ground level.

ADDITIONAL SPECIES, CULTIVARS, OR VARIETIES
'Cardinal' has bright-red stems and nice fall foliage color. 'Flaviramea' has yellow twigs and reddish-purple fall foliage. *Cornus alba* 'Argenteo Marginata' is quite unusual, producing variegated white-and-green leaves. Its stems are bright red in winter. This variety does best in part shade; it is subject to leaf scorch in hot exposures. 'Isanti' has a denser, lower-growing habit (5 to 6 ft.) with brilliant-red stems in winter. If you want a small tree, try *Cornus alternifolia*, or Pagoda dogwood. It grows to 15 ft. or more and makes a handsome specimen tree in an east or north exposure.

Rocky Mountain Sumac

Rhus glabra var. *cismontana*

Height: 3 to 6 ft.
Spread: 3 to 12 ft.
Flowers: Yellowish green (not showy)
Bloom Period: Summer
Zones: 2, 3, 4, 5, 6

Light Requirement:

Some of our finest native shrubs are often relegated to the "plant thugs" category because of their rampant growth and wild characteristics. As these natives become more available in the nursery trade, it is time to take another look at them. Most native plants are drought resistant, tolerate a variety of soils, and produce beautiful foliage and texture. The native Rocky Mountain sumac is considered an "untamed" plant due to its tendency to sucker and produce new plants in all directions, but its fine attributes as a groundcover make it an excellent choice for the water-wise landscape. Its compound leaves give it a fern-like appearance; its foliage is bright-green in summer and turns brilliant scarlet in autumn. Rocky Mountain sumac can be used on steep banks or hillsides, and in waste areas that have poor soil. If you think golden aspen is beautiful, you will find Rocky Mountain sumac's intense scarlet autumn coloration breathtaking.

WHEN TO PLANT
Plant container-grown shrubs in early spring through fall.

WHERE TO PLANT
Locate plants in a sunny, open area where they can spread out and grow naturally. Avoid planting this shrub in the shade; it will become straggly and leggy. Do not plant Rocky Mountain sumac as a foundation plant because it will soon consume the area and become a nuisance.

HOW TO PLANT
Dig the planting hole twice as wide as the rootball. Inspect the root systems of container-grown plants. If the roots form a tight mass that encircles the rootball, the shrub has been in the pot for a while and is rootbound. As long as the plant is healthy, it is acceptable for

purchase. To ensure its survival, use the "butterfly technique" to plant a rootbound plant. Lay the plant and rootball on their sides. Using a knife or sharp shovel, cut through the lower portion of the rootball. Insert the knife in line with the main trunk or stems and slice through the bottom of the rootball halfway up its length. This will allow you to spread the lower halves of the rootball apart. When positioning the shrub in the planting hole, place the roots that were growing at the bottom of the container nearer the surface, where soil conditions are more favorable for vigorous root development. Mulch the area with shredded wood or pine needles.

CARE AND MAINTENANCE

Sumac is an aggressive plant, so you may want to temper its vigorous growth by occasionally cutting it back to ground level in early spring. New growth will soon result, allowing the plant to reestablish its territorial hold. It adapts well to dry conditions; indeed, it will not survive in extremely wet sites.

ADDITIONAL INFORMATION

It is important to plant Rocky Mountain sumac where it will not become invasive and encroach on shrub borders or flower beds. It is a tough, resilient, water-thrifty shrub that is just right for problem spots in your landscape.

ADDITIONAL SPECIES, CULTIVARS, OR VARIETIES

There are several sumac species that can be effectively used in Colorado landscapes. Some can be trained to grow as small trees. *Rhus typhina*, or staghorn sumac, is quite attractive. Its stout terminal twigs are covered with a fine brown velvet coating that resembles the covering on deer antlers. This unique characteristic helps soften staghorn sumac's coarse winter habit. It has an upright growth habit and can grow to 18 ft. or more. 'Dissecta' and 'Laniniata' are cultivars with finely dissected leaflets that produce a fern-like effect. *Rhus trilobata*, or three-leaf sumac, is another native; its three-lobed leaves turn reddish orange in the fall. It has a spreading, upright habit (6 to 8 ft.) that makes it an excellent choice for an informal hedge. Its sticky red berries are wild bird favorites.

Rose-of-Sharon

Hibiscus syriacus

Other Name: Shrub Althaea
Height: 8 to 12 ft.
Spread: 6 to 10 ft.
Flowers: White, pink, red, purple, lavender
Bloom Period: Late summer
Zones: 4, 5, 6

Light Requirement:

---

*S*hrub althaea, also known as rose-of-Sharon, is one of our favorite old-fashioned shrubs. Its eye-catching blossoms appear from late summer to frost. Depending on the variety, flowers range from 2¹/₂ to 4 in. and can be single, semi-double, or double. Althaea makes an excellent focal specimen in the landscape. It can also be planted as a group in a shrub border. Though the plant may die back to ground level in winter, it endures Colorado's erratic climatic conditions well and will grow new, vigorous stems in spring. This "Nature's Pruning" will result in a smaller shrub with much bigger flowers. If you prefer, you can selectively prune the shrub to maintain shape, height, and flower development.

WHEN TO PLANT

Plant container-grown plants from spring through early fall. Bare-root plants should be planted in early spring as soon as the soil can be worked.

WHERE TO PLANT

Though althaea will tolerate light shade, but try to choose a planting site that receives full sun. Avoid areas that are too wet or soils that are poorly drained. Place it against a garden shed or garage; althaea will hide a bare wall with a showy display of flowers from summer through frost.

HOW TO PLANT

Dig the planting hole 2 to 3 times wider than the rootball. Inspect the root systems of shrubs grown in containers. If the roots form a tight mass that encircles the rootball, the shrub has been in the pot for a while and is rootbound. As long as the plant is healthy, it is acceptable for purchase. To ensure its survival, use the "butterfly technique" to plant a rootbound plant. Lay the plant and rootball on their sides. Using a knife or sharp shovel, cut through the lower portion of the rootball. Insert the knife in line with the main trunk or stems and slice through the bottom of the rootball halfway up its length. This will allow you to spread the lower halves of the rootball apart. When positioning the shrub in the planting hole, place the roots that were growing at the bottom of the container nearer the surface, where soil conditions are more favorable for vigorous root development. When planting bare-root plants, be sure to spread the roots into the planting hole without cramping them. Add backfill soil and water slowly to eliminate any air pockets under the roots. Spread a 2-in. layer of mulch under the shrub. Keep the soil evenly moist for at least one month.

CARE AND MAINTENANCE

Shrub althaea will experience drought stress in extremely dry sites or in sandy soils. The application of mulches will help reduce moisture loss and keep the soil cool. Water regularly during the summer months. Thinning out crowded branches or pruning for renewal in late spring will encourage more vigorous and floriferous stems. Apply a 5-10-5 all-purpose granular fertilizer at the rate of $1/4$ cup per ft. of shrub height in spring and then again in midsummer. Broadcast fertilizer at the dripline and water-in thoroughly.

ADDITIONAL INFORMATION

Rose-of-Sharon is slow to start out in spring, so be patient when waiting for the leaves to emerge. Pruning the previous season's growth to two or three buds in spring will result in fewer but larger flowers.

ADDITIONAL SPECIES, CULTIVARS, OR VARIETIES

'Diana' is a tetraploid variety with large 4-in. flowers. It does not produce seed, so you won't have to worry about weeding hibiscus seedlings each summer. 'Bluebird' has beautiful sky-blue single flowers. 'Aphrodite' is especially attractive and has large 4- to 5-in. dark-pink flowers with prominent darker-red eyes. 'Collie Mullens' bears large double lavender-purple flowers in late summer.

Scotch Broom

Cytisus scoparius

Height: 4 to 5 ft.	**Light Requirement:**
Spread: 4 to 6 ft.	
Flowers: Yellow, red, orange, some bicolors	
Bloom Period: Late spring to summer	
Zones: 4, 5, 6	

*T*he unique linear leaves of Scotch broom give this shrub a leaf-less appearance. This adaptation allows it to withstand Colorado's dry, windy conditions. The bright, pea-like, golden-yellow flowers bloom profusely, creating a very showy display in late spring. The long arching stems remain green to yellow-green year-round and present a nice texture in the winter garden. Use this shrub as a specimen plant, in a shrub border, as a foundation planting, or anywhere where you have dry, poor soils. Scotch broom has the ability to fix nitrogen from the atmosphere; this enables it to thrive in infertile soils. It is truly a rugged, well-adapted plant for our region and deserves more use in Colorado landscapes.

WHEN TO PLANT
Plant Scotch broom in spring. This will give the plants a full season to become established before winter.

WHERE TO PLANT
Scotch broom does best in full sun and well-drained soils. Plant as a shrub border, in mass plantings, or as an accent shrub.

HOW TO PLANT
Container-grown plants are easy to transplant. Though brooms are tolerant of sandy, infertile soils, heavy clay soils should be amended with organic matter to improve drainage. In sandy soils, add compost to help retain moisture during extended dry periods. Dig the planting hole twice as wide as the rootball. Inspect the root systems of shrubs grown in containers. If the roots form a tight mass that encircles the rootball, the shrub has been in the pot for a while and is rootbound. As long as the plant is healthy, it is acceptable for purchase. To ensure its survival, use the "butterfly technique" to plant a

rootbound plant. Lay the plant and rootball on their sides. Using a knife or sharp shovel, cut through the lower portion of the rootball. Insert the knife in line with the main trunk or stems and slice through the bottom of the rootball halfway up its length. This will allow you to spread the lower halves of the rootball apart. When positioning the shrub in the planting hole, place the roots which were growing at the bottom of the container nearer the surface, where soil conditions are more favorable for vigorous root development. Add the backfill soil to the planting hole and water slowly to eliminate any air pockets under the roots. Check the soil moisture by digging down 4 to 6 in. If it has begun to dry out, give the shrub a good drink. Apply a mulch of pea gravel or shredded wood chips to conserve moisture.

CARE AND MAINTENANCE

Once established, brooms need little maintenance. Water deeply and infrequently throughout the growing season. Young shrubs can be pinched for shaping, but older shrubs do not respond well to pruning. Allow the shrub to grow in its natural form. Because bacteria on the roots help to fix atmospheric nitrogen, additional fertilizer is generally not required.

ADDITIONAL INFORMATION

Scotch broom's profusion of flowers is stunning. Use it along pathways, driveways, or in a shrub border. Smaller varieties will work nicely as accent plants in rock gardens.

ADDITIONAL SPECIES, CULTIVARS, OR VARIETIES

Cytisus scoparius 'Moonlight' broom is a nice rounded shrub with nodding branches that are peppered with narrow, bright-green leaves. The creamy-yellow flowers create a showy display in late spring. *Cytisus* × 'Lena' has a more compact growing habit (2 to 3 ft.) and showy red-winged, bright-yellow blossoms. It makes a nice accent plant in the rock garden.

Sea Buckthorn

Hippophae rhamnoides

Height: 12 to 20 ft.	**Light Requirement:**
Spread: 10 to 15 ft.	
Flowers: Yellow	
Bloom Period: Early spring	
Zones: 3, 4, 5, 6	

*S*ea buckthorn is an excellent shrub for the water-thrifty landscape. Its spiny stems and linear, silvery leaves provide a nice contrast to other plants in the landscape. This shrub is great for planting in a naturescape to attract wildlife. It produces yellowish flowers in early spring before the leaves emerge. The showy orange berries on the female plants persist into winter and have a very high Vitamin C content. Both male and female plants are needed to produce berries. Sea buckthorn's growth habit can be somewhat varied. Male plants exhibit a more upright growing habit, while female plants tend to spread, forming an irregularly rounded shape. Use this shrub as a screen or informal hedge. It does well in roadside and street plantings where salt is used for winter de-icing. Sea buckthorn seems to do best in infertile soils rather than soils that are rich in organic matter. It is not bothered by insects or diseases.

WHEN TO PLANT

Container-grown shrubs can be planted from early spring through fall. You may have to look around for this uncommon plant. If you cannot find sea buckthorn at local nurseries, your best bet is to order it through a mail-order source. We have planted several of these shrubs in our windbreak and find sea buckthorn to be a rugged yet interesting landscape shrub with attractive silvery foliage and bright fruits.

WHERE TO PLANT

Locate sea buckthorn in a sunny, open area. Plant it as an informal hedge, a privacy screen, or an accent plant in the background of your landscape.

How to Plant

Dig the planting hole 3 times wider than the rootball. As long as the soil has been broken up and is not lumpy, no soil conditioner is necessary. Inspect the root systems of shrubs grown in containers. If the roots form a tight mass that encircles the rootball, the shrub has been in the pot for a while and is rootbound; as long as the plant is healthy, it is acceptable for purchase. To ensure its survival, use the "butterfly technique" to plant a rootbound plant. Lay the plant and rootball on their sides. Using a knife or sharp shovel, cut through the lower portion of the rootball. Insert the knife in line with the main trunk or stems and slice through the bottom of the rootball halfway up its length. This will allow you to spread the lower halves of the rootball apart. When positioning the shrub in the planting hole, place the roots that were growing at the bottom of the container nearer the surface, where soil conditions are more favorable for vigorous root development. Add backfill soil to the planting hole and water slowly to eliminate any air pockets under the roots. Mulch with shredded wood chips, cedar shavings, or other organic mulch. Water when the soil dries out to a 4- to 6-in. depth. Avoid light, frequent waterings.

Care and Maintenance

Once the sea buckthorn has become established, it will thrive in Colorado's unpredictable weather conditions. Water occasionally, applying water thoroughly with a soaker hose or drip irrigation system. Because it is a nitrogen-fixing plant, supplemental fertilizer is generally not required.

Additional Information

Both male and female plants are needed to produce berries. It has been suggested that a ratio of 6 female plants to one male is sufficient for good pollination. We have enjoyed growing this plant on the High Plains; it has endured drought and the ever-changing climatic conditions.

Additional Species, Cultivars, or Varieties

This is the only species currently available.

Serviceberry

Amelanchier alnifolia

Height: 8 to 12 ft.	**Light Requirement:**
Spread: 8 to 12 ft.	
Flowers: White	
Bloom Period: Spring	
Zones: 3, 4, 5, 6	

*S*erviceberry is a handsome mountain native shrub that is often grown as a small tree in landscapes with limited space. It offers year-round interest with showy, billowy clusters of white blossoms in spring, berries in summer, orange-yellow fall foliage, and attractive ascending trunks during winter. The berries don't last long; as soon as the fruit begins to turn reddish-purple, wild birds move in for the feast. The Saskatoon serviceberry is a good selection for a water-wise garden. It is drought-enduring, tolerates alkaline soils, and is adaptable to moist meadow sites, stream banks, and to drier mountain slopes. We have several serviceberries in the windbreak of our Green Thumb landscape, where these shrubs have proven themselves tough enough to survive the plain's winds and drought conditions. The wild birds they attract to our landscape add more seasonal interest.

WHEN TO PLANT

Plant serviceberry in spring through early fall. Shrubs are available as container-grown or balled-and-burlapped plants.

WHERE TO PLANT

Serviceberry prefers partial shade but will perform admirably in full sun if provided with good air circulation. Combine it in a naturalized setting with Gambel oak (*Quercus gambelii*), chokecherry (*Prunus virginiana*), or apricot (*Prunus armeniaca*).

HOW TO PLANT

Dig the planting hole 2 to 3 times wider than the rootball. Serviceberry prefers a well-drained, loamy soil with a neutral to slightly acidic pH. Amend the soil with a 50/50 mixture of compost and sphagnum peat moss. Mix 25 to 30 percent by volume of this soil conditioner with the backfill soil and add some to the hole, mixing it into the bottom and sides. Inspect the root systems of shrubs grown in containers. If the roots form a tight mass that encircles the rootball, the shrub has been in the pot for a while and is rootbound. As long as the plant is healthy, it is acceptable for purchase. To ensure its survival, use the "butterfly technique" to plant a rootbound plant. Lay the plant and rootball on their sides. Using a knife or sharp shovel, cut through the lower portion of the rootball. Insert the knife in line with the main trunk or stems and slice through the bottom of the rootball halfway up its length. This will allow you to spread the lower halves of the rootball apart. When positioning the shrub in the planting hole, place the roots that were growing at the bottom of the container nearer the surface, where soil conditions are more favorable for vigorous root development. Set the plant level with the surrounding grade and remove any nylon twine or rope. If the plant is balled and burlapped, remove the upper portion of the wire basket. Mulch with 2 to 3 in. of pine needles, compost, or other organic material to conserve moisture and prevent drought stress during the summer.

CARE AND MAINTENANCE

Though serviceberry will adapt to less-than-ideal conditions, it performs best when grown in organic soils with good drainage. Be sure to provide several deep, thorough waterings during the heat of summer to prevent severe drought stress and leaf scorch. A groundcover planted at the base of the shrubs will act as a living mulch; or you can mulch the soil with a heavy layer of pine needles or shredded cedar shavings. Except for needing occasional removal of unwanted sucker growth, this shrub usually requires very little pruning.

ADDITIONAL INFORMATION

Serviceberry is a well-adapted shrub or small tree that should be used more often in Colorado landscapes. It can be occasionally bothered by fire blight, powdery mildew, and aphids. Avoid applying high-nitrogen fertilizers to this shrub. If you can get the fruit before the birds do, it makes delicious jam or jelly.

ADDITIONAL SPECIES, CULTIVARS, OR VARIETIES

The Shadblow serviceberry (*Amelanchier canadensis*) has a larger growth habit, reaching up to 20 ft. in height with a spread of 8 to 12 ft. Its showy white flowers appear in early spring before the leaves emerge. Fall color is yellowish red. *Amelanchier alnifolia* 'Regent' is a smaller selection of Saskatoon serviceberry that has a larger, heavier fruit set. Its bluish-black fruit resemble blueberries and ripen in early summer.

Siberian Pea Shrub

Caragana arborescens

Height: 10 to 15 ft.
Spread: 6 to 12 ft.
Flowers: Yellow
Bloom Period: Late spring
Zones: 2, 3, 4, 5, 6

Light Requirement:

The Siberian pea shrub is native to the cold, windy regions of northern Asia, which makes it widely adaptable to the High Plains of Colorado. It is a valuable shrub that works well as a screen, hedge, or windbreak where growing conditions are less than ideal. Siberian pea shrub tolerates winter temperature extremes and can withstand dry, hot, windy conditions. Charming clusters of fragrant yellow pea-like flowers appear in late spring, followed by small slender pods in summer. Its foliage is pinnately compound with 8 to 12 leaflets; it resembles feathers. The stems are yellow-green with pale horizontal lenticels in the bark. The pea shrub is effective for use in naturescapes, water-thrifty gardens, or difficult spots in your landscape.

WHEN TO PLANT

Container-grown pea shrubs can be planted from early spring through fall. Bare-root plants should be planted as soon as the soil can be worked in early spring. This will allow for good root establishment before hot weather appears.

WHERE TO PLANT

Siberian pea shrub will grow in moist, well-drained soils, but it prefers sandy soil and full sun. If soil is compacted, be sure to loosen it up thoroughly to encourage good root development. This shrub makes a hardy windbreak or privacy screen.

HOW TO PLANT

If planting Siberian pea shrub as a hedge, place the plants 2 to 3 ft. apart. Dig the planting hole twice as wide as the rootball. As long as the soil has been broken up, no soil conditioner is necessary. In sandy soils, it is beneficial to add some compost or well-rotted manure to help retain moisture; add 25 to 30 percent by volume to native soil and incorporate the amendment into the soil to a depth of 8 in. or more. When planting bare-root plants, spread the roots into the planting hole and add backfill soil. Inspect the root systems of shrubs grown in containers. If the roots form a tight mass that encircles the rootball, the shrub has been in the pot for a while and is rootbound. As long as the plant is healthy, it is acceptable for purchase. To ensure its survival, use the "butterfly technique" to plant a rootbound plant. Lay the plant and rootball on their sides. Using a knife or sharp shovel, cut through the lower portion of the rootball. Insert the knife in line with the main trunk or stems and slice through the bottom of the rootball halfway up its length. This will allow you to spread the lower halves of the rootball apart. When positioning the shrub in the planting hole, place the roots that were growing at the bottom of the container nearer the surface, where soil conditions are more favorable for vigorous root development. Water-in thoroughly. Water as needed throughout the year to promote good growth.

CARE AND MAINTENANCE
Once established, this shrub requires little care. Pruning will encourage denser growth. Remove the previous season's growth by 1/3 to 1/2 after the shrub has finished blooming. To rejuvenate older shrubs, cut them back to ground level in early spring.

ADDITIONAL INFORMATION
Siberian pea shrub resists most pests but may suffer an occasional attack from leafhoppers and leaf cutter bees.

ADDITIONAL SPECIES, CULTIVARS, OR VARIETIES
The weeping Siberian pea shrub, *Caragana arborescens* 'Pendula', is an unusual ornamental with weeping branches that give it an umbrella-like shape. 'Lorbergii' has narrower flowers and thread-like leaflets that produce a ferny appearance. Pygmy pea shrub, *Caragana pygmaea*, is a very attractive form that grows 3 to 4 ft. tall with 4 dark-green leaflets per leaf.

Silver Buffaloberry

Shepherdia argentea

Height: 8 to 15 ft.
Spread: 6 to 12 ft.
Flowers: Yellowish
Bloom Period: Spring
Zones: 2, 3, 4, 5, 6

Light Requirement:

The leathery, silvery green leaves of buffaloberry make this shrub a handsome addition to the landscape. It is one of the most drought-resistant plants for our state and tolerates conditions that other shrubs cannot survive. Its dense growth and rounded, upright growth habit make buffaloberry useful as a screen or informal hedge, or in mass plantings for a windbreak. The stems are silvery-gray and contrast nicely with the foliage. One- to 2-in. thorns grow from the ends of the branches. Buffaloberry is extremely tolerant of both drought and cold, and it grows well in alkaline soils. Its orange-red berries are favored by wildlife, making it excellent for planting in a naturescape. We have planted several of these shrubs in our windbreak. The silvery foliage and stems add landscape interest year-round.

WHEN TO PLANT

Container-grown shrubs can be planted from spring to early fall. If you purchase bare-root plants, plant them in early spring as soon as the soil can be worked.

WHERE TO PLANT

Place in a sunny, open exposure. Buffaloberry is very useful in dry, alkaline soil conditions.

HOW TO PLANT

Dig the planting hole 2 to 3 times wider than the rootball. As long as the soil has been broken up to relieve soil compaction, no soil amendment is necessary. When planting bare-root plants, spread the roots into the planting hole without cramping them. Inspect the root systems of shrubs grown in containers. If the roots form a tight mass that encircles the rootball, the shrub has been in the pot for a while and is rootbound; as long as the plant is healthy, it is acceptable for purchase. To ensure its survival, use the "butterfly technique" to plant a rootbound plant. Lay the plant and rootball on their sides. Using a knife or sharp shovel, cut through the lower portion of the rootball. Insert the knife in line with the main trunk or stems and slice through the bottom of the rootball halfway up its length. This will allow you to spread the lower halves of the rootball apart. When positioning the shrub in the planting hole, place the roots which were growing at the bottom of the container nearer the surface, where soil conditions are more favorable for vigorous root development. Add backfill soil to the planting hole and water slowly to eliminate any air pockets under the roots. Add a layer of mulch to maintain moisture during establishment.

CARE AND MAINTENANCE
Once established, buffaloberry is extremely durable and hardy. Water when the soil dries out to a depth of 4 to 6 in. Water thoroughly but not frequently. Because buffaloberry fixes atmospheric nitrogen, additional fertilizer is generally not necessary. Prune out dead wood in early spring.

ADDITIONAL INFORMATION
Both male and female plants are required to produce the fruit, which can be used to make jelly.

ADDITIONAL SPECIES, CULTIVARS, OR VARIETIES
Shepherdia canadensis, russet buffaloberry, is a native of rocky slopes. It grows as a loosely rounded shrub with a height of 6 ft. or more and a comparable spread. The dark-green leaves have silvery undersides and a "gritty" texture. Fruit on female plants is yellowish-red and bitter.

Spirea

Spiraea spp.

Height: 1 to 7 ft.
Spread: 2 to 8 ft.
Flowers: White, pink
Bloom Period: Spring or summer,
depending on species
Zones: 3, 4, 5, 6

Light Requirement:

*T*ake a drive through any neighborhood in spring and you are sure to find the arching branches of *Spiraea* × *vanhouttei*, bridal wreath spirea, laden with clusters of small white flowers. It is a testimonial to this plant's adaptability that settlers brought cuttings of it westward with them. Today, there are many species and cultivars ranging in size from 12 in. tall to 6 ft. or more. The profuse clusters of blossoms in early spring and summer are sure to provide weeks of enjoyment for gardeners who want an easy-to-grow shrub. Spirea can be used as foundation plantings, informal hedges, or background plantings for flower beds; or use in mass plantings and borders.

WHEN TO PLANT

Plant in early spring through fall. Container-grown nursery plants are readily available. Bare-root plants can be found through various mail order sources.

WHERE TO PLANT

Though they are tolerant of many soil conditions, spireas do best in well-drained soils. Avoid areas that tend to stay wet. Locate in full sun to part shade.

HOW TO PLANT

Dig the planting hole 2 to 3 times as wide as the rootball. Compost can be added if the soil is extremely sandy or has poor drainage. Loosen the soil in the area where the plants are to be grown. Inspect the root systems of shrubs grown in containers. If the roots form a tight mass that encircles the rootball, the shrub has been in the pot for a while and is rootbound. As long as the plant is healthy, it is acceptable for purchase. To ensure its survival, use the "butterfly technique" to plant a rootbound plant. Lay the plant and rootball on their sides. Using a knife or sharp shovel, cut through the lower portion of the rootball. Insert the knife in line with the main trunk or stems and slice through the bottom of the rootball halfway up its length. This will allow you to spread the lower halves of the rootball apart. When positioning the shrub in the planting hole, place the roots that were growing at the bottom of the container nearer the surface, where soil conditions are more favorable for vigorous root development. Add backfill soil and water thoroughly after planting. Keep the soil evenly moist for the first month. Use a mulch of compost, pine needles, or shredded cedar to maintain and conserve moisture.

CARE AND MAINTENANCE

Once established, spireas are easy to maintain. Most types are very drought tolerant. Be sure to water deeply and thoroughly during the summer to ensure more prolific flowering. You can apply an all-purpose 5-10-5 fertilizer according to directions in April, May, and June. After the flowers have faded, use hedge clippers or hand pruners to remove 6 in. of foliage from all around the plant. The new growth that appears will usually produce a second flush of flowers later in summer. Older shrubs should be thinned out and renewed every 3 years. Remove the oldest canes to ground level to encourage new growth from the base.

ADDITIONAL INFORMATION

Most spireas are easy to propagate from softwood cuttings or from sprouts that grow beneath the bush.

ADDITIONAL SPECIES, CULTIVARS, OR VARIETIES

There are so many species and cultivars of spirea that we can include only a few favorites. Check with your nursery or a reputable mail-order source for additional information. *Spiraea japonica* 'Froebelii' is a low-growing shrub that sports flat clusters of rose flowers in late May or June. 'Goldflame' has bright-golden leaves with red tips; its foliage turns yellow-green in summer and dark-pink flowers appear in summer. 'Gumball' is an excellent summer-blooming shrub with a compact growth habit. In early summer, it produces beautiful pink blooms and contrasting medium-green leaves. *Spiraea cineria* 'Grefsheim' has an arching growth habit and produces cascades of white flowers all along its branches in late April or early May. *Spiraea japonica* 'Alpina' has a low growing habit (12 in.) and makes an attractive fine-textured groundcover. Clusters of light-pink flowers appear in midsummer.

Tatarian Honeysuckle

Lonicera tatarica

Height: 8 to 10 ft.
Spread: 6 to 8 ft.
Flowers: Red
Bloom Period: Spring through early summer
Zones: 3, 4, 5, 6

Light Requirement:

The tubular flowers of honeysuckle possess a fragrance that brings back memories of my grandmother's garden. She planted 'Zabelii', a variety that has since become severely plagued by the honeysuckle aphid. These pests cause a "witches' broom" on the terminal growth, primarily affecting tender new growth: the leaves become stunted and develop into distorted bunches. Despite this invasion, the honeysuckle bush will still flower prolifically. Flowering is followed by ornamental berries; they are a favorite of robins and disappear quickly. One of the better cultivars for Colorado gardens is *Lonicera tatarica* 'Arnold's Red'. It has characteristic pinkish-red blossoms in late spring followed by glossy red berries that robins consume in mass quantities. It is a good choice for gardeners in the High Country.

WHEN TO PLANT
Container-grown honeysuckle shrubs can be planted from spring through early fall. Bare-root plants are also available and should be planted as soon as the soil can be worked in early spring.

WHERE TO PLANT
Honeysuckle prefers full sun, but it will adapt to partial shade. It does best in well-drained, loamy soils that have moderate moisture.

HOW TO PLANT
Dig the planting hole 2 to 3 times wider than the rootball. Honeysuckle is easy to transplant and quick to establish. Inspect the root systems of shrubs grown in containers. If the roots form a tight mass that encircles the rootball, the shrub has been in the pot for a while and is rootbound; as long as the plant is healthy, it is acceptable for purchase. To ensure its survival, use the "butterfly technique" to plant a rootbound plant. Lay the plant and rootball on their sides.

Using a knife or sharp shovel, cut through the lower portion of the rootball. Insert the knife in line with the main trunk or stems and slice through the bottom of the rootball halfway up its length. This will allow you to spread the lower halves of the rootball apart. When positioning the shrub in the planting hole, place the roots that were growing at the bottom of the container nearer the surface, where soil conditions are more favorable for vigorous root development. Add backfill soil to the hole and water slowly. Apply a 2-in. layer of mulch to maintain uniform moisture during the first growing season.

CARE AND MAINTENANCE

Once established, honeysuckle is very drought-enduring. Avoid overwatering—water deeply but infrequently during the summer. To maintain vigor and health, prune honeysuckle after it has flowered; remove the oldest canes to ground level to help rejuvenate older shrubs.

ADDITIONAL INFORMATION

Some varieties are susceptible to honeysuckle aphids, depending on the geographical area. Distorted growth can be pruned off as it appears.

ADDITIONAL SPECIES, CULTIVARS, OR VARIETIES

The blueleaf honeysuckle, *Lonicera korolkowii*, is a selection with gray-blue leaves and rose-pink blossoms. It bears bright-red berries in late summer and is not bothered by aphids. *Lonicera involucrata*, or Twinberry honeysuckle, is a compact-growing oval shrub (3 to 6 ft.) with pairs of yellow flowers in late spring to early summer. Twin berries rest in its reddish floral leaflets. *Lonicera syringantha*, or tiny trumpet honeysuckle, is hardy to an elevation of 11,000 ft. It has arching branches with small, strongly fragrant, pale-violet, trumpet-like flowers that bloom in late spring. The bluish green leaves contrast nicely with the newer red stems. *Lonicera maackii*, or Amur honeysuckle, has an upright growth habit and medium- to dark-green leaves. Fragrant white flowers are borne in clusters in May to June, followed by bright-red fruits that are much loved by birds. This variety is not affected by honeysuckle aphids.

Viburnum

Viburnum spp.

Height: 4 to 12 ft.	**Light Requirement:**
Spread: 3 to 10 ft.	
Flowers: White, pinkish white	
Bloom Period: Spring	
Zones: 2, 3, 4, 5, 6	

*V*iburnums comprise a large group of adaptable shrubs that have handsome foliage and attractive flowers. They are easy to grow and tolerate most soil types throughout Colorado. The berry-like fruit is a favorite food for wild birds. *Viburnum × rhytidophylloides* 'Alleghany' has shown excellent adaptability and thrives in hot, dry conditions as well as in fertile cool soils near evergreens. The flowers are flat, showy white panicles that produce handsome red berries in late summer and fall. The glossy green foliage makes this shrub an excellent choice for use in mass plantings, hedges, foundation plantings, or shrub borders.

When to Plant
Plant from spring through fall.

Where to Plant
Viburnums do best in well-drained soils but will tolerate various soil conditions. Locate in full sun to part shade.

How to Plant
Dig the planting hole 2 to 3 times as wide as the rootball. Because viburnums prefer moist soils, it is helpful to amend the soil with compost (at the rate of 30 percent by volume to the native soil). Mix the compost uniformly with the backfill soil. Inspect the root systems of shrubs grown in containers. If the roots form a tight mass that encircles the rootball, the shrub has been in the pot for a while and is rootbound; as long as the plant is healthy, it is acceptable for purchase. To ensure its survival, use the "butterfly technique" to plant a rootbound plant. Lay the plant and rootball on their sides. Using a knife or sharp shovel, cut through the lower portion of the rootball. Insert the knife in line with the main trunk or stems and slice through the bottom of the rootball halfway up its length. This

will allow you to spread the lower halves of the rootball apart. When positioning the shrub in the planting hole, place the roots which were growing at the bottom of the container nearer the surface, where soil conditions are more favorable for vigorous root development. Water the newly set plant thoroughly and mulch with pine needles or shredded cedar.

CARE AND MAINTENANCE

Once established, viburnums are easy-to-maintain. Only minor pruning after the plant flowers will be necessary to keep the shrub in shape. Water throughout the summer to prevent scorch and severe wilting.

ADDITIONAL INFORMATION

The European cranberry bush, *Viburnum opulus*, is frequently attacked by aphids. Early detection and control will help prevent a severe problem.

ADDITIONAL SPECIES, CULTIVARS, OR VARIETIES

Viburnum acerifolium, or maple-leaved viburnum, is a low-growing shrub (4 to 6 ft.) with bright-green foliage that changes to reddish purple in fall. It withstands shade and grows in dry-to-moist soils. *Viburnum* × *burkwoodii* has glossy leaves and fragrant blossoms that are followed by clusters of black berries in summer and wine-red foliage in fall. *Viburnum carlesii,* the Koreanspice viburnum, is valued for its fragrant pinkish white flowers and crimson fall foliage. *Viburnum opulus,* or European cranberry, has maple-like leaves and lacy white blooms that are followed by bright-red fruit. 'Nanum' is a dwarf form that seldom grows more than 2 ft. tall. It is non-fruiting and displays excellent wine-red fall color. 'Compactum' is a smaller rounded shrub (4 to 5 ft.) that produces persistent scarlet fruit. *Viburnum lantana,* or wayfaring tree, is a taller-growing shrub (to 15 ft.) with handsome leathery dark-green leaves. Large white flower clusters are followed by crimson fruit which turns black in fall. Its autumn foliage is a beautiful maroon. 'Mohican' has a more compact growing habit (6 ft.) with red-orange fruit that persists. *Viburnum prunifolium,* or blackhaw, is a fine tall shrub that works well in mass plantings and shrub borders, or as a single specimen in the landscape. The leathery, dark-green leaves are pest-free. Fall color is a brilliant red. *Viburnum trilobum* 'Compactum' is a smaller form of the American cranberry, with three-lobed leaves that turn vibrant red in fall. *Viburnum dentatum,* or arrowhead, is one of our favorites. It has upright spreading branches and striking bluish-black berries in late summer. Autumn foliage is a rich red.

CHAPTER ELEVEN

Vines

*V*INES ARE VERSATILE PLANTS IN COLORADO. Growing vines can be rewarding if you understand their habits and know some attractive ways to use them in the landscape. Many vines that grow in Colorado have handsome foliage, beautiful flowers, and edible fruits, and their clinging, twining, or upright growth makes a nice visual contrast to the plants around them. One of our favorites, Virginia creeper, makes a beautiful autumn display.

Annual vines will produce the largest leaves and bear more flowers when planted in full sun. Perennial vines often reward the gardener with flowers, interesting foliage, and ornamental stems and bark for winter interest. For vines to grow and prosper, it is important to select them thoughtfully and consider their location well. Many of them do not like to be disturbed.

How They Climb

Vines are different in the ways they climb. Clematis climb using tendrils or leaf-like appendages that grow out from their stems and wrap themselves around some kind of support. Some vines, including Boston ivy, Virginia creeper, and trumpet vine, have non-coiling clinging tendrils and a climbing part called an *adherent pad*. Their stems bond to a rough surface or support structure like a super-strength adhesive. English ivy and climbing hydrangea have aerial rootlets called *holdfasts* that cement themselves to walls, trees, or other objects in their growing paths.

Whatever the climbing mechanism, most vines climb by twining themselves around a structure. In the wild, the structure is often a tree; in your landscape, it can be a post, a pillar, a downspout, or a dead tree. A vine will start to twine when it touches an object, producing growth faster on one side of the vine than on the other. This causes twisting; the vine grows and continues to bend around and around the object. Just as people are right- or left-handed, so are twining vines. A vine will twist around its support either clockwise (to the right) or counterclockwise (to the left). This growth habit is easy to see when you observe a honeysuckle, which grows clockwise, or bittersweet, which grows counterclockwise. It helps to know this habit so that when a vine starts to grow you won't inadvertently twist it in the wrong direction. Let nature takes it course.

TRAINING

Matching a vine to a support is one of the secrets of growing success. A twining vine will not grow up a brick wall, and you can't expect an ivy to climb a wire. Vines can be trained on arbors, trellises, pergolas, gazebos, fence posts, lattices, and trees. Clematis are often at their best when climbing through trees and shrubs. Some vines can be left to grow as a groundcover to hold the soil; they are attractive when cascading over walls and embankments. We find vines useful on chain-link fences, and annual vines can be easily grown on twine or string.

The list of vines in this chapter is not exhaustive, but it includes some of the best tried-and-true vines for Colorado. Most are hardy throughout our area, although it is helpful to provide some protection to newly planted vines by applying a winter mulch in late November or early December. We use evergreen boughs and coarse compost at the base of our vines to protect the roots and crowns from heaving. A *Colorado Green Thumb rule of thumb*: Water vines monthly in the absence or rain or snow. Then water as needed as long as the soil remains unfrozen and will accept moisture, and when temperatures are above freezing.

American Bittersweet

Celastrus scandens

Height: To 25 ft.
Flowers: Yellowish white
Bloom Period: Late spring; orange berries
  in autumn
Zones: 3, 4, 5, 6

Light Requirement:

American bittersweet is a remarkable vine prized for the colorful fruit that clings to its stems throughout fall and winter. We especially like to use cuttings of this vine in dried flower arrangements. American bittersweet grows relatively quickly and will cover a trellis, arbor, fence, or rocks if given vertical support. The foliage provides a thick screen in summer and turns lime green to yellow in fall. Clusters of creamy-white flowers appear in June. The female plants produce yellow and orange berries that burst open in autumn to reveal bright orange-red seeds. This is when bittersweet is at its showiest. For an elegant display, pick a bouquet of berries and display them in a bottleneck gourd. Be sure to plant both male and female plants if you desire the berries.

WHEN TO PLANT

Plant container-grown vines from spring through fall. If you purchase bare-root vines from a mail-order nursery, soak the roots in a bucket of warm water for a few hours before planting. Clip off any damaged or broken roots down to live, healthy tissue.

WHERE TO PLANT

Bittersweet prefers full sun but will grow in partial shade. When planted in full sun, the vine will produce more colorful fruit for drying. It is adapted to most soil types and tolerates poor soil conditions. If the soil is too rich, bittersweet may threaten to grow and cover everything in sight. This vine climbs by twining and needs a strong support.

HOW TO PLANT

Dig the planting hole 3 times wider than the rootball. There is generally no need to amend the soil, but if it is compacted, take time to loosen it. This will aid in root development. If your soil is a heavy clay, adding an organic amendment will improve drainage; if the soil is extremely sandy, add an organic amendment to help retain moisture. Mix $1/4$ to $1/3$ compost into the soil that has been removed from the planting hole. This will help get the bittersweet vine off to a more vigorous start. Sandy soils will need more compost (up to 40 percent by volume) to help retain moisture. If the roots in the container have become rootbound, gently pull them apart and loosen the longest roots so that they can be spread into the hole. Add backfill soil and water-in thoroughly. Spread a mulch of compost or bark beneath the plant and water only as needed when the soil starts to dry out.

CARE AND MAINTENANCE
Once established, bittersweet requires little care other than occasional pruning in spring to increase flowering and fruiting. Vines that have become overgrown can also be kept in bounds with periodic pruning. Should the vine begin to grow out of bounds by means of underground roots, you can "root prune": Using a sharp shovel, cut unwanted plants out by the roots. Water bittersweet thoroughly and deeply, but not frequently, during the growing season. Avoid overwatering. Fertilizer is generally not necessary, but if desired, a complete 5-10-5 can be applied in spring.

ADDITIONAL INFORMATION
The yellow and orange berries of bittersweet are a favorite for autumn's dried table arrangements and for use in wreaths. Both male and female plants are necessary to produce fruit. Unless you learn the sex of the plant from the place of purchase, it will be necessary to plant several to ensure efficient pollination and fruit production.

ADDITIONAL SPECIES, CULTIVARS, OR VARIETIES
Two other bittersweets that are adapted to our region are Loesener bittersweet, *Celastrus loeseneri*, and Oriental bittersweet, *Celastrus orbiculatus*, which can grow to 25 ft. Cultural requirements for both varieties are the same as those for *C. scandens*.

Clematis

Clematis spp.

Height: 10 to 25 ft.
Flowers: Purple, pink, blue, white, red, yellow, bicolors
Bloom Period: Late spring, summer, or late summer
Zones: 4, 5, 6

Light Requirement:

One of the showiest vines in the landscape, clematis produces an abundance of exquisite blooms on vigorous, fast-growing vines. The flowers are made up not of petals but of sepals, the outer parts of the blossom that surround and protect the bud before it opens. C. × 'Jackmanii' is a popular variety with rich-purple blossoms; there are a rainbow of colors available in other varieties, including pink, red, rose, blue, lilac, mauve, purple, lavender, and white. The small, nodding yellow flowers of *C. tangutica* resemble tiny lanterns that glow in the evening garden. The secret to success with clematis is to grow this vine with its head in the sun and its feet in the shade. This will protect the roots from summer heat. You can keep a deep layer of mulch at the base of the vine or grow a groundcover around the plant to shade the crown. Clematis does remarkably well in our alkaline soil. This vine is recommended for trellises, arbors, mailboxes, posts, fences, and other structures around which stems and petioles can twine.

WHEN TO PLANT

Plant in spring. When possible, buy 2-year-old plants. Bare-root plants are available in early spring and transplant easily.

WHERE TO PLANT

Choose a site that receives full sun to part shade, keeping the roots cool. An east- or north-facing site is ideal, though vines will thrive in full sun if air circulation is good and if even moisture is provided. *Clematis montana* var. *rubens* is right at home climbing through shrubs.

HOW TO PLANT

Prepare the planting area by loosening the soil deeply to provide good soil aeration and drainage. Amend soil by adding 1/3 compost to the native soil. Dig the hole 2 to 3 times wider than the rootball and set the crown of the plant 1 to 2 in. below the soil grade for added protection. Gently firm the backfill soil around the rootball and water-in well to eliminate air pockets. Cover the crown with a few inches of organic mulch. A trellis or other support on which the clematis vine can be trained should be anchored in the ground at the time of planting to reduce root and stem damage.

CARE AND MAINTENANCE

Clematis prefer soil that is kept evenly moist but not waterlogged. Once clematis is established, avoid cultivating around it or you may damage its shallow roots. Vines are hardy and need only occasional pruning to maintain shape, height, and flowering. Pruning methods vary according to the flowering time of the individual variety. Spring-blooming types that bloom on previous year's growth should be pruned after flowering (no later than mid-July) to allow for the production and ripening of new growth for the next season. Remove dead wood and damaged tips. Deadheading old flowers after they fade can often stimulate new blooms in summer and early fall. Summer-flowering and early-fall-blooming varieties do best if cut back in early spring. Prune stems back to a pair of plump buds and thin out weak and dead wood. Late-flowering cultivars and species produce flowers on the current season's growth, so prune in early spring. Remove the previous season's stems down to a pair of plump, healthy buds 6 to 12 in. above the ground.

ADDITIONAL INFORMATION

Clematis can often lose vigor and become too woody, producing lots of bare stems at the base. To overcome this problem, prune hard: cut the vine back to 4 to 6 in. from the ground. This will promote vigorous new growth and more flowers, and keep the vine in bounds.

ADDITIONAL SPECIES, CULTIVARS, OR VARIETIES

There are many hybrids of *Clematis* that have resulted in large flower size and beautiful soft colors. 'Henryi' has 6- to 8-in. flowers; 'Madame Edouard André' has 4-in. scarlet-purple blooms; 'Nelly Moser' has large 6-in. pale mauve-pink flowers with darker central bars; 'Mrs. Cholmondeley' has rich light-lavender-blue blooms; and 'Marie Boisselet' produces huge 8-in. pure-white flowers that last for several weeks. The spring-flowering *Clematis montana*, or anemone clematis, has fragrant 2-inch blossoms. *Clematis tangutica*, yellow lantern clematis, displays glowing yellow 3- to 4-inch lantern-like flowers in June and July. It makes a nice ground cover or climber. Western Virgin's Bower, *Clematis ligusticifolia*, is a Colorado native that produces white 4-petaled flowers in summer. It is effective as a groundcover but can become invasive if not kept in bounds.

Climbing Hydrangea

Hydrangea petiolaris

Height: To 40 ft. or more **Flowers:** White **Zones:** 4, 5, 6	**Light Requirement:**

When we think of a hydrangea, most of us think of a shrub rather than a vine, and indeed most hydrangeas are shrubs. The climbing hydrangea is, however, an excellent vine for Colorado landscaping. It grows well on north and northeast walls. It is a true clinging vine that uses aerial rootlets called "holdfasts" to cement itself to almost any structure. Pressing its stems flat against a wall, climbing hydrangea can easily support itself and its lateral or side branches. As it matures, the vine requires a strong support for its weight, and to keep it somewhat tame. Climbing hydrangea does well growing up a large tree and will not cause any harm. It can also be planted as a groundcover and looks nice spilling over a rock wall. The attractive dark-green leaves have serrated edges and are 2 to 4 in. long and about as wide. Huge (8- to 10-in.) white flower clusters open in June and July. Peeling reddish-brown bark adds winter interest. Though this vine is somewhat slow to get started, your effort will be rewarded with an attractive addition to the landscape.

WHEN TO PLANT

If you purchase bare-root plants from a mail-order nursery, plant them as soon as the soil can be worked in the spring. Container-grown plants can be planted from spring to early summer. This vine needs plenty of time to establish, so be patient.

WHERE TO PLANT

Climbing hydrangea prefers partial shade with a rich, moist, well-drained soil that is a bit on the acidic side. Plant it against barren walls, on fences, spilling over a retaining wall, or over rocks.

HOW TO PLANT

Climbing hydrangea prospers in somewhat acidic soils. Whether sand or clay, it will be necessary to add a combination of compost and sphagnum peat moss to our native soils. Dig the planting hole 2 to 3 times wider than the root system and about 18 in. deep. Mix $1/2$ compost or sphagnum peat moss to the soil removed from the hole. To prevent later damage to the developing roots, drive a wooden stake into the planting hole at the time of planting. This stake can be removed once the vine has begun to climb on its own. Gently untangle any crowded roots and spread them into the planting hole before adding the backfill soil. Position the vine in the hole so that the crown will be planted at the same level it was growing in the container. Add backfill soil about halfway, and water slowly to eliminate any air pockets and allow for settling. After this water has soaked in, add more soil to complete the planting, and water again. Mulch with pine needles to maintain even moisture and insulate the soil. Finish by tying the stems loosely to the stake with soft twine or plastic-coated wire. Water climbing hydrangea again when the soil begins to dry out to a depth of 3 to 4 in.

CARE AND MAINTENANCE

For the first few years, while climbing hydrangea is being established, it is important to keep the soil evenly moist. Once established, this vine will tolerate drought if you keep it well-mulched with pine needles. Prune the vine to keep it shapely and within bounds. Apply a complete fertilizer such as 10-10-10 in spring as new growth begins, and once again in early summer. Water thoroughly after each application. Older hydrangea vines that have been neglected tend to lose vigor and produce few flowers. Prune in early spring to rejuvenate the vine. The holdfasts that attach the vine may cause structural damage over time, so keep an eye on older brick and wood siding. This is where regular pruning can be helpful.

ADDITIONAL INFORMATION

Climbing hydrangea transplants are slow to get started. Their initial energy goes into establishing roots. Once acclimated to its new home, the vine will begin to grow, rapidly covering its intended support.

ADDITIONAL CULTIVARS, SPECIES, AND VARIETIES

There are no cultivars of this vine. Just look for climbing hydrangea, *Hydrangea petiolaris*.

Common Hops

Humulus lupulus

Height: To 40 ft.
Flowers: Yellowish green
Bloom Period: Summer
Zones: 3, 4, 5, 6

Light Requirement:

---

*H*ops are vines that can be both annual and perennial, depending on growing conditions and the area in which the vine is planted. The common or perennial hop is used to flavor beer and is becoming naturalized in our region. The hop vine is very attractive as an ornamental. It twines as it grows. You will have to provide a strong support such as a trellis, arch, or pillar; or plant hop vine under a Ponderosa pine, Douglas fir, or spruce. The variety 'Aureus', golden hop, has handsome foliage that will bring light to shady places. We recommend hop vine for screening unsightly areas or drab walls. It grows rather quickly and can reach 25 ft. or more in a single season. It is tolerant of Colorado's low humidity and wind. The bright 6- to 8-in.-wide leaves provide nice, dense cover on a fence, lattice, or other support. Female plants produce greenish-yellow pinecone-like flowers.

WHEN TO PLANT

Plant the common hop vine as soon as the soil can be worked in the spring. The Japanese hop, *Humulus japonicus*, is an annual grown as a fast-growing vine that dies back to the ground in fall. Plant the annual species in spring after all danger of frost has passed. If soil conditions are good it will reseed and germinate the following spring.

WHERE TO PLANT

Hop vine will grow in a wide range of soil types, but the soil must be well drained. This vine is easy to grow. Plant it in full sun to part shade. Use hop vine to cover fences, unsightly walls, or rocks.

HOW TO PLANT

The common hop vine is an easy-to-grow vine that does well in ordinary garden soil. If you want quicker growth, heavy clay or sandy soils should be amended with organic matter. Add 1/3 compost or well-rotted manure to the soil removed from the planting hole; these organic amendments will improve soil structure and drainage. Dig the planting hole as deep as the depth of the rootball and 2 to 3 times as wide. Drive a stake into the planting hole before setting in the vine; this will prevent later damage to the developing roots. Loosen the rootball and gently untangle the longest roots so they can be spread into the hole. Position the vine in the hole so that the crown will be planted at the same level it was in the container. Fill in the planting hole with backfill soil, and water slowly to eliminate any air pockets. Mound a rim of soil 3 to 4 in. high around the edge of the hole to hold water. Tie the stems loosely to the stake using soft twine or plastic-coated wire. Apply an organic mulch at the base of the vine to maintain moisture during establishment and to conserve water. Water again when the soil begins to dry out 4 to 6 in. deep.

CARE AND MAINTENANCE
The common hop vine will grow rather quickly and cover a support for the summer season. Once established, it is well adapted to withstand drought conditions. Soak the soil deeply, but not frequently. Depending on the severity of the winter, the common hop vine can be cut back to the ground each spring, and it will quickly grow back. If the stems survive, prune them back to live buds to clean out the dead wood and thin out the crowded stems. The annual hop vine will often reseed in the fall and start anew the following spring.

ADDITIONAL INFORMATION
The hop vine is an effective vine to naturalize in some of the older evergreens that have lost lower branches. The stems will twine around the trunk and lower branches to lighten up the darker foliage.

ADDITIONAL SPECIES, CULTIVARS, OR VARIETIES
In addition to the common hop vine, look for *Humulus lupulus* 'Aureus', or golden hops. It has bright, golden-green foliage that lightens up shady spots.

English Ivy

Hedera helix

Height: To 30 ft. or more
Flowers: Not showy
Zones: 4, 5, 6

Light Requirement:

*E*nglish ivy is a very popular evergreen vine which clings tenaciously to most surfaces. It clings to mortar, walls, and other structures with special adaptations called "holdfasts." Holdfasts adhere the ivy so tightly to a surface that it takes great strength to loosen their grip. The shiny, leathery leaves are 3- to 5-lobed and often have whitish veins. Ivy foliage forms a dense blanket on masonry walls. It can be grown on trellises, rock walls, and other strong supports, and can used as a groundcover in shady areas. As an evergreen groundcover, it can be trained to grow both under and up into trees for a special effect. Ivy's roots prevent erosion on shady slopes by knitting the soil together. English ivy can be planted to enhance the beauty of other plants in the shade garden or allowed to sprawl along the ground to edge a pathway.

WHEN TO PLANT

Container-grown plants should be planted in spring to allow time for good root growth before the onset of hot weather. Bare-root plants purchased from mail-order nurseries should be planted as soon as the ground can be worked in spring.

WHERE TO PLANT

English ivy grows best in moist, organic-rich soils in part to full shade. Winter sun can bleach or scorch exposed leaves. A north-facing exposure is ideal for this outdoor ivy. Its small aerial roots cling tenaciously to walls, fences, tree trunks, trellises, or other supports.

HOW TO PLANT

Dig the planting hole 2 to 3 times wider than the root system and about 18 in. deep. If the soil in the planting area has not been prepared previously, mix 1/3 compost, well-rotted manure, or sphagnum peat moss to the soil removed from the hole. To prevent later damage to the developing roots, drive a wooden stake into the planting hole at the time of planting. This stake can be removed once the vine has started to climb on the support you have provided for it. Gently untangle the crowded roots and spread into the hole before adding the backfill soil. Set transplants 1 in. below the soil surface to help in establishment and for added winter protection. Position the vine in the hole and use the backfill soil to fill the hole about halfway. Water slowly to eliminate any air pockets. After the water has soaked in, add more soil to complete the planting, and water again. Mulch with shredded cedar or pine needles to maintain moisture and insulate the soil. Finish by tying the stems loosely to the stake with soft twine or plastic-coated wire. Water again when the soil begins to dry out at a depth of 3 to 4 in.

CARE AND MAINTENANCE

Once established, English ivy is quite drought tolerant and requires only periodic watering during dry periods. Water thoroughly as needed. If the foliage begins to turn yellow from lack of nutrients, apply a slow-release or organic nitrogen fertilizer in spring. Prune the plant back as needed to restrict or train growth in early spring. Pinch back growing tips to keep the vine compact and bushy. Ivy is resilient and generally cannot be overpruned.

ADDITIONAL INFORMATION

As this vine matures and produces woody stems, clusters of small green flowers will appear, followed by tiny, poisonous purple-black berries.

ADDITIONAL SPECIES, CULTIVARS, OR VARIETIES

Some cultivars with good cold hardiness are 'Bulgaria', 'Hebron', and 'Thorndale'. If winter weather is very cold and harsh, ivy may die back to ground level but will grow back from its roots in spring.

Honeysuckle

Lonicera spp.

Height: To 30 ft.
Flowers: Pink, yellow, white, orange
Bloom Period: Spring
Zones: 3, 4, 5, 6

Light Requirement:

*T*he fragrance of the honeysuckle vine evokes memories of grandma's garden and the sounds of busy bees working the flowers. Honeysuckle vines are generally hardy, vigorous plants that thrive with a minimum of care. The vines can become invasive, and pruning is necessary to keep them in bounds. The tubular, sweetly fragrant flowers of red, orange, coral, yellow, or white are borne in whorls or clusters. In late summer and early autumn, berries are a source of food for wild birds. Growing honeysuckle as a vine requires a sturdy support such as a strong trellis, arbor, fence, or wall onto which the stems can intertwine. Honeysuckle vines can also be allowed to grow along the ground, where they make an effective groundcover.

WHEN TO PLANT

Plant in spring through fall. Bare-root plants transplant easily in early spring. If you purchase plants from a mail-order catalog, be sure to inspect the roots and clip any broken or damaged roots down to fresh tissue. Soak the roots in a bucket of tepid water for a hour before planting.

WHERE TO PLANT

Choose a site that receives full sun or partial shade. The soil should be well drained and enriched with compost. Train honeysuckle on trellises and fences, or grow it as a sprawling groundcover.

HOW TO PLANT

Dig the planting hole 2 to 3 times wider than the root system and about 18 in. deep. If the soil in the planting area has not been prepared previously, mix 1/3 compost, well-rotted manure, or sphagnum peat moss into the soil removed from the planting hole. To prevent later damage to the developing roots, drive a wooden stake into the planting hole at the time of planting. This stake can be removed once the vine has begun to climb the support you have provided for it. Position the vine in the hole so that the crown is planted at the same level it was growing in the container. Fill the hole about halfway with backfill soil and water slowly to eliminate any air pockets. After the water has soaked in, add more soil to the planting hole to complete the planting, and water again. Mulch with shredded cedar or pine needles to maintain moisture and insulate the soil. Finish by tying the stems and tendrils loosely to the stake with soft twine or plastic-coated wire. Water again when the soil begins to dry out to a depth of 3 to 4 in.

CARE AND MAINTENANCE

Once established, honeysuckle vines will endure drought conditions. Keeping a layer of mulch beneath the plants will help conserve moisture and prevent weed invasion. Honeysuckles do not usually need fertilizer unless the soil is of poor quality; if this is the case, apply a complete 5-10-5 or 10-10-10 fertilizer in spring. To keep the plants growing vigorously and to promote prolific flowering, prune when the blooms fade. Prune honeysuckle in the spring to maintain the desired shape and to control growth. Thin out the oldest stems to ground level to encourage new growth from the crown.

ADDITIONAL INFORMATION

The fragrant, tubular flowers of many honeysuckles will attract hummingbirds during the day and sphinx moths in the evening.

ADDITIONAL SPECIES, CULTIVARS, OR VARIETIES

One of our favorites is Hall's honeysuckle, *Lonicera japonica* 'Halliana'. It has light-green leaves and delightfully fragrant creamy-white flowers that mature to yellow. It also works well as a groundcover. *L. sempervirens*, coral or trumpet honeysuckle, is a hardy native with coral blooms. The goldflame honeysuckle, *Lonicera heckrotti*, has handsome blue-green leaves. Its red buds open to blossoms with yellow corollas and pinkish outer petals. One of the hardiest varieties is Brown's honeysuckle, *Lonicera* × *brownii*, with fragrant orange-red blooms from May to June. It is a sure lure for hummingbirds.

Perennial Pea

Lathyrus latifolius

Height: To 10 ft. or more	Light Requirement:
Flowers: White, rose, magenta	
Bloom Period: Late spring	
Zones: 4, 5, 6	

*P*erennial pea is the sweet pea's rugged, reliable cousin. It comes back year after year, and its old-fashioned charm is a welcome addition to the garden. Peas climb by tendrils that coil around wires, lattice, or other upright structures. The deep magenta-pink flowers add color to a chain-link fence or trellis over the summer season. The natural vining habit can form a screen on fences or other structures. This perennial can tolerate summer's heat and thrives in a wide range of soils. The bluish green leaves grow in pairs along the stems. The clusters of 1- to 1 1/2-in. flowers in white, rose, or magenta bloom profusely throughout the summer. Perennial pea makes excellent long-lasting cut flowers.

WHEN TO PLANT

Perennial pea seeds should be planted as soon as the soil can be worked in the spring. If you have a brightly lighted space indoors, you can start pea seeds in peat pots to be transplanted outdoors in mid- to late spring.

WHERE TO PLANT

Choose a sunny site with well-drained soil. Be sure to provide the vine with a sturdy support. Plant peas where they can easily climb on a chain-link fence, netting, trellis, lattice, or other upright support up the side of a garden shed or building.

HOW TO PLANT

Loosen soil thoroughly in the area where perennial peas are to be planted. Amend the soil with a good organic soil conditioner. Mix 1/3 to 1/2 compost by volume into the planting area. This will improve soil structure as well as drainage, and it will help retain moisture in sandy soils. Make a trench about 2 in. deep with a sharp garden hoe. Plant the seeds about 1 in. deep and 15 to 18 in. apart.

Mulch lightly with compost to keep the seedbed moist and to ensure successful germination. Peas are vulnerable to rot, so be sure not to overwater them.

CARE AND MAINTENANCE

Once established, the perennial pea is drought-enduring and will last for years. Fertilize in spring with an organic or organic-based complete fertilizer such as 5-10-5. Remove spent flowers to extend the blooming season. In late winter or early spring, cut the dead growth back to the ground. New growth will eagerly return. Periodic pinching of the growing tips will help promote more branching to cover a trellis or fence more quickly.

ADDITIONAL INFORMATION

Though perennial pea, or everlasting pea, is not fragrant like the annual sweet pea, *Lathyrus odoratus*, it is a rugged vine that can still be found clinging to fences at abandoned homesites.

ADDITIONAL SPECIES, CULTIVARS, OR VARIETIES

Two varieties of perennial pea are *Lathyrus albus*, which has white flowers, and *L. rosea*, whose flowers are a clear pink. There are many varieties of the annual sweet pea, *Lathyrus odoratus*, which have good heat resistance and large blooms in an dazzling array of colors. Their sweet fragrance is especially delightful when planted near the patio or porch. Plant annual sweet peas for accent and quick summer cover. They are ideal for use as cut flowers.

Porcelain Vine

Ampelopsis brevipedunculata

Height: Up to 20 ft.
Flowers: Greenish
Bloom Period: Summer (followed by turquoise-blue fruit)
Zones: 4, 5, 6

Light Requirement:

*P*orcelain vine is a vigorous, attractive vine from Asia that will grow rapidly to cover a trellis or arbor. Its dense foliage resembles grapevine leaves and works well as a screen. This vine's outstanding feature is its colorful turquoise-blue fruit; its flowers are not showy. The foliage of *Ampelospis brevipedunculata* 'Elegans' has pink-tinged foliage that is splashed with creamy white. It adds visual interest to the garden. Porcelain vine can be used to cover unsightly walls, fences, or poles, and can even be trained over large rocks.

WHEN TO PLANT

Plant container-grown nursery plants from spring through early fall. Bare-root plants can be planted as soon as the soil can be worked in the spring.

WHERE TO PLANT

Porcelain vine needs support for climbing. To produce the most abundant and colorful fruit, plant the vine in a location that gets full sun or filtered shade. Soil should be well drained. Porcelain vine can be used on trellises, arbors, or large trees. If you have a dead tree you don't want to remove, consider planting this vine at the base for landscape interest.

HOW TO PLANT

Porcelain vine is available as a container-grown plant that is easy to transplant. If you plan to plant this vine near a tree or post, fasten chicken wire loosely around the tree trunk or post to help the vine's tendrils cling. Dig the planting hole beyond the root spread of the tree and use a wooden stake to lead the vine to the tree's trunk; dig this planting hole as deep as the rootball and 3 times as wide. If the soil in the planting area has not been previously prepared, mix

¹/₃ compost into the soil you remove from the hole. Loosen the root-ball and gently untangle the longest roots so that they can be spread into the hole. Add backfill soil, gently firm the soil around the roots, and water thoroughly. If the vine is attached to a stake in the container, carefully untie it after planting and spread out the stems. Tie them loosely to the support. Prune off any damaged stems. Apply a 2-inch layer of mulch or compost to protect the crown, enrich the soil, and conserve water.

CARE AND MAINTENANCE

Porcelain vine is somewhat slow to establish, but it is long-lived and prolific. Once established, it adapts well to Colorado's climatic conditions. You can prune to control or direct vine growth as needed. For more rapid growth, fertilize in early spring with a complete fertilizer such as a 5-10-5 or 10-10-10, following the directions on the label.

ADDITIONAL INFORMATION

To produce the best display of fruit, porcelain vine must be planted in a site that gets full sun. Without support of some kind, it will grow rangy and spread over the ground. You can easily start a new vine by layering a stem into the ground in spring. This will cause the plant to develop roots along the stem. You can cut the layered stem from the mother vine and transplant it the following spring.

ADDITIONAL SPECIES, CULTIVARS, OR VARIETIES

The common porcelain vine has attractive 3-lobed emerald-green leaves. The cultivar *Ampelopsis brevipedunculata* 'Elegans' has hand-some pink-tinged foliage that is variegated with greenish white.

Silver Lace Vine

Polygonum aubertii

Height: To 30 ft. **Flowers:** White **Bloom Period:** Late summer **Zones:** 4, 5, 6	**Light Requirement:**

*S*ilver lace vine is prized not for its foliage, but for its masses of fleecy, greenish-white blossoms that persist through the summer. This vine grows so vigorously that it will cover a fence or trellis in one growing season. It is very tolerant of wind, drought, and urban pollution. Silver lace plants can be found growing in alleys and waste sites, testifying to its ability to survive in a variety of soil conditions. Though it may die back to the ground in severe winters, the vine will recover rapidly in the spring and produce many new vigorous shoots. Silver lace is a fast-growing deciduous vine that supports itself by twining. With the proper support from a trellis or arbor and some careful pruning, it will be an attractive addition to your landscape.

When to Plant

Plant container-grown plants in early spring. If you purchase bare-root plants from a mail-order source, unpack the vine as soon as it arrives and clip the roots lightly to remove broken or damaged ends. Soak the roots in a bucket of water for an hour or so before planting.

Where to Plant

Plant silver lace vine in full sun where its growth will be the most vigorous. This vine makes a fast-growing screen and is ideal for fences or as a rambling groundcover. It is an excellent water-thrifty plant for hot, dry sites.

How to Plant

Dig the planting hole 2 to 3 times wider than the root system and about 18 in. deep. If the soil in the planting area has not been prepared previously, mix $1/3$ compost, well-rotted manure, or sphagnum peat moss into the soil removed from the planting hole. To prevent later damage to the developing roots, drive a wooden stake into the planting hole at the time of planting. This stake can be removed once the vine has begun to climb on the support you have provided for it. Position the vine in the hole so that the crown will be at the same level it was in the container. Add the backfill soil about halfway and water slowly to eliminate any air pockets. After the water has soaked in, add more soil to complete the planting and water again. Mulch with shredded cedar or pine needles to maintain moisture and insulate the soil. Finish by tying the stems and tendrils loosely to the stake with soft twine or plastic-coated wire. Water again when the soil begins to dry out to a depth of 3 to 4 in.

CARE AND MAINTENANCE

The silver lace vine is a true survivor that tolerates dry conditions and thrives in most Colorado soils. Water thoroughly and infrequently. Avoid overwatering and overfertilizing. If desired, apply a complete 5-10-5 or 10-10-10 granular fertilizer in spring as new growth appears. This vine flowers on new wood and does best if pruned back hard (even to ground level) in early spring. You can easily start new vine plants from stem cuttings or plant divisions.

ADDITIONAL INFORMATION

The silver lace vine is often called "mile-a-minute vine" because it grows so rapidly, even in difficult sites. It spreads by rhizomes and can sometimes become weedy. Dig out unwanted sections to keep the vine in bounds.

ADDITIONAL SPECIES, CULTIVARS, OR VARIETIES

There are no cultivars. The long-lived silver lace vine is perhaps the best selection Mother Nature herself could make.

Trumpet Vine

Campsis radicans

Other Name: Hummingbird Vine
Height: 20 to 40 ft.
Flowers: Orange, orange-red
Bloom Period: Summer
Zones: 4, 5, 6

Light Requirement:

Trumpet vine's orange-scarlet trumpet-shaped blossoms highlight the landscape in summer at a time when other vines have finished flowering. It is a magnet for hummingbirds and sphinx moths. If you have ever driven through Grand Junction, you may have seen the bright-orange flowers on telephone poles and wondered what they were. Trumpet vine is a quick-growing plant that anchors itself to trellises, poles, and flat surfaces with aerial rootlets called "holdfasts." Its pinnately compound leaves are glossy green and provide a nice background or screen. In late summer or early fall, this vine may produce 3-in.-long spindle-shaped seed capsules that contain many winged seeds. If killed to the ground by a hard winter, it will quickly send up new shoots in spring.

When to Plant

Plant in spring through fall. Container-grown plants, cuttings, and root suckers are all easily transplanted. Bare-root plants are available from mail-order nurseries and should have their roots soaked in water for a few hours before planting.

Where to Plant

The sunniest locations suit the trumpet vine, which flowers well into fall. Soil should be well drained and can be amended with compost to improve porosity and drainage. Plant this vine against a garden shed, fence, or wall. It readily attaches itself by means of ivy-like aerial roots that cling to walls or other supports.

How to Plant

Have the vine supports in place before planting. If you purchased a bare-root vine, soak the roots in a bucket of water for a few hours before planting. If your soil is a heavy clay or is extremely sandy, amend it with compost. Add approximately 30 percent by volume of a high-quality compost to the soil removed from the planting hole. Mix the compost uniformly with the soil. Dig the planting hole 2 to 3 times wider than the rootball or wide enough to accommodate the spread of bare roots. If the roots are crowded in the container, gently unwind the longest ones and spread them into the planting hole. Fill the planting hole halfway with backfill soil and water-in slowly to eliminate any air pockets under the roots. After the water has soaked in, add the remaining backfill soil to complete the planting, and water again. Mulch with additional compost or shredded cedar shavings. This will help maintain even moisture during the vine's establishment. Water when the soil begins to dry out to a depth of 4 to 6 in.

CARE AND MAINTENANCE

Once established, trumpet vine is a hardy trouble-free vine for Colorado gardens. It performs best in full sun and requires little or no fertilizer; too much fertilizer will stimulate leafy growth and few flowers. Don't be afraid to prune this vine. It requires pruning to keep it in bounds. Flowers appear on new growth each year, so prune the vine back to its desired height every spring.

ADDITIONAL INFORMATION

The most successful trumpet vine is the old-fashioned *Campsis radicans*. Most of the hybrid varieties are not fully winter hardy and will die back to ground level every winter unless they are provided proper protection. Trumpet vines can be started from stem cuttings, root cuttings, or seed. If you see a sprout at the base of a vine, dig it out carefully and transplant it to a new spot.

ADDITIONAL SPECIES, CULTIVARS, OR VARIETIES

You will find several selections in the nursery trade: 'Flava' has soft, yellow flowers; 'Crimson Trumpet' has pure-red flowers; and 'Atropurpurea' has scarlet trumpets. These varieties are not as hardy in Colorado and will often die back to ground level after a harsh winter. Stick with the tried-and-true species, *Campsis radicans*, for reliable flowering every season.

Virginia Creeper

Parthenocissus quinquefolia

Other Name: Woodbine
Height: To 30 ft.
Flowers: Not showy
Zones: 3, 4, 5, 6

Light Requirement:

---

*V*irginia creeper makes a striking display in autumn, when its dense growth turns brilliant scarlet-red. This rapidly growing vine quickly produces a blanket of foliage that covers rough walls, trellises, arbors, fences, or unsightly surfaces. Virginia creeper climbs by means of twisting tendrils that are often tipped with adhesive discs. It produces dark bluish-black berries that birds love to eat. It is especially effective in a naturalized setting where it can grow around and spill over large rocks.

WHEN TO PLANT

Plant container-grown plants in spring through fall. Vines transplant easily from rooted cuttings or plant divisions.

WHERE TO PLANT

Plant Virginia creeper in full sun to ensure vigorous growth and spectacular coloration in fall. It will tolerate partial shade. Plant this vine on chain-link fences, against walls, or where it will cascade over rocks.

HOW TO PLANT

Set plants $2^1/2$ to 3 ft. apart near supports or walls where their growth is desired. Dig the planting hole 2 to 3 times wider than the root system and about 18 in. deep. If the soil in the planting area has not been prepared previously, mix $^1/3$ compost, well-rotted manure, or sphagnum peat moss into the soil removed from the planting hole. To prevent future damage to the developing roots, drive a wooden stake into the planting hole at the time of planting. This stake can be removed once the vine has begun to climb on the support you have provided for it. Position the plant in the planting hole and add the backfill soil until the hole is about halfway full. The plant should be placed in the hole so that the crown (the point at which the stem meets the roots) is at the same level it was in the container. Water slowly to eliminate any air pockets. After the water has soaked in, add more soil to cover the crown with about 2 in. of soil, and water again. Mulch with shredded cedar or pine needles to maintain moisture and insulate the soil. Finish by tying the stems and tendrils loosely to the stake with soft twine or plastic-coated wire. Water again when the soil begins to dry out to a depth of 3 to 4 in.

CARE AND MAINTENANCE

Once established, Virginia creeper is the undisputed champion of fast vine growth; it will need periodic pruning and thinning to keep it in bounds. Prune vines back as needed in early spring and throughout the summer. Water thoroughly and deeply as needed during the growing season. Avoid overwatering.

ADDITIONAL INFORMATION

Virginia creeper will usually get powdery mildew in late summer or early fall. Use a cedar mulch to keep the soil dry, and increase air circulation to help prevent this disease. A homemade spray using 1 tsp. baking soda in 1 qt. of water can be applied every 3 to 5 days to reduce the proliferation of powdery mildew spores.

ADDITIONAL SPECIES, CULTIVARS, OR VARIETIES

Parthenocissus quinquefolia var. *engelmann*, Engleman ivy, is not as vigorous as the species, but has nice green foliage that also turns bright red in autumn. Provide it with some support or, if you prefer, use it as a groundcover. Boston ivy, *P. tricuspidata*, is self-climbing with glossy dark-green foliage that turns orange-to-red in fall. This vine grows best on east- or north-facing exposures.

Wintercreeper

Euonymus fortunei

Height: To 20 ft. or more
Flowers: Not showy
Zones: 4, 5, 6

Light Requirement:

This broadleaf evergreen vine clings to a trellis, arbor, or wall with tiny roots that sprout along its stems. Wintercreeper also makes a good groundcover. It performs best when planted in moist, well-drained soil in partly shaded sites. The 1- to 2-in. glossy green leaves provide year-round color, turning purplish-red in fall and winter. Wintercreeper can be grown as a free-standing shrub form or as a vine that will climb 20 ft. or more. The small greenish-white flowers develop berry-like, pea-sized pale-pink fruits that burst open in late summer or fall, exposing showy orange seeds that persist into winter.

When to Plant

Container-grown plants can be planted from spring through early fall. If you purchase bare-root plants, get them into the soil as soon as the soil can be worked in early spring.

Where to Plant

Though wintercreeper tolerates full sun, it thrives best in shady exposures or in sites that get morning sun. Planting in partial shade will reduce the chances of sunscorch and winter desiccation. Wintercreeper is widely adaptable to Colorado soils that have been amended with moisture-retentive organic matter. It is often used as a groundcover for underplanting with spring bulbs.

How to Plant

Dig the planting hole 2 to 3 times wider than the root system and about 18 in. deep. If the soil in the planting area has not been previously prepared, mix 1/3 compost, well-rotted manure, or sphagnum peat moss into the soil removed from the planting hole. To prevent later damage to the developing roots, drive a wooden stake into the planting hole at the time of planting. This stake can be removed once the vine has begun to climb on the support you have provided for it. Position the vine in the hole so that the crown will be planted at the same level it was growing in the container. Fill the planting hole about halfway with backfill soil and water slowly to eliminate any air pockets under the root system. After the water has soaked in, add more soil to the planting hole to complete the planting, and water again. Mulch with shredded cedar or pine needles to maintain moisture and insulate the soil. Finish by tying the stems and tendrils loosely to the stake with soft twine or plastic-coated wire. Water again when the soil begins to dry out to a depth of 3 to 4 in.

CARE AND MAINTENANCE

Wintercreeper grows best in soils that remain evenly moist throughout the spring and summer. Water as needed when the soil begins to dry out, but avoid overwatering, which can result in crown or root rot. A topdressing of mulch in spring and a complete fertilizer of 10-10-10 will promote vigorous growth. Prune out dead stems or portions that may have been "winterkilled" by desiccation. The plant will generate new growth rather quickly to fill in any voids.

ADDITIONAL INFORMATION

It is not uncommon for wintercreeper to suffer from sunburn or scorch in winter. If planted in a highly exposed site, its leaves may require wind and sun protection in winter.

ADDITIONAL SPECIES, CULTIVARS, OR VARIETIES

'Sarcoxie' is a cultivar with large, lustrous green leaves and whitish venation. It has an upright growth habit of 3 to 4 ft. 'Ivory Jade' has handsome green foliage with ivory margins that develop a tinge of pink in cold weather. 'Sparkle'n'Gold' is a gold-leaf variety whose large leaves have dark-green centers bordered in gold; it produces a nice mounding growth form that reaches 12 to 18 in. in height with a spread of up to 6 ft.

GLOSSARY

Gardening Terms

Alkaline soil: Soil with a high pH (above the neutral rating of 7.0).

Annual: A plant that starts from seed, flowers, and produces seed to complete its life cycle in one growing season.

Backfill soil: Soil removed from the planting hole that is returned to the hole during the planting process.

Balled-and-burlapped: A method of wrapping the rootball of a large tree or shrub with burlap, rope, twine, and wire basket during the digging process so it can be transported safely.

Biennial: A term describing a plant with a two-year life cycle. It grows from seed and produces foliage during the first year. The second year is typified by foliage growth, flowering, and seed production.

Bloom: 1) The flower of a plant. 2) Also, the bluish-gray coating on evergreen needles, fruit, or foliage that can be wiped off or removed with certain pesticide sprays.

Bract: A modified leaf at the base of a flower or flower clusters.

Broadleaf weed: A weed with broad, flattened leaves as distinguished from thin, grass-like foliage.

Calcareous soil: Soil that is alkaline due to high amounts of calcium carbonate.

Canopy: Refers to the height and width of a tree's branch area.

Chlorosis: A condition where plants develop a yellowing of otherwise normal green foliage.

Corm: A solid, bulb-like underground stem (such as that of crocus and gladiolus).

Crown: 1) The highest portion of a tree. 2) The point on an herbaceous plant where stem and root meet.

Cultivar: A variety or strain of a plant that has originated and persisted under cultivation. Cultivars are given a specific name, usually distinguished by single quotation marks: *Acer rubrum* 'Autumn Blaze'.

Cyme: A more or less flat-topped flower.

Glossary

Deadheading: Removing dead or spent flower heads by pinching or with scissors. This is generally done to tidy the garden and promote more blooms.

Deciduous: A term used to describe plants that shed their leaves during the fall.

Dormant period: The resting period in a plant's life cycle when no growth occurs.

Dripline: The imaginary line at ground level where water dripping from the outermost branches of a tree or shrub will fall.

Fireblight: A bacterial disease that infects the tips of a tree's branches and progresses toward the trunk. The foliage will appear to have been scorched.

Frog-eyes: One of the oldest and best sprinklers that delivers water with coarse droplets and in a low arc so that there is little waste from evaporation. It is also known as the "twin-eye" sprinkler.

Gall: A swollen growth that can occur on the stems, branches, or foliage of a tree. It is caused by insects or fungus, is generally harmless, and may be pruned out.

Germinate: The term used to describe a sprouting seed.

Hardening off: The process of gradually acclimating plants that have been started indoors or in a greenhouse to outdoor growing conditions.

Hardy: A term used to describe a plant's ability to grow in a specific area and to survive low temperatures without protection.

Heeling in: The technique of temporarily planting plants in a protected spot until they can be transplanted. The roots are protected from drying by covering with loose soil or shredded wood chips.

Hellstrip: The term we coined during the drought of 1977 to describe the area between the street and sidewalk that is traditionally planted with grass and trees.

Herbaceous: This pertains to a plant whose above-ground parts are not hardy and will die back to the ground each winter.

Glossary

Holdfast: A root-like structure by which a plant clings to a wall or other structures.

Humus: The well-decomposed, fertile, and stable part of organic matter in the soil.

Layering: A method of starting plants by bending and securing a stem to the soil. Roots and shoots form along this stem to produce a new plant. Once the roots are established, the shoot is cut from the parent plant and transplanted.

Limbing up: A type of pruning in which the lower limbs are removed from a tree. This is often referred to as "skirting" in regard to evergreen trees.

Mulch: 1) Any of the various organic and inorganic materials that are used to cover soil to prevent moisture loss, discourage weed growth, and keep the soil cool. 2) To spread mulch.

Naturalize: To establish plants in the landscape so that they adapt, grow, and spread unaided as though they were native.

Pinching back: Snipping or pruning the tender tip of a shoot to stimulate side-branching or to make a plant grow bushier.

Perennial: A plant that continues to live from year to year.

pH: The measure of a soil's acidity or alkalinity on a scale from 0 to 14, with a value of 7.0 representing neutral, while the lower numbers indicate increasing acidity and the higher numbers indicate increasing alkalinity.

Pole peelings: An organic mulch made when branches, stems, and other woody byproducts are run through a grinder or wood chipper. The thin wood slivers that result will knit together; this prevents them from blowing away.

Rhizome: A thickened underground stem or root that produces shoots above and roots below. Plants with rhizomes include bearded iris and bluegrass.

Saline soil: Soil containing a high level of soluble salts, which can be injurious to plant growth.

Glossary

Scarification: Breaking the seed coat, such as by filing, to hasten seed germination.

Side dress: 1) To work fertilizer into the soil around the root zone of a plant. 2) Also, to spread mulch around the base of plants.

Stolon: A horizontal stem that grows along the ground or just below the surface, rooting along its nodes or tip and giving rise to new plants. Strawberry grows in this way.

Sucker: A soft, fast-growing shoot that originates from the base of a tree trunk, on limbs, or from roots.

Translocation: The movement of water, minerals, and nutrients within a plant.

Tuber: A short, thickened underground organ which usually, but not always, grows as a stem.

Waterlogged: This refers to a soil so saturated with water that it has poor aeration and is not conducive to healthy root growth.

Whorl: The arrangement of several leaves, flowers, or other organs around a common growth point or node.

Zone: An area restricted by a range of average minimum temperatures. Used to describe a plant's hardiness.

SOURCES

Mail-Order Sources

MANY OF THE PLANTS INCLUDED IN THIS BOOK are readily available at local garden retailers. Some of the rarer plants may be purchased via mail-order seed and nursery catalogs. The following list is not exhaustive. *Gardening By Mail* by Barbara Barton (Houghton Mifflin Company, 1994) gives the names and addresses of many other sources.

The Daffodil Mart
7463 Heath Trail
Gloucester, VA 23601
Bulbs

Dutch Gardens, Inc.
P.O. Box 200
Adelphia, NJ 07710
Bulbs

Forest Farm
990 Tetherow Rd.
Williams, OR 97544-9599

Geo. W. Park Seed Co., Inc.
1 Parkton Ave.
Greenwood, SC 29647-0001
Seeds, Perennials

Henry Field's Seed & Nursery
415 North Burnett
Shenandoah, IA 51602-0001
Seeds, Perennials, Bulbs, Shrubs, Trees

High Country Gardens
2902 Rufina Street
Santa Fe, NM 87505-2929
Perennials

Jackson & Perkins
1 Rose Lane
Medford, OR 97501-0702
Roses

Klehm Nursery
4210 N. Duncan Rd.
Champaign, IL 61821
Peonies, Perennials, Grasses

Roses of Yesterday & Today
803 Brown's Valley Road
Watsonville, CA 95076-0398
Roses

Royall River Roses
70 New Gloucester Road
North Yarmouth, ME 04097
Roses

Thompson & Morgan
P.O. Box 1308
Jackson, NJ 08527-0308
Seeds

W. Atlee Burpee & Co.
Warminster, PA 18974
Seeds

Sources

Wayside Gardens
1 Garden Lane
Hodges, SC 29695-0001
Perennials, Shrubs

White Flower Farm
P.O. Box 50
Litchfield, CT 06759-0050
Perennials, Shrubs, Roses

Another valuable resource for mail-order catalogs and suppliers:

Andersen Horticultural Library's Source List of Plants and Seeds

Available from:
Andersen Horticultural Library
Minnesota Landscape
Arboretum
3675 Arboretum Drive
P.O. Box 39
Chanhassen, MS 55317-0039

SOURCES

Bibliography

Bailey Hortorium. *Hortus Third*. Macmillan Publishing Company, 1976.

Bryan, John E. *John E. Bryan on Bulbs*. Macmillan Publishing Company, 1994.

Clausen, Ruth Rogers and Nicolas H. Ekstrom. *Perennials For American Gardens*. Random House, 1989.

Crandall, Barbara and Chuck. *Flowering, Fruiting & Foliage Vines*. Sterling Publishing Company, 1995.

Darr, Shelia and Helga and William Olkowski. *Common-Sense Pest Control*. The Tauton Press, Inc., 1991.

Dirr, Michael. *Manual of Woody Landscape Plants*. Stipes Publishing Company, 1990.

Evison, Raymond J. *Making the Most of Clematis*. Burall Floraprint Ltd., 1991.

Fairchild, D. H. and J. E. Klett. *Woody Landscape Plants for the High Plains*. Colorado State University, 1993.

Harper, Pamela. *Designing with Perennials*. Macmillan Publishing Company, 1991.

Jimerson, Douglas A. *Successful Rose Gardening*. Meredith Books, 1993.

Kelly, George W. *Trees For The Rocky Mountains*. Rocky Mountain Horticultural Publishing Company, 1976.

——. *Rocky Mountain Horticulture*. Pruett Publishing Company, 1957.

Meyer, Mary Hockenberry. *Ornamental Grasses*. Charles Scribner's Sons, 1975.

Pesman, M. Walter. *Meet the Natives*. Pruett Publishing Company, 1988.

Phillips, Roger and Martyn. *Perennials*. Volumes 1 and 2. Random House, 1991.

Shigo, Alex L. *A New Tree Biology*. Shigo and Trees, Associates, 1986.

Still, Steven. *Manual of Herbaceous Ornamental Plants*. Stipes Publishing Company, 1994.

Strauch, Jr., J. G., and J. E. Klett. *Flowering Herbaceous Perennials for the High Plains*. Colorado State University, 1989.

Turgeonn, A. J. *Turfgrass Management*. Prentice Hall, Inc., 1991.

Wyman, Donald. *Ground Cover Plants*. Macmillan Publishing Company, 1976.

——. *Shrubs and Vines for American Gardens*. Macmillan Publishing ompany, 1969.

INDEX

Index

Index

Index

Index

Index

ABOUT THE AUTHOR

*J*OHN L. CRETTI, known as Colorado's Plant Doctor to many residents, shares more than twenty years of valuable, down-to-earth gardening experience in the *Colorado Gardener's Guide*.

Horticulturist and Colorado native John Cretti is known regionally and nationally as "Doctor Green Thumb" from his far-reaching radio shows, newspaper columns, and television appearances. He is a Rocky Mountain horticulturist with degrees in horticulture from Colorado State University and has served as a CSU home horticulture specialist for twelve years. He received the Scotts Horticultural Professional Improvement Award for lawn and garden communications, the National Association of County Agricultural Agents award of excellence in horticulture communications, and was recognized for outstanding community service for garden and education programs by Xeriscape Colorado.

John and his wife Jeri, also a horticulturist, host "Colorado's Green Thumb Radio Show," which received the prestigious Award of Excellence for garden communications in 1990 and Quill and Trowel Awards from the Garden Writers Association of America in 1988, 1989, 1990, 1993, 1995, and 1997. They have received numerous awards for their garden writing for newspapers and television garden features. John and Jeri are the regional editors for the "Rocky Mountains and High Plains in Flower and Garden" magazine. At home in eastern Colorado with Jeri, sons Jason, Justin, and Jonathan, and daughter Jinny, John takes gardening to a different level: an active relationship between human, environment, and plants. As John would say, "To grow plants successfully, you have to *think* like a plant."

COLORADO GARDENING
ONLINE

www.coolspringspress.com

Now available, exclusively for Colorado gardeners!

To serve the needs of today's gardeners, Cool Springs Press has created one of the most advanced home pages in America devoted exclusively to gardening. It offers expert advice on how to make Colorado gardening more enjoyable and the results more beautiful.

Consult the Cool Springs Press home page for monthly information from the *Colorado Gardener's Guide.* Keep up-to-date with Colorado gardening on the Internet.

— LOCALIZED GARDENING CALENDAR FOR THE MONTH

— SELECTED "PLANT OF THE MONTH"

— DISCUSSION ROOM FOR CONVERSATION AND ADVICE, JUST FOR COLORADO GARDENERS

www.coolspringspress.com